Dandyism and Transcultural Modernity

This book views the Neo-Sensation mode of writing as a traveling genre, or style, that originated in France, moved on to Japan, and then to China. The author contends that modernity is possible only on "the transcultural site"—transcultural in the sense of breaking the divide between past and present, elite and popular, national and regional, male and female, literary and non-literary, inside and outside.

To illustrate the concept of transcultural modernity, three icons are highlighted on the transcultural site: the dandy, the flâneur, and the translator. Mere *flâneurs* and *flâneuses* simply float with the tide of heterogeneous information on the transcultural site, whereas the dandy/flâneur and the cultural translator, propellers of modernity, manage to bring about creative transformation. Their performance marks the essence of transcultural modernity: the self-consciousness of working on the threshold, always testing the limits of boundaries and tempted to go beyond them. To develop the concept of dandyism—the quintessence of transcultural modernity—the Neo-Sensation gender triad formed by the dandy, the modern girl, and the modern boy is laid out.

Writers discussed include Liu Na'ou, a Shanghai dandy *par excellence* from Taiwan, Paul Morand, who looked upon Coco Chanel the female dandy as his perfect other self, and Yokomitsu Riichi, who developed the theory of Neo-Sensation from Kant's the "thing-in-itself."

Peng Hsiao-yen is a research fellow at the Institute of Chinese Literature and Philosophy, Academia Sinica. She has published *Antithesis Overcome: Shen Congwen's Avant-gardism and Primitivism* and, in Chinese, *Beyond realism and Desire in Shanghai: From Zhang Ziping to Liu Na'ou.*

Academia Sinica on East Asia

Published in association with Academia Sinica, Taiwan

Series Editor: Dr Ts'ui-Jung Liu, Vice-President, Academia Sinica, Taiwan

ACADEMIA SINICA

Academia Sinica was founded in Mainland China in 1928. During its early stage of development ten institutes were created, three of which were in the field of humanities and social sciences. Then came the turbulent years and in late 1948 Academia Sinica followed the government move to Taiwan. Only two of its institutes, History & Philology and Mathematics, ever arrived and these were established in Nankang, an eastern suburb of Taipei. From these difficult beginnings Academia Sinica has developed over the years into a prestigious full-scale research institution with 31 institutes and research centers.

The fields of humanities and social sciences have eleven institutes and one research center between them and the extensive team of researchers are devoted to the study of archaeology, history, literature, linguistics, philology, philosophy, anthropology, economics, sociology, political science, and law as well as interdisciplinary research.

The Academia Sinica on East Asia series will incorporate the Academia's best research on East Asia from the humanities and social sciences institutes. It will strive to make an important contribution to the field.

Taiwan in Japan's Empire-Building
An institutional approach to colonial engineering
Hui-yu Caroline Ts'ai

Divine Justice
Religion and the development of Chinese legal culture
Paul R. Katz

The Poet-historian Qian Qianyi
Lawrence C.H. Yim

Beyond Confucian China
The rival discourses of Kang Youwei and Zhang Binglin
Young-tsu Wong

Dandyism and Transcultural Modernity
The dandy, the flâneur, and the translator in 1930s Shanghai, Tokyo, and Paris
Peng Hsiao-yen

Dandyism and Transcultural Modernity

The dandy, the flâneur, and the translator in 1930s Shanghai, Tokyo, and Paris

Peng Hsiao-yen

LONDON AND NEW YORK

First published 2010
by Routledge
2 Park Square, Milton Park, Abingdon, Oxfordshire OX14 4RN

Simultaneously published in the USA and Canada
by Routledge
711 Third Avenue, New York, NY 10017

First issued in paperback 2014

*Routledge is an imprint of the Taylor & Francis Group,
an informa business*

© 2010 Peng Hsiao-yen

The right of Peng Hsiao-yen to be identified as author of this work has been asserted by her in accordance with sections 77 and 78 of the Copyright, Designs and Patents Act 1988.

Typeset in Times by RefineCatch Limited, Bungay, Suffolk

All rights reserved. No part of this book may be reprinted or reproduced or utilized in any form or by any electronic, mechanical, or other means, now known or hereafter invented, including photocopying and recording, or in any information storage or retrieval system, without permission in writing from the publishers.

British Library Cataloguing in Publication Data
A catalogue record for this book is available from the British Library

Library of Congress Cataloging-in-Publication Data
Peng, Hsiao-yen.
  Dandyism and transcultural modernity : the dandy, the flâneur, and the translator in 1930s Shanghai, Tokyo, and Paris / Hsiao-yen Peng.
    p. cm.—(Academia Sinica on East Asia)
  Includes bibliographical references and index.
  1. Oriental literature—20th century—History and criticism.
  2. Cultural pluralism in literature. 3. Dandyism in literature.
  I. Title.
  PJ312.P46 2010
  809'.93355—dc22   2010002030

ISBN 13: 978-1-138-87907-2 (pbk)
ISBN 13: 978-0-415-58428-9 (hbk)

For Daw-hwan,

for our new home at Rich-Muraue

Contents

List of figures	ix
Preface: transcultural modernity	x
Acknowledgments	xiv

Introduction: dandyism, the quintessence of transcultural modernity   1

Prologue: Louis XIV, the dandy par excellence *1*
The dandy/flâneur and transcultural modernity 5
The dandy, the modern girl, and the modern boy 10

1 A dandy, traveler, and woman watcher: Liu Na'ou from Taiwan   22

A perpetual traveler: transcultural practice 22
A dandy par excellence *and misogyny 26*
The neo-sensation mode and the modern girl 32
Dandyism and the Shanghai type 41
A Taiwanese in Shanghai and Tokyo 50
The macaronic and transcultural modernity 56

2 A traveling subgenre: the palm-of-the-hand story   59

The modern girl gazing back 59
A subgenre from France to Japan and China 63
Dandyism as a life calling 67
How to be a modern girl? 70
Commodifying the modern girl 74
Dandyism and misogyny 77
When a dandy meets a female dandy: Morand and Chanel 83
Neo-sensation from Paris to Tokyo to Shanghai 92
Je n'aime que le movement (I like nothing but the movement) 95

3 The flâneur and the flâneuse: Yokomitsu Riichi's Shanghai   99

Neo-sensation and symbolism 100
"On Neo-Sensation" and the thing-in-itself 104
Miyako: the modern girl in the war of nations 110
Olga in a seizure: Russia's lost angel 113
Hō Shūran: the mysterious Chinese woman revolutionary 114
Yamaguchi: the Asianist and scavenger 119
Sanki and Ōsugi: Japan's lost children 125
From the masses to the flâneur and the flâneuse 128

4 A traveling text: *Souvenirs entomologiques*   131

Personal agency in translation 131
The three modern boys and the science of love 132
Souvenirs entomologiques *and Ōsugi Sakae 137*
Lu Xun and Konchūki 142
Jean-Henri Fabre and Charles Darwin 146
A traveling text 156
What Lu Xun would think of Dandyism 161

5 A traveling disease: the "malady of the heart" and the modern boy   163

Translation and transcultural modernity 163
"You have cured me of misogyny, but given me neurasthenia" 165
Psychology as a discipline in Japan and China 169
How to name the five senses and the malady of the heart 174
How to say "I love you" 185

Conclusion: to connect   192
Notes   199
Bibliography   237
Index   257

Figures

Intro.1	The Sun King	2
Intro.2	"The war is so long..."	12
Intro.3	Miss Modern Girl and Master Modern Boy	14
Intro.4	Miss Modern Girl and Master Modern Boy	16
Intro.5	Miss Modern Girl and Master Modern Boy	16
Intro.6	Miss Modern Girl and Master Modern Boy	17
Intro.7	Wild Prophesy of the Future Cityscape of Shanghai	19
Intro.8	Sex Histories	19
Intro.9	Wild Prophesy of the Future Cityscape of Shanghai	20
1.1	The Touch of 1933: The Enchantment of a Machine	39
2.1	*The Women's Pictorial*	60
2.2	The most fashionable man's dress startles a girl in the public toilet	61
2.3	"Mr. Huang, allow me to introduce Miss Chen."	62
2.4	A Body without Soul	78
2.5	A Model of Modern Women	80
2.6	All Contents in a Modern Woman's Brain Cells	81
2.7	All Contents in a Modern Woman's Brain Cells	82
2.8	Marie Bell in the movie *La garçonne*	87
2.9	Josephine Baker as Black Venus in 1926	88
2.10	Sketch of mannequin wearing Chanel's April 1926 collection in French *Vogue*	89
4.1	Black, Red, Cruelty, and Women	135
5.1	Nishi Amane's handwriting	170
5.2	A Hundred-Year-Old Machine	182
5.3	Doan's Nerve Tonic Tablets	183
5.4	Doan's Backache Kidney Pills	184
5.5	Blutose	185
5.6	Burutōze	186

Preface: transcultural modernity

This book views the Neo-Sensation mode of writing as a traveling genre, or style, that originated in France, moved on to Japan, and then to China. Paul Morand, to whom the Japanese attributed the invention of this style, never used the term himself. In studying the relationships of 1930s Shanghai Neo-Sensation writers with their Japanese and French counterparts, my major concern goes beyond influence or parallel study. Nor am I interested in simply pointing out the exotic in their writings; "exoticism" was a common phenomenon in both Japanese and Chinese literatures at the time. Rather, I am trying to connect the routes through which people, genres, concepts, expressions, and texts circulated in the Euro-Asian context. In other words, how they "traveled" from the "points of origin" in the West to Japan and China, and then were transformed along the way, while transforming the reception cultures at the same time. So the chapters in this book are about stories of how people, genres, concepts, expressions, and texts travel. When traveling happens, the effect is never the "one-way imposition of the dominant culture," but a "two-way give and take," as the Latin American concept of transculturation indicates.[1]

With the Neo-Sensation mode as a point of departure, I propose the concept of "transcultural modernity" to rethink the nature of modernity. It is my contention that modernity is possible only on "the transcultural site"—transcultural in the sense not only of transnational and translingual, but also of breaking the divide between past and present, elite and popular, national and regional, male and female, literary and non-literary, inside and outside.[2] "Transcultural" is perhaps a more inclusive concept to use. In a word, the concept of transcultural modernity challenges both language and disciplinary boundaries. In my conceptualization, modernity does not refer to any specific period in history. In any period of time of any culture, whoever makes it their goal to pursue the new by breaking the traditional divide is one of those who engage in transcultural practice; they are the propellers of modernity. Cultural inventors who are on the threshold of modernity always live and act at the frontiers; it is through the act of constant border crossing that they find inspirations to create. The transcultural site, where cultures meet and overlap, is where the creative energy of artists, literary men and women, translators, thinkers, and so on finds expression. So this book is mainly about the transcultural site where transformative creativity is possible. It talks about linguistic, literary, and cultural creativity rather than imitation, assimilation, or influence of the foreign. I am especially interested in the linguistic flux and fluidity accompanying the process of creative transformation, rather than stability and stasis, which are signs of a culture or language dying out.

The trascultural site is the space for cultural translation. In a way, all of us in today's global and multi-ethnic societies are participating in cultural translation on a day-to-day basis. With or without our awareness, the visible or invisible "foreign" in our daily lives necessitates constant acts of cultural translation, from archaic expressions to scientific language, from translated texts to borrowed terms, from foreign tongues to dialects, from professional jargon to slang. However, those who take it as their vocation to engage in cultural translation are the subjects of this study. They are modernists who consider themselves harbingers of a new horizon. It is through cultural translation that the transcultural site becomes a fecund space for their transformative creativity.

Comparative theorists often talk about the "contact zone" or "translation zone" where cultures meet. Both terms are suggestive of the "war zone."[3] With the term "transcultural site," I intend to reduce the military overtones. I am more interested in how different cultures are connected and transform each other than how they conflict and "clash."[4] Furthermore, instead of merely talking about cultural memories inscribed in the "contact zone" of cultures,[5] this book especially looks at intellectuals who are cultural translators acting on the transcultural site and setting the trends. If we use stage performance as a metaphor, they are conscious actors working on the site, rather than mere characters who are the site itself.[6] While characters may be unconscious that they are caught in the intricate network of transcultural communication, actors, going through the same experience, are highly aware of their own performance. Of course, as actors, they are not completely in control of the roles they play and are often carried away by it; as characters as well, they could be likewise merely half-conscious of all the information flowing in and out of their bodies and minds. Judith Butler's notion of "psychic excess," the concept that the psychic "exceeds the domain of the conscious subject," can certainly complicate the issue.[7] What I want to emphasize is that, more than mere characters, they are artists who perform on the transcultural site, and whose personal agency transforms elements from both sides of the divide.

Some may think East–West cross-cultural relationship is an unequal one, and express anxiety over the center/periphery hierarchy.[8] It is also said that personal agency or individual choice is impossible while facing institutional powers.[9] Note that, for poststructuralists like Foucault, Homi Bhabha, or Judith Butler, personal agency, as a rule exercised in the crisscrossing of multiple institutional powers, is always possible through uneven positions. Power relations are not simply domination versus subjugation. Foucault never advocates "equality" when he talks about power relations. Rather, he talks about the "practice of freedom" of individuals constantly testing institutional limits in order to jostle for a space for creative transformation. Equality is an ideal. However we strive for regulations that promise equality, any regulating norms would not be able to ensure all the specs necessary to achieve an equal society; all that the law can do is provide guidelines. Whatever norms we have, there is always room where we need to test the limits and negotiate. People act under constraints, but they do not just conform to norms; they violate them.[10] With the practice of freedom we are allowed to reshuffle power relations. As the old saying goes, if there is equality, there will be no freedom.[11] All imaginings of future societies indicate that standard equality always leads to absolute constraints.

Another point I want to emphasize is that, in translation, not only does linguistic competence matter, but it is crucial, because languages represent the cultural traditions which both the translator and the translated inherit. In this book I try to show that in both modern Japan and China the act of translation was always (indeed, has always been) a negotiation between foreign intellectual institutions—such as Darwinism, anarchism, and psychology—and various domestic institutional powers, including classical and vernacular language traditions, classical medical concept, Confucianism, Buddhism, and so on. During the process of translation, the translator whose neologisms have become part of our daily or academic language today managed to bring about creative transformation through individual free choice, or personal agency, while testing the intellectual limits of both domestic and foreign institutions. The bottom line is, to have freedom, one needs to know where the limits are.

To illustrate the concept of transcultural modernity, this book highlights three icons on the transcultural site: the dandy, the flâneur, and the translator. In my conceptualization, the dandy/flâneur and the cultural translator are propellers of modernity on the transcultural site, whereas mere flâneurs and flâneuses, such as characters in Neo-Sensation stories, simply float with the tide of heterogeneous information. In a sense, we are all travelers in life. Along the way, while most people collect memories and transmit them without much thinking, a select few transform them with their creative power. Their performance marks the essence of transcultural modernity: the self-consciousness of working on the threshold, always testing the limits of boundaries and playing on the temptation to go beyond them. After the concatenations of transformative creation carried on throughout history, what is not ours has become an inseparable part of our everyday reality, whose "foreignness" we do not often even think about. This book tries to trace how the foreign becomes part of our own. More importantly, it shows how constant transcultural practices—mainly, but not exclusive to, traveling and translating—connect human beings and ideas from different cultures.

The Introduction lays out the theoretical framework of this book. It develops the concept of dandyism as the quintessence of transcultural modernity, with a view to distinguishing the dandy/artist/flâneur from the flâneur who roams the city, pursuing any objective other than art. Chapter 1 centers on the Shanghai Neo-Sensation writer Liu Na'ou, a dandy/flâneur and translator. Chapter 2 shows the connections between the Shanghai and Japanese Neo-Sensation writers through the concept of dandyism and their links with Paul Morand, a perfect French dandy. Chapter 3 concentrates on Yokomitsu Riichi's *Shanghai*, analyzing him as a self-conscious artist practicing transcultural modernity, as a contrast to characters in the novel who are simply flâneurs and flâneuses floating on the transcultural site. Chapter 4 shows how translators practice transcultural modernity and their crucial role in connecting cultures. It uses a Shanghai Neo-Sensation story of human love and insects as a point of departure to connect Lu Xun's advocacy of Fabre with the Japanese anarchists who translated Fabre and the dispute between Fabre's natural theology and Darwinism. Chapter 5, starting with another Shanghai Neo-Sensation story, demonstrates how neurasthenia was recognized as a modern disease in Japan and China through the efforts of translators. The Conclusion extrapolates one of the main purposes of this book: How the practices of transcultural modernity connect cultures. In lieu of the prevalent confrontational approaches of current cross-cultural studies, this book's central concept is "to connect."

Acknowledgments

This book began as a National Science Council research project from 2004 to 2007, which enabled me to do research in Paris, Tokyo, and the United States. A Fulbright grant for six months in 2007 allowed me to do research at Harvard University, whose rich library holdings in Japanese and French greatly facilitated my work.

The origin of this book dates in fact long before 2004. It would have been impossible without the experience of compiling the fourteen-volume *Complete Works of Yang Kuei* from 1997 to 2001, a Council for Cultural Affairs project that forced me to learn Japanese from scratch. The mastery of the language has enabled me to work on the China–Japan–Europe triangular connection and has made a significant difference in my career as a researcher at Academia Sinica. I owe the luxury of learning a new language while doing research to the excellent academic environment there, where I have always considered myself a student.

Many people are indispensable to my intellectual development. In the United States, Patrick Hanan, David Wang, Lydia Liu, Shu-mei Shih, Faye Kleeman, Emily Apter, Tani Barlow, Chen Xiaomei, Yan Haiping, Larissa Heinrich, and Andrea Bachner either read the manuscript, in part or in its entirety, or listened to my talks on the project and shared their thoughts along the way. In Hong Kong, Leo Ou-fan Lee and Leung Ping-kwan's interests in my work are always encouraging. Leo's study of Shanghai modernism, Lydia's concept of translated modernity and translingual practice, and Shu-mei's study of the Neo-Sensation School are particularly inspiring. This book is basically a continuation of their work, while trying to push some key issues further. I especially appreciate the intellectual exchange with Andrea, whose theoretical acuity has helped shape this book. In France, thanks are due to Isabelle Rabut and Angel Pino for their expertise on the Shanghai Neo-Sensation School and long-term support over the years. In England, my thanks go to James St. André for his useful insight on hybridity and transculturation. In Japan, I thank Inaga Shigemi and Suzuki Sadami for their invaluable suggestions. In China, I am indebted to Wang Zhongchen, Dong Bingyue, Wang Cheng, and Wang Zhisong, who have invited me to join their East-Asian Humanities Lecture Series and carefully read the Chinese versions of the chapters. Peichen Wu from Taiwan has read the chapters and made useful suggestions. I would like also to thank my anonymous reviewers for their comments and suggestions, and the editorial assistants for guiding me through the long and complicated process of publication.

The theoretical framework of this book is owed to my colleagues of the Forum for Literary Theory and Philosophy Group at Academia Sinica: Fabian Heubel, Yang Xiaobin, Huang Kuan-min, and Chen Hsiang-yin. I have benefited more than I can say from the East Asia Study Group organized by my colleague Liao Chao-heng. My students at the University of Chicago during the spring term of 2006, including Valerie Levan and Xiang Song, have either listened to my thoughts on the project or read the chapters and helped me with their feedback. My assistants over the years, Walter Jen-hao Hsu, Olivier Bialais, Vanissa Ying-chen Chen, Helen Yi-lun Huang, Shannon I-hsien Lee, Lily Yin-chun Wang, and Bell Ko-ching Tang, have been most helpful and generous with their time. It is a treasure to be able to learn and grow with them. Thanks are due to Julie Hu, who has patiently read all the chapters without being bored. Last but not least, the biological anthropologist Wang Daw-hwan, my best friend and spouse, has transformed me into what I am, as scholar as well as person.

Four of the five chapters were published in either English or Chinese and have been extensively revised. An earlier version of part of Chapter 1 appeared in Ping-Hui Liao and David Wang (eds) *Taiwan Under Japanese Colonial Rule, 1885–1945: History, Culture, and Memory,* New York: Columbia University Press, 2006. An earlier Chinese version of part of Chapter 2 was published by Academia Sinica under the title "Dandyism and Border Crossing: Gender, Language, and Travel in Neo-Sensation" in *Bulletin of Chinese Literature and Philosophy*, no. 28, March 2006. An earlier version of Chapter 4 was published by National Taiwan University in *NTU Studies in Language and Literature*, no. 17, June 2007, and by Beijing Sanlian Books in Chinese in *Dongya renwen* (East Asian Humanities), Inaugural Issue, October 2008. A Chinese version of Chapter 5 was published in *Bulletin of Chinese Literature and Philosophy*, no. 34, March 2009.

For the images in this book:
1) After Hyacinthe Rigaud, Portrait of Louis XIV, 18th Century, oil on canvas, 289.6 × 159.1 cm. Courtesy of The J. Paul Getty Museum, Los Angeles
2) Miss Modern Girl and Master Modern Boy: Courtesy of Tanaka Ruriko
3) Cartoons of Zhang Wenyuan, Guo Jianying, and Shangbanyu: Courtesy of The Shanghai City Copyrights Protection Center for Literary Men and Artists
4) Josephine Baker as Black Venus: Courtesy of AKG-Images London
5) Nishi Amane's Handwriting: Courtesy of Satō Tatsuya

Translations in this book are mine unless otherwise indicated.

Introduction
Dandyism, the quintessence of transcultural modernity

Prologue: Louis XIV, the dandy *par excellence*

To illustrate my definition of the dandy, I would like to refer to Hyacinthe Rigaud's 1701 portrait of Louis XIV, an oil painting on canvas I saw at the Paul Getty Museum in Los Angeles in March 2007. At the time, as a Fulbright grantee doing research at Harvard, I was invited to give talks on three campuses of the University of California. After the talks at UC Davis and Berkeley, UCLA was the last stop. The visit to the museum there was unexpected, but it turned out to be the most rewarding experience in my weeklong trip to the west coast. Louis XIV in the painting manifests perfectly the dandy in my mind, a concept I had been deliberating for years, trying to lay out the principal theoretical frame of this study. How much more can an image say than words!

In the portrait, Le Roi Soleil (The Sun King) is shown in his ermine coronation robes, wig, scepter, and sword—the usual regalia representing a mighty ruler. What is unusual is the ermine robes lifted like drapes hanging down from his left shoulder, deliberately exposing his short balloon skirt, semi-bare legs in tights with beige knitted straps beneath the knees, and beige high-heeled shoes decorated with two buckled windmill ties beneath the ankles. The high heel and the upper windmill tie of each shoe are scarlet red. Together with the grayish, pale legs, the red/beige high heels form a stark contrast with the dark blue/whitish, dotted fur robes. More telling is that Louis is standing in a ballet pose, with his left shoulder and flank towards the viewers, eying them aslant. The posture also suggests a model enticingly displaying fashion on a catwalk. It is a perfect image of the female in male, or an artist/dandy inventing and defining femininity, one of the main characteristics of the dandy in my mind. The Sun King, famous for saying "L'état, c'est moi" (I am the state), seems to be stating in the portrait, "La mode, c'est moi" (I am fashion), or, better still, "La Femme, c'est moi" (I am Woman) (Figure Intro.1).

There is one thing I found most intriguing about the exhibition of the painting. Since the huge painting (114 × 62 5/8 in.) is hung nearly four feet above the ground, the first thing that catches the viewer's attention is the

2 *Dandyism and Transcultural Modernity*

Figure Intro.1 The Sun King.

semi-bare legs with the high-heeled shoes. But the legend of the painting, emphasizing the stateliness and pompous gesture of the king, surprisingly mentions nothing of this deliberate display of androgyny.[1] The bare legs and the high-heels of the king in the portrait are so outstanding that not even a child would overlook. In fact, when I was pondering this, I heard children passing by commenting delightfully on the red high heels in the painting. Why is this aspect of the female in male omitted in the caption?

The next day after I returned to Harvard, I hastened to check out Peter Burke's book on the representations of the Sun King, *The Fabrication of Louis XIV*. I was thrilled to find that the painting in question, in black and white facsimile, is the first image included in the book. But, again astonishingly, although Burke returns time and again to mention the painting, the androgynous aspect is left totally unsaid. He describes the painting as portraying "the dignified old age" of the king[2] and achieving "a certain equilibrium between formality and informality," with "a studied informality in the way in which he holds his scepter, the point down, as if it were the cane he usually carried in public."[3] He mentions a historian who points out "the elegant legs and the 'ballet pose' of the feet, a reminder of the king's dancing days."[4] I was hoping that in the chapter titled "The Crisis of Representations," something different would be said about the painting. But Burke says here, "His wig and his high heels helped to make Louis more impressive." In a later reference to the same portrait, remotely close to what I have in mind, he says, "Louis wears the royal mantle, but it is open so that his modern clothes are visible underneath."[5]

Shown underneath Louis's royal robes is something, I venture to say, more than "modern clothes." Of course, it was indeed "modern clothes," in the sense that in the seventeenth century it was fashionable for men to wear short balloon skirts with tights and for both men and women to wear high heels.[6] It is widely known that Louis was a patron of modern fashion in all areas. In the realm of footwear alone, he unprecedentedly appointed a cobbler from Bordeaux, Nicolas Lestage, as the king's official "master shoemaker" and raised him to noble rank. It is said that Louis even had Lestage's portrait painted and displayed in his art gallery, labeled "Maître Nicolas Lestage, il est miracle de son âge" (Master Lestage, he is the miracle of his age).[7] Nevertheless, fashion in itself is not what I have in mind. Rather, what I intend to point out is that, in France at the time, when cross-casting and cross-dressing on stage were common practices,[8] the sartorial signs of masculinity and femininity were perhaps not as categorically defined as it is today. The Sun King's androgynous image in the famous Rigaud painting would probably not have raised many eyebrows among viewers at the time.

It is perhaps our own age, which prides itself on its liberal point of view, that imposes fixed definition of sex differentiation and stringent rules of gender performance. Our age requires each person, as it were, to follow strict dress codes indicating clearly his or her position and identity as either straight, homosexual, or lesbian. It is likely that it is we who are less tolerant with dress styles blurring the boundaries of the sexes and thus label them cross-dressing and transvestism. In Louis's days, men wearing high heels or powdering their faces were not declaring they were gay and would not be considered as such; they were just pursuing fashion. On the other hand, this is exactly why I see Louis in the painting as displaying proudly and tauntingly the female in male—he could do so without being labeled homosexual.[9] Why is it regarded "effiminate" or "unmanly" for a man to display qualities that are deemed to be "feminine" today? Can we consider the possibility that there is a woman in every man, and vice versa?

There is so much we could learn from ancient wisdom. In Plato's *Symposium*, from section 189 on, we are told through Aristophanes' words that, instead of two genders, originally there were three: male, female, and androgyny. The episodes could be conveying a symbolic meaning, of course. The way homosexual and heterosexual orientations are looked at in the Platonic dialogues is lovely: each male, female, and the androgynous are split in two; losing the other half, each half is searching for the other that is his or her matching half,[10] a trope we are familiar with. But here I would like to propose a hyperbole that pushes the concept of androgyny further: There is a female in each male, and a male in each female. Louis's portrait is a telling illustration of this nuanced ambiguity of human sexuality, which is one of the key aspects of what I call dandyism in this study. Whether one is biologically male or female does not prevent one from possessing the character traits deemed belonging to the opposite sex. When did the outward display of androgyny, a symbolic concept of the male in woman and the female in man, become unacceptable in our culture?

Not only does Louis in this painting proudly demonstrate the androgynous nature of humans, but he tells us something more: He is announcing the position of an artist/dandy inventing and defining femininity, the way male actors such as Mei Lanfang in early twentieth-century Beijing opera immortalized the female roles they interpreted on stage.[11] Following the court ballet tradition since the sixteenth century, Louis XIV and his male courtiers often played female roles in performances. But although the convention of cross-casting still persisted, Louis's court ballet began to include more and more female courtiers and professionals in performances.[12] This is in line with the unprecedented freedom women enjoyed in social life and the intellectual education for women during his reign.[13] One may as well say that he heralded women's liberation before the term and concept were even invented.

Louis was also keen on the professionalization of ballet as an art form. Right after he began his personal reign in 1661, he established the Académie Royale de Danse and signed the "Letters Patent of the King" to legalize the academy's patent privilege to train professional dancers and its responsibility to bring ballet art to perfection. The 23-year-old monarch, at the crucial moment when he should have been tending to more urgent state affairs, was eager to "centralize all arts under his personal control" as well. The Academies of Inscriptions et Belles Lettres (1663), Sciences (1666), Opéra (1669), and Architecture (1671) followed.[14] As Louis's political and military power extended to Austria, Germany, England, the Dutch Republic, southern Netherlands, Alsace, Spain, and so on, his cultural influence also became dominant in Europe.

A monarch who displayed arrogantly "La femme, c'est moi," who put the perfection of art on his list of priorities, and whose power transgressed the confinement of national borders, Louis XIV is the archetypal dandy I have in mind. Hence in my definition, a dandy *par excellence* comprises these three main aspects: taking the opposite sex as one's other self, preoccupation with artistic perfection and self-invention, and constant transcultural practices.

Come to think of it, can we not say that there is something of a dandy in each of us, in every man and woman on the transcultural site who is preoccupied with self-perfection and invention?

The dandy/flâneur and transcultural modernity

For my conceptualization of the dandy/flâneur, I am indebted to Charles Baudelaire. Known as "Bōdorēru" in Taishō Japan, or "Potelai'er" in republican China, he was one of the numerous colossal European writers and thinkers whose images and works loomed large in modern Japanese and Chinese literatures, infiltrating into writers' psyche as well as writings.[15] Chapter 1 of this book, centering on Liu Na'ou, the leader of Shanghai Neo-Sensation writers, testifies to this fact. For Baudelaire in China or Japan, quite a few studies are already available.[16] What I want to refer to here is Baudelaire's famous treatise on the dandy as a modernist, *Le peintre de la vie moderne* (*The Painter of Modern Life*), which has inspired a great number of thinkers and literary critics in Western academe,[17] among whom the most prominent are Walter Benjamin and Michel Foucault. The major difference between their views is helpful to this study.

Benjamin concentrates on the concept of the flâneur in his studies of Baudelaire written during the 1930s. To him, both Baudelaire the poet and the painter Constantin Guys in *The Painter of Modern Life* manifest the qualities of the flâneur. In his Marxist interpretation, not only does the flâneur succumb to the fetish of commodity and women, but, similar to the prostitute, he is the commodity itself. According to Benjamin, the flâneur, strolling the street and the arcades,

> is someone abandoned in the crowd. He is thus in the same situation as the commodity. He is unaware of this special situation, but this does not diminish its effect on him; it permeates him blissfully, like a narcotic that can compensate him for many humiliations. The intoxication to which the flâneur surrenders is the intoxication of the commodity immersed in a surging stream of customers.[18]

Benjamin further points out that the modern artist, as a flâneur, is seeking to commodify his literary production, even though he is unconsicous of the process of capitalization: "In the flâneur, the intelligentsia sets foot in the marketplace—ostensibly to look around, but in truth to find a buyer."[19]

Note that Benjamin's terms such as "abandoned in the crowd," "unaware of this special situation," "the intoxication to which the flâneur surrenders" repeatedly emphasize the flâneur's lack of awareness of his own commodification in the capitalized modern world. He also compares the flâneur to a detective, but again stresses his passiveness in acting like one: He is "turned into an unwilling detective," for whom the posture of being a detective incognito "legitimates his idleness," but behind his apparent indolence "there is the watchfulness of an observer who does not take his eyes off a miscreant."[20] Benjamin is saying that the "unwilling" detective, like a "physiognomist," is observing and studying the "miscreants" to sketch their caricatures. Among the hoodlums teeming in the Paris of Napoleon III, Benjamin singles out the *bohème*, the amateur or professional conspirator who imagined the overthrow of the regime, as a metaphor for the intelligentsia floating with the tide of historical transition[21]: "In this intermediate stage, in which it [the inteligentsia] still has patrons but is already beginning to familiarize itself with the market, it appears as the bohème."[22] Furthermore, Benjamin's flâneur shows empathy with the ragpicker:

> A ragpicker cannot, of course, be considered a member of the *bohème*. But from the littérateur to the professional conspirator, everyone who belonged to the *bohème* could recognize a bit of himself in the ragpicker. Each person was in a more or less blunt state of revolt against society and faced more or less a precarious future.[23]

Icons such as the bohème and the ragpicker indicate that for Benjamin, Baudelaire "sides with the asocial,"[24] while the flâneur is at the dawn of the proletarian revolution. Benjamin is implying that the flâneur is on the threshold of a major historical shift in modern civilization, but he is unconscious of it: He is experiencing the onset of capitalization when the old patronage system is still working; he is between the ages of bourgeois dominance and proletarian revolution.[25] Benjamin does not distinguish the modernist from the flâneur. For him, the modernist/flâneur is part of the crowd, unconsciously going through the historical transition. He says, "As rich as Baudelaire is in knowledge of his art, he is relatively lacking in stratagems to face the times."[26] On the other hand, Foucault has an entirely different interpretation of Baudelaire's mindset, making a clear distinction between the Baudelaireian modernist/flâneur and the ordinary flâneur as part of the crowd. For him, the modernist is a conscious actor who both represents and transgresses the age he lives in. In this sense, Foucault's theory of dandyism is in fact critiquing, or revising, Benjamin's theory of the flâneur, as I will discuss below.

Let us begin with "Qu'est-ce que les lumières" (What is enlightenment),

Foucault's 1983 course at Collège de France. Here he explicates Kant's 1784 article "Was ist Aufklärung" (What is enlightenment)[27] and refers to Baudelaire's famous treatise on the dandy in *The Painter of Modern Life* in order to define dandyism and modernity. In the following passage from Foucault's "What is Enlightenment," note how he juxtaposes someone caught unawares in the flux of time and one consciously facing his own task in the transitional moment of history:

> To be modern is not to accept oneself as one is in the flux of the passing moments; it is to take oneself as object of a complex and difficult elaboration: what Baudelaire, in the vocabulary of his day, calls dandyism.[28]
>
> (Être moderne, ce n'est pas s'accepter soi-même tel qu'on est dans le flux de moments qui passent ; c'est se prendre comme objet d'une élaboration complexe et dure : ce que Baudelaire appelle, selon le vocabulaire de l'époque, le "dandysme".)[29]

Foucault is saying here that in Baudelaire, to be a dandy, or a man of modernity, it requires a kind of "élaboration ascétique de soi" (an ascetic elaboration of the self), while dandyism is the quintessence of modernity.[30] Foucault's reading of Kant helps him develop this idea. He finds in Kant's article the indication that modernity is not only a form of relationship with the present, but also a mode of relationship that one should establish with oneself when facing the present.

In Foucault's interpretation, Kant is saying that modernity is neither an epoch, nor "a set of features characteristic of an epoch"; nor is it the "consciousness of the discontinuity of time: a break with tradition, a feeling of novelty, of vertigo (*vertige* in French) in the face of the passing moment."[31] (Note the word "vertigo" here, reminiscent of Benjamin's word "intoxication," or *Rausch* in German.[32]) Rather, it is an attitude, or an *ethos*. It is

> a mode of relating to contemporary reality; a voluntary choice made by certain people, in the end, a way of thinking and feeling; a way, too, of acting and behaving that at one and the same time marks a relation of belonging and presents itself as a task.[33]

To make it short, this *ethos* is "a voluntary choice" (un choix volontaire) made by the man of modernity to relate himself to contemporary reality (actualité). The expressions "voluntary choice" and "the elaboration of the self," or "technologies of the self," are recurrent concepts in Foucault's lectures at Collège de France in the 1970s and 1980s, and a key to understanding his theory on power relations.

How does one relate to contemporary reality, then? Foucault uses Constantin Guys, the artist in Baudelaire's *The painter of modern life*, as an example to illustrate his point. In Foucault's mind, to relate to contemporary reality, or the present, a modernist such as Guys faces three tasks: (1) Modernity is the ironic heroization of the present (cette ironique héroïsation du présent)[34]; (2) The modernist transforms the world of reality (il le transfigure)[35] through the difficult game played between the truth of reality and the exercise of freedom (jeu difficile entre la vérité du réel et l'exercice de la liberté); and (3) Modernity compels the artist to face the task of the elaboration of the self (elle [modernity] l'astreint à la tâche de s'élaborer lui-même).[36] For Foucault, it is impossible for these tasks to be accomplished in society or in body politics. The only realm where they can be achieved is in art: "They can be produced only in another milieu which Baudelaire calls art (Ils ne peuvent se produire que dans un lieu autre que Baudelaire appelle l'art)."[37]

According to Foucault, in Baudelaire the man of modernity is not a mere flâneur, who "captures it [the present moment] as a fleeting and interesting curiosity," or is "satisfied to keep his eyes open, to pay attention and to build up a storehouse of memories."[38] In contrast, the man of modernity

> hurrying, searching, has an aim loftier than that of a mere flâneur . . . He is looking for that quality which you must allow me to call 'modernity.' He makes it his business to extract from fashion whatever element it may contain of poetry within history.
>
> (Il cherche ce quelque chose qu'on nous permettra d'appeler la modernité. Il s'agit pour lui de dégager de la mode ce qu'elle peut contenir de poétique dans l'historique.)[39]

So Foucault is saying that it is the modernist's priority to extricate poetry from fashion, or to transform fashion into poetry—this is exactly what he means by the "ironic heroization of the present": the creative transformation of the present moment.

The thing to note is that, for Foucault, the heroization of the present is "ironic," because "The attitude of modernity does not treat the passing moment as sacred in order to try to maintain or perpetuate it."[40] He is saying that the modernist, adopting an ironic attitude towards the present, transforms the present rather than simply catches it in its fleeting moment: "Constantin Guys is not a flâneur . . . when the whole world is falling asleep, he begins to work, and he transforms that world."[41] Yet transforming the present does not mean denying it; for Foucault, the modernist, holding the present in high value, is urged "by a desperate eagerness" to imagine it and to transform it: Baudelairean modernity is an exercise in which extreme attention to *le réel* (l'extrême attention au réel) parallels the practice of freedom that simultaneously respects this reality and violates it. *Le réel* in Foucault, as well as in French structuralism, is always contrasted with imagination, or fiction. For Foucault, *le réel* connotes also the established order, or institutional powers; we, as subjects of knowledge and as subjects of our own actions, are always functioning under the limits of *le réel*. How can an artist both "respect" *le réel* and "violate" it at the same time? According to Foucault, through the practice of freedom, one manages to know where the limits are and to what extent one is free to transgress them. He uses the term "a limit-attitude" (une attitude limite) in order to further explain what he means by "the attitude of modernity":

> This philosophical ethos may be characterized as a limit-attitude. ... We have to move beyond the outside–inside alternative; we have to be at the frontiers. ... The point, in brief, is to transform the critique exercised in the form of inevitable limitation into a critique of practice in the form of a possible transgression.
>
> (Cet *êthos* philosophique peut se caractériser comme une attitude limite. ... On doit échapper à l'alternative du dehors et du dedans ; il faut être aux frontières. ... Il s'agit en somme de transformer la critique exercée dans la forme de la limitation nécesaire en une critique pratique dans la forme du franchissement possible.)[42]

Thus to Foucault, the attitude of modernity is to position oneself neither inside nor outside the limits of the established order, but to be both inside and outside at the same time: The modernist has to be always at the frontiers, constantly testing the limits of institutional powers in order to find possibilities to transgress them. For him, it is a game (un jeu) played between the practice of freedom and *le réel*. It is exactly through the practice of freedom that individual agency is possible when confronting institutional powers.

To sum up the discussion above, while Benjamin's flâneur, swayed by the commodity and the crowd, is unaware of his own condition on the threshold of modern history, Foucault's dandy/modernist, on the other hand, constrained by the limits imposed on him but impatient for freedom,[43] is fully conscious of his own position at the frontiers, ready for any possible transgression. In seeing modernity as an *ethos* and the modernist as a conscious actor who is keen on self-invention and changing the status quo, Foucault is approaching the attitude of modernity as an ethical or philosophical enquiry: It is an ontological critique of ourselves with "a historico-practical test of the limits that we may go beyond," and thus it is "work carried out by ourselves upon ourselves as free beings" (travail de nous-même sur nous-même en tant qu'êtres libres).[44] Furthermore, this historico-critical attitude has to be an experimental attitude (une attitude expérimentale).[45] In short, for Foucault, the attitude of modernity is a voluntary choice we make when, confronting our own era, we experiment by testing our thoughts, words, and actions against the limits of the established order in order to transgress them and bring about creative transformation. If there is no personal freedom or personal agency in the face of institutional powers, how could revolution or creativity ever be possible?

While the idea of the personal agency of the cultural translator intervening on the transcultural site to effect creative transformation runs throughout this book, the concept of dandyism in connection with the Shanghai Neo-Sensation writers will be fully developed in Chapters 1 and 2.

The dandy, the modern girl, and the modern boy

In developing the concept of dandyism, I lay out the Neo-Sensation gender triad formed by the dandy, the modern girl, and the modern boy. First, there should be a few words on the so-called Neo-Sensation School.

As explained in the preface, this book uses the Shanghai Neo-Sensation School as a point of departure to develop the concept of transcultural modernity. It was in practice briefly from the late 1920s to the late 1930s, featuring a small group of burgeoning writers, including Liu Na'ou 劉吶鷗, Mu Shiying 穆時英, Shi Zhicun 施蟄存, Guo Jianying 郭建英, Ye Lingfeng 葉靈鳳, and Heiying 黑嬰.[46] In fact, in the beginning they never called themselves by that name. A pejorative label attached by a contemporary critic, it implied the copying of their more prominent Japanese counterparts, among whom were Yokomitsu Riichi 橫光利一 and the Nobel Prize winner Kawabata Yasunari 川端康成. Unlike the Japanese group, who consistently wrote articles defending their Neo-Sensation position and agenda, the Shanghai group never officially declared they were a "school." Shi Zhicun even denied in later years that he had been a so-called "Neo-Sensation writer." But as I will show in Chapter 1, at least in 1934 the cartoonist Guo Jianying already called their group by that name.

The Japanese Neo-Sensation School flourished in the period from 1923, the year of the Great Tokyo Earthquake, to the early 1930s. As short-lived as it was in both China and Japan, the practice of this unique genre manifested splendidly the ongoing cross-cultural exchanges in the Euro-Asian context. We should be aware that the transcultural phenomenon I point out in connection with the Neo-Sensation writers was by no means exclusive to them at all; most writers during the time in both countries were engaging in similar transcultural practices. I will not elaborate on this now, but concentrate on the Neo-Sensation writers. To me the most prominent feature of their writing is the triad formed by the dandy, the modern girl, and the modern boy. Before I delve into this, the term "Neo-Sensation" needs some clarification first.

The term immediately reminds one of the Romantic concept of sensibility, of course. But there are essential differences between these two kinds of sensibilities. To make it short, the Romantic tradition stresses the subjectivity of the poet, who transforms the external reality into something transcendental, whereas Neo-Sensation emphasizes the semi-objective position of the writer, who absorbs external stimulations and presents them through the filtering of his eye and language, without aiming at the transcendental. Synesthesia, or the harmony and fusion of the five senses, represents for Romanticism the transcendence of the soul. The concept of the soul, on the other hand, does not concern Neo-Sensation at all. In contrast to the Romantic preoccupation with nature and transcendental experiences, what the Neo-Sensation writer seeks is a new mode of expression, what I would call the Neo-Sensation mode, that can capture the new type of sensations aroused in a cosmopolitan, fast-moving world marked by superficial commercialism and the speed brought about by modern technology. For Yokomitsu Riichi, the Neo-Sensation captured in their new language represents the "thing-in-itself" that escapes the ordinary eye. His article "On Neo-Sensation" 新感覺論 imbues this concept with an epistemological dimension by responding to and critiquing Kant, as I will show in Chapter 3.

Most studies of the Neo-Sensation School in China or Japan center on the image of the modern girl portrayed in their stories, as does Shu-mei Shih's 2001 book *The Lure of the Modern: Writing Modernism in Semicolonial China, 1917–1937*.[47] Miriam Silverbers's 2006 book, *Erotic Grotesque Nonsense: The Mass Culture of Japanese Modern Times*, on the other hand, looks at the Japanese modern girl as "a creation of the mass media,"[48] which was true of the Chinese modern girl as well. On the other hand, I intend to approach the topic from a different perspective. As I see it, the modern girl, who has become the subject of cross-cultural, transnational studies in recent years, is basically a creation of the dandy's gaze. Both the Japanese and Shanghai Neo-Sensation writers, deeply indebted to Paul Morand, were more or less self-styled dandies like him, who made it a rule not only to live but to write in the dandyish style. Without looking at the modern girl from the perspective of dandyism, one will fail to see the modern girl as the essence of modernist construct both embodying and critiquing the pursuit of modernism. If we borrow Foucault's concept, the modern girl's image represents the dandy's ironic attitudes towards "the modern" embodied in her. The modern girl epitomizes the dandy's "heroization of the present," in other words.

Some clarification is needed between the modern girl and her predecessor who emerged one or two decades earlier, the New Woman. The two certainly overlapped somewhat in time and shared certain characteristics. The French *fin-de-siècle* new woman, "who lived and worked independently from her family" because of depleted family fortunes or inflation, also represented a global phenomenon.[49] In Japan, the Seitōsha 青鞜社 (Blue Stocking Society) women writers were famous examples of the new woman, who was marked by her avant-garde, bohemian way of life.[50] In China, the new woman could be a middle-class girl aspiring to enlightenment and free love, struggling to support herself through college in big cities such as Beijing, Shanghai, Tokyo, or even Paris by writing stories or working freelance. Thus she gained to some extent sexual freedom and economic independence as an intellectual. Stories are well known of how Bai Wei 白薇 (1894–198?) and Lu Yin 廬隱 (1899–1934) became renowned women writers in the literary circles in Beijing and Shanghai dominated by May Fourth male writers.[51] One of the most memorable images of the new woman in China is the decadent woman writer portrayed in the 1934 silent film *Xin nüxing* 新女性 (The New Woman), in which she is contrasted with a "progressive" leftist woman worker.

Both the new woman and the modern girl were criticized for being

12   *Dandyism and Transcultural Modernity*

decadent and departing from traditional mores. But the new woman's struggle for independence and intellectual achievements commanded respect to some degree, whereas the modern girl as a rule was relentlessly ridiculed by contemporaries for her ignorance and looseness, or her behavior manifesting *teisō kannen ga nai* 貞操観念がない (without the concept of chastity), as the Japanese would say. In France also she was an object of ridicule. Louis Icart's (1888–1950) 1916 sketch in the wartime magazine *A coups de Baïonnette* (At the Thrust of the Spear) is most telling in this regard. In the sketch, in a shop for *haute couture*, a modern girl is trying on clothes. At the corner of the dressing room, her escort, in army uniform, is waiting for her. Looking at herself in the new outfit in the mirror, she says to him in a nonchalant way, "The war is so long. . . . " The officer, yawning, says, "Oh! But by no means as long as trying on clothing" (Figure Intro.2).[52] The

Figure Intro.2 "The war is so long. . . . "

modern girl living a life of luxury and decadence despite the onset of war and human suffering was a transnational topic. Wherever she was—in France as *la femme moderne*, in Japan as *modan gāru* モダン．ガール, or in China as *modeng nülang* 摩登女郎—the modern girl embodied the quality of *ero guro nansensu* エロ．グロ．ナンセンス, or "érotique grotesque nonsense," a phrase imbued with French, English, and Japanese connotations. The term, transported to Shanghai in the 1930s, turned the original concept as well as her dandyish observer into the target of ridicule, as I will show in the analysis of a Shanghai cartoon in Chapter 2.

Like the new woman, the modern girl during the 1920s and 1930s had, of course, a historical existence aside from being a creation of the male gaze. The overlapping and interplay between the real being and the constructed image of the modern girl would certainly be a meaningful topic of investigation. What interests me in this book, however, is her image as a cultural construct. Distinct from similar studies of the modern girl in Japanese, English, or French gender culture, I propose to decode her image through the concept of dandyism, the mindset that created her cultural image. To me, dandyism represents the essence of transcultural modernity.

In my concept of dandyism, first and foremost, the dandy has to be defined by his relationship with the modern girl. The dandy and the modern girl are two sides of the coin; the modern girl is the reflection of his self—his obsession with her is a manifestation of narcissism. In addition, without the modern girl, the dandy would lose the *raison d'être* of his existence: He needs her to reinforce his role as a dandy. But the modern girl is his inferior other self. A defender of good taste and *préciosité*, the dandy takes upon himself the duty of teaching the modern girl how to behave and dress. While he is infatuated with her looks and refinery, he is highly suspicious of her intelligence and fidelity, disclosing a deeply rooted misogyny on his part. Most intriguing is that, as much as he despises her intellectual inferiority and infidelity, the dandy is nevertheless powerlessly drawn towards the modern girl and overcome by her. Or one should say, he half willingly puts up with her ignorance and suffers her betrayal and mistreatment; masochism is no doubt involved. In fact, it is a relationship of mutual torture between the dandy and the modern girl.

One can say that, to the dandy, the modern girl has nothing but a face and a body. If the dandy assigns the modern girl the role of mannequin, he himself is the designer. Or, to be more exact, he combines the roles of designer and mannequin. He invents himself, whereas the modern girl is incapable of self-invention. But Coco Chanel, a modern girl who becomes a fashion designer and thus is capable of self-invention, would be recognized by a dandy like Paul Morand as a female dandy. He embraces her as his perfect other self and gives her the role of narrator, allowing her to tell her own story in his book. This is discussed in Chapter 2.

"Misogyny," the word that I employ to indicate the love–hate relationship between the dandy and the modern girl, is used humorously in a

Neo-Sensation story about the modern girl and the modern boy, as is discussed in Chapter 5. The modern boy, on a par with the modern girl in every way, is also the dandy's inferior other self. A dandyish figure emerging during the late Taishō and early Shōwa periods and known as *modan boi* モダン．ボイ, or *mobo* モボ, he was the male counterpart of *moga* モガ, or *modan gāru*. It was the cultural critic and journalist Nii Itaru 新居格 (1888–1951) who invented neologisms such as *moga, mobo, Marukusu boi* マルクス．ボイ (Marxist Boy), and *Engurusu gāru* エングルス．ガール (Engels Girl).[53] For a telling illustration of the image of the *moga-mobo* pair during the period, we can look at Tanaka Hisara's 田中比左良 1929 comic strip with 48 boxes, "Mogako to moborō" モガ子とモボ郎 (Miss Modern Girl and Master Modern Boy). In box 19, a modern girl and a modern boy are all dressed up in their fashionable Western clothes but look absolutely frustrated in front of a little girl in the countryside. The bandana worn as headdress and the baby carried on her back indicate that, as young as she is, she already functions as part of the workforce. With a singsong line, she is making fun of the pair for their good-for-nothingness: "If the modern girl were human, flowers would bloom on the power poles." Crouching beside her feet, a frog croaks in refrain: "Modern girl! Silly! Modern boy! Silly!" (Figure Intro.3).[54] The whole series is about how the modern girl craves fashion, prefers sea bath to traditional hot spring bath, tortures the modern boy with her coyness, and challenges him to modern sports such as tennis and skating.

Unlike the modern girl, who has become a prominent subject of interdisciplinary studies worldwide, the modern boy in Japan and China has drawn little scholarly attention so far. Exactly like the modern girl, he is a conspicuous figure in commercials for hats, cigarettes, hairstyles, tailored clothes, and so on, and always referred to in a pejorative fashion, if ever mentioned at all. Both the modern girl and the modern boy are denounced as

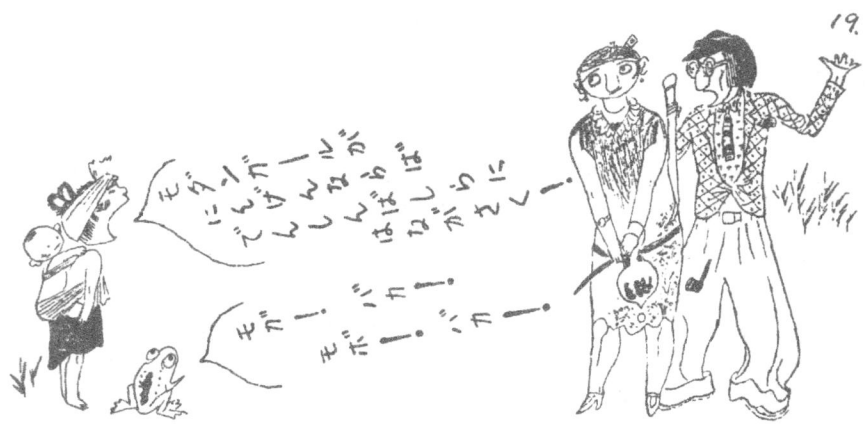

Figure Intro.3 Miss Modern Girl and Master Modern Boy.

symbols of decadence and "ero-guro-nansensu." In a sense, the modern boy is the dandy's inferior same-sex other self.

We should say that there is something of a dandy in every modern girl and modern boy, and vice versa. But the dandy is different from his male and female other selves in age—the modern boy and girl are relatively young, say, from the late teens to early thirties, whereas the dandy has no age limit. Yet, the major feature that distinguishes a dandy from his other selves is not age difference, but his status as an artist. In contrast to the modern girl and the modern boy who may have a job as a taxi dancer, a shop girl, a journalist, or even a lawyer—apart from a possible sideline career as a kept woman or a gigolo—the dandy's major, most often sole, occupation is art, a profession that allows him the luxury of being idle and creative at the same time. In addition to the predilection for fashionable dress and living that the modern girl and the modern boy share, the dandy aims at an aesthetic project. Dandyism connotes an aesthetic statement as well as a fashionable lifestyle, as is discussed in Chapters 1 and 2. Chapter 1 is devoted to Liu Na'ou as a dandy *par excellence*. Born in colonial Taiwan and educated in Tokyo, he established his literary career as the leader of the Neo-Sensation writers in Shanghai. His diary kept in 1927 as well as his other writings illustrate well the dandy as a person and dandyism as an aesthetic project. Chapter 2 uses the concept of dandyism to connect Paul Morand with his Japanese and Chinese followers. The modern girl and the modern boy are recurrent figures in the book as a contrast to the dandy/cultural translator.

The concept of dandyism, yet to be fully problematized in Chapters 1 and 2, is an area invested with significant theoretical energy. According to my concept of transcultural modernity, the dandy is a conscious actor who works on the transcultural site and brings about creative transformation in art, language, and culture; he sets the trends. In contrast, the modern boy or the modern girl is the site itself, floating with the trends without being aware of their historical significance. While the dandy, acting as a cultural translator, transforms the influx and outflow of heterogeneous information through the transcultural site, his inferior other selves are receptacles through which information is received and then flows out. The first three boxes in Tanaka Hisara's comic strip discussed above can serve as a telling illustration.

In box 1, the modern girl, reading the newspaper, repeats what she reads: "What . . . How about it . . . Japanese-style light, transparent clothes (*usumono* 羅物) are strictly forbidden . . . says MPD (Metropolitan Police Department) . . . All for it!" (Figure Intro.4). In box 2, she says to a woman wearing a *usumono* on the street, "It is shameful to wear this kind of *usumono*, so stop wearing it. It is Japanese women's shame." Taken by surprise, the traditional woman asks her, "What about your own *usumono*?" (Figure Intro.5). In box 3, the modern girl, in a Chanel-style chiffon dress exposing her knees, responds with a series of adjectives formed with the suffix "teki" 的 to distinguish the clothes both were wearing: "Mine is aesthetic (*shinbiteki* 審美的), artistic (*geijutsuteki* 藝術的), creative (*dokusōteki* 獨創的), cultural

16 *Dandyism and Transcultural Modernity*

Figure Intro.4 Miss Modern Girl and Master Modern Boy.

Figure Intro.5 Miss Modern Girl and Master Modern Boy.

(*bunkateki* 文化的), expressive of virgin beauty (*shojobi hakkiteki* 處女美發揮的). Whatever it looks like, it is different (*teki wa teki demo teki ga chigau* 的は的でも的が違う). Yours is lascivious (*chōhatsuteki* 挑發的) and decadent (*taihaiteki* 頹廢的)" (Figure Intro.6).[55]

Here the modern girl's behavior is typical of a receiver/transmitter of knowledge. First, she takes in the information learned from the newspaper

Figure Intro.6 Miss Modern Girl and Master Modern Boy.

and, following the MPD's order to ban traditional clothes, starts policing the street on her own. Second, the latest Parisian fashion she is wearing and the Japanese flag in her hair form an incongruous combination which is emblematic of the Meiji patriotic slogan: "out of Asia, into Europe" (*datsua nyūō* 脱亜入欧), a concept that envisions a stronger Japan on a par with European imperialist nations. (See Chapter 3 for a more detailed discussion.) Third, her language full of "teki" is reflexive of the Europeanized Japanese language during the Meiji period. According to *Social History of the Meiji, Taishō, and Shōwa Periods* (Meiji Taishō Shōwa sesōshi 明治大正昭和世相史):

> After the tenth year of Meiji [1877], philosophers began to use terms such as positive [*sekkyokuteki* 積極的], collateral [*bōkeiteki* 傍系的], and abstract [*chūshōteki* 抽象的]. This led to concocted terms such as literary [*bungakuteki* 文學的], barbarian [*yabanteki* 野蠻的], and womanly [*fujoteki* 婦女的], with "teki" added to compound words. This practice became popular in common usage around the twenty-second year of Meiji [1889].⁵⁶

While the modern girl and the modern boy are parroting back information, be it ideological or linguistic, language innovation is a prominent feature for the Neo-Sensation mode of writing. I use the concept of "the macaronic" (the free combination of expressions from different language systems) to discuss the transcultural hybridity of the Neo-Sensation language. To me the macaronic, highlighting the cultural translator's negotiation between foreign/ native, national/regional, classical/vernacular, elite/popular language codes, is emblematic of the essence of transcultural modernity. By analyzing the macaronic, we see how cultural translators, juggling between different institutional powers, manage to invent new expressions through creative transformation while introducing new concepts.

Chapter 3 calls attention to the modern girls and modern boys in Yokomitsu Riichi's novel. Swept to Shanghai by revolutions and imperial wars, they are unconscious of the historical significance of what they are going through. They are the flâneurs and flâneuses in the Foucaldian sense, constituting part of the crowd and caught in the "vertigo" of the flitting moments. In contrast, those who create their images in stories and cartoons are dandies, writers, and cultural translators who adopt an ironic attitude towards their era, accomplishing creative transformation with a brand new mode of expression. Chapters 4 and 5 also begin with modern boys and modern girls. We will see how they parrot slogan and scientific terms in a tongue-in-cheek fashion, throwing into light the writers' ridicule of the modernist pursuit characteristic of their times. The laughable images of the modern boy and the modern girl are also a form of self-mockery reflecting how much Neo-Sensation writers are conscious of their own roles as propellers of modernity on the transcultural site. These two chapters are mainly about the traveling of texts and cultural translators who, encountering them on the transcultural site, resort to personal agency to effect creative transformation. They are juxtaposed with modern girls and modern boys who are simply repeating information learned from fiction and the mass media.

To illustrate the dandy/cultural translator's self-mockery and self-consciousness, I would like to refer to a 1936 comic strip published in the magazine *Modern Sketch* (Shidai manhua 時代漫畫). Titled "Wild Prophesy of the Future Cityscape of Shanghai" (Weilai de Shanghai fengguang de kuangce 未來的上海風光的狂測), it comprises twelve boxes that depict an army of modern girls, militant and nearly stark naked, as future leaders of the metropolitan city. As seen in box 1, in this future society, thongs are the only permitted clothing. So they patrol the street to prohibit men from wearing pants, which are "remnants of feudalism" (*fengjian de yunie* 封建的餘孽) (Figure Intro.7).[57] All jobs are taken up by women, including pulling the rickshaw, while men, becoming unemployed, stay at home. Hiring beautiful men as waiters turns out to be a sensational attraction, whereas it becomes fashionable for women to take several husbands at the same time, a practice that leads to a rampage of sexual diseases. As a result, "there are more hospitals for venereal diseases than tobacco shops." As shown in box 7, magazines on men are bestsellers, while pornography is sold on the street, including *Sex Histories* (Xingshi 性史, 1926), a collection of Havelock Ellis-style case studies of personal sexual experiences reputed to be compiled by the legendary "Dr Sex," Zhang Jingsheng 張競生 (Figure Intro.8).[58] It is obvious that this future society ruled by modern girls is a ridicule of the gynecocracy envisioned in Zhang's utopian works in 1925, *An Aesthetic Outlook on Life* (Mei de renshengguan 美的人生觀) and *Organization of an*

Figure Intro.7 Wild Prophesy of the Future Cityscape of Shanghai.

Figure Intro.8 Sex Histories.

20 *Dandyism and Transcultural Modernity*

Aesthetic Society (Mei de shehui zuzhifa 美的社會組織法). In his imagined future world women rule with their sexual power, while their aesthetic instincts transform all aspects of society, including sartorial reform promoting scanty clothes and the progressive practice of nude sea bathing.[59] In our Shanghai dandy's parodic future world dominated by women, men are virtually turned into sex slaves. It is no doubt the dandy's self-mockery of his own obsession with the modern girl: He is always at her mercy.

Furthermore, as box 8 indicates, the pastime *du jour* for modern girls is walking turtles and snakes on the streets (Figure Intro.9).[60] In the Chinese context, turtles connote cuckoldry—a husband whose wife commits adultery is called a "turtle." Snakes, the traditional symbol of *la femme fatale*, may refer to gigolos, *les hommes fatals* in this future gynarchy. But one aspect is more interesting to this study: Those who are familiar with Walter Benjamin's 1938 work, "The Paris of the Second Empire in Baudelaire," will be instantly reminded of the connection between the turtle and the flâneur. As he writes:

> He [the flâneur] goes his leisurely way as a personality; in this manner he protests against the division of labor which makes people into specialists. He protests no less against their industriousness. Around 1840 it was briefly fashionable to take turtles for a walk in the arcades. The flâneurs liked to have the turtles set the pace for them. If they had had their way, progress would have been obliged to accommodate itself to this pace.[61]

Figure Intro.9 Wild Prophesy of the Future Cityscape of Shanghai.

For Benjamin, walking the turtles in the arcades seems to indicate the dandy's boredom and the dreamer's nostalgia for bygone days,[62] but in fact symbolizes the Baudelairean flâneurs' gesture of countering industrialization marked by the division of labor, industriousness, and progress; it is a symbolic resistance against modernization. But our Shanghai dandy here, who envisions this fantastic rhapsody of the future Shanghai, reverses the Baudelairean prototype by transforming the flâneur into the militant flâneuse. The modern girl in this future Shanghai is walking not only turtles, but dandies and modern boys—including Baudelaire the archetypal dandy—who willingly submit themselves to her enchanting power. Our Shanghai dandy's playful mimicry, while introducing a European modernist concept into China, is mocking not only the subject of his study—the militant modern girl—but the "original copy" of the concept as well as himself. This is possible only through his art of creative transformation.

1 A dandy, traveler, and woman watcher
Liu Na'ou from Taiwan

The end of life is lonely; saying goodbye especially makes us feel alone. *Bon voyage ! O ! frère !*

(Happy voyage! O! brother!)

A perpetual traveler: transcultural practice

On 5 May 1927 Liu Na'ou (1905–40), watching his younger brother leave for Tokyo from their home in Tainan, Taiwan, wrote in his diary, "*Bon voyage ! O ! frère !*"[1] (Liu's own French). He himself, though thirsting to return to Shanghai, had to remain in Tainan until his grandmother's funeral. Inspired by Baudelaire's famous line, "*Hypocrite lecteur,—mon semblable,—mon frère !*" (Hypocrite reader, my likeness, my brother!),[2] Liu's seafaring feeling sounds a mumbo jumbo of transcultural blending and affectation. Liu's diary volume, dated "the sixteenth year of Taishō," was made by Shinchōsha 新潮社 in Tokyo. The Emperor Taishō in fact ruled for only 15 years before he died on 25 December 1926, too late for publishers to change the publication year of titles to be released. In all likelihood Liu bought the diary in Tokyo late that year, when he revisited there, or in Shanghai, where he was staying then.

Born into a landlord's household and having lost his father when he was 12 years old, Liu Na'ou always had a problem with his mother, who represented the "feudal system" to him. Fortunately enough, his mother, though uneducated herself, did what most wealthy Taiwanese parents were doing at the time, sending her two sons and one daughter to Japan and China to study while generously providing for them. At the age of 22 Liu Na'ou was already an experienced traveler, constantly journeying to Taiwan, Japan, and China. Like the language in his diary, written in awkward Chinese vernacular studded with English, French, Japanese, German, and Taiwanese expressions, he was very much "a man of the world," a phrase concocted by one of his closest friends after his much disputed murder in Shanghai in 1940.[3] This phrase was intended to connote a transcultural artist who aspires to artistic freedom and perfection while transcending national, linguistic, and cultural boundaries.

Indeed, his everyday life was by no means free from limitations. Born in colonial Taiwan in 1905 and a Japanese by nationality, in 1920 he transferred from the Presbyterian School in Tainan to the high school division of Aoyama College in Tokyo, because there were limited opportunities for a colonized citizen to continue higher learning in the colony.[4] He continued to study at the Advanced Learning Division (Kōtō gakubu 高等学部) of Aoyama College in 1923 and graduated with honors from the English Department in March 1926.[5] In the summer of 1926 he entered the special French program at L'Université L'Aurore in Shanghai and became Dai Wangshu's 戴望舒 classmate; Shi Zhicun and Du Heng 杜衡 entered the program the following year.[6] Liu's diary relates how in January 1927 these students, who would later make a name for the Shanghai Neo-Sensation School, dreamed together about an aborted plan of establishing a journal called *Modern Heart* (Jindai xin 近代心), which, incorporating illustrations and light-hearted vignettes, was intended to bridge the chasm between elitism and popular tastes.[7] Such a dream would not come true until January 1934, when Guo Jianying, a cartoonist and fellow Neo-Sensation writer, became the editor-in-chief of *The Women's Pictorial* (Furen huabao 婦人畫報) with the support of Liu's coterie in January 1934. More will be said about this in Chapter 2.

Liu Na'ou was not alone in his experiences of diaspora and in resorting to art to defy the predicament of identity during the Japanese occupation in Taiwan. There were numerous others, for instance, to name just a few, Yang Kui 楊逵 (1905–85), who studied in Tokyo from 1924 to 1927 and then became the foremost of the proletarian writers in Taiwan; Zhang Wuojun 張我軍 (1902–55), a leader of the vernacular literature movement in Taiwan who studied Chinese literature and taught Japanese in Beijing off and on from 1921 to 1946; and Zhang Shenqie 張深切 (1904–65), who studied in Japan from 1917 to 1921 and in Shanghai from 1923 to 1924, and then became a writer, playwright, screenplay writer, and filmmaker in Taiwan and China. It was not easy for Taiwanese at the time to live and work in colonial Taiwan or China during the Sino-Japanese war. One example will show how Taiwanese struggled through living in the conflicts of nations. In the 1930s Zhang Wuojun worked as a Japanese translator for the Beijing government, but the night before the Japanese invasion in July 1937 all the government officials evacuated from the city clandestinely with the army without telling him, because they were afraid that, being a Taiwanese, he might inform the Japanese of the evacuation plan. As a result he and his family were left in the occupied capital. After the war until his death in Taiwan in 1955, he was never cleared of collaborating with the Japanese in wartime Beijing.[8]

During the time Liu Na'ou was in Shanghai he pretended to be Fukienese, because he was aware that in the semicolonized metropolis in China a Taiwanese was likely to be suspected of being a Japanese spy.[9] There were contemporaries, such as Ye Lingfeng, who thought he was half-Japanese.[10] But, even though he was aware of the inconvenience of his Taiwanese identity in wartime China, he was not alert enough to keep himself away from danger. Perhaps due to his lack of territorial or national allegiance as a Taiwanese in semicolonial Shanghai, during his literary and film careers he did not hesitate to engage in transcultural/transnational practices, associating with the various contending political institutions there: the leftists, the Nationalist government, the Wang Jingwei 汪精衛 puppet regime, and the Japanese.

On the other hand, it might also indicate that as an artist, his only allegiance was to art: He was eager to embrace as many opportunities as possible to further his film career. For that purpose, he had to test the limits of institutional powers to find possibilities for breakthroughs. He served for sometime as the director of Screen Playwrights and Film Directors Committee of the Central Film Studio, run by the Nationalist government in Nanjing.[11] In that capacity he made an anti-Japanese movie, *Secret Code* (Midianma 密電碼), in 1937. He also made movies for several leftist companies. For the Star Studio, he directed *The Everlasting Smile* (Yongyuan de weixiao 永遠的微笑) in 1936, starring the famous actress Hu Die 胡蝶. For the Artistic China Film Studio, he wrote the screenplay and undertook the directorship of *First Love* 初戀 (Chulian) in 1936. For the Light Studio, he adapted Pearl Buck's novel *Mother* into the screenplay for *Daughter of the Earth* (Dadi de nüer 大地的女兒) in 1937. Then, during the Sino-Japanese war, he was hired in 1939 as manager of the China Film Studio, established by the Cultural Bureau under the Japanese Kōa'in 興亞院 (The Asia Development Board).[12] With such complicated involvement in the entanglement of semicolonial politics, he was walking on thin ice. Engaging in transcultural practices while relentlessly testing the limits of national boundaries, he ended up being a victim of his own recklessness.

The cause of his murder on 3 September 1940 by an unidentified gunman, who ambushed him from the staircase of a restaurant and shot him three times,[13] has been a mystery in literary history. The murder took place right after a lunch party held in his honor by a group of Japanese and Chinese friends, celebrating his succession to the directorship of *National Subjects' Daily* (Guomin xinwenshe 國民新聞社) after Mu Shiying (1912–40), a fellow Neo-Sensation writer and filmmaker. After the assassination, Liu was immediately taken to a nearby hospital in his Japanese friend's car, but died before arriving there.

National Subjects' Daily was a news agency run by the Wang Jingwei puppet regime. On 28 June of the same year, while functioning as its founding director, Mu had likewise been shot and died on the way to the same hospital.[14] No one knew if these two murders were connected or instigated by the same agency. There were rumors that Liu's murder was committed by the Japanese secret agency because they thought he was a double agent for the Nationalist government. Some, on the other hand, believed that the Nationalist Party secret agency had him killed because he was thought to collaborate with the Japanese.[15] Shi Zhicun even suspected that Liu's killer was sent by the notorious Du Yuesheng's 杜月笙 gang for outstanding gambling debts.[16]

Whatever the real cause was, Liu's tragic death points to the danger inherent in the semicolonial society in Shanghai, where no single government enforced its laws and protection was not guaranteed to subjects of any nationality; Liu's transcultural practice and ambiguous identity certainly did not assist him in this regard.

A man with multiple identities imposed on him, Liu eventually chose to be a self-styled modernist, an identity that accorded with his personality and lifestyle as a dandy. Like many of his contemporary writers in China, he began his literary career with a few mediocre stories written in the proletarian vein, while the bookstore he established in 1929 with his own funds was a *rendevouz* for leftist intellectuals before it was eventually closed down by the Nationalist government.[17] He switched to modernism almost immediately, because he was tired of the proletarian emphasis on content at the expense of form.[18] The modernist stories his coterie wrote were criticized by the contemporary critic and editor-in-chief of *Literary News* (Wenyi xinwen 文藝新聞), Lou Shiyi 樓適夷, who perceptively pointed out in 1931 that his group "transported Neo-Sensation to Shanghai from Japan."[19] In fact, before that Liu and his coterie never called themselves the Neo-Sensation School. But in April 1934 Guo Jianying, acting as editor-in-chief of *The Women's Pictorial*, acknowledged the label and wrote in the editor's afterword, "Mr Hei Ying is a newcomer to the modern Chinese Neo-Sensation School."[20]

For Liu Na'ou acquiring the aesthetic values of modernism required a complex process of acculturation, which is "a process of intercultural borrowing marked by the continuous transmission of traits and elements between diverse peoples and resulting in new and blended patterns."[21] In the context of Latin American mixed culture, the term "acculturation" emphasizes the "one-way imposition of the dominant culture," whereas the Cuban anthropologist Fernando Ortiz concocted the term "transculturation" to indicate that intercultural dynamics are a "two-way give and take."[22] Although writers or artists in the third world seem to imitate the dominant culture, the "two-way give and take" is basically a process of creative transformation. Thus while it was prerequisite for Liu to imitate and show allegiance to international modernism, at the same time the modernist traits and elements manifested in him were inevitably blended with the characteristics of his own cultural traditions and personal history. Liu, disguised as a Fukienese in Shanghai with Baudelaire as his mentor and the Japanese Neo-Sensation writers as his models, remained Taiwanese at bottom, though certainly transformed. The "new and blended patterns" manifested in Liu's modernism were no longer the original patterns found in Baudelaire or the moderated patterns found in the Japanese Neo-Sensation writers, while Liu, acculturated in these international trends through the experiences of diaspora, was in a sense emancipated from the limited visions of insulated islanders. His life and work manifested the essence of transculturation.

Denouncing the injustice of the colonial policy and the loss caused by exile, forced or self-willed, does not prevent one from recognizing the modernization brought about by colonialism, which benefits the colonized as well as the colonizer. Nor does it prevent one from appreciating the liberating capacity resulting from the experiences of diaspora. The question is, if for writers such as Liu Na'ou the aesthetics of universal literary laws created the possibility of liberating the self, how did they come to terms with the particular? Terry Eagleton, dealing with a similar situation confronting Irish writers, points out that the contradictions are not so unresolvable that "Particularity is either suppressed in the totality of universal Reason, the concrete Irish subject sublated to a citizen of the world, or celebrated as a unique, irreducible state of being impenetrable to all alien Enlightenment rationality."[23] Indeed, while governed by a universal aesthetic law, the work of art manifested in each artist is inscribed with individual emotions, sensations, and impulses as well as local, regional, and national particularities.

For 1920s Taiwan there was no totalizing vision that could easily conciliate the radical view of individual enlightenment and the regionalist particularity of twentieth-century Taiwanese nationalist consciousness, especially when that consciousness was divided among Japan the colonial sovereignty, China the motherland, and Taiwan the native land. As Seamus Deane puts it when he refers to the Irish condition, it is not oppositions to be erased or a theoretical paradox to be resolved, "it is a condition to be passionately lived."[24]

Liu Na'ou and his contemporary Taiwanese writers did live passionately through the contradictions facing their artistic lives during the Japanese occupation. Liu, as a dandy philandering in Shanghai, Yang Kui, writing as a proletarianist in Taiwan, and Zhang Wojun, advocating Taiwanese literary reform from Beijing, infused their personal tastes and lives into their literary beliefs. They were all transcultural artists who constantly tested the limits of national boundaries. Their respective literary practices, inseparable from their literary or socialist activities that implicated them in the semicolonial politics in Shanghai, Beijing, or colonial politics in Taiwan, eventually brought dangers to their lives. Liu's death by assassination in Shanghai and Yang's constant imprisonment both during and after the Japanese occupation bespeak the insurmountable laws of semicolonial or colonial politics that entangled individual identities while leaving the universal aesthetic laws powerless.

A dandy *par excellence* and misogyny

Liu Na'ou's modernism is most effectively manifested in his dandyism. In my conceptualization, dandyism is as much a literary mode as a lifestyle.

As far as lifestyle is concerned, a dandy by definition is a man with means and leisure, who pays meticulous attention to his dresses and appearance. Liu had particular tastes about his clothes, as can be seen in his 1927 diary. It was his habit to go to specific stores for different styles of clothes, all tailor-made. For instance, on 5 April he writes: "Had a suit and two summer outfits made at Wang Qingchang's 王慶昌"; on 8 December he writes: "Had a tuxedo made at Wang Shunchang's 王順昌"; and on 12 December: "Tried on the clothes at Wang Shunchang's."[25] In a family film with an English title, *The Man Who Has the Camera*, probably made in the mid 1930s in Shanghai, Liu is seen in different scenes wearing a white suit and a white hat, apparently his favorite outfit.[26] In addition, he is a devout dancer with the nickname "The Dancing King," regularly frequenting dance halls and exercising dance steps with his friends as well as studying dance manuals to perfect his skill. For instance, on 3 February Liu writes, "Returned to his home and taught him fox-trot."[27] Here "him" refers to his childhood friend from Tainan, Lin Chengshui 林澄水, who was at the time working in Shanghai. On Liu's July reading list there are two dance manuals with French titles: "Apprenons à danser" (Let's Learn to Dance) and "Danses modernes" (Modern Dance Steps). On the August reading list there is another dance manual with an English title, "Dancing Do's and Don'ts."[28] The thing to note is that the performance of the dandy, no less than a task, needs constant practice in order to achieve perfection.

On the surface, dandyism in Liu seems to be a lifestyle, or a matter of taste; it is the taste of the affluent class in metropolitan Shanghai—the new aristocracy in democratic China. Yet, for a dandy, to strive for perfection is more than a lifestyle or taste. It is an attitude, the urge for self-invention. These dance manuals recorded in his diary tell us that Liu is not satisfied as simply a good dancer; he spares no effort in perfecting his dancing art. To illustrate my point of the dandy's urge for self-invention, it is necessary to bring in here Liu's European mentor, Baudelaire. As much as Liu demonstrates a fine specimen of a Shanghai dandy in the 1930s, however, we should not forget that the lineage of the dandy can be easily traced to Baudelaire in Paris or Oscar Wilde in London in the latter half of the nineteenth century. Baudelaire, though not exactly a dandy himself, wrote the single treatise on dandyism that defined the dandy as a species. The dandy as a species has crossed the boundaries of nations and time.

If we check the passages titled "La Modernité" and "Le Dandy" in Baudelaire's *The Painter of Modern Life*, it is clear that Foucault's interpretation of modernity comes mainly from Baudelaire, as I have mentioned in the introduction, while the meaning of the so-called "ascetic elaboration of the self," which is the central idea in Foucault's *History of Sexuality*, becomes much clearer.

In "Le Dandy" the dandy is defined as "L'homme rich, oisif" (the rich, idle man), whose only occupation is "l'élégance," and who is raised in luxury and, from youth on, accustomed to the obedience of other people. He enjoys at all times "une physionomie distincte" (a distinct appearance), with a love for "distinction." In addition, dandyism is "une institution vague," meaning it is an institution without written laws. According to Baudelaire, dandyism as an institution is "en dehors des lois" (outside of laws), but has its own rigorous laws to which all its subjects strictly submit themselves, in spite of the fieriness and independence of their characters. For the adepts in the unwritten doctrines of this institution the main driving force is "le besoin ardant de se faire une originalité" (the ardent need to make oneself an original).[29]

Besides the idea that dandyism is an "institution," Baudelaire also points out that dandyism verges on "spiritualisme et . . . stoicisme." In his mind, all the extravagant taste and material elegance a dandy subjects himself to are only a symbol of the "supériorité aristocratique de son esprit" (aristocratic superiority of his spirit). Baudelaire claims that dandyism is a sort of religion, with the most rigorous doctrine of all religions, namely that of elegance and originality. According to him, dandyism appears mostly in transitory periods, when democracy is not yet fully in force and aristocracy is partially faltering, with a view to engaging in "le projet de fonder une espèce d'aristocratie" (the project of founding a new species of aristocracy). Thus dandyism, an institution with the unwritten doctrine of elegance and originality, is a class marked by the distinction of taste that separates itself from the mediocre and the trivial. (For Baudelaire, being trivial is an irreparable dishonor.) One can easily see that Bourdieu shares with Baudelaire the idea of the distinction of taste.

In addition, dandyism embodies a particular attitude towards woman, as one can tell from the passage titled "La Femme" (Woman) in *The Painter of Modern Life*. A dandy like Liu Na'ou is a woman lover and a relentless misogynist at the same time, in whose mind only man is capable of intellectual thinking and performance, while woman, a creature indulged in lust and using man to gratify her sexual desire, is totally alien to the realm of intellect. On the other hand, ironically enough, a dandy like Liu, a frequenter of dance halls and brothels, is always involved in carnal relationships with women. As Baudelaire puts it, "Si je parle de l'amour à propos du dandysme, c'est que l'amour est l'occupation naturelle des oisifs. Mais le dandy ne vise pas à l'amour comme but spécial." (If I speak of love in regard to dandyism, it is that love is the natural occupation of the idle. But the dandy does not aim at love as a special goal).[30]

From Liu Na'ou's 1927 diary one can tell that the image of woman as *femme fatale*, alluring but destructive at the same time, is deeply rooted in his psyche. That in his diary he should call his wife a "vampire" sapping his energy and blood is illuminating. She was one year older than he was and his first cousin, their mother being sisters. They were married in 1922, when Liu was only 17 years old. Right from the beginning he was dissatisfied with the marriage, the reason being partly that it was an arranged marriage, a "feudal remnant" in his eye, and partly that the two were incompatible in education and personality. Like most women of her time, his wife was educated at home by private tutors. The fact that the two did not get along can be told from his wife's scarce appearances in his 1927 diary. In January that year, having finished his French courses at L'Université L'Aurore in Shanghai, he was living the leisurely life of a dandy there, idling and philandering, without doing anything specific. She is first mentioned in the diary entry of

17 January, in which Liu complains that her letter in Japanese is so poorly written that he can hardly understand what she intends to say. On 1 February he mentioned writing several letters, to his mother, grandmother, wife, and friends. On 17 April he returned from Shanghai to Tainan for his grandmother's funeral, but he did not mention his wife in the diary until 18 May. This is also the third time she ever appears in the diary.

In the entry of that day and the next one his description gradually takes her as a representative of "woman," or even *femme fatale*, in general. In the 18 May entry he says:

> Ah! Marriage is truly the gate to hell. . . . Woman is dumb, good for nothing. . . . Ah! that I should have been raped by her, the unsatiable man-beast, the goblin-like vampire, knowing nothing except indulgence in sexual desire![31] [Ellipses are mine]

In the following entry he says:

> Women, whatever types they are, may be said to be the emblem of sex. Their life and existence depends entirely on the gratification of sexual desire. At the time of . . . compared with what men can feel, how much more powerful is their orgasm! The center of their thought, behavior, and act is sex. Therefore besides sex they are completely devoid of intellectual knowledge. They don't like to learn things and they are incapable to learn. You see, aren't most women idiots and stupid jerks? Her stupidity really makes me mad.[32]

Those who are familiar with Baudelaire know his poem titled "Le Vampire" in *Les Fleurs du Mal* (The Flowers of Evil). Here the speaker is tormented by his own "esclavage maudit" (accursed slavery), always at the mercy of the woman to whose bed he is "bound like a convict to his chain," or "like the maggots to the corpse." At the end he curses her and calls her the "vampire."[33] One may as well compare Liu's passage quoted above with the description of *femmes fatales* in verse 5 of Baudelaire's "Spleen et idéal" and see the similarity:

> Et vous, femmes, hélas ! pâles comme des cierges,
> Que ronge et que nourrit la débauche, et vous, vierges,
> Du vice maternel traînant l'hérédité
> Et toutes les hideurs de la fécondité ![34]
> (And you, women, alas! pale as candles,
> Whom Debauch gnaws and feeds, and you, virgins,
> Who trail the heritage of the maternal vice
> And all the hideousness of fecundity!)[35]

In Liu's mind woman, incapable of true feelings or love, wants nothing but sex, while her sexual drive more often than not causes man's downfall. In the vocabulary of the dandy, man is the emblem of intellect and ruler of the spiritual, and woman, a sex symbol and physical creature. To him woman has only two functions, all tied to her body: to bear children and to make love. Yet as much as Liu calls his wife a "vampire" à la Baudelaire, if we read between the lines there are strong indications in the diary that he passes on syphilis to his wife, which causes her miscarriage. On 11 May he realized that he might be afflicted with a kind of "poisonous measles" (*duzhen* 毒疹). On 17 May he had a serum test, which indicates that the disorder was indeed syphilis. The following day he complained about the relapse of the disorder. On 20 May he had an injection of some sort at a hospital. When his mother asked about the cause of the disorder, he said he had probably got it from the public baths in Shanghai. Then his wife disclosed that according to the doctor, her miscarried child had been damaged by "*sōdoku*" (poisonous pus 瘡毒), which means syphilis in Japanese. She said she had had the serum test twice, completely of her own volition, for "women's disease" (*fujinbyō* 婦人病; she did not know Mandarin Chinese). Liu's reaction is typical of a male chauvinist who never puts the blame on himself: "Hearing her say it, I really don't know where the poison came from."[36] Syphilis, the lethal disease known for causing Baudelaire's death, did not spare our Shanghai dandy and philanderer either.

Yet despite his deep-rooted misogyny, the dandy is also a keen observer of woman's physical form, which to him has a deeper meaning than a body. In Liu's diary we can see that, as a flâneur, he is constantly strolling the street and back alleys, moving from one café or dance hall to another, looking for images of women that would meet his taste. Like Baudelaire's "À une passante" (To a Passer-by), these women are passers-by, or chance encounters in a café or a brothel, unknown to him, but all of them reveal the same quality: an intensity of desire that draws out their beholder's passions more than their own. When he is observing a woman silently and leisurely on the street or in quarters of pleasure, he is engaging in *flânerie*—the sketch art of physiognomy capturing the distinctive traits that reveal "nothing more than the elements of a new type," as Walter Benjamin says of Baudelaire's art.[37] The "new type" that Liu and his coteries are obsessed with is the modern girl.

Observing the modern girl as a new type, he is not concerned with what she thinks or feels, since to the dandy a woman is an unthinking and unfeeling creature; rather, he is concerned with her physical form with all its adornments and refinery adding to her allurement, which is the quintessence of modernity, or "the 'heroic' aspect of the present moment," in Foucault's words.[38] On 24 October, Liu records in his diary two girls whom he observes on the street. One, sitting in a horse carriage passing by, seems to be gesturing (the English word "gesture" is inserted in Liu's diary) with her eyes when she speaks; gazing at her, he forgets himself. The other, passing by in a car, has a lascivious look. Images of women on the street for him are specimens of the "fugitive beauté" Baudelaire describes in "À une passante." (The French word "fugitif" is inserted in Liu's text.)[39] A reader familiar with Baudelaire will be reminded of these famous lines, "Fugitive beauté/Dont le regard m'a fait soudainement renaître,/Ne te verrai-je plus que dans l'éternité ?" (O fleeting beauty,/By whose glance I was suddenly reborn,/Will I see you no more before eternity?)[40]

With his sketch art of *flânerie*, Liu is more than a mere flâneur; he is a peripatetic artist whose first occupation is modernity. The French word "la modernité," the emblem of Baudelairean aestheticism, appears twice in his diary, both in connection with prostitutes. Once in a brothel, looking at a young prostitute who awaits his patronage, he sighs, "Ah, my hungry heart! Ah, the translucent eyes that I can hardly devour, the face of *Modernité*!"[41] (Liu's own French). On 27 November the word "modernité" is used again to describe an unknown prostitute's eyes: "I chose her because of the look of *modernité* in her eyes."[42] Under the dandy's gaze, an insignificant brothel girl is instantly transformed into a symbol of modernity. As Foucault's interpretation of Baudelaire's dandy, Liu "has an aim loftier than that of a mere flâneur," who is "the idle, strolling spectator . . . satisfied to keep his eyes open, to pay attention and to build up a storehouse of memories." In contrast, a dandy like Liu is "looking for that quality which [is called] 'modernity.'"[43]

If we compare Foucault's words with Baudelaire's definition of the modernist in "La Modernité," we can see that he nearly quotes the latter verbatim. Baudelaire equates the modernist to a loner:

[C]e solitaire doué d'une imagination active, toujours voyageant à travers *le grand désert d'hommes*, a un but plus élevé que celui d'un pur flâneur, un but plus gégéral, autre que le plaisir fugitif de la circonstance. Il cherche ce quelque chose qu'on nous permettra d'appeler *la modernité*.[44]

(This loner endowed with an active imagination, always voyaging across the great desert of men, has an aim more elevated than that of a pure flâneur, an aim more general than the fugitive pleasure of the moment. He is looking for the thing that we are allowed to call modernity.)

From the point of view of the laboring class, the modernist, like the flâneur, seems idle and unproductive, but in fact it is his vocation—*flânerie*—that compels him to stroll the city. His idleness is his labor.[45] As an artist, more than a mere flâneur and *l'observateur*, his imagination transforms the physical form he encounters into something spiritual and eternal. The flitting, transient pleasure of the moment is thus transformed into modernity—the "heroisation of the present." Woman as a real-life being is not what attracts him; it is the woman in his imagination, seen through the dandy's eye—he is in fact gazing at his own soul, his inferior other self. Thus to the dandy the complex image of woman is bewildering and agonizing. No words are more telling than Baudelaire's own in "La Femme" (The Woman) in *The Painter of Modern Life*: "C'est une espèce d'idol, stupide peut-être, mais éblouissante, enchanteresse, qui tient les destinées et les volontés suspendues à ses regards." (She is a kind of idol, stupid perhaps, but dazzling and bewitching, who holds wills and destinies suspended on her glance.)[46] It is clear that Liu inherited the misogyny and idolization of women from Beaudelaire's concept of dandyism. The modern girl is disconcerting, because she is gazing back at the dandyish gazer. Men are nothing but her "gigolos," as we will see later in this chapter and in later chapters.

The neo-sensation mode and the modern girl

Analyzing a full entry from Liu's 1927 diary will suffice to illustrate how women's images are transformed through the aesthetics of the dandy—the art of flânerie. While quoting the entry, I am also going to point out the macaronic feature of Liu's language at the same time, using italics and parenthesis to highlight the foreign text and classical expressions incorporated into his new vernacular. This may interrupt the smooth flow of the reading, but is necessary to make my point clear.

From 28 September to 3 December, he went to Beijing from Shanghai for an extended visit. On 10 November he went to see the performance of Jin Youqin 金友琴, a renowned Beijing opera singer. The beginning part of the entry reads like this:

> After finishing reading the *Introd.* by *G. Apollinaire* in the morning, I went to Jin Youqin's show in the Star Theater in the market place. . . . The singing was not bad, while the voice was really good. People say Beijing women are good at speech, but I don't think so. Whether one is good at speech is determined by one's education. They may have mistaken women's talkativeness for excellence in speech. But everyone is willing to listen to Beijing women, because their voices are really melodious. In this barbarous country where natural beauty [Ch. *ziranmei* or *shizenbi* 自然美] is lacking, a woman's voice is the only comfort [*weile* or *iraku* 慰樂] for men. To say that it resembles swallows chirping and nightingales singing [classical Ch. *yanyu yingti* 燕語鶯啼] may seem vulgar, but the comparison is right. When I read about this in poetry, thinking it was only a beautiful adjective [*xingrongxing* or *keiyōkei* 形容形], I never knew it could be reality [*shigan* or *jikkan* 實感].[47] [Ellipses and italics are mine]

With the italics and parenthesis, what I am drawing attention to here is the macaronic, the free mixture of foreign text and classical language with the Chinese vernacular, a linguistic feature highlighting the transcultural characteristic of the Neo-Sensation mode of writing. The words in italics in the above passage, *Introd.* and *G. Apollinaire*, are originally in French in the diary. The term "swallows chirping and nightingales singing" (*yanyu yingti*) is a classical Chinese proverb eulogizing a woman's melodious voice. The terms for which I provide both Chinese and Japanese pronunciations in parenthesis are modern Japanese *kanji* expressions. Their pervasive presence in Liu Na'ou's vernacular is astonishing. Some of them, such as "nature" (*ziran*), are already commonly used in modern Chinese, while a native speaker could hardly detect their japonaiserie. Some are Liu's own borrowings that seem to be awkward Chinese and would never catch on. These attempts at borrowing, successful or failed, show both the instability and infinite possibility of the new vernacular at its experimental stage during the early decades of the twentieth century. In addition, as I will show in the following analysis, Chinese tradition, though seemingly denounced in the rhetoric of the New Vernacular Movement, is a persistent presence in the Neo-Sensation writers' macaronic practice. Consciously or unconsciously retained in their macaronic, tradition is a problematic that cannot be easily brushed aside. The so-called "May Fourth ideology of total Westernization," which they indeed absorbed as Shu-mei Shih points out in *The Lure of the Modern: Writing Modernism in Semicolonial China, 1917–1937*, in no way completely blocked the overflow of the traditional Chinese in which they had been well trained.[48]

Using the hybrid language he created, Liu is demonstrating in this passage the Neo-Sensation tendency to view women as a collective entity, as accorded with his art of flânerie: Even though he went to see the performance of a particular actress, in his description of her it is clear that he looked upon her as a type, the representative of the collective noun "Beijing women." In other words, the Beijing opera singer Jin Youqin in his imagination was not a woman endowed with personal thoughts, emotions, or life history, but the sample of Beijing women. His association of ideas connected with this particular Beijing woman's voice and body discloses his prejudices against women in general. First, according to him, the idea that Beijing women are good at speech is probably wrong, because speech belongs to the realm of the intellect, and one needs to be well educated in order to be good at speech. In his view, since Beijing women are totally uneducated, they cannot possibly be good at speech; they are talkative. Second, even though Beijing women are talkative, the only function of their beautiful voices is to please men. Third, this particular Beijing woman's voice reminds him of the reality of the panegyric "swallows chirping and nightingales singing," a classical expression. But, according to him, this voice only reaches the realm of "reality" (*shigan* or *jikkan*). In other words, in his mind's eye Beijing women, or any other women in general, are incapable of being associated with spiritual beauty and sublimation.

We should note, however, that here it is his dandyish gaze that turns this particular woman into the sample of Beijing women; he is concerned with types rather than real women. In the following, we will see that in his dandyish gaze, she becomes nothing but a sex symbol: a voice and a body to satisfy men's erotic pleasure; what she wears only highlights her seductiveness. From the initial description of the Beijing woman's voice, Liu continues to comment on her body:

Even though she had a good voice, her body was not beautiful from the viewpoint of a modern man [Ch. *xiandairen* or *gendaijin* 現代人], since the part under her waist was too short. But it was tiny and lovely, indeed a northern woman's body, able to dance on a big man's palm of the hand [classical Ch. *zhangshangwu* 掌上舞]. Such a *delicate* woman sleeping with a big man [*danan* or *ōotoko* 大男]. Right! They like to see her itching and suffering beyond forbearance [*suanyang nandang* 酸癢難當], pretending to be dying of pain. Ah, how *cruel*! When she sang, the mouth was really lovely to see. The triple coordination of lips, teeth, and tongue was like an over-ripe [*guoshou* or *kajuku* 過熟] pomegranate splitting up. The white cloth dress could not show the curves [*quxian* or *kyokusen* 曲線] of her body, but the crimson red stockings revealed some *erotic* elements.[49] [Italics mine]

Here in this concluding part we continue to see the intricate working of the macaronic. In this passage, "delicate," "cruel," and "erotic" are originally in English. The terms followed by Chinese and Japanese pronunciations are again Japanese *kanji* terms. Like the previous part, here classical allusions abound, too. At first Liu points out the deficiency of her body from the point of view of a "modern man" like himself, who considers long legs as the criterion of a modern beauty. This implies, of course, that she could be called a beauty from the traditional standard. Then, with the term "to dance on a palm of the hand," which is a classical expression, he is comparing her to Zhao Feiyan 趙飛燕 (flying swallow), a beauty during the Han Dynasty famous for her slender figure and singing and dancing skills. It is said that Emperor Cheng 成帝 was so enchanted by her that he abandoned his wife and made her the Empress, and even tolerated her continual adulterous relationships in court. The story ends with the Han Dynasty eventually losing its reign because of her—a typical story of a *femme fatale* who as a rule would destroy a nation. In Liu's dandyish gaze, the Beijing woman as an enchantress certainly can be traced back to her genealogy from classical times. Next, with the phrase "to see her itching and suffering beyond forbearance, pretending to be dying of pain," he is resorting to a stock description in traditional pornographic texts. Although the exact wording may change from text to text, the basic idea is the same: Man likes to see a woman pretending that she is being ravished. The image of the "over-mature pomegranate splitting up," describing the opening mouth of a beauty, is also associated with sex in traditional pornography. In Liu's macaronic practice, "traditional" and "modern" are indeed juxtaposed, but they are not exclusive to each other. The narrator is highly self-conscious of himself as a "modern man" who should be promoting a new set of aesthetic standards, but cannot help describing the woman's beauty with traditional set phrases. In Liu Na'ou's time, the great divide between tradition and the modern was not as easily drawn as one may imagine.

Under the narrator's salacious gaze, the Beijing woman singer's clothes seems to have no other function than reveal her "erotic" elements. In this diary entry, as in his other diary entries that focus on women's bodily forms, it is more the dandyish mindset that is disclosed than the woman gazed at. Liu's prejudices against women as shown in the aesthetics of a dandy certainly mold the images of the modern girls constructed in his work. This is true to Shanghai Neo-Sensation writers in general, as can be amply exemplified by Mu Shiying's story "Craven 'A,'" in which the features and body of the woman gazed at by the male narrator is turned into a sight-seeing spot fit for men's short visits.

Mu, a follower and friend of Liu Na'ou and known as "the Chinese Yokomitsu Riichi" among contemporary writers, was famous for his dandyish lifestyle and Neo-Sensation mode of writing. He was born in Shanghai, came from a well-to-do family, and studied Western literature at Guanghua University 光華大學. At the tender age of 18 he made his literary debut with a proletarian story, "Our World" (Zamen de shijie 咱們的世界), which was published in *La nouvelle littérature* (Xinwenyi 新文藝) in February 1930 with Shi Zhicun as the editor-in-chief. Shi, though pointing out that the story is "incorrect in *ideology*," praises the author as the most promising young writer whose artistic technique would shame veteran writers.[50] Mu was known as an excellent fox-trot dancer, with "permed hair, a well-pressed Western suit, and the style of a modern artist," and even married a taxi dancer in 1934. It is said Craven "A" was his favorite cigarette brand.[51] Here the modern girl in the story, smoking his favorite cigarette, is equated to his female other self, so to speak. The concept of the modern girl as the inferior other self of the dandy will be developed further in Chapter 2.

In "Craven 'A'" the male narrator uses the trope of "a map of a country" to describe the modern girl he is gazing at. Note the numerous geographical terms used in his language. She is sitting alone and smoking Craven "A" in a dance hall. Her eyes in his view are "two lakes" that sometimes get icy cold, sometimes hot beyond boiling point. Her mouth is a "volcano" that spews forth the smoke and odor of Craven "A." Inside the volcano the milky larva (teeth) and the flame in the middle (tongue) can be seen. "The people here are still quite primitive, using men as sacrifice at their volcano festival. For travelers this country is by no means a safe place," says the narrator. Then he describes the landscape under the "thin clouds" of a black-and-white checkered design, apparently a blouse made of semitransparent material. As a result the "purple peaks" (nipples) of the "two hills (breasts) ostensibly juxtaposing each other on the plain" seem to "protrude from the clouds."

Then the lower part of the map, blocked from view by the table at which the woman sits, is likened to the landscape of the "South," which is even more enchanting than that of the "North." The narrator imagines how the "two breakwaters" (legs) under the table join to form a "triangular alluvium plain," and how the "important harbor" with "the majestic entrance of the giant steam boat" arouses "billows and splashes on the prow." When the narrator finds out the woman's name from an acquaintance, he says:

I know many of her stories. Almost all of my friends have traveled in that country. Since the traffic there is convenient, almost all of them manage to visit the whole country in one or two days. . . . Experienced ones are able to land on the harbor right from the start. . . . Some sojourn for one or two days, while others stay on for a week. When they return they boast to me about the alluring landscape of that country, and all look upon it as a wonderful sightseeing spot for short visits.[52]

The language of the story is again an ample illustration of the macaronic, showing how the writer is testing the limits of the new vernacular by creating a bold mixture of linguistic possibilities. The title of the story "Craven 'A'" is originally in English. Transliterations that imitate the sound of foreign words abound, for instance, the jazz (*jueshi* 爵士) music in the dance hall; the girl's Parisian style (*balifeng* 巴黎風) face; her velvet-like (*weiyelerong side* 維也勒絨似的) gray eyes. Here *feng* 風 (wind) is borrowed from the Japanese suffix *fū*, indicating appearance, customs, tendency, or style. *Side* 似的 is a traditional vernacular Chinese expression used after a noun to form an adjective compound. These suffixes combined with any nouns can create endless lists of new terms. Expressions directly borrowed from Japanese *kanji* are numerous, including those concerning denominations of modern knowledge, e.g., country (Ch. *guojia* or *kokka* 國家), people (*minzu* or *minzoku* 民族), pessimism (*beiguan* or *hikan* 悲觀), order (*zhixu* or *chitsujo* 秩序), national defence (*guofang* or *kokubō* 國防). Most of the *kanji* expressions concern science and technology, for instance, weather (*qihou* or *kikō* 氣候), rainfall (*yuliang* or *uryō* 雨量), freezing point (*bingdian* or *hyōten* 氷點), boiling point (*feidian* or *futten* 沸點), lava (*rongyan* or *yōgan* 熔岩), volcano (*huoshan* or *kazan* 火山), clay stratum (*niantuceng* or *nendosō* 黏土層), triangular alluvium plain (*sanjiaoxing de chongji pingyuan* or *sankakukeiteki chūseki heigen* 三角形的沖積平原), harbor (*gangkou* or *kōkō* 港口), steamboat (*qichuan* or *kisen* 汽船). It is nearly impossible to name all of them.

Not only is the modern girl in the story described as a loose woman, but she is seen as capricious. The set of vocabulary used to describe her forehead and eyes (the prairie and the two lakes) deliberately highlights her fickleness: "Here the inhabitants have double national character: the typical pessimism of northerners and the brightness of southerners; unpredictable weather, sometimes below freezing point, sometimes above boiling point; fierce seasonal wind, with limited rainfall." "Limited rainfall" refers to her eyes that seldom shed tears, which indicate, of course, that she shows no mercy for men. The Neo-Sensation writer's fascination with science and technology is playfully combined with his obsession with the modern girl. It is through the macaronic that the humor and mocking tone is brilliantly conveyed.

In "Craven 'A,'" with a literary mode and language unique to the Neo-Sensation School, the modern girl's attitude towards man is highlighted: She treats men as her "gigolos." The word appears four times in the story, as, for instance, when the narrator says to the girl, "I love you so," she responds with a question, "You want to be my *Gigolo* (original in French), too?"[53] It indicates the kind of man-and-woman relationship characteristic of metropolitan Shanghai, in which no love is involved. It is mainly one-night stand, purely for fun on both sides. As Guo Jianying writes in the caption to "The Way of Love" (Ai zhi fangshi 愛之方式), one of the three cartoons in "The Touch of 1933" (Yijiusansan nian de ganchu 一九三三年的感觸), he is all for the kind of love described by Kollontai (1872–1953), the Russian revolutionary woman writer:

> In Kollontai's work, *The Loves of Three Generations*, a woman called Genia sleeps with her mother's lover repeatedly. Her reason is like this: Although she loves her mother dearly, and although one cannot live without one's mother's love, she needs a man's physical love at the same time. Her carnal relationship with this man, her stepfather, is purely by chance. Therefore she believes that this fact will never damage her mother in any way.[54]

According to Guo, there should be no sentimentality, sorrow, or tragedy in modern love. He further mentions modern American men and women experimenting with "weekend love" (his own English), which has nothing to do with "right" or "wrong" at all.[55]

In other words, in Neo-Sensation love stories, psychological stress or ethical judgment is not at issue, unlike in the stories of erotic love by Creation writers such as Yu Dafu 郁達夫 or Zhang Ziping 張資平,[56] generally considered to be their predecessors. For instance, the male protagonist in Yu Dafu's *Lost Lamb* (Miyang 迷羊), tormented by his love for the fickle actress who walked out on him, ends up in an asylum. The new women in Zhang Ziping's stories, though aspiring for sexual freedom, constantly lament and complain about the inability to be really free in a society still bound by "feudal" ethics. In contrast, the light-hearted theme of Neo-Sensation stories is marked by a playful tempo, as if the scenes were flickering with the male narrator's dandyish eye seeing through the camera. In these stories, man never weeps for the modern girl or himself over her. With the modern girl always viewed from the outside and described as a type through the writer's art of flânerie, it is no wonder that her heart and mind remains a mystery to the reader as well as the narrator.

In another cartoon in Guo's "The Touch of 1933," "The Enchantment of a Machine" (Jixie de meili 機械的魅力), a woman is literally transformed into a creature without heart and mind in the narrator's dandyish eye. In the cartoon, a man leaning on his left arm, bent in an angle on the left center corner, is showing only the back of his head, hair flowing down, and torso. He is turning his head and body downward, contemplating a woman sleeping with her face up in the picture. Both are stark naked. While he shows less than half of his body on the side of the picture, her body stretches across the whole scene, from the lower left corner to the upper right, with her feet beyond the frame of the picture. His small torso seems insignificant compared with her huge, elongated body that is the center of attention. But on a closer look, there is no doubt that the woman, lying motionless with her eyes tightly closed and seemingly smiling, is a machine or robot, because the joints connecting her forearms, elbows, hands, knees, and neck can be clearly seen. The man, reminding one of Rodin's pensive thinker, seems to be intimidated and tortured by the faint mocking smile on the woman's face, even though she is sleeping. The caption reveals the dandyish attitude towards women:

> He is a man who is engrossed in the enchantment [Ch. *meili* or *miryoku* 魅力] of a mechanical female body [*nüti* or *jotai* 女體].
>
> The uncanny touch [*ganchu* or *kanshoku* 感觸] belonging particularly to metal [*jinshu* or *kinzoku* 金屬] and the cold, gray glitter are grabbing tightly his emotions at this moment.
>
> Exactly because it is a lifeless object [*wushengwu* or *buseibutsu* 無生物], he can feel its tireless sexual desire [*xingyu* or *seiyoku* 性慾].
>
> Here, due to its lifelessness, one can discover its *Grotesque* [original in English] and peculiar coyness, pride, and subjugation [*qucong* or *kutsujū* 屈從].
>
> Sometimes, in an enclosed dark room, he indulges [*taozui* or *tōsui* 陶醉] in its brand new touch. Its materiality [*wuzhigan* or *bushitsukan* 物質感] can lead his senses [*ganjue* or *kankaku* 感覺] to a poetic world [*shijie* or *shikai* 詩界].
>
> Sometimes, he indulges in its untiring sexual desire. Here there is no human [*renlei* or *jinrui* 人類] hatred, sorrow, anger, or jealousy.
>
> Here there is no illness or ugliness pertaining to human psychology [*xinli* or *shinri* 心理] or feelings. Only here is there bright and boundless love, the pioneering [*jianduande* or *sentanteki* 尖端的] touch of 1933! (Figure 1.1)[57]

Again this macaronic passage shows the free blending of English and Japanese *kanji* characters with the new vernacular. The great number of *kanji* characters mixed in Guo Jianying's new vernacular can be easily ignored, since they have become standard modern Chinese expressions. Some of them are expressions concerning perception and feelings: enchantment, touch, sexual desire, subjugation, indulgence, senses, and so on. Others concern scientific categories: machine, female body, metal, a lifeless object, materiality, world, human, psychology, pioneering. Modern Japanese and Chinese intellectuals' obsession with science and how they learned to name the five senses and describe their feelings through translation of Western texts will be discussed in Chapters 4 and 5.

What I want to emphasize about this cartoon here is how the dandyish gaze transforms a modern girl's body into a lifeless machine, without any feelings and psychological reactions. The image wonderfully captures the dandyish complex towards women: idolization of her body coupled with the fear of her

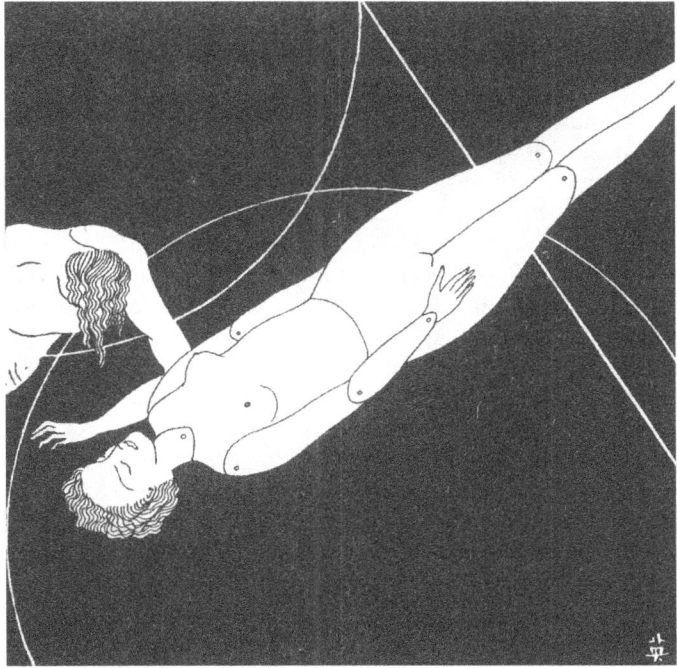

Figure 1.1 The Touch of 1933: The Enchantment of a Machine.

gaze—only when her eyes are closed can he look at her at ease. Underlying the fascination with the mechanical female body is the man's unuttered dread of a living modern girl with tempestuous emotions that could make a man's life miserable. Here, becoming a machine, she is deprived of the agency of a human being and presents no threat to man; her only function at this moment is her tireless sexual desire that would satisfy him. Or one should say, her sexual desire should be as persistent as he wants it to be—he should be the one in control. Reducing the modern girl to a sex machine shows in fact the dandy's own psychology: his fear of a living woman exerting power over him —he despises her inferiority but is helplessly overpowered by her. Only when she is a machine can he be in total control of their relationship. While the cartoon reveals the dandy's idolatry of the female body and misogyny at the same time, it also discloses the dandyish indulgence in artifice and materiality —nature is ugly, transient, and fearful, while artifice and materiality are beautiful and everlasting. Hence "Its materiality can lead his feelings to a poetic world," or to the sublime. The word "machine," denoting scientific modernity, gives the modern girl an inhuman splendor transcending the mundane.

Here it would help to refer to Baudelaire again. As he states in "Éloge du maquillage" (Eulogy of Make-up), the dandy is a species of man who believes in artifice rather than nature: " ... la nature n'enseigne rien, ou presque rien. ... la nature ne peut conseiller que le crime. ... La vertu, au contraire, est *artificielle* ... "[58] (Nature doesn't teach anything, or almost nothing. ... nature can advise nothing but the crime. ... Virtue, on the other hand, is artifice.) Hence the dandy's heavy dependence on materiality. Fashion, the quintessence of materiality, reinforces woman's beauty, of course. Yet fashion is by no means an end in itself; it is the manifestation of the ideal to surpass and reform nature, where the unrefined, the terrestrial, and the squalid are accumulated. For Baudelaire, fashion is "une déformation sublime de la nature" (a sublime deformation of nature).

Seen in this light, the Neo-Sensation mode of writing is a distinct contrast to the realistic mode. Unlike realistic stories such as those written by Creation writers, which often resort to the technique of psycho-narration to render the characters' psychology transparent,[59] the characters in Neo-Sensation stories as a rule are a-psychological. We are told of the characters' looks, behavior patterns, and words, but their psychology remains opaque. As a result these characters are almost like *actants* in the stories, often without names. Even with names they are exchangeable. It makes no difference at all if one character is moved from one story to another, since all the characters are endowed with the same single character trait: seductiveness. Thus the modern girl in the aesthetics of dandyism is not a real woman who has heart and feelings, but a collective noun with a symbolic meaning beyond the real woman herself. Looked at from another perspective, these characters share the nameless characteristic of the masses that were becoming the central subject matter of proletarian literature at the time. The main difference is that the characters in Neo-Sensation stories are members of the bourgeois class enjoying cosmopolitan life, whereas those in proletarian literature are either lower-class people described as victims of social injustice or the bourgeois as targets of attack.

With outer looks becoming the most important element to describe, it does not come as a surprise that fashion and material elegance turn out to be the focus of attention in Neo-Sensation stories. In addition, fashion should not be considered in itself; it should be imagined when vitalized and vivified by the women who wear it.[60] The modern girls in Neo-Sensation stories are exactly like mannequins that display fashion and make it alive. They usually wear reformed *qipao* 旗袍 (renovated Manchu dresses transformed into the latest fashion) or Western dresses, which were *à la mode* in 1930s Shanghai. Fashion in these stories is certainly more than an end in itself; it is a marker of class. The hooligan in Mu Shiying's 1930 story "Fingers" (Shouzhi 手指), with an envious eye for modern girls, describes in fitful ejaculation their fashionable outfit: "Today they crave Western products, tomorrow National goods. Their *qipao*, either long or short, in soft silk, satin, American chiffon, or Indian rayon ... fashion shows, exhibitions ... silk stockings, high-heeled satin shoes, tea-time dresses, party dresses, wedding gowns, salacious dresses, casual wear, short wear ... "[61] Fashion, an inseparable part of the modern girl, adds to her dazzle and enchantment, while marking her off as belonging to a class that the hooligan both envies and hates. Not only does the class distinction here involve the differences of taste between the high and the low, the bourgeois and the proletariat, but it also involves the native and the foreign. It is the conflict between nationalism and colonialism that is at work here.

Based on the discussion so far, I would conclude that the Neo-Sensation mode of writing is marked by three characteristic features: (1) The dandyish narrator's incorrigible male chauvinism and misogyny; (2) The modern girl transformed into a modernist artifice through the dandy-observer's sketch art of *flânerie*; (3) The marcaronic that highlights the hybridity of his transcultural practice. Since woman is only a symbol, or a concept, for Neo-Sensation writers, they are not interested in what is going on in her heart, not to mention in her mind. This aspect is best revealed in Liu Na'ou's 1927 diary, which faithfully records his readings of literary or non-literary works on a day-to-day basis. All of them are works by male authors; no women writers are ever mentioned. This is hard to imagine. From the nineteenth century on there were quite a few well-known women writers, Chinese or foreign. With Liu's wide literary knowledge, it is impossible that he was unaware of their existence. The only explanation is that he was not interested in women writers' works at all. On 2 December, when he was visiting Beijing with Dai Wangshu, he mentioned in the diary that Dai went to visit the woman writer Ding Ling 丁玲: "Dai went to see the woman in no. 20 and her *amant* (original in French), Hu Yepin 胡也頻." For Liu Na'ou, Ding Ling did not even have a name. Of course, she was not that famous then, but neither was Hu, her Communist lover who would be executed by the KMT in 1931. Liu's interest in Ding Ling as shown in the diary entry was simply limited to the fact that she was a woman in Room 20, with a lover. Without her lover's name mentioned in the diary, we would not even know who she was.

Dandyism and the Shanghai type

Dandyism as a matter of taste is also manifested in Liu Na'ou's preferences for friends and associates. The year 1927, in which he wrote the diary extant today, was also the year the Nationalist regime started the Northern Expedition and Party Purge. In the 1920s and the 1930s fluxes of writers immigrated to Shanghai to either take shelter from the war in the north or seek opportunities of artistic development there, since, with big publishing companies continually moving from Beijing to Shanghai starting in the early 1920s, it had become the new cultural center in China. Famous literary men such as Lu Xun 魯迅, who came to Shanghai in September 1927, and Shen Conwen 沈從文, who moved there in early 1928, gathered in the metropolis and struggled for their livelihood. Teaching and writing were the main sources for them to earn a living, while writing gradually emerged as a full-time profession during that period.

Liu Na'ou, who came to Shanghai in 1926 and lived the life of a dandy there, did not get along with writers like Lu Xun or Shen Congwen. Or one should say more exactly, he did not bother to associate with them at all. He was intimate with friends from Taiwan, frolicking with them together and often letting them stay in his apartment. They included schoolmates from the Presbyterian School of Tainan and the renowned advocate of the vernacular literature movement in Taiwan, Huang Chaoqin 黃朝琴, who had studied in Tokyo and Illinois and in 1923 had written one of the earliest important treatises on that subject.[62] He was at that time looking for a position in Shanghai and from 1928 on would work for the Overseas Chinese Bureau of the Ministry of Foreign Affairs of the Nationalist government. From September 1927 on he often called Liu on the telephone. When they met, the usual activities they engaged in were conversing, eating in restaurants, frequenting dance halls, and playing mahjong. They became neighbors on 21 December, when Liu moved to the apartment next door to the Huangs.

There was also a schoolmate from Aoyama college, Ōwaki 大脇, who was living in Shanghai and often stayed over in his apartment. Liu's brother visited him in April and stayed a month. In addition, Liu was closely connected with friends he had met at L'Aurore. They worked as a team in his bookstore, and after work they would frequent dance halls and brothels, ogling women together. In the dance halls he was always marveled at when he tangoed; people would stop dancing, spread out, and leave room for him to perform. He taught his L'Aurore friends Japanese whenever there was time in between work and play. Even during the trip to Beijing with Dai Wangshu in October, they still continued their Japanese lessons.[63] The Beijing trip had another goal: They attended courses at the l'Institut Franco-chinois (Sino-French Institute) there, including "Préscis de la Littérature Française" (Outline of French Literature) and "La Poésy Française" (French Poetry), taught by French teachers, "History of Chinese Literature" taught by Feng Yuanjun 馮沅君, and "Poetry and *Ci* Poetry" by Feng Yinmo 馮尹默.[64] Liu and his friends were held together by ties of common interests and taste. From the courses they took, we also know that classical Chinese literature as well as French literature was on their list of priorities when it involved their agenda of self-formation.

Of the leaders of the many literary coteries in Shanghai, Liu and his companions chose to befriend the renowned modernist poet Shao Xunmei 邵洵美 (1906–68), who, also from a wealthy family, was a dandy of great renown like Liu. Shao's residence in Shanghai, a palace-like marble building and a legend in itself, became a salon where literary men and artists gathered for meals and conversation.[65] Among the distinguished guests constantly invited were people like the poet Xu Zhimo 徐志摩, the writers Zeng Jinke 曾今可 and Zhang Ruogu 張若谷, and the painter Xu Beihong 徐悲鴻, besides Liu and his friends.[66] In contrast, Liu's coterie and Lu Xun's never hit it off. There could have been, in fact, a great many opportunities for these two parties to meet and associate with each other. When Liu was experimenting with proletarian literature during the late 1920s, *Trackless Train* (Wugui lieche 無軌列車), the journal he established with Dai and Shi Zhicun, often published Feng Xuefeng's 馮雪峰 articles. Feng belonged to Lu Xun's coterie, but Liu and his friends never had direct contact with Lu. Shi did write Lu some letters concerning matters of the bookstore, but thought he was a "narrow-minded man."[67] As a matter of fact, Shi was living two blocks from Lu Xun's house at the time, but they somehow or other missed the chance to get to know each other, or they never intended to, since the two parties lived such distinct lives and gradually developed diametrically opposed literary beliefs.[68]

When the Shanghai types (*haipai* 海派) controversy broke out in the early 1930s, Lu Xun and Shen Congwen, though they never befriended each other, both became fervent enemies of the Shanghai types. From the language they used in the debate, one senses that the contention lay as much, if not more, in taste as in literary convictions. Today literary critics often talk about these two types of writers as if they had been two distinct literary schools.[69] As a matter of fact, during the time of the controversy, there were no such literary schools as the Shanghai School or the Beijing School at all; the formation of these two schools of writers was a later invention. The controversy concerned mainly the incorporation of popular taste into literary works and the commercialization of literature in Shanghai, as opposed to the "serious" May Fourth literary tradition represented by the north, which Shen embraced so dearly even while he was living in Shanghai and had to conform to the popular taste there one way or other.[70]

In a 1934 essay, Shen connected Creation writers such as Yu Dafu and Zhang Ziping and Neo-Sensation writers such as Mu Shiying with the Saturday School writers by calling the latter the "Shanghai types" and their followers the "New Shanghai types." Shen said that Zhang Ziping, like the Saturday School writers, was a master of "low, vulgar taste," or "popular taste." He adds, "The most suitable place of appreciating Zhang Ziping's works is at the desk of those college students who, while looking at the beauty queens of girls' colleges in *The Young Companion* (Liangyou 良友), talk about ways of kissing in the movies."[71] As for Mu Shiying, Shen says, "His works are almost like romance (with man-and-woman relationships as the subject matter, romance in Shanghai, so to speak). It is suitable for him to write works for pictorials or design magazines, or write for women, movies, and playful magazines. The city has made this writer, and yet limited him at the same time."[72] One is instantly reminded of *The Young Companion* and *The Women's Pictorial*, to which Liu and his coterie constantly contributed articles.

The ridicule, and even contempt, in Shen's attitude towards the Shanghai types is unmistakable. On the other hand, Lu Xun, who did not have anything nice to say about either of the two contending parties, pointed out the stereotypical views connected with regional prejudices, stating that "the literati in Beijing is akin to officials, those in Shanghai, to merchants. . . . In a word, the 'Beijing types' are the protégés of officials, while the 'Shanghai types' are the protégés of businessmen."[73] It was clear that Lu Xun himself never considered himself a "Beijing School" writer as later critics would.

It was in fact unfair for people like Shen Congwen to single out the Creation and Neo-Sensation writers to be targets of satire for their catering to popular taste. Those who often wrote for *The Young Companion* included writers whom he would consider to be "serious," for example, Mao Dun 茅盾, Ding Ling, Lao She 老舍, Zheng Boqi 鄭伯奇, Feng Zikai 豐子愷, Lu Yan 魯言, Ba Jin 巴金, and Zhang Tianyi 張天翼. Even Hu Shi 胡適, one of the leaders of the vernacular literature moment, and Cai Yuanpei 蔡元培, the president of Academia Sinica at the time, were no exceptions. In the December issue of 1931, Hu Shi's translation, in classical Chinese, of Alphonse Daudet's "The Siege of Berlin" was published, while in the September issue of 1932 Cai endorsed the magazine for its contribution to "introducing the customs of our nation to overseas readers with the help of photographs."[74] Around 1933 *The Young Companion* sold 40,000 copies,[75] a wide circulation that probably no literary men who had to sell their writings to make ends meet in Shanghai during the tumultuous times of civil war and foreign invasions could afford to turn their backs on.

If Neo-Sensation writers were despised for their metropolitan taste, Shen showed remarkable perception in singling out their fetishizing of the "Modern Girl," who in their stories was placed on the pedestal, as it were. She represented the spirit of an affluent society marked by the aesthetics of commodities, cult of things Euro-American, japonaiserie, light-hearted entertainment, and the fanfare of *la bourgeoisie*. It was the popular taste promoted by pictorials such as *The Young Companion* and *The Women's Pictorial*, a taste shared by college girl students, call girls, taxi dancers, and gentlemen's and merchants' wives, concubines, and daughters. In fact, we see the representations of modern girls not only in Neo-Sensation stories, but in contemporary leftist writers' works such as Mao Dun's *Midnight* (Ziye 子夜, 1933), in which the call girl Xu Manli 徐曼麗, impersonating the *carpe diem* spirit of the age, pursues carnal pleasures till the end of the story despite the ravaging of civil war and the financial crises that are destroying people's lives.

In such stories, types like the modern girl become enemies of the proletariat; they exist simply to highlight the necessity of proletarian revolution. In 1935 the leftist movie *Xin nüxing* (The New Woman), featuring the famous actress Ruan Lingyu 阮玲玉, depicts a decadent woman writer who commits suicide in the end. In the movie the hard-working women laborers who are always in the background throw into relief the decay and decline of the woman intellectual who indulges in sensual pleasures and pursues her own destruction. The fact that the star Ruan Lingyu did commit suicide shortly after the movie was released[76] seemed to point to the apocalyptic vision of art and its inevitable unification with life.

After Liu Na'ou reverted from proletarianism to modernism during the late 1920s and the early 1930s, the collision between his coterie and the proletarianists eventually erupted in the "hard films/soft films" debate. In 1933

Liu, together with Huang Jiamou 黃嘉謨, a friend from Taiwan, and others, established the magazine *Xiandai dianying* 現代電影 (*Modern Screen*, the editors' own English title). In the mission statement of the journal Huang states that with the importation of foreign movies into the Chinese market, the editors of the journal hope that Chinese will "produce movies that represent the Chinese spirit and flavor," so that Chinese movies can be exported to the world and compete with foreign movies.[77] One article in the same issue points out that Chinese enterprises, especially the movie industry, are facing bankruptcy because of "the infiltration of foreign capital and the penetration of imperial culture. . . . This explains the bankruptcy of our national capital in a semicolony."[78] In 1933 and 1934 there was in China a general movement to promote national products and enterprises in order to boycott Euro-American products and prevent further draining of agricultural population, which would eventually deplete rural areas.

Besides answering the call to promote national enterprises, Huang makes it clear that *Modern Screen* is completely free from the control of any ideology or the demand of propaganda, implying the existence of unwanted ideological domination by revolutionary literature and nationalist literature at the time. He points out that the movie is more than a kind of entertainment; it is "the highest-class entertainment in modern times." It is in the second issue of the journal that Liu Na'ou further spells out the entertainment function of the movie. He says that it functions

> like sleeping pills that help people escape reality. . . . If we eliminated from current movies the sleeping pills like sentimentalism, irrationalism, fashionableness, intellectual fun, and romanticism and fantasy, would not this favorite of modern man become a great desert?[79]

For Liu the success of the movie depends not on the content, but on the way the subject matter is handled and adapted into the movie. In other words, it is the form and autonomy of art that matters.[80] From the fifth issue on, he wrote a series of articles on movie techniques, for instance, "A Brief Essay on the Rhythm of the Camera" (Dianying jiezou jianlun 電影節奏簡論) in 1933, and "On the Mechanism of the Camera—The Function of Angle and Position" (Kaimaila jigou—weizhi jiaodu jineng lun 開麥拉機構—位置角度機能論) in 1934,[81] as a way to demonstrate his thesis that technique and form were everything for the movie. Worthy of our attention here is a 1932 article published in *Cinéma Weekly* (Dianying zhoubao 電影周報), "On Cinematic Art" (Yingpian yishulun 影片藝術論). In this article he analyzes the techniques of montage and *ciné-oeuil* (kino-eye) developed by Russian directors Vsevolod Pudovkine (1893–1953) and Dziga Vertov (1896–1954). Since quite a few French translations of technical terms are inserted into the article, we can infer that Liu learns about Russian films and directors through readings in French.

Often compared with his contemporary director Sergei Eisenstein, who used montage to extol the "monumental heroics" of the masses, Pudovkine preferred to portray "typical individuals caught up in the mass movements of history."[82] In his article, Liu distinguishes the concept of "cinématographique" from "photographique." According to him, the visual images captured by the pointless camera movement is photographic, "dead" or "without purpose," whereas with the technique of montage, the distinct images purposefully juxtaposed and arranged into an organized whole are endowed with cinematic "life and value." In his mind, montage "creates a new dramatic time and space, or 'film-truth,' which has nothing to do with real time and space."[83] Using this concept he analyzes two of Pudovkine's movies, *The End of St. Petersburg* (1927) and *Mother* (1926), Victor Tourjansky's *Le Chanteur inconnu* (The Unknown Singer, 1931), and two contemporary Chinese films, *Marriage in Tears and Laughters* (Tixiao yinyuan 啼笑姻緣, starring Hu Die, 1932) and *The Grandeur of One Night* (Yiye haohua 一夜豪華, starring Ruan Lingyu, 1932).

Liu praises *The Unkown Singer* as "the best sound film since the production of sound movies":

> The director Tourjansky is able to use silent images to emphasize the musical effect. The unknown singer's enchanting voice, transmitted from the broadcast station, flies over clouds and mountains, into different countries on the European continent, into families, until it fills the hearts of girls longing to be loved and men and women loving each other. This passage is really a great demonstration of montage, enabling music to instill the rhythmic intoxication in the audience."[84]

In contrast, Liu criticizes *Marriage in Tears and Laughters* as an inferior movie, since the director fails to use montage to give the audience the necessary "visual pleasures" during the flute-playing scene under the moonlight. He points out the unforgivable mistake of the director: In this prolonged scene the man and the woman are outdoors facing the moon, but their shadows proceed them. Liu comments: "Other directors use unreal things to create 'film-truth,' but this director is turning reality into the unreal."[85] The concept of film-truth, *kino-pravda*, was in fact developed by Vertov. It is translated into French as *cinéma vérité*, a concept that would influence many filmmakers of the generations to come.[86] From this emerged his "kino-eye" (kinoglaz) technique, the basic concept of which is to show "Life-As-It-Is" on the screen by "shooting life-unawares."[87]

In the section on "kino-eye" of his article, Liu discusses the documentary Vertov made in 1929, *Living Russia, or the Man with a Movie Camera*. He says, "Vertov was the leader of the group known as 'kinoglaz' (or kino-eye), and took the same position as Madame Esther Shub, a leader of Russian constructivism."[88] The group of film artists surrounding Vertov was called *kinoks* (*kinoki*), whose ideal was to promote the proletarian newsreel or the "unstaged film," as opposed to the traditional fictional film. Vertov, his wife

Elizabeth Svilova, and his brother Mikhail Kaufman formed the Council of Three, and were responsible for the production policy of the cooperative.[89] *Kinoglaz* was the title of a series of newsreels Vertov and his coterie made in 1924, recording children mobilized as "The Young Pioneers" in Soviet village centers, the movement for a healthy populace, and the workers' education. The part about the children, called also "The Young Leninists," is most moving, a masterpiece beautifully combining ideology with movie aesthetics. They are seen joyfully pasting propaganda posters on walls, distributing pamphlets to extort all "to buy from the cooperative" instead of the private sector, building their own training camps, and so on. In their efforts to "fight for the workers' state," we see them marching into the marketplace to investigate the prices of food, helping to cut customers' hair at the barber's, shining tin utensils, and assisting a widow with the harvest. The two scenes with "time backwards" as the theme humorously depicts how meat and bread in the market are produced. For instance, the meat being sold is traced back to the skinned bull in the slaughter house, the entrails stuffed back into its stomach, the skin stuck back, the bull coming alive and then marching back into the barn. It is a fantastic demonstration of how the editing technique can play with our perception of time. The logo of the series, a huge human eye framed in the movie camera's lens, became a recurrent motif in *The Man with the Movie Camera*. The basic principles of Vertov's group, "Without a script, without actors, outside the studio," opens up all the films of the *Kino-Eye* series, including *The Man with the Movie Camera*.

Esther Shub, on the other hand, originally worked for the Constructivist theatre of Meyerhold and Mayakovsky and became in 1922 a creator of the compilation film, the nonfiction film created by editing the footage made for another purpose. She worked closely with Vertov. According to Richard Barsam, Shub believed in the "ontological authenticity of the images," and thus her concept of the nonfiction film is more akin to Vertov, as against Eisenstein, whose films were "theatrical reenactments of history."[90] Associating Vertov with Shub, Liu is clearly well informed of the connection between Vertov's film theory and the constructivist movement. His analysis of Vertov's kino-eye technique is to the point:

> He [Vertov] is a machinist through and through, therefore his theories are inclined towards this direction. According to his opinion, "kino-eye," equipped with high speed, microscopic accuracy, and other scientific qualities and proficiency, is more thorough than the human eye. Its metaphysical nature allows it to penetrate the outer layers of things and perceive all the minutiae. All phenomena, dissected, analyzed, and interpreted through it, are reorganized to form a work related to the central theme. Thus to portray "life" one needs no actors but a camera that is able to incorporate the fragments of "life" in a proper way.[91]

So Liu knows very well that the purpose of Vertov's "kino-eye" technique, deemed much more superior to the human eye, is to create "film-truth," a reality "truer" than the reality perceived by the human eye. The passage also shows his understanding of the basic concept of the technique: unperformed film created with the montage of fragments of life caught unawares rather than the acting of professional actors. His valorization of the "high speed, microscopic accuracy, and other scientific qualities and proficiency" of the kino-eye technique indicates he is aware that Vertov shared with constructivism the fascination with machines. When he points out that Vertov's movie *The Man with the Movie Camera* is created with these concepts as principles, he gives its title in French: *L'homme à l'appareil de prises de vues* (Man with the Machine of Snapshots). According to him, there are two basic elements in the film: life of the masses in the city, and the cameraman who walks into the masses and controls the representation of their lives. Note that while introducing Vertov to the Chinese reader, Liu carries out a critique of him as well. As much as he praises Vertov for his excellent movie technique, he criticizes him for his excessive worship of machines, and doubts if his kind of *film san acteurs*, movie without actors, would prevail in the long run.[92]

We should keep in mind that Liu Na'ou's mid-1930s documentary, mentioned earlier in this chapter, has an English title, *The Man Who Has the Camera* (a Japanese title *Kamera wo motsu otoko* カメラを持つ男 is also given), apparently paying homage to Vertov. As many critics have pointed out, Vertov's documentary, besides recording Russian life, is marked by its self-reflexivity that runs throughout the work. It is as much about the life of the masses as about the technique of movie making, with the cameraman appearing in the movie: walking among the crowd, climbing a tower, riding in a fast-moving car, and lying on the ground to take the best shots. We also see the woman editor working with the film reels, the film being shown in the movie theater, and so on.[93] Furthermore, the whole film is a dazzling demonstration of the montage technique. In contrast, Liu's documentary does not share at all that self-referential quality and the montage technique that distinguish Vertov's movie.[94] The reason for the difference is worth thinking about.

Liu's 31-minute documentary, resuscitated by Chinese Taipei Film Archive in 1997 and now kept in its library, contains five parts: "Human Life" (Renjian 人間), "The Temple Parade" (Youxing 遊行), "Fengtian" (奉天, a harbor in Manchuria), "Canton" (廣州, the Canton City), and "Tokyo." Except for the part on the temple parade, it is mainly a sort of home video recording his personal life and travels, certainly unable to cope with the scope of Vertov's work intending to show Russian life in its entirety. We see Liu, his brother, mother, wife, and children in "Human Life." The masses, whose dominating image is overwhelming in Vertov's documentary, feature briefly in Liu's as well. In "Canton," they are seen thronging to a sight-seeing spot, quite distinct from the masses rushing on the streets in Vertov's film. The young women on an oceanliner in Liu's film are apparently posing for the camera, not shot "unawares" at all. The only part vaguely reminiscent of the "unstaged" principle is the temple procession, with all the usual features of such an occasion in Taiwan, including walking on stilts, the lion dance, characters in *Journey to the West* such as the monkey and the pig, the folklore ghosts Lord VII and Lord VIII, and so on. The presence of the men in Japanese costumes dancing in the procession indicates that this part was made either in Taiwan, Nanjing, or Manchuria during the Japanese occupation.

Film production has been an expensive business since its invention, requiring highly complex technical as well as personnel apparatus. A home video like Liu's was in no way comparable with a professional production such as Vertov's *The Man with the Movie Camera*. We know that Vertov struggled with different film institutions to secure financing for his filmmaking, as Liu did after him. Due to the controversies with Eisenstein and other colleagues, in 1927 Vertov was dismissed from Sovkino, the centralized state cinema trust established in 1924 to finance filmmaking in the entire Soviet Union. He was then invited to work for VUFKU (All-Ukranian Photo-Cinema Administration), the Ukranian film studios in Kiev. It was there that he created *The Man with the Movie Camera*.[95] In Liu's case, it is known that he was amply provided for by his mother, and that he established two bookstores consecutively in Shanghai, and published journals and books with his own means. Starting from the early 1930s he even invested in real estate in Shanghai. He built the block of houses where his family lived after moving from Taiwan and lent two units for friends such as Dai Wangshu and Mu Shiying, while renting the rest of the units to Japanese. In addition, he bought nearly a whole block in a business area.[96] The cost of making movies would far surpass that of establishing literary journals and bookstores and could well consume all the money he invested on properties. This may explain why, as a filmmaker, he needed to work for studios controlled by conflicting political parties; where there is funding, there is work. But as I have said, while he was negotiating with the political systems to pay for his movie career, he exceeded the safe limits and endangered his own life. To ensure personal freedom, one needs to know exactly where the limits are.

Because of his proficiency in foreign languages, especially French, Liu was well informed on avant-garde Russian film theories and became the first significant film theorist in China. It does not come as a surprise that his strong arguments for film aesthetics led to a debate between his coterie and the leftist filmmakers, who, though having learned from Russia the use of film for propaganda purposes, were falling largely behind in aesthetic theory.[97] In this regard, Liu stood out as a unique phenomenon among his contemporary filmmakers. The article that directly triggered the debate with the leftist camp, though, was Huang Jiamou's "Yingxing yingpian yu ruanxing yingpian" 硬性影片與軟性影片 (Hard Films and Soft Films) in December 1933, in which he complained that the leftist "revolutionary movies" have "hardened" the soft films of the movie, and as a result meaningless slogan and didacticism drive away audiences who used to throng to the movie theaters. He emphasized the entertainment function of the movie by saying, "Movies are the ice-cream for the eye, and the sofa for the soul."[98]

Liu's coterie's movie theories met with severe opposition from the leftist writer Tang Na 唐納, who published from 19 to 27 June 1934 a series of articles in *Morning Post* (*Chenbao* 晨報) rebutting their emphasis of form over content. In the article "Purging the Soft-Film Theory—The Entertainment Theory of Soft-Film Theorists" (Qingsuan ruanxing dianying lun—ruanxing lunzhe de quwei zhuyi 清算軟性電影論—軟性論者的趣味主義) on 19 June, Tang states that "art expresses not only emotions, but also thoughts. . . . These emotions and thoughts are derived from the world of reality, and should be aroused from the inside of a person. Therefore on the one hand there is the reality that exists objectively, while on the other, there is the subjectivity of the writer in society." He emphasizes the social function of art and its didactic value, as opposed to the entertainment theory of Liu's coterie. Tang says that since Liu and his coterie "fail to understand the unification of content and form," they criticize the leftists for "overemphasizing content," and thus insist on "the superiority of form over content in a work of art."[99]

Liu's coterie's modernist stance, which valorized the autonomy of art, their literary practice manifested in the aesthetics of the dandy, and their entertainment theory were poles apart from the politicized aesthetics of proletarian literature. A controversy of this nature was inevitable.

A Taiwanese in Shanghai and Tokyo

Modernism seems to be a celebration of the metropolitan mode of life and an ironic embrace of capitalism, while the modernist dandy belongs to an affluent class that is ignorant of poverty and suffering. A dandy such as Liu Na'ou, though marked by an aestheticism defying bourgeois mediocrity, is undeniably a product of bourgeois culture and capitalist expansion. A dandy like he is can be considered the product of the amalgamation of bourgeoisie, capitalism, and colonialism. In 1920s Taiwan, young men aspiring for literary careers like Liu Na'ou did not lack international models to emulate. Practicing Baudelaire's theory of the dandy in writing as well as in lifestyle, he as a writer and filmmaker in Shanghai found himself in a predicament. As much as he aspired to the universal aesthetic values of modernism, the laws of national boundaries still cornered him in the end.

As the language of creative writing became an issue with Taiwanese writers of his generation, so was Liu, living and writing in Shanghai, highly concerned about his own Taiwanese origin and the inadequacy of his Chinese proficiency. In his 1927 diary we can see his self-consciousness of being a nonnative speaker of Mandarin Chinese and the efforts he made to improve his Mandarin. For instance, on 3 January he wrote, "Practiced Mandarin Chinese conversation tonight." On 5 January, when he was reading a Japanese translation of the Russian writer Alexandre Kuprin's (1873–1938) novel *Yama: The Pit* (1901–15) he wrote, "The author has really a great ability to tell a story. . . . I keenly feel that my ability to tell stories is limited. Perhaps because Fukienese has a limited vocabulary, I often fail to come up with the right expression to say what I have in mind." But even though he was highly conscious of his Minnan 閩南 origin, Minnan expressions pop up from time to time in the diary, probably without himself being aware of it. For example, in the 6 April entry where he writes, "The trains to Jiangning 江甯 were all full of soldiers," the Minnan expression *bingmuanmuan* 兵滿滿, full of soldiers, is used instead of something like *manzai junren* 滿載軍人 in Mandarin.[100] In the 14 July entry where he writes, "This telegraph awakened my illusion of five or six years," the Minnan expression *meimang* 迷夢, illusion, is used instead of *menghuan* 夢幻 in Mandarin.[101] In the 9 December entry, "Went with Huang to Odeon and saw a shitty bad movie," the expression *kaoyao* 考友, shitty, is used instead of something like *tamade* 他媽的 in Mandarin. The Minnan dialect is certainly an inevitable component in his macaronic practice of the new vernacular.

There is no doubt that Liu considers himself Taiwanese, as distinguished from Chinese. In the 20 January entry he writes about his decision to rent a room from someone from Tianjin, and describes the landlord as *un bon chinois*, a good Chinese, in French. The combination of languages in his vernacular is free; when he would use which language does not seem to have a rule. But there are indications that when he gets sick he is likely to switch to Japanese, sometimes with the whole entry written in it. For example, the 10 January entry starts with these sentences and goes on in Japanese until the end: "Atama wa itamu, hana wa tsumaru, mune wa kurushii, mata iyana kaze da" 頭は痛む、鼻はつまる、胸は苦しい、又いやな風邪だ (Head hurts, nose is stuffy, chest burns. Again a lousy cold).

The same happens during his visit to Tokyo—the entries from 1 to 3 August are completely in Japanese. It seems he does not find Tokyo up to his taste. In the 1 August entry when describing a restaurant he writes, "Omoshiroku mo nai dentōtekina teikyū ajisa, tada suzushikatta" 面白くもない傳統的な低級味さ、只涼しかった (not interesting at all, low-class traditional taste, just refreshing). The 2 August entry has these sentences, "Ginbura wo shita. Sakuya no daikenkyo de chichinda mono ka, mobo moga no kage ga akatsuki no hoshi no yōtadda. Hajimete *Mon Ami* e haitta. Bōi ga po'anchi wo shiranai" 銀ぶらをした。昨夜の大檢舉で縮んだものかモボ、モガの影が曉の星の樣つだった。始めてMon Ami へ入った。ボーイがポアンチを知らない。 (Loitering in the Ginza area. Perhaps due to the mass police roundups last night, people were thwarted. Modern boys and modern girls were as scarce as the morning stars. Went to *Mon Ami*, My Friend, for the first time. The waiter knew nothing about punch). The 3 August entry is a self-examination of his own good-for-nothing conduct and a criticism of Tokyo lagging behind in the way of the modern: "Yoku mo anna muchina mobo, moga wo aite ni shite asonda mono da. Koremo sabishii kara darō. Ah Shanghai no wu-ru-tsu ga koishii" よくもあんな無智なモボ、モガを相手にして遊んだものだ。これも淋しいからだろう。あフ、上海のワルツが恋しい。 (Always frolicking with those ignorant modern boys and modern girls. Maybe it is because of loneliness. Ah, how I miss the waltz in Shanghai!)

Apparently Liu prefers Shanghai to Tokyo. From his diary we see Tokyo policemen cracking down on the pleasure quarters. Shanghai with its many foreign concessions was a semicolony where foreign infiltration was felt everywhere. In his 1927 diary we see an ordinary citizen's daily life in Shanghai inconvenienced by English or Japanese soldiers who set up roadblocks or check people's identifications. In the 19 February entry, he writes: "Hangzhou 杭州 was lost, General Sun's army is retreating to Songjiang 松江"; "The southern army has arrived in Shanghai"; "A general strike has started in Shanghai." 21 March: "On the border of the Ahrui Precinct 阿瑞里 soldiers in plain clothes conflicted with foreign soldiers." 27 March: "The traffic in the settlement was likewise blocked." 3 April: "Frisked by lousy British soldiers." 6 April: "Made a detour through Gansu Road 甘肅路, but was blocked by the British army." 9 April: "When passing through Diswell Road, was checked by Japanese mariners several times."[102]

With all the inconveniences caused by the multinational military presence and the threat of war (sometimes he could hear the gunfire the whole night), Liu managed to lead the life of a dandy in 1927 Shanghai. He was quite conscious of his own decadent lifestyle and often engaged in self-criticism, but would relapse into self-indulgence time and again. For example, he writes in the 5 February entry:

> These few weeks have been spent in *bexiang* [playing 白相, Shanghai dialect]. I have not studied at all. Having spent all my money, I borrowed. Now I have borrowed from almost all of my friends in Shanghai. My health [Ch. *jiankang* or *kenkō* 健康] is deteriorating. I almost sleep the whole day every other day. Learning? It has become a fairyland in the fog [*wuli de xianxiang* 霧裡的仙鄉]. Dates tomorrow, and the day after. Aiya!

"Bexiang" in Shanghai dialect means doing nothing useful, or living a decadent life. As is recorded in the diary, Liu's mother constantly sent him money, usually in large sums. But apparently he spent faster than he could receive. In 1927 Shanghai the *carpe diem* mentality seemed to be pervasive among people of his class. Names of cafés, dance halls and movie houses fill the pages of his diary. Movie houses mentioned include Carlton, Odeon, Donghua Theater, Central Theater, Barrymore, Apollo, Atlantic, Shanghai Grand Theater. The movies he sees include *Variété* (1925), starring Emil Jannings and Lya de Putti (28 May); *The French Doll* (1923), starring Mae Murray (21 September); *The Law of the Lawless* (1923), starring Dorothy Dalton (23 September); Charlie Chaplin's 1918 movie *Shoulder Arms* (23 September); *Paris* (1926), starring Joan Crawford and Charles Ray (25 September), and so on. He especially likes Lya de Putti as an actress, thinking that she has the eyebrows, eyes, facial features, figure, waist, and feet of a *majo* 魔女, enchantress (*monü* in Chinese). He goes to performances such as Beijing opera, *kunju* opera 昆劇, or folk vaudeville. He likes soccer and basketball games as well. Cafés and dance halls he frequents are numerous: Bluebird (Burubādo, ブリューバード or initiated as B.B.), Momoyama 桃山 (Peach Mountain), Lion Café (Rai'on Kafei ライオン・カフェー), Golden Star, Madame Café, Park Pavillion, Sanmingong 三民宮 (Three Peoples' Palace), Nora, Eastern, Lodge, Eden Café, The Black Cat (kuro neko クロネコ), The Little Cherub, Del Monte; the list goes on. But it is not all play without work. Bookstores where he is a regular customer are many as well: Uchiyama 内山 Bookstore (for Japanese books and magazines), Zhonghua 中華 Bookstore, the Commercial Press, Guanghua 光華 Bookstore. We can see that reading and literary criticism as well as pleasure seeking are among his main occupations.

At the end of each month of his diary there is a reading list, from which we can see that his reading, covering Japanese, French, English, classical and modern Chinese, is a demonstration of transcultural practice. The works of Paul Morand and Japanese Neo-Sensation writers such as Yokomitsu Riichi and Kataoka Teppei 片岡鐵兵 are included, of course. When Liu comments on Yokomitsu's story "Skin" (Hifu 皮膚) in the November reading list, he writes: "Only the *style* (original in English) is worth mentioning. The content is *nonsense* (original in English)."[103] This criticism, though short, is quite to the point. Most Japanese and Shanghai Neo-Sensation works share similar overemphasis on stylistic experimentation. Apart from that, it seems, indeed, nothing much meaningful could be said about its content—always a male narrator gazing at modern girls. "Nonsense" is connected with the Japanese expression "ero guro nansensu," which would be transmitted to one of Guo Jianying's cartoons in 1934, as we will see in the next chapter. The term could refer to the decadence in 1930s Shanghai as well as pre-war Japan.[104] Since Chapter 2 will be devoted to the Shanghai Neo-Sensation writers' connections with their Japanese counterpart and Paul Morand, here I will not delve into it. I would just mention his brief comment on the latter in the 23 October entry: "Finished Morand's poetry collection tonight. Many difficult words, crude but not elusive. Though densely modernist, not deep, just furnished with a few Neo-Sensation words."[105]

Liu's interests in contemporary Japanese literature certainly went beyond the Neo-Sensation group. Included in the first three months' reading lists are Horiguchi Daigaku's poetry collection *Gekka no ichigun* (Gathering in Moonlight), Kikuchi Kan's 菊池寬 story "Fuji Jūrō's Love" (Fuji Jūrō no koi 藤十郎の戀), Tanizaki Jūn'ichirō's *Collection of Modern Stories of Satyriasis and Nymphomania* (Kindai jōchi shū 谷崎 潤一郎の近代情痴集), Mushanokōji Satsuane's 武者小路實篤 play *Desire* (Aiyoku 愛慾), Satō Haruo's 佐藤春夫 "Devil's Toy" (Akuma no omocha 惡魔の玩具), Itō Kaishūn's 伊藤介春 poetry collection *Eye to Eye* (Me to me 眼と眼), and so on. These are either single volumes or pieces found in Japanese magazines such as *Women's Forum* (Fujin kōron 婦人公論), *New Tide* (Shinchō 新潮),

and *Central Forum* (Chūō kōron 中央公論) published in the same year. Liu was certainly very much *au courant* with the Japanese literary scene. It is not necessary to go on with the other months' lists.

Liu's interests in classical Chinese works are wide and varied. The following titles are included in his monthly reading lists: *Annotations on Ancient Ci Poetry Collected in the Book of Folk Rhymes* (Yuefu gucikao 樂府古辭考, Han Dynasty), *Complete Tang Poetry, Anecdotes of the Xuanho Period of the Great Song* (Dasong Xuanho yishi 大宋宣和遺事), *Water Margin, Six Chapters of a Floating Life* (Fusheng liuji 浮生六記, 1808), to name just a few. What I am more interested in is Liu's criticism of his contemporary Chinese writers and literature in general. He read all schools of writers, but apparently preferred the Creation school. About Yu Dafu's story "The Past" (Guoqu 過去) he writes in the 9 May entry: "It describes two Chinese new women. Though some descriptions are crude, the language is juicy. He is a story writer with the quality of a poet." He writes about Zhang Ziping in the 10 May entry: "He is a realist, skilled at subtle psychological depictions. But the language, heavily influenced by Japanese, is a spoiler." He likes Zhang's novel *Taili* 苔莉, in which Taili, the concubine of a man, falls in love with his cousin, and the two lovers commit suicide because of pressure from society. The 15 May entry has this to say: "Its description of Chinese society, especially the sexual desire of Chinese people, is succinct. Although unevenness is seen here and there—the imperfection of writing skill is his shortcoming, and although there is too much Japanese influence, he is a good writer." In contrast, Liu's evaluation of the Literary Research Society (Wenxue Yanjiuhui 文學研究會) is low. According to him, its organ, *Short Story Monthly* (Xiaoshuo yuebao 小說月報), is not up to standard. He comments in the 1 July entry: "The second issue of *Short Story Monthly* arrived. Lousy indeed. Literary men in China are dying out! . . . In comparison, the writings in *Creation Monthly* are much better."

Though Liu liked American movies as much as European ones, he was totally averse to American taste in literature. No American literary works are recorded in his diary. In the 1 May entry he comments on *The Best French Short Stories of 1926*, a collection of French stories edited by an American:

> Several people have written about the topic "Americans and literature." No one denies that there is literature in America, but for me the Americans don't know anything about literature at all. The editor of this book is a journalist living in Paris this year. He has edited a few similar volumes, but what he calls *the Best* [original in English] contain nothing worth reading. I believe what can be called *the Best* French stories of 1926 must be something other than these—the term America is an eyesore.[106]

The volume he mentions is part of a series of collections of French short stories published by Small, Maynard Co. in Boston from 1924 to 1927.[107] Liu, addicted to things French, seems to have inherited French prejudices against Americans as well. He sometimes reads English works through French translation, for instance, John Cleland's *Mémoirs de Fanny Hill, femme de plaisir* (*Fanny Hill: Memoirs of a Woman of Pleasure*, 1748–49).

Reading, frolicking, loitering and women watching constituted Liu's life in Shanghai. The people, known and unknown, recorded in his diary cover all nationalities: Filipino, Danish, French, Indian, Japanese, English, American, German, and so on. The names of women of pleasure, Yuriko ユリ子, Isshi 一枝, Chiyoko 千代子, Kimiko キミ子, Lily リリ, Lüxia 綠霞 (Green Twilight), and so on, dot the pages of his diary. There are entries in which he expresses the fascination for the enchanting transcultural hybridity of the semicolonial human landscape there, as the 12 January entry indicates, where he engages in an enraptured eulogy of Shanghai:

> Shanghai, Ah! Shanghai of enchanting power [Ch. *moli* or *maryoku* 魔力]!
> . . . .
> O what a golden pit (*huangjinku* or *ōgonkutsu* 黃金窟] you are! Look at the sparkling trinkets!
> O Land of beauties! Red, white, yellow, black, a shaft of light in the night [*yeguang* or *yakō* 夜光], from the hands of narrow waists [*xiyao* or *saiyō* 細腰]!
> A smile with the floating gaze [classical Ch. *hengpo* or *yokonami*], the hybridity [*hunzhong* or *konshu* 混種] of short hair [*duanfa* or *danbatsu* 斷髮] and bare knees.[108]

Here "the floating gaze," a classical expression, refers to the modern girl gazing coyly back at her gazer. The phrase "short hair and bare knees" refers to her fashionable short hairstyle and modern outfit baring her knees. *Xiyao*, literally meaning "narrow waist" in Chinese characters, is in fact borrowed from the Japanese *saiyō*, a phrase indicating a beauty. Again we see the free mixture of classical Chinese and foreign text with the new vernacular, which is a demonstration of the linguistic hybridity of the Neo-Sensation mode of writing, paralleling the delightful hodgepodge of different races seen on the streets of Shanghai. In contrast to this eulogy of the metropolis, there are also passages showing Liu's aversion to foreign presences. For instance in the 19 January entry, after mentioning an unhappy episode with a Caucasian woman in the tram, he says, "An eye for an eye, the fire of hatred, you devil-like white women! Stand steady, or the oriental man burning with indescribable fire would rush you to the tramway hell!"[109] Reading through Liu's diary one senses that on the one hand the diarist feels genuine resentment towards foreign exploitation and colonial expansion, while on the other he undeniably enjoys the cosmopolitan atmosphere and luxurious foreign products.

While Liu does not seem to feel for Caucasians, he does not feel akin to the Japanese way of life, either. After his grandmother's funeral in Taiwan, he went to Tokyo and stayed there from 26 May to 8 September. His sister, living in Tokyo with her husband, came to meet him at the train station; she was studying at Japan Women's University at the time. Once when he visited her, she was practicing the piano.[110] He studied French and Latin briefly at the Athena-Français Language School (Atene.Furanse in *kana*), but was bored and missed Shanghai tremendously. On 6 June he complained about the teaching method of the language school, which did not help one learn French at all. He writes in the 17 June entry, "In these few days I feel suffocated. There is nothing serious, but I simply don't like the '*Japanese way*' (original in English)!"[111] On 12 July when he received his mother's letter permitting him to go back to Shanghai, he gladly planned to make it his "land of the future" (jianglai de di 將來的地). Later, around 1934, he would bring his wife and three children to Shanghai, where two more would be born.[112] But a compulsive traveler like Liu was nonetheless constantly suffering from the feeling of homelessness. As he writes in the 3 May entry, his deceased grandmother as well as all human beings are travelers in life until death: "Life is travel; we are all visitors away from home." A "man of the world" is also a homeless man, driven by the urge to leave the domicile and move on. More will be said about this in Chapter 2.

As a Taiwanese during the Japanese occupation who became famous and was murdered in Shanghai, it took more than half a century for Liu Na'ou to be re-established in Taiwan as a literary man. In the summer of 1997 when Liu's family entrusted his 1927 diary to me, they were still uncertain whether it was "safe" or appropriate to have its content meet the public eye. Even though it was already ten years after the lifting of the martial law in Taiwan, his second daughter, the fourth of his five children, was still uneasy when talking about her father's murder. It had been a subject of taboo since her return to Taiwan from Shanghai with her mother and siblings shortly after the violent event. A child of seven as she was at the time, she keenly felt the shock and horror that would persist for decades to come, over the years of the postwar handing over of Taiwan to the Nationalist government, the 28 February Incident in 1947, and the White Terror from the 1950s to the 1970s. In summer of 1997 she vaguely remembered her mother's description of her father having been active in Shanghai's literary circle and film industry during the 1930s, but until the publication of his five-volume *Complete Works* in 2001 she would not know his stature and significance as a literary man.

The macaronic and transcultural modernity

Liu Na'ou has been included in the canon of modern Chinese literature since the late 1980s, when the Neo-Sensation School, long fading into oblivion, was revived as a reaction against the realistic trend that had dominated the critical scene since the May Fourth.[113] Liu and his fellow Neo-Sensation writers wrote at a time when China was facing a representation crisis—traditional language was no longer efficient in conveying the meaning of a modern world beset with free love, speed, and modern technology.

Critics like Edward Gunn have pointed out that the classical prose created by popular writers such as Su Manshu 蘇曼殊 and Xu Zhenya 徐枕亞 coexisted with the "Japanization period" approximately after 1900 and the "Europeanization period" from 1918 on.[114] But, instead of talking about these different periods and separating popular writers' classical prose and traditional vernacular from the new vernacular, I prefer to draw attention to the macaronic of the Neo-Sensation mode of writing. With the term "the macaronic" I intend to show that the stylistic creativity of their new vernacular is reflected in its free mixture with classical expressions, dialects, and foreign texts, Japanese or European, a linguistic emblem of transcultural modernity. Rather than dividing Japanese and European influences into approximately fixed periods, my conceptualization of the macaronic shows the inclusive nature and the creativity of the new vernacular at its experimental stage. It crosses the borders between not only national languages, but also traditional and modern, national and regional, literary and scientific. Its transcultural/translingual hybridity results in the fluidity and instability of the new vernacular that I find most fascinating.

No national language is an enclosed system; infiltrations of foreign elements are never stoppable. While the Vernacular Movement in modern China advocated an all-out effort to create a new national language, what was "national" became all the more suspect. Those who participated in the movement, writers and laymen alike, were highly sensitive to the divide between the traditional and the modern, as can be attested by innumerable documentations. Yet simultaneous to the enunciation of this great divide and the general obsession with the "nation," what can be witnessed in practice was the loosening up of all tangible and intangible borders and the tug-of-war between institutional powers vying to gain control. What is "modern" may turn out to be the creative transformation of the classical. What is considered "native" may be the foreign that has taken roots in local culture. What is "national" may be the combination of different dialects. There is no "pure" Chinese anymore, as there has never been.

In addition to the macaronic marked by transcultural linguistic performances, the Neo-Sensation mode of writing also transgresses the boundary between high and low cultures. While critics often talk about the influence of film techniques on the Neo-Sensation School, its connections with popular magazines in Shanghai should not be ignored, either. We are more familiar with the high-brow journals that functioned as its organs, such as *Trackless Train* (September to December 1928), a biweekly, and the two monthlies *La Nouvelle Littérature* (1929–30) and *Les contemporaines* (Xiandai 現代; 1932–35).[115] On the other hand we should not ignore the fact that Liu Na'ou, Mu Shiying, Shi Zhicun, and Hei Ying often published in popular magazines such as *The Young Companion*. More worthy of attention is that, starting in 1934, *The Women's Pictorial*, published since 1933, would be taken over by them as their official organ. It would be the medium through which their art of dandyism is fully expressed, as will be discussed in Chapter 2. In addition, we will see how the Neo-Sensation mode of writing traveled from France to Japan and then to China.

2 A traveling subgenre
The palm-of-the-hand story

> A lightning flash . . . then night! Fleeting beauty
> By whose glance I was suddenly reborn,
> Will I see you no more before eternity?
> Elsewhere, far, far from here! Too late! Never perhaps!! For I know
>   not where you fled, you know not where I go,
> O you whom I would have loved, O you who knew it!
>   —Charles Baudelaire, "To a Passer-by," trans. William Aggeler

The modern girl gazing back

In Baudelaire's poem "To a Passer-by," the fleeting beauty, appearing as a lightening flash in the night, would be a monumental leitmotif that reverberates in the works of Paul Morand and his Japanese and Chinese followers. It tells of a chance encounter between the dandy/flâneur and the modern girl/flâneuse. The modern girl is the symbolic Other whom the dandy yearns to catch sight of in his wandering route through the metropolis till eternity, just for the enchanting glance that will grant him his rebirth. Gazing boldly back at him, the modern girl is more titillating than a traditional object of desire that remains modest and passive. Thus, with her returned gaze indicating that man is nothing but her "Gigolo," as discussed in Chapter 1, she is adopting, and thus reversing, the dandy's role as womanizer. The cover of the October 1934 issue of *The Women's Pictorial* features a short-haired modern girl in a man's suit with a scarf for tie, indicating how the modern girl's cross-dressing was attracting public attention at the time (Figure 2.1).[1] Two of Guo Jianying's cartoons in 1934 also depict the modern girl in a man's suit. In Figure 2.2, the modern girl, wearing a man's suit and tie and carrying a stick, walks into a lady's room and startles another modern girl.[2] In Figure 2.3, a modern girl-cum-painter, wearing a short-sleeved shirt, a bow-tie with a scarf hanging down, and trousers, is introducing, in a calm and matter-of-fact way, her naked female model to a man, who stands in a rigid posture, completely stunned and speechless.[3] When the modern girl behaves like men, she stirs up gender trouble.

The dandy's endless obsession with the modern girl is spurred by his

Figure 2.1 The Women's Pictorial.

age-old narcissism. Agonized and compelled to follow her, he lives and dies for her, his other self in the mirror, as Baudelaire says: "vivre et mourir devant le miroir" (live and die before the mirror). In this chapter we will see how the dandy follows the modern girl to eternity, marveling at her enchanting beauty while resenting her inferiority and ignorance at the same time, as discussed in Chapter 1. In this chapter we will see how he shows infinite patience in his didacticism and condescension towards her, teaching her how to behave and dress—how to be his perfect other self.

Thus, here I continue to develop the concept of dandyism while studying the Shanghai Neo-Sensation writers, with special emphasis on their interactions with their Japanese counterparts and the French modernists Paul Morand (1888–1976) and Maurice Dekobra (1885–1973). In my definition, dandyism manifests itself in three aspects: (1) The dandy's *préciosité* of writing in the macaronic, which is emblematic of the hybrid nature of

A traveling subgenre 61

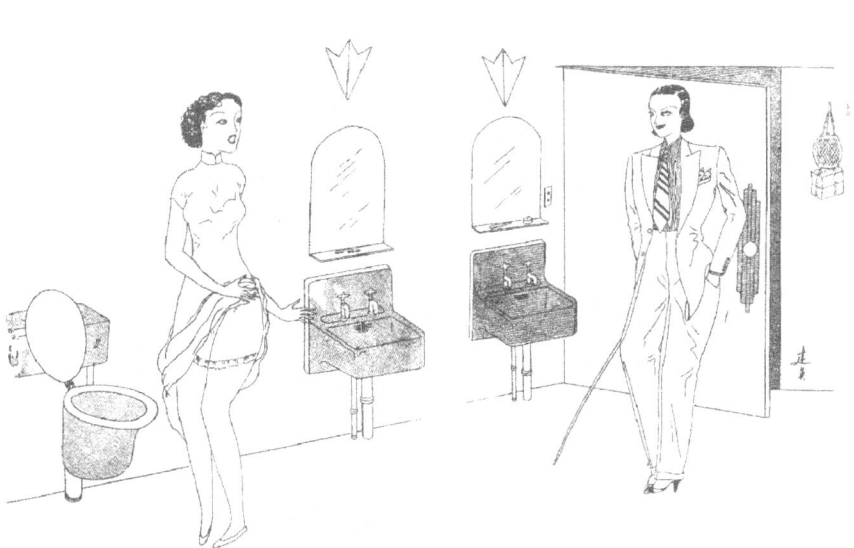

最时髦的男装吓死了公共厕所的姑娘

Figure 2.2 The most fashionable man's dress startles a girl in the public toilet.

transcultural modernity; (2) the dandy's love–hate relationship with the modern girl, who represents his inferior other self; (3) the dandy's stance as a perpetual traveler and his art of *flânerie* depicting women as types. In this chapter I will begin with the palm-of-the-hand story, a subgenre that traveled from Paris to Japan and then was appropriated by the Shanghai Neo-Sensation writers in the 1920s and 1930s. Always featuring a dandyish male narrator ogling a modern girl, this subgenre throws into light the essence of dandyism.

As a continuation of the previous chapter, I will analyze again in detail the macaronic, which mixes classical expressions, dialects, foreign text, transliterations, neologisms, and so on, as the emblem of the Neo-Sensation mode of writing. To me, this linguistic experimentation exemplifies perfectly the essence of transcultural modernity: It creates a transcultural space, or a meeting ground, where the traditional/new, elite/popular, native/foreign, national/regional, literary/non-literary overlap and interact. It is the transcultural site where creative transformation is possible. How did the Shanghai Neo-Sensation writers boldly engage in this practice of linguistic reform? How did they use the new media, including the vernacular and visual images such as cartoons, to understand the relationships between the two sexes in the modern metropolis, which totally reversed traditional concepts of gender

Figure 2.3 "Mr. Huang, allow me to introduce Miss Chen."

performance? How did they establish the symbiotic relationships between the dandy and the modern girl through the experimentation of the new media at their disposal? These are the issues I will try to address in this chapter.

As a contrast to the palm-of-the-hand story, Paul Morand's novel *L'allure de Chanel* will be discussed in order to illustrate my conceptualization of the dandy/modern girl symbiotic relationship. Unlike the usual modern girl who is as a rule described by the male narrator, Chanel, the modern girl-cum-designer, is the narrator of her own story. She is recounting her life, desire, and aspirations to excel in the international fashion world. If, as I have said in the previous chapter, for the dandy the modern girl is incapable of intellectual activities and thus despised by him, Chanel combines the characteristics of a modern girl and a female inventor for Morand. We will see how, in creating the character Coco Chanel, Morand is in fact formulating his perfect other self, a female dandy.

A subgenre from France to Japan and China

One intention of this book is to show that Japan as a vector of European concepts and ideas for China is an indispensable area of study when we look at modern Chinese literature. During the traveling process of the subgenre, the palm-of-the-hand story, this necessity is incontestable.

The cartoonist Guo Jianying (1907–79) took over the editorial job of *The Women's Pictorial* in January 1934. The magazine had published nine issues since April 1933 without drawing much attention from the literary circle in Shanghai. It derived its name *Furen huabao* from *Fujin gahō* 婦人畫報, a Japanese popular magazine established in 1905 and continuing publication until after the war, with famous modernists such as Kikuchi Kan, Kataoka Teppei, and Kawabata Yasunari as contributors. *The Women's Pictorial* was a sister journal of *The Young Companion*, likewise published by the Liangyou Company. At first it seemed to be simply one of the women's pictorials devoted to fashion, cosmetology, love and marriage that were booming in 1920s and 1930s Shanghai. But Guo intervened with the creation of a column titled "Collection of Palm-of-the-Hand Stories" (Zhangpian xiaoshuoji 掌篇小說集) and invited his Neo-Sensation friends such as Liu Na'ou, Mu Shiying, and Heiying to contribute stories, with the exotic modern girl as the central motif. This kind of mini-story, quite popular in 1930s Shanghai, created liminal or in-between spaces that allowed the Neo-Sensation writers to cross the borders between the elite and the popular, display the dandyish fascination with the modern girl and misogyny, and transform the modern girl into a materialized symbol of modernist artifice.

Literally, *zhang* 掌, the Chinese character for the "palm," indicates that these are tiny stories which can be written or held in the palm of the hand. Yet *Zhangpian xiaoshuo* is in fact adapted from *shōhen shōsetsu* 掌篇小説 or *tenohira no shōsetsu* 掌の小説 (Palm-of-the-Hand Story), a subgenre Kawabata Yasunari started experimenting with and made famous during the 1920s.[4] During the later years of the Taishō period in Japan, in *Literary Times* (Bungei jidai 文藝時代), the organ of the Japanese Neo-Sensation writers, there was a trend in writing mini-stories. Writers such as Nakagawa Yoichi 中川與一, Okada Saburō 岡田三郎, and Takeno Tōsuke 武野藤助 tried their hands at the subgenre, but not for long. According to Kawabata's 1926 article "The Booming of Palm-of-the-Hand Stories" (Shōhen shōsetsu no ryūkō 掌篇小説の流行), the term *shōhen shōsetsu* was invented by Nakagawa Yoichi, inspired by a palm-of-the-hand story published in *Literary Spring and Autumn* (Bungei shūnshū 文藝春秋). At the time, this subgenre had two or three other names, for instance, the "twenty-line story" used by Okada Saburō, the "ten-line story" by Nakagawa Yoichi, or the "one-sheet story" by Takeno Tōsuke. Because of Okada's article "On *conte*" (Konto ron コント論), it was generally known as *conte*.[5] Of course, anyone familiar with Paul Morand's mini-stories would know that he often named them *contes*.

Kawabata's opinion about the Japanese name of this subgenre discloses his general view on how to translate a foreign term into Japanese. According to him, using the *katakana* expression *konto* may seem more "natural" than using strange translated terms, but he is not satisfied, because using *katakana* to transcribe a foreign term gives the impression of professional jargon and may discourage the general reader. In addition, in French a *conte* does not necessarily refer to a mini-story, according to him. Convinced that in Japan this kind of mini-story had a specific history of development, he prefers to use the Japanese term *shōhen shōsetsu*. Arguing that this subgenre is a revival of past tradition, he takes as examples precedents in traditional Japanese narratives, including "The Pillow Book" (Makura no sōshi 枕草子) in the eleventh century and Ihara Saikaku's 井原西鶴 (1642–93) "Twenty Unfilial Children in Our Dynasty" (Honchō nijū hukō 本朝二十不孝), apparently a parody of the "24 Filial Children" (Ershisi xiao 二十四孝) in China.[6]

Kawabata's stories in this subgenre are called *tenohira no shōsetsu*. He began experimenting with it from the 1920s on. Taking it as a form for perfecting writing techniques, he continued writing in this subgenre and wrote 127 pieces altogether in forty years. Most of his palm-of-the-hand stories were written between 1923 and 1930, the Neo-Sensation period. Thirty-five of them were collected in *Decoration of the Emotions* (Kanjō sōshoku 感情装飾) in 1926.[7] The first edition of *Tenohira no shōsetsu* by Shinchōsha was published in 1971. Revised in 1989, the new edition collected 111 pieces. Here one tends to ask, what are the aesthetic characteristics of this subgenre that drew Kawabata to it for a period of forty years? In the "Exposition" (Kaisetsu 解説) to the 2001 edition, Yoshimura Teiji 吉村貞司 writes:

> The so-called palm-of-the-hand story refers to a story that can be written in the palm of the hand, or a mini-story that can be held in the palm. As short as it is, by no means is its content simple or skimpy. Nor is it written with the leftover materials of a novel, just as a *haiku* 俳句, though the shortest form of poetry, is far from being a coarse piece of work made with the leftover materials of a long poem or a *tanka* [short poem 短歌]. Just as a superb *haiku* contains a whole universe, its content on a par with a long poem, so does a palm-of-the-hand story. Its richness of content, complexity of psychology, sharpness of human nature, and so on, are by no means inferior to ordinary novels. Exactly because it is short, its characteristics are succinctness and directness, devoid of any redundancy.[8]

As is manifested here, a palm-of-the-hand story is often compared to a *haiku*, indicating this subgenre's experimental characteristic and poetic style. In his 1927 article "On Palm-of-the-Hand Stories" (Shōhen shōsetsu ni tsuite 掌篇小説について), Kawabata states that a palm-of-the-hand story is a super mini-story, exactly the way a *haiku* is a super mini-poem. He explains the four superb characteristics of the subgenre as a literary form as follows:

(1) It coincides with Japanese tradition and the unique qualities of Japanese national character such as humor, sarcasm, and pungent social criticism; (2) It records the sparkling of senses that people experience in modern times, when feelings become sharper, finer, and more fragmented than before; (3) Demanding much less time and labor, fewer sheets of paper (more economical in that sense), and less complicated writing technique, this subgenre invites even common people to write; (4) Compared with a novel, a short story is the essence of fictional art, while a palm-of-the-hand story no doubt represents its quintessence. His conclusion is that, like an impromptu poem, a palm-of-the-hand story can catch the "sensitive heart and purity of emotion at the flash of a moment."[9]

Kawabata wrote in the "Postscript" (Atogaki あとがき) of the first volume of *Selected Works of Kawabata Yasunari* (Kawabata Yasunari senshū 川端康成選集) in 1938:

> Among my past work, those that I miss most, love most, and even today would still like to give to many people as presents are palm-of-the-hand stories. Most pieces in this volume were written during the 1920s. A great deal of literary men wrote poetry during their youth, but I wrote palm-of-the-hand stories instead of poetry. Even though some of them were written forcibly, not a few of them flowed naturally from the heart. From today's point of view, though I am somewhat reluctant to call this volume "My Specimen Room," I do think that the poetic spirit of my youth fairly lives on.[10]

My Specimen Room (Boku no hyōhonshitsu 僕の標本室) is the title of the second collection of his palm-of-the-hand stories published in 1930, comprising 47 mini-stories. Despite the fact that in 1948 upon the publication of his complete works, Kawabata overturned his own words and criticized himself, "Now I feel the self revealed in these palm-of-the-hand stories unbearably disgusting.... That step of my writing career as manifested in these samples was a mistake,"[11] there is no denying that he did devote considerable creative energy to this subgenre. It crystallizes the Neo-Sensation spirit, while many scenes and motifs described in these mini-stories find fuller expression in his longer works. His attachment to this subgenre manifests itself in the fact that the last work he wrote and published before his suicide in 1972 was "The Snow Country Sketch" (Yukiguni-shō 雪國抄), a mini-story based on his 1935 novel *The Snow Country* (Yukiguni 雪國).[12] It is worth mentioning that this mini-story published in *Sunday Everyday* (Sandei mainichi サンデー毎日) is typeset like a poem.

Kawabata used the succinct form of palm-of-the-hand stories to describe traditional rural scenes in Japan. There are autobiographical stories such as "Bone Collecting" (kotsuhiroi 骨拾い) and "Toward the Sun" (Hinata 日向), about memories of the author's deceased grandfather. Stories about girls in the countryside abound, for instance, "The Virgins' Prayers" (Shojo no inori

處女の祈り) and "Hair" (Kami 髪). There are also stories about the enchanting *geisha* girls in the Izu Peninsula, for instance, "Ring" (Yubiwa 指環) and "The Custom of the Dancing Girls' Tours" (Odoriko-tabi hūzoku 踊子旅風俗). Some of these mini-stories capture in a single moment the fascinating energy of a capricious, teenaged girl (usually under 15 and a virgin), which allows the male character to perceive at an instant the essential meaning of something that seems trivial. In "Toward the Sun," the narrator is meeting his first love at an inn on the beach. When suddenly the girl shyly covers up her face with the sleeves of her *kimono*, he realizes that he has been embarrassing her with his peculiar habit of staring at people's faces. How and when did he get that habit? He searches in his memory: Was it at his parents' home during his childhood, or was it when they took shelter at a friend's place after they had lost their own? To avoid looking at the girl, he turns away and looks at the beach bathed in the autumn sunlight. All of a sudden the beach extending towards the sun awakens his buried memories. It was after his parents passed away, when he went to live with his grandfather in the countryside for nearly ten years. His grandfather, being blind, always sat at the same corner in the same room, facing the east. Almost every five minutes he would turn his head like an electric doll to face the south, towards the sun, but never turned towards the north. The narrator, surprised that even a blind man could be so sensitive to the sunlight, often sat in front of the old man and stared into his face, wondering if he would turn to the north only for once. So that was how he got into the habit of staring at people's faces. This moment of epiphany draws the girl closer to him. Turning a little red, she says something to solicit his attention in a childlike manner and makes him laugh heartily.[13]

That all through his life Kawabata was fascinated with the enchantment of young girls is a known fact. He even declared in an interview with a journal that rather than a wife he preferred to take an ignorant young girl as concubine, with as little cultural upbringing as possible.[14] It is widely known that Hiteko 秀子, whom he lived with for years but finally took as his wife, fits this category perfectly. It is true that the young girls in his palm-of-the-hand stories are bewitching but ignorant. They are traditional Japanese girls, whether with *danbatsu* 短髪 (short hair) or a *geisha*'s hairstyle, in traditional rural settings. Yet despite their ignorance, they serve as the catalyst that provokes the male characters' emotions and actions and thus suddenly brings about an intuitive grasp of reality.

In comparison, in Shanghai Neo-Sensation mini-stories the modern girls are likewise ignorant, entertaining, and a pleasure to the male gaze. Their presence in the stories serves simply to reflect the male narrator's dandyish mindset. They are the synonym of the metropolis, with Westernized clothing and lifestyle. They are the symbol of materiality, void of any possibility of intellectual excellence. But the truth is that it is the dandyish male gaze scrutinizing them which fails to see anything beyond their bodily forms and refineries. While ogling at women, the narrator-dandy reveals instead, in an

A traveling subgenre 67

ironic fashion, his own state of mind, which reflects a way of life and an attitude towards the semicolonial metropolitan world in Shanghai. Self-irony revealing the narrator's playful attitude towards both his own stance as a dandy and the modern girl as his object of desire is an important element in Shanghai Neo-Sensation stories, as I will demonstrate bellow.

Dandyism as a life calling

The narrator in Shi Yan's 史炎 "Music on the Cruising Route" (Hangxianshang de yinyue 航線上的音樂) is a typical dandy in the palm-of-the-hand stories in *The Women's Pictorial*. Since the setting is on a river cruiser and he is wearing a white suit, one can assume that he is a man of some means. Seeming to be free from any occupation, he has all the leisure at hand to ogle women. Trying to idle away a pleasant morning on the cruiser, he strolls from bow to stern to scan one by one the young girls aboard. The first one that catches his eye is a 12- or 13-year-old country girl, who returns his stare by looking aslant at his white suit. Then, unable to bear his relentless gaze, she turns around in a flutter. The second girl who catches his attention is around 15 or 16. Sensing that she is being looked at, she starts to flirt with a middle-aged woman, and then blushes and looks away from his gaze. The third girl is 18 or 19 years old. The narrator describes her in the following way:

> Her face is shaped like a chicken egg, as if seen through the magnifying glass [Ch. *kuodajing* or *kakudaikyō* 擴大鏡], with a cherry-like small mouth shaped like a heart, cheeks as fresh as the color of apples [*linqin*, or *ringo* 林檎], a pair of translucent, *feverish* eyes shining with a watery light, a waist as slender as a willow in the spring, a back shaped like a violin [*fanyaling* 梵啞鈴], long legs like lotus stems, ample figure. . . . Her manners show the purity of St. Maria [*Maliya* 瑪利亞].
> My eye lingered on the final destination of its trip.[15]

What is most noticeable is not only the male narrator ogling the young girls, but the macaronic he uses. Transliterations of foreign words such as "violin" and "St. Maria" can be seen. The words followed by both Chinese and Japanese pronunciations are modern Japanese *kanji* terms, e.g., *kakudaikyō*, the magnifying glass. The *kanji* term for *ringo*, no longer in use today, is likely to be taken for poor Chinese pronounced as *linqin*. Like many Japanese *kanji* terms, *ringo* is a return loanword originally from classical Chinese, meaning "apple" since the Tang and Song Dynasties. In addition, English text directly inserted into the narrative abounds. The word "feverish" in "a pair of translucent, *feverish* eyes" as quoted above is originally in English. Earlier in the narrative when the first girl shies away from the narrator's gaze, he says, "My gaze has become an *artful* single rail," with "artful" written in English. When the second girl looks away, too, he says, "But I am a quiet sleep walker (*mengyouzhe* 夢遊者), carrying on my monopoly (*zhuanli* 專利, meaning ogling girls) with a *spiritual* prowess." Here "spiritual" is originally in English. The three-character term *mengyouzhe* and two-character term *zhuanli* are semantic translations from "sleep walker" and "monopoly." When she and the middle-aged woman are giggling, he comments in English, "*A loving caress.*" When he senses that the third girl finally responds to his gaze with meaningful glances, he begins to whistle and feels that the melody of his whistling is mingled with the music flowing from her glances, "as if relishing mutually the taste of a trembling *kiss*" ("Kiss" in English).

Classical expressions, apparently transformed here, are an integral part of the passage. To say a girl's face is "shaped like a goose egg" (*edanlian* 鵝蛋臉, or *eluanxing* 鵝卵形) is a traditional trope, meaning an oval-shaped face, the first criterion of being a beauty. But the expression in the passage, "shaped like a chicken egg," is twisted and hilarious, showing both the narrator's intention to depart from tradition and his inability to get rid of trite expressions completely, hard as he may try. The same clumsiness is witnessed in another term, *chanxing outui* 長型藕腿, long legs like lotus stems. In traditional vernacular, a woman's arms with extremely delicate skin disclosed from her long sleeves are often described as tantalizing as "lotus stems," as can be seen in the sentence, "Liangzhi gebo, nen ru huaxia de lian'ou" 兩隻胳膊，嫩如花下的蓮藕 (The two arms are as tender as lotus stems under the flowers).[16] But comparing a woman's long legs to lotus stems invites laughter. Our author certainly finds it difficult to describe a modern girl's body part exposed by her fashionable outfit. Take another example: *chun zhi liu zhi yaozhi* 春之柳之腰支, a waist as slender as a willow in the spring. In classical Chinese, *liuyao* 柳腰, willowy waist, is used to describe a beauty's slender waist. But in "Music on the Cruising Route," the classical expression comprising two characters is translated into six characters in the vernacular, with *zhi* 之, a function word in classical Chinese, inserted twice into the new phrase, and with the character *chun* 春, spring, added in the beginning. Furthermore, the single word *yao* 腰, waist, is transformed into two characters, *yaozhi* 腰支, waist-branch, quite redundant. Heavily dependent on classical expressions, this newly "invented" term, *chun zhi liu zhi yaozhi*, is as awkward as it can be. Here we see how the author tests the limits of both the classical and the vernacular, and thus in the transcultural site where they overlap, creativity finds unlimited room—one could indeed "translate" the classical expression *liu yao* into endless possible vernacular expressions following this example. This kind of inept performance shows the author caught in the tug of war between tradition and invention. How could one pinpoint where the old ends and where the new begins?

The macaronic certainly represents a new hybrid culture already well bred in 1930s Shanghai, where foreign concessions had been established since 1842. Foreign languages and cultures mixed with local tongues and life were an everyday reality in the semicolonial metropolis. An indicator of the evolution of linguistic style, the macaronic in 1930s Shanghai Neo-Sensation stories was no doubt a marker of a mixed new culture which combines the foreign and the exotic with the newly reformed Chinese vernacular. It was not too long since the vernacular movement had been promoted by Hu Shi in 1917. With classical language and its obscure allusions and trite expressions abandoned, writers were struggling to find new expressions. Whereas the result of Hu's own experiments with the new poetry, critics tend to agree, were mediocre and banal, the Neo-Sensation experimentation with the macaronic, though likewise awkward and premature, was indicative of a whole generation of Chinese literary men trying to grapple with the new vernacular as a literary medium.

Another important element in the above-quoted paragraph worth analyzing is the use of imageries of technology and Western music. To say a girl's face looks as if it were "seen through a magnifying glass" is totally unconventional. Yet though far-fetched, it works like a modern version of metaphysical conceit: It combines a scene of beauty with science. To say a beautiful girl's back is "shaped like a violin" is odd. But given a second thought, the term "shaped like a violin" may well be connected with the music imagery later on in the story. In fact, during the 1930s the expression "Woman is like a violin" was a new expression translated from the words of a French modernist defining woman as an instrument awaiting the right musician. More will be said about this later in this chapter.

Let us examine another passage in "Music on the Cruising Route." Many a passage such as the following sounds like a soggy mishmash at first, but becomes delightfully lively after several readings:

> Rocks in a motley of patterns lined the river banks. Sparrows perching on the electric cables on the banks were like musical scores and notes. I transmitted turbulent torrents of wireless messages to that girl. The returned messages, though scarce, were full of meaning. The overture of my fantasy began.

Here the "wireless messages," *wuxiandian* 無線電 in Chinese, could be either telegrams or radio transmissions. But since in the story these refer to silent messages transmitted from the narrator's eye, it would be logical to say that the term here should mean telegrams. To sum up the discussion so far, we see a distinct pattern in the narrator's mode of expression. Not only is he a practitioner of the macaronic, but he is interested in two sets of imageries, mostly deriving from Japanese *kanji* terms: those of modern technology such as steamship (Ch. *qichuan* or *kisen*), magnifying glass, electric cables (*dianxian* or *densen* 電線), and telegram (*wuxiandian* or *musenden*); and those of Western music such as violin, overture (*xumu* or *jomaku* 序幕), musical scores (*yuepu* or *gakuhu* 樂譜), notes (*yinfu* or *onpu* 音符), imageries unknown in traditional narratives. Even though seemingly at odds with each other, these two sets of imageries combined imbue the narrative with an unusual poetic dimension. The title "Hangxianshang de yinyue" could mean either "music on the cruising route" or "music on the gazing route." I would venture to say that the author is consciously engaged in a stylistic invention, even though from our point of view today, most of his language is awkward. In the scanty space of less than two pages, he has created a metropolitan prose poem commemorating the advent of modern technology and the dandy's "monopoly" of scrutinizing women.

The word "monopoly" appears twice in the narrative. The first time it appears, the narrator, bewitched by the first girl's innocent beauty, says, "I wanted to take up the duty of my monopoly, and began to stare at her like a fool." The implication of that word may escape a careless reader at this instance, but will probably seize his attention the second time it appears, when the narrator, trying to catch the second girl's eye, says, "But I am a quiet sleep walker, carrying on my monopoly with a spiritual prowess." "Monopoly," a term indicative of the modernist concept of the protection of intellectual property, is certainly too emphatic a word to use, yet no doubt emblematic of how the narrator/dandy looks upon woman watching as his exclusive legal privilege and dandyism as his life calling.

How to be a modern girl?

While most studies on Shanghai Neo-Sensation writers center on the modern girl, I emphasize the dandyish male gaze that shapes her image. As I see it, they are a group of self-styled dandies, who make it a rule not only to live but to write in style. The Neo-Sensation mode of writing highlighting the macaronic throws into relief their transcultural performance that is elitist in nature. Yet at the same time they embrace the mass media culture and demonstrate the ease with which they cross the borders between elite and popular. In *The Women's Pictorial*, we often see the Neo-Sensation writers adopt a dandyish persona, positing himself as a preacher of good taste while infiltrating popular culture with his insignia of transcultural stance.

Viewing the modern girl as his inferior *alter ego*, he spares no effort in teaching her how to become his ideal other self. Always dogmatic, he lays out all the rules for her of how to behave and dress, writing treatises included in such special issues as "Odes to Chinese Women's Beauty" (Zhongguo nüxingmei zanli 中國女性美讚禮).[17]

This special issue, published in April 1934, was inspired by a French journalist and modernist writer Maurice Dekobra, who made his literary debut in 1927 with *La sirène des tropiques* (The Siren of the Tropics) and *La madone des sleepings* (Madonna of the Sleeping Cars). His love stories and travel accounts were extremely successful in France and North America during the late 1920s and 1930s. He was translated into 75 languages and his books sold more than 90 million copies, but he is unjustly forgotten today. In his 2002 biography, Philippe Collas placed him in the same rank of dandies as Paul Morand and Scott-Fitzgerald.[18] Dekobra was a passionate traveler. As a journalist he had a chance to work in Berlin for a period of time and then in London. He was among the first Westerners to visit the Kingdom of Nepal.

In November 1933, in order to write a love story based on an oriental woman, he began his trips to the Far East that lasted for months. He arrived in China and provoked the fair sex with his Orientalist views on the beauty of Chinese women, went to Japan, and then stopped by Shanghai before he returned to France. In Shanghai, he offended his own sex by stating that "Chinese men do not know the art of love."

But the anger of Chinese men did not seem to last long. In the March 1934 issue of *The Women's Pictorial*, Mo Ran 默然 published an article advising Chinese men and women to listen to Dekobra with patience:

> Dekobra is a true nuisance, his words being unbearably provocative. But, have patience and read carefully the words of this Western expert on love. What he said might be out of context, or too impolite; he might have evaluated the oriental art of love from Parisian-Hollywoodist perspectives. But Misses, Ma'ams, Mesdames, Mademoiselles, Misters, Masters, Messieurs, if you want to be angry, please hold your temper and get angry only after you read his words.[19]

What wisdom is there at all in the words of this "Western expert on love" that eventually subjugates our Shanghai dandy? First, Dekobra says, Chinese men should improve their manners; they are not aware that, before kissing women, they should take off their hats—a basic rule of politeness when courting the fair sex. Second, because Chinese men are not competent in the art of love, marital problems arise in Chinese society. They should know that, unlike Japanese women who constantly bow and prostrate to show that they are men's slaves, Chinese women are like Tartars and Mongols, full of fighting spirit. They are untamed, looking for equality. In parties or social functions, they are quick in repartee, leaving men no leeway during debates. When you incite them to anger, they are extremely uncontrollable. They are panthers in human form, ready to jump and grab your throat. Third, Chinese men are to blame for their women's untamed behavior, because they lack imagination, do not understand the art of love, and are not willing to spend more energy on women. They have no intention of understanding their partners, or studying their likes and dislikes, their sensitivity and vulnerability. Fourth, Chinese men should know that woman is like a violin lying on a table, waiting to be tuned and played by a musician who knows it well. The key issue is not a good or bad violin, but an artist who can play true music with it. Whether an instrument responds depends on the skills and talent of the player. Fifth, Chinese men, when tired of their wives, marry concubines inferior to their wives and place them under the same roofs, thus resulting in endless domestic misfortunes. Instead, Chinese men should learn the art of having affairs from their Western counterparts, who go clandestinely to their mistresses for diversions, but always come home telling their wives how much they love them. This is "hypocrisy of the highest class," an art in which Chinese men still fall far behind.[20]

Not only does our Shanghai dandy willingly agree with the Parisian dandy on the shortcomings of Chinese men in the amorous art, but he imitates his mentor in his taste for Chinese women. In "Chinese Women's Beauty in a Foreigner's Eye" (Wairen muzhong zhi Zhongguo nüxingmei 外人目中之中國女性美), Mo Ran further recounts the Parisian dandy's views on Chinese women. In Dekobra's opinion, the standard Chinese beauty should have "a pair of almond-shaped slanting eyes, a pair of pink, sea-shell like ears, a tiger's mouth, an eagle-like nose, a spoon-like chin, a forehead like a crescent-moon, a face shaped like a watermelon seed; her shoulder, thighs, and shins should be a little plump with curves, her height five feet two inches. Her beauty is mysterious, enchanting." All these are stereotypical views on the Oriental beauty.

Mo Ran is highly conscious of the shortcomings of a Chinese beauty seen against her Western counterpart. Adopting the gesture of a mentor like Dekobra, he further instructs Chinese women to use eye shadow in order to enlarge the contours of their eyes, a cosmetic technique that they should learn from Western women:

> There is a shortcoming in Chinese women's cosmetic skills. They have not paid enough attention to coloring the eyelids; they should apply some blue to the eyelids to enhance their beauty. If their eyes are narrow, this will especially make them look bigger.[21]

It is not just the face, though. Beauty of the bodily figure is a must, too. Dekobra declares that flat breasts were already *passé*; in the twentieth century, not only is a protuberant, ample bosom a sign of health, but it is an element of beauty. He advises Chinese women to stop binding their breasts and allow their shoulders and thighs to develop attractive curves.[22]

The Shanghai dandies, mostly echoing Dekobra's views, are highly concerned with the Chinese woman's "Chineseness." In "Chinese Women's Innocent and Ignorant Beauty" (Zhongguo nüxing de zhizhuomei 中國女性的稚拙美), Hu Kao 胡考 says that the traditional Chinese women with "cherry-like lips, longish narrow eyes, and willow-leaf eyebrows" should be dead and buried. Instead, the modern Chinese beauty should have "big eyes with unbalanced whites, long eyebrows drawn with harmonious lines, lips with thirty-degree upward curves, a brown skin that recalls the south-Pacific beach, dark hair dyed with blond streaks," apparently totally transformed by the Western art of cosmetics.[23]

It turns out that Chinese women's facial expressions should be improved, too, also by imitating Western women. Ōgai Kamome 鷗外．鷗 (or Ouwai Ou in Chinese), a Hong Kong poet who made his name by writing palm-of-the-hand stories for *The Women's Pictorial*, cautions Chinese women against wearing a *poker-face* (original in English) and advises them to learn vivid facial expressions from foreign actresses' performance in movies. To him, Chinese women imitating foreign actresses are in an "evolutionary process," meaning progressing towards a more civilized or modernized state:

> It is quite effective to save one's flat and unemotional face by trying hard at facial expressions. Due to the popularity of foreign movies in this great metropolis [meaning Shanghai] of our country, Chinese women' flat faces have shown some emotional aspects. This is something to celebrate. ... Learning from the actresses' zoomed in faces in the movies, they have cleverly transformed their own unblessed faces to those full of emotional beauty. Today the beauty of the facial features of China's daughter is in an evolutionary process. If we may joke about it, her face has become foreign, so to speak, by imitating the screen-faces of *Hollywoodism* [the author's own English]. ... Besides crying and smiling, our daughter's face, having transcended pure nationality, has acquired various expressions. She knows how to show her sadness, knit her eyebrows, and look unhappy, surprised or shocked. She is capable of making a pass at someone, putting on airs, or even acting as if longing for someone. It is not ungrounded to say that the facial features of the metropolitan girl in our country, surpassing national boundaries, have adopted more and more transnational beauty.[24]

The irony and tongue-in-cheek tone disclosed in the passage are subtle, while the dandyish didacticism towards the modern girl is unmistakable. As much as Ōgai Kamome adulates the modern girl's "transnational beauty," he insists on her *chinoiserie* as well. To him, dark hair and dark eyes are her natural beauty; it is wasting nature's gift if she dyes her hair blond. He agrees that the Chinese girl should paint her eyebrows so that they would look longer, like those of Westerner women, but in his view, compared with Japanese women's "samurai eyebrows" (meaning wide and short eyebrows, without curving towards the end), the Chinese girl's can be already considered blessed. He strongly suggests that she wear *qipao* to fully reveal the contours of her breasts, slender waist and buttocks. He agrees that "a few years ago, our women's breasts, having long been tied up, seemed to have never existed on their bodies. But lately their breasts have been liberated and grown a few times larger than before. *Qipao*, which further enhances the beauty of our women's breasts, "has established an immortal career." Thus, while paying homage to transnational and transcultural hybridity, the dandy is also extremely conscious of the differences of nations and national characteristics, a paradox that marks the complexity of dandyism.

Dandyism and misogyny are inseparable. It is said in "Chinese Women's Innocent and Ignorant Beauty" that the Chinese modern girl, with her peculiar tone, should speak with "an incorrect diction, showing childish innocence and ignorance. Ah, this ideal beauty, what an image in a Cézanne painting! This is the fetishism of the beauty of innocence and ignorance in modern age, the Chinese beauty in my heart!"[25] The dandy, though infatuated with the modern girl's looks, despises her infidelity and ignorance, disclosing his deep-rooted misogyny. The term "misogyny" was actually used in a tongue-in-cheek fashion in Mu Shiying's 1933 story to tease a modern boy infatuated with a modern girl. This will be the central topic in Chapter 5. As we will see in the following, to the dandy the modern girl's infidelity is incorrigible, whereas her lack of intellect is constantly ridiculed in the Neo-Sensation mode of writing.

Commodifying the modern girl

Like his Shanghai counterparts discussed so far, the Tokyo Neo-Sensation writer Yokomitsu Riichi was no stranger to the dandy–modern girl pair bond. He published a story in the Neo-Sensation organ *Literary Times* in 1927, "The Exercise of Seven Floors" (Nanakai no undō 七階の運動), which has received little critical attention so far. Liu Na'ou's translation of this story was included in *Erotic Culture* (Seqing wenhua 色情文化), a collection of his translations of Japanese proletarian and Neo-Sensation stories published by his own bookstore in Shanghai in 1928.

The story is about Kuji 久慈, a dandy/womanizer whose father owns a department store. He makes the salesgirls, vying for his attention and favor, jealous of each other. His everyday duty, or monopoly, is going up and down the seven floors of the department store to inspect the salesgirls responsible for a wide range of merchandise. The first paragraph of the story, juxtaposing each girl with a commodity item, throws into light an analogy between the fetishism of commodity and that of the modern girl:

> Today is the continuation of yesterday. The elevator continued its ejection. The girl flying into chocolates. The girl diving into socks. *Robes montantes* and opera bags. Sticking her face out of the wall of parasols is Nōko 能子. Pocket mirrors in compacts. Next to the embankment of soaps were pillars of hats. Down pillows surrounded the wood of walking sticks. In the mountains of perfume Kyōko 競子 had been indulging since morning. Waves of people flowed through the depths of wallets and knives. Valleys among cans and cliffs of shoes. Ribbons and laces climbed onto flowers.[26]

Yokomitsu's language, with short, succinct sentences juxtaposing terse phrases, is reminiscent of Paul Morand's linguistic innovation, as will be discussed later in this chapter. His Japanese is shockingly unconventional compared with that used in the Meiji and Taishō periods, or in the Shōwa period and today. There is no doubt that he is testing the limits of the Japanese language which favors grammatically complex sentences and tends to be quite evolved, with long strings of modifiers before nouns and extensive uses of particles that can be crucial to the meaning of the sentences. Yokomitsu's and his fellow Neo-Sensation writers' experiment in literary language was an effort that reflected how during the Taishō period avant-garde writers, inspired by foreign influences, were boldly transgressing traditional boundaries.

What I would like to delve into here is Liu Na'ou's Chinese translation of Yokomitsu's text. Liu's translation defamiliarizes Chinese while refreshing our perception, even though it takes effort and repeated readings to understand it. Thanks to the interchangeability between many *kanji* and Chinese characters without the risk of blurring the meaning, Liu is able to keep, or borrow, as many of the original *kanji* phrases as he can, for instance *tosha* 吐瀉 (*tuxie* in Chinese, ejection), *kaichūkyō* 懷中鏡 (*huaizhongjing*, pocket mirror), "bōshi" 帽子 (*maozi*, hat), "kōsui" 香水 (*xiangshui*, perfume), "hōtō" 放蕩 (*fangdang*, indulge), and so on. The *katakana* terms, on the other hand, pose a problem in translation, because they are used to transliterate foreign terms of which there are no Japanese equivalents. Here Liu Na'ou likewise resorts to Chinese transliteration and thus shows his ingenuity in inventing Chinese phrases—for instance, he renders "ribon" (ribbon) into "li-feng" 禮鳳 (gif-phoenix), a phrase no one could understand unless compared with Yokomitsu's original. This free rendering manages to keep to some extent the sound of the original while mimicking the meaning, even if it is a strain on readability. Sometimes the meaning is deplorably undecipherable in the Chinese transliteration, when, for instance, "shikuramen o dē colon" シクラメン・オー・デ・コロン (Cyclamen eau de cologne) is rendered into "xikeraman.aodikelang" 西客拉曼．奧迪可郎 (west-guest-pull-svelte deep-wise-allow-lad).[27]

Kanji and *katakana* terms are more or less "transmittable," in a way, but when it comes to gender indicators in Japanese, the translation can be totally disastrous, because there are no counterparts in Chinese. For instance, when Kyōko says to Kuji, "Anata, ī wa" あなた、いいわ (My love, good day), anyone who speaks Japanese knows right away it is a woman speaking to her lover or husband. "Anata," あなた meaning "you," is strictly used by a woman to address her loved one, otherwise it shows condescension and can be very impolite, even offensive. In addition, the particle "wa" わ ending a spoken sentence is only used by women. Liu Na'ou's rendering of this simple sentence is awkward and confusing as to who is speaking to whom: "Hao, ni zhege ren!" 好，你這個人！ (Good day, you!) In Chinese "ni zhege ren," indicating the speaker's coyness, surprise, or even displeasure towards the interlocutor, can be used by both men and women to address a loved one, a friend of either sex, or an unknown person. If one reads only the Chinese translation, one gets completely lost as to the sexes of the speakers and the relationships between them, even though there are only three people speaking in this scene—Kyōko, her lover Kuji, and Nōko, who is jealous of her and tries in vain to keep him for herself.

The formal structure innate to a foreign language may be untranslatable, for instance, the sentence structure and the gender indicators, if they are different or non-existent in the translating language. In cross-cultural translation, what may be better transmitted is the content, or the story, even though the translatability of these elements may be impaired because of the unsuccessful rendering of the formal structure. What is unmistakably transmitted in Liu Na'ou's translation is the concept of the commodification of the modern girl, as can be seen in the above-quoted paragraph, and, especially, her image constructed by Kuji the dandy/womanizer.

Calling him the department store owner's "dandy son" or "playboy son" (*dōraku musuko* 道楽息子), the narrator says, "Kuji does not stick around the counters because he has to make a living. This department store owner's dandy son intends to invent the everlasting woman." The everlasting woman, *ei'en no josei* 永遠の女性, instead of referring to a particular woman or a woman *per se*, turns out to be a montage of multiple women's body parts: "To him the everlasting woman is made of a composite of bits and pieces collected from here and there." It is a montage of Kyōko's torso, Nōko's head, plus "the shoulder, hands, and feets [are] stirring in the middle of towels and tables on the seventh floor." These minor parts belong to Hiroko 容子, Toriko 鳥子, Makotoko 丹子, Momoko 桃子, Utsuko 鬱子, and so on. For instance, Utsuko, on the second floor, is "the right foot" of the everlasting woman.[28] Kuji, an incorrigible dandy, is collecting the body parts he fancies most of each of the salesgirls to create his everlasting woman—no woman is perfect; it is only by combining the best parts of each of them that a perfect one can be invented.

Furthermore, Kuji the dandy/womanizer gets what he wants by generously handing out 10-yen bills to the salesgirls whenever he visits their departments, a gesture that highlights the commodification of the modern girl. All but Nōko gladly accept the money. When he proposes to give her money, she always mocks him with her sharp tongue and it has never worked with her—he has not been able to get her into bed yet. In his mind she is the head of the everlasting woman, exactly because, distinct from the other girls, she has a brain of sorts. The narrator makes it clear that, to Kuji, this is a game he plays with all the salesgirls, and Nōko manages to outwit him: "To him, Nōko is a tough match. It is only with this head of the 'everlasting woman' that his 10-yen bills have never once worked. Therefore his knowledge of psychology is shattered here."[29] She seems to see through him by clairvoyance, teasing him: "You are like a machine that tests the degree to which people would respond to money."[30] A clever modern girl, she knows how to distinguish herself from the others so that she is more enticing to him, but eventually she loses the courtship game, because she is in love. The narrator tells us that in her heart she is willing to go anywhere with him, even though up to now she has not yet succumbed to his temptation.

In the end, she does go with him to a hotel. Everything goes well, except that she makes a fatal mistake by suggesting marriage. When Kuji keeps silent and does not commit himself, she walks out of the hotel room alone. Kuji comments that Nōko is the only girl who is behaving "counter to the principle of the department store" (hyakkaten no hōsoku kara gyaku ni shinkō shite

ite 百貨店の法則から逆に進行してゐて).³¹ The so-called "principle of the department store" is simple and clear: money in exchange for the modern girl's sexual favor as commodity. Asking anything more than monetary exchange is against the commodity principle. The next day when Kuji goes up the seven floors of the department store to inspect the salesgirls again, the narrator says, "Whenever it was break time, Kuji again climbed up, bickering all the way to the seventh floor, just to gaze at the hands and feet of the 'everlasting woman' with her head removed" (atama no toreta 'ei'en no josei' 頭のとれた永遠の女性).³² The story ends on this note.

The meaning of these last words is quite ambiguous. They could mean that Nōko has lost her head because she consented to sleep with Kuji; she is no longer considered a modern girl with a brain. Or, since she wants marriage, she violates the commodity principle of the department store and should therefore be removed from the money/sex game. No doubt the narrator is saying that, to Kuji the dandy/womanizer, the everlasting woman does not need a head—all she needs is a torso and hands and feet.

Dandyism and misogyny

Pejorative depictions of the modern girl abound in Japanese and Chinese literatures and popular magazines during the 1930s. To see how the idea of the headless modern girl indeed traveled far, it would be interesting to look at "A Body without Soul" (Wu linghun de routi 無靈魂的肉體), a comic strip of twelve boxes published in the magazine *Modern Sketch* in 1936.

In box 1, the middle-aged man wearing a suit, a tie, a vest, and a hat is looking intently at a mannequin displaying a *qipao* in a shop window. He is gentlemanlike, with a fat belly indicating he is a sugar-daddy type. In box 2, he suddenly steals the mannequin and runs away with it, carrying it on his shoulder. In box 3 he arrives at a secret spot where a huge trunk is found. Taking off his jacket, he starts to measure the height of the mannequin. In box 4, he stands on a stool and uses a saw to cut off the head of the mannequin. In box 5 he measures the height of the mannequin again, and then begins to saw off its legs in box 6. In box 7 he measures the width of the trunk, and then saws off the arms of the mannequin in box 8. In box 9 he is finally able to put the torso of the mannequin into the trunk, and it begins to dawn on the reader that this man has taken all the trouble so far in order to store the mannequin in the trunk as jewelry in a treasure box. In box 10 the cover of the trunk is closed, with the mannequin inside. He buries the head, hands, and legs of the mannequin in the ground. In box 11 a policeman comes along at night and, aided by a flashlight, discovers this mysterious trunk. In the last box, we see the open trunk at the upper-right corner and the Venus-like torso of the mannequin on a table that apparently serves as an altar. The policeman, kneeling piously on the ground with his palms closed, is worshiping the torso of the mannequin (Figure 2.4).³³

This comic strip is a telltale story: Men worship the modern girl's body; her

78 *Dandyism and Transcultural Modernity*

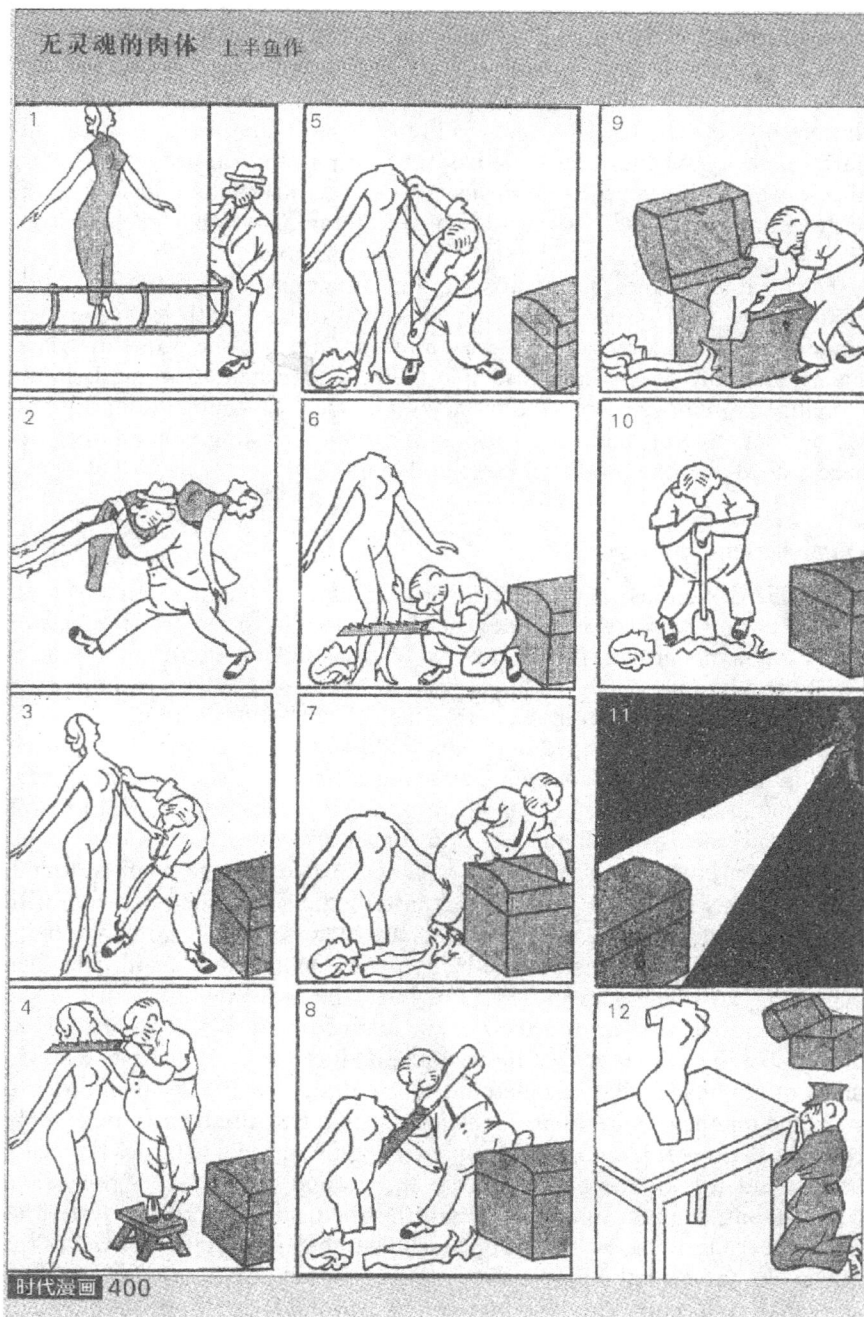

Figure 2.4 A Body without Soul.

head, hands, and feet are of no value, because she does not think, labor with her hands, or walk with her feet—with money, there are maids hired to do the house chores and cabs or carriages to take her anywhere. Or, we should say that men are not worshiping her for her thought, diligence, frugalness, and so on; all they want is her body and sex.

Here, for comparison, we are going to look at two of Guo Jianying's cartoons collected in *Collection of Cartoons by Jianying* (Jianying manhuaji) in June 1934. The one titled "A Model of Modern Women" (Xiandai nüxing de muoxing 現代女性的模型, 1930) depicts in the center a short-haired woman in a standing position, wearing nothing but a bra, panties, and high-heeled shoes, with her long, naked legs split in an upside-down V shape. She lifts her left arm towards her head, caressing her hair and looking aslant, with a luscious smile on her face. Two electric wires are connected to the back of her head, producing heat waves of "It" (original in English) emanating from her head. The wires are traced to a generator controlled by a man standing in the background on the lower right hand corner of the picture. This man's small figure makes her stature look like a giant. He is shuffling money bags (represented by the dollar sign) to empower the generator. The other ends of the wires lead to the lower left hand side of the picture, near her right ankle, with two male figurines named respectively "Shengzhi Yuansu" (reproductive essence 生殖元素) and "Hormone" (original in English) tied to each end of the two wires. Hormone's legs are intertwined with her right ankle (Figure 2.5).[34]

A doggerel of five lines serving as a caption of the cartoon is printed at the lower-left corner of the picture, right beneath the two figurines at the woman's right ankle:

> *Nonsensical* (無內容的) [without content] brain cells,
> *Grotesque* (怪異奪目的) [eccentric and eye-catching] torso,
> *Erotique* (肉感的) [sensual] lower part—
> The generative power is money and *Hormone* (生殖元素) [reproductive essence]
> *It* (熱) [heat] is her weapon of livelihood. [italics mine][35]

The five italicized words are originally in English or French. The five expressions in parentheses are original Chinese characters explaining their meanings. The caption wonderfully reinterprets the Japanese term *ero guro nansensu* in the 1930s, indicating the sensual, silly mass culture represented by the modern girl.[36] This visual statement is more telling and powerful than any language alone could convey. The message is unmistakable: The modern girl has nothing in her head but sex (represented by heat); her sexual strength, powered by men's money and hormone, lies in her sensual body, which she is proud to display.

Another cartoon titled "All Contents in a Modern Woman's Brain Cells" (Xiandai nüzi naobu xibao de yiqie 現代女子腦部細胞的一切) can be viewed

80 *Dandyism and Transcultural Modernity*

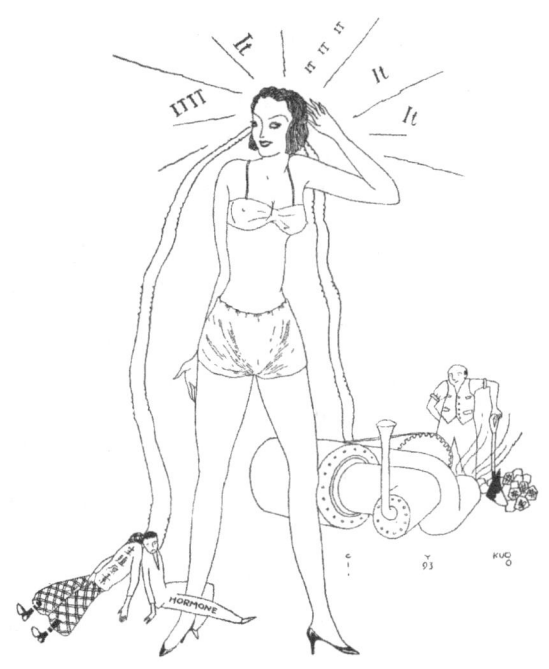

现代女性的模型

Nonsensical(无内容)的头脑细胞，
Grotesque(怪异夺目)的上身，
Erotique(肉感)的下身——
原动力是金钱与 Hormone(生殖原素)，
It(热)是她的生活武器。

Figure 2.5 A Model of Modern Women.

as complementing the previous one. It draws a woman's head and naked torso. A halo around her head looks like her profile, filled with images and words, disclosing what is inside the head. They include images such as a wine bottle, a filled wine glass, a saxophone, a cigarette, money bags, and poker cards, and words such as HORMONE, EROTICISM, and *Great Light* (Daguangming 大光明, a movie theater in Shanghai) (Figure 2.6).[37] The caption (Figure 2.7) on page 82 reads:

> Movies—cocktail—"jazz"—*Garbo, Deitrieh* [Dietrich]—materials for qipao—ice-cream—Saxophone—rouge—Daguangming—kisses—hugs —"waltz" dance—Mr—introduction—*Rendezvous* (蜜會)—Hollywood—rent a hotel room—*Eroticism*—art of love—celibacy—art of

现代女子脑部细胞的一切

Figure 2.6 All Contents in a Modern Woman's Brain Cells.

controlling a husband—policy of wheedling—cars—*Revue*—non-stocking-ism—walking dogs—rapture—stimulation—*Nonsense*-ism—*A. B. C.*—dance halls—"heat and charm of the other sex"—speed and power—non-sentimentalism—*Hormone, Hormone, Hormone* (生殖元素)—money, money, money, money, money! [Italics originally in English][38]

In these two cartoons, the modern girl as a lover of entertainment businesses such as the movie theater and the dance hall is emphasized. Her sole occupation is seeking pleasure, fortune-hunting, and men-hunting. She enjoys wine, jazz, speed, and stimulation. To highlight her image as a sex symbol, the

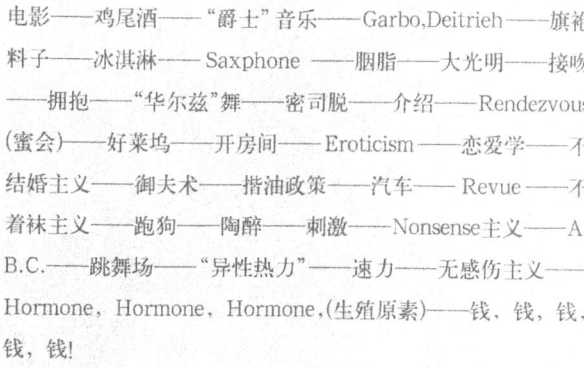

Figure 2.7 All Contents in a Modern Woman's Brain Cells.

cartoons connect her with Hollywood movie stars such as Greta Garbo (1905–90) and Marlene Dietrich (1901–92). The latter as the *femme fatale* in *The Blue Angel* (1930) is unforgettable. More revealing is the reference to "The It Girl" Clara Bow (1906–65), who starred in the silent movie "It" in 1927 and became the spokeswoman for the new social mores the movie was presenting: Sex means having fun. In the movie, "It" refers to the sexual appeal of the female protagonist, a shop girl who attracts wealthy men with her overwhelming charm dubbed as "It": a *je ne sais quoi*, indescribable, power.

The two cartoons and captions disclose clearly the misogyny of the dandy. To the dandy, not only is the modern girl bewitching and luring, a gold-digger who will take every opportunity to victimize sugar-daddies, but her greatest sin is ignorance. In fact her meticulously adorned appearances and pursuit of pleasures in modern life reflect the dandy's own penchant in every possible way, yet her lack of intellect and incapability of self-invention only mark her out for his inferior other self.

To the dandy, the modern girl, with a fascinating face and body, needs his instructions to learn how to dress and behave. He is the designer and creator, while the modern girl is nothing but the mannequin that wears the clothes he designs. Furthermore, the dandy, combining the roles of designer and mannequin, is capable of self-invention. The modern girl, beautiful but ignorant, is incapable of self-invention, and thus is his inferior other self. Hence Maurice Dekobra's maxim meant to teach Shanghai dandies about the truth in the man–woman relationship: Woman is like a violin awaiting the right musician.

But when a modern girl-cum-designer such as Coco Chanel (1883–1971) appeared on the scene, even a cocksure dandy like Paul Morand could not help marveling at her as his perfect other self—a female dandy, as we will see in the next section. He immortalized her in his 1976 work: *L'allure de Chanel*, the last book in his writing career spanning nearly sixty years.

When a dandy meets a female dandy: Morand and Chanel

L'ange exterminateur d'un style dix-neuvième siècle[39]
(the angel-exterminator of the nineteenth-century style)
—Morand, *L'allure de Chanel*, 1976

In the preface to *L'allure de Chanel*, Paul Morand recounts how on New Year's Eve in 1921 he became one of the familiar guests at the frequent gatherings in Coco Chanel's boutique on the Rue Combon in Deauville, a city in central Normandy. It was an internationally renowned resort, symbolic of elegance and the art of living. Among the guests were celebrities and rising talents such as Philippe Berthelot, Élisabeth Jouhandeau, Pablo Picasso, Jean Cocteau, Raymond Radiguet, and Pierre Reverdy. It was the time before Chanel conquered the fashion world in Paris, and it did not occur to Morand or the other guests that she would one day be "the angel-exterminator of the nineteenth-century style," a term indicative of Chanel's aggressiveness and militancy in his mind. To Morand, she was on the threshold of the new era for fashion: She ended the old style marked by salon elegance and heralded the modernist fashion of the twentieth century that "walked into the street."

In conjuring up Morand's association with Chanel, I am concerned less with Chanel as a real-life person than as a character in *L'allure de Chanel*. The first woman to share the fashion industry dominated by male designers, Chanel was a groundbreaking inventor who has inspired numerous studies. With all the available literature on her, Morand's fiction is particularly relevant to this study, because it represents a dandy's view of a female dandy. Unlike Morand's usual short or mini-stories of the modern girls, *L'allure de Chanel* is a full-length book. Most interesting of all, Chanel the female protagonist is telling her own story. Why does Coco Chanel as a modern girl deserve a book and why is she given a voice of her own? My reading is that Morand's dandyish stance is camouflaged with the autobiographical mode: He is speaking through Chanel's voice, his perfect other self.

The modern girls in Morand's stories are as a rule described by the dandy/modern boys who watch them closely. They are the object of the dandyish gaze and desire, without any personal history or psychological depth. In *L'allure de Chanel*, however, the female protagonist is given not only a voice but also complexity of character, distinct from the other modern girls created by him. In his usual dandyish condescension towards modern girls, Chanel is no doubt one of them in his mind, but he emphasizes at the same time that she is distinctly superior to them.

First, concerning her controversial relationships with a series of lovers,[40] she is described by Morand as a typical modern girl, capricious and constantly changing sexual partners at will. For instance, in the story, the first man in her life is M. B., whom she happens to meet in a teahouse when she is only 16 years old. The next day when he invites her to share his good living, she consents and goes away with him instantly. A little later, she meets a handsome English man, Boy Capel, and falls in love with him. She immediately abandons M. B. and gets on the train to Paris with her new lover.

In Morand's description, like a modern girl, she is content to be a kept woman—since Boy Capel, an English industrialist, prefers to stay home with her alone; she dresses up every night to please him without ever pleading to go out. Morand makes her say, "[J]'ai un côté femme de harem qui s'accommodait fort bien de cette reclusion."[41] (I have the quality of a woman in the harem who was well adapted to being a recluse.) In the meantime her doting lover spoils her with expensive gifts such as diamonds. Once, upon her request, he even sends her a bouquet of flowers every half hour for two days on end until she gets bored—a detail that highlights her capriciousness as a modern girl.[42] In another relationship, her English lover of ten years, the Duke of Westminster, grants her every wish before she even finishes her sentence. But she eventually leaves him because she is bored by the distasteful tedium of leisure and wealth. (Je m'ennuyais, de cet ennui sordide de l'oisiveté et des riches.)[43] When she declines to marry him, she says to him, "I don't love you. It's not amusing to sleep with a woman who doesn't love you, right?" Indeed a *femme fatale*. She tells the reader that upon hearing this, "[T]he men with whom I was brutal always became docile right away." (Les hommes avec qui j'ai été brutale sont tout de suite devenus très gentils.)[44]

Yet, unlike ordinary modern girls, Morand's Chanel does not exploit her lovers simply for fun or on the spur of the moment; she stays with them mainly because they most often serve as her mentors and because their wealth brings about independence for her. In M. B.'s case, according to Morand, he provides a chance for her to run away from her rigid aunts who have taken her in since her parents died. With her second lover Capel, Morand points out that it is the lifetime opportunity for her to start a millinery with the money provided by him. But here Morand carefully devises a scene in which it is clear that, due to her ignorance of how the business world functions, all the time she writes a check and the bank cashes it, she thinks she is withdrawing her own money earned from the millinery. When Capel discloses the truth that she owes the bank money and that the bank pays her simply because he has acted as her guarantor, her pride is hurt. She says in the story, "L'orgueil est une bonne chose, mais ce jour-là, c'en fut fini de ma jeunesse inconsciente."[45] (Pride is a good thing, but that day ended my ignorant youth.) From that day on she toils like a workaholic until her death, and she manages to clear the debt in a year.

She tells the reader that for her, work means money, and money means liberty: "[I]l me fallait acheter ma liberté, la payer n'importe quel prix."[46] (I had to buy my freedom, paying whatever price it takes.) In a word, her dependence on men buys her the freedom she needs to pursue what she wants, but her success is a result of her work, not of luck. According to her in the story, "The secret of my success is that I worked feverishly."[47] Her pride is emphasized throughout the novel, and it is interesting to find at the end that she compares it with the pride of Louis XIV, the inventor of French high fashion: "As I told you in the beginning, I am all pride ... the true pride ... is the pride of Louis XIV, or that of the British nature." (Ainsi que je l'ai dit au début, je suis tout orgueil ... le vrai orgueil ... c'est l'orgueil de Louis XIV, ou celui de la nature anglaise).[48] We should keep in mind that it is Morand the novelist who makes her compare herself to Louis XIV, probably the most eminent dandy in French cultural history.

Thus in Morand's description, like the usual modern girls, Chanel is capricious, proud, masochistic, destructive, as retributive as Nemesis (Chanel, c'était Némésis), goddess of vengence.[49] In short, a "belle dame sans mercy" (merciless beauty), as he says in the preface to the novel:

> C'est là le côté ombre de Chanel, sa souffrance, son goût de faire mal, son besoin de châtier, sa fierté, sa rigueur, ses sarcasms, sa rage destructive, l'absolu d'un caractère soufflant le chaud et le froid, son génie invectif, saccageur; cette Belle dame sans mercy ...[50]
>
> (This is the shadowy side of Chanel, her suffering, her sensation for doing harm, her urge to punish, her pride, her severity, her sarcasm, her destructive rage, her extreme character of blowing hot and cold, a genie of invective, pillager, the merciless Beauty ...)

Yet, despite the downside and negative qualities she shares with all the modern girls in his creation, she is nonetheless not a usual, ignorant modern girl in his eye. Rather, she is championed as an inventor, the indispensable quality of being a dandy. In his description, she is a revolutionary in fashion design who mocks high-class snobbism with provençal taste: She invents a semblance of poverty and simplicity for millionaires (all the time dining with tableware of gold), transforms high society women into maids (transformant les altesses en femmes de ménage), tones down the glitter of silk by neutralizing it with jersey, and so on. Her "stunning paucity" (paupérisme rageur) delights in devaluing precious jewelry and turns it into common stones.[51] The series of oxymoron used in Morand's preface to eulogize Chanel's invention points to one of the criteria of my definition of dandyism: crossing the bounderies between high and low, elite and popular. Drawn as a relentless modern girl endowed with the capacity of artistic creation and adept at transcultural practice, Coco Chanel is a perfect female dandy in Morand's eye.

Morand's story of Chanel is about an orphan who strives to make a future in the high society of Paris, but eventually conquers it with the "puritanical taste" (puritanisme) of her aunts imprinted on her since her life with them in the province of Auvergne. We know today that in her real life after her mother died, Chanel in fact lived in a monastery for seven years and learned the trade of a seamstress before she went away with M. B.[52] It was probably due to lack of information that Morand made the mistake, since Chanel herself recounted different versions of her childhood. Yet, at any rate, the image of a Chanel who has acquired the taste for simplicity and honesty from the stringent aunts, and who is a "quakeresse" conquering Paris, seems well-wrought. This plot line ties in seamlessly with Morand's analysis of Chanel's unique taste for fashion that revolutionized the salon taste for elaboration and redundancy.

Most intriguing is how Morand the dandy is concealed (or revealed) in Chanel the narrator when she embarks on analyzing her taste for fashion, one of the primary occupations of a dandy. The mirror effect is most clear in the sections titled "La rue Cambon" and "De la mode ou Une trouvaille est faite pour être perdue" (On fashion or An invention is accomplished to be lost). In the former, when Chanel tells the success story of her boutique in Deauville and later in Paris, one senses that Morand the dandy is personified in Chanel the narrator. In the story the dominating gaze, scrutinizing women and meticulously considering what makes them ugly and how to enhance their beauty, belongs as much to Morand as to Chanel. The ambiguity of this dandyish, condescending gaze is most pronounced in passages such as the following:

> Comme elles [les femmes] mangeaient trop, elles étaient fortes, et come elles étaient fortes et ne voulaient pas l'être, elles se comprimaient. Le corset faisait remonter la graisse dans la poitrine, la cachait sous les robes. En inventant le jersey, je libérai le corps, j'abandonnai la taille (que je ne repris qu'en 1930), je figurai une silhouette neuve; pour s'y conformer, la guerre aidant, toutes mes clients devinrent maigres, "maigre comme Coco". Les femme venaient chez moi acheter de la minceur.[53]
>
> (Since they [the women] ate too much, they were fat, and since they were fat and didn't want to be like that, they compressed themselves. The corset squeezed the fat onto the chest, covering it under clothes. Inventing the jersey, I liberated the body, I abandoned the waistline—which I did not resume until 1930, I delineated a new silhouette. In order to conform to it, thanks to the war, all my clients became slim, "as slim as Coco." Women came in to my shop to buy slenderness.)

Here the dandyish arrogance cannot be made clearer: the despise for the stupidity and inferiority of women who lack self-discipline and allow themselves to grow unbearably fat, and the mockery of how the corset squeezes the fat up and results in the shockingly huge bosom that was once fashionable. The description is ruthless and the fat women look hideous. The dandy behind the persona is perhaps "le Beau monsieur sans mercy"—is it not, after all, Morand the dandy who projects his own mind on Chanel, when he calls her the "Belle dame sans mercy"? In "De la mode" is it not the misogynistic dandy who speaks through Chanel that "Women are like children; their function is to wear out fast, to break, to destroy at a monstrous rate"?[54]

In "La rue Combon" and "On Fashion," when referring to her innovation of style that liberates woman's body from the corset, Morand is ostensibly making her a female dandy highly conscious of her own position at the frontiers. She says to the reader: "Les révolutions de la mode doivent être

A traveling subgenre 87

conscientes, les changements graduals et imperceptibles."[55] (The revolutions of fashion should be conscious, the changes gradual and imperceptible.) Sentences such as "I liberated the body," "I abandoned the waistline," and "I delineated a new silhouette," on the one hand reveal the arrogance of a female dandy, and on the other, make the reader suspect that it is rather Morand the dandy/male chauvinist who is making the value judgment and approving of Coco Chanel, his female counterpart.

Morand repeatedly emphasizes Chanel's dandyish gift of self-invention and self-reproductivity—whatever self-image she creates for her own person catches on and becomes contagious, inviting countless enthusiastic imitators. If Chanel is slender, every woman wants to be slender. If Chanel cuts her hair short, every woman does the same. Her famous "la garçonne" hairstyle fashionable in the 1920s is highlighted in the narrative. Yet, in real life who

Figure 2.8 Marie Bell in the movie *La garçonne* (1936).

88 *Dandyism and Transcultural Modernity*

was the one that originated this hairstyle can be debated. This term, indicating a boyish girl, became famous due to a Victor Margueritte 1922 novel *La garçonne*, which was banned in 1925 for its description of a boyish girl defying religion and ethics[56] (Figure 2.8). Another celebrity to whom could be attributed the invention of this hairstyle was Josephine Baker, the American black performer who arrived in Paris in 1925 and conquered the entertainment industry[57] (Figure 2.9). Fashion critics at the time were often struck by how the hairstyle of Chanel's mannequins reminded one of Baker[58] (Figure 2.10). But in the book Chanel claims that she cuts her hair short in 1917 and turns it into fashion. According to Chanel in the story, people praise the fact that with her new hairstyle she resembles "a young boy, a little swan" (un jeune garçon, un petit pâtre); the style instantly becomes popular, while comparing a woman to a young boy becomes a compliment.[59]

The section "On Fashion" is also worth delving into for our purpose. Here Chanel claims that she is the original for others to copy: There is only one

Figure 2.9 Josephine Baker as Black Venus in 1926.

A traveling subgenre 89

Figure 2.10 Sketch of mannequin wearing Chanel's April 1926 collection in French *Vogue*.

original, but the copies can be infinite. The dandyish obsession with originality and reproductivity as disclosed in Baudelaire's "Le dandy" is underscored. Chanel says, "At the origin of creation, there is invention ... Then this form is expressed, translated, diffused by millions of women who conform to it."[60] In another paragraph, she says, "[O]nce created, an invention is done in order to be lost in anonymity. My ideas are never exhausted, and it gives me great pleasure to see them realized by others ... What for them (my colleagues) is a grandiose drama never exists for me: the copy." She makes fun of her competitors who "toil secretly at night with their workers." She ridicules the "counterfeit process," "the samples that disappeared," the "spies" (espions) trying to steal her invention, and the vying for patrons "as if it were the formula of an atomic bomb."[61] Her confidence, dandyish pride, and mockery of inferior minds and performers are clearly revealed here. She mentions that there is an exclusive club of around twenty fashion designers in Paris, le PAS (Protection des Arts Saisonniers; Protection of Seasonal Arts), its mission being the prevention of illegal copying. She questions if such a mission, aiming to hamper the livelihood of 45,000 people for the privileges of 20, is indispensable, concluding arrogantly in an unrhymed couplet, "Que peuvent-ils faire, ces petits,/sinon interpreter les grands?"[62] (What can they do, these small potatoes,/other than interpret the great?)

Most important to the purpose of this study is that the entire section of "On Fashion" is a dandyish definition of fashion as an art form. Morand, or Chanel, is stating that fashion, as a form of modern art, is subject to the law of mass reproduction; in fact, existence itself is governed by the law of "movement and exchange." The world has abided by French inventions, while France herself has abided by the elaboration or the realization of the ideas invented by other peoples.[63] Furthermore, what is implicated here is not fashion alone, but the age-old dialectic of originality and imitation concerning artistic production. Morand the dandy/literary man, speaking through Chanel, analyzes in the following way:

> Si ces couturiers sont les artistes qu'ils prétendent être, ils sauront qu'il n'y a pas de brevets en art ... Les Orientaux copient, les Américains imitent, les Francais ré-inventent. Ils ont ré-inventé plusieurs fois l'Antiquité : la Grèce de Ronsard n'est pas celle de Chénier ; le Japon de Bérain n'est pas celui des Goncourt, etc.[64]
>
> (If these fashion designers are the artists they pretend to be, they will know that there is no patent in art ... The Orientals copy, the Americans imitate, the French reinvent. They reinvented Antiquity many times: The Greece of Ronsard is not that of Chénier; the Japan of Bérain is no longer that of Goncourt, etc.)

This is a perfect delineation of transcultural modernity. In artistic and literary production, how does one pinpoint what is pure French, German, American, Japanese, or Chinese? How could one claim that an artistic production, introduced into another country, often copied or transformed, belongs to the country of origin exclusively? The Chanel style triumphs in great metropolises of the world; in London, Tokyo, New York, or Shanghai, we see numerous imitations of her invention. Likewise, the Greco-Roman and Christian traditions, the *kanbun* 漢文 (classical Chinese) tradition, and the Arab and Muslim traditions have been the rich cultural resources that transgress national boundaries. When we consider the East–West transculturation process, it is by no means one-directional. While modern Asia has been overwhelmed by a progressive West, Europe has been drawn to a mysterious East since the eighteenth century. Coco Chanel, or Morand, highly conscious of the distinction of nations and peoples, recognize fully that all national cultures are already "tainted" by foreign cultures, be they French, American, Japanese, or Chinese.

In "On Fashion," maxims abound, indicating that Chanel, or Morand, is declaring her/his treatise on dandyism. For instance: "Creation is an artistic gift, a collaboration of the fashion designer (la couturière) with her age";

"Fashion should be the expression of place and time" (La mode doit exprimer le lieu, le moment);[65] "Fashion, like landscape, is a state of mind (un état d'âme)"; "Where lies the ingenuity of the fashion designer (le couturier)? It lies in his power to foresee the future. More than the great politician, the great fashion designer is a man who has the future in his spirit."[66] These maxims best exemplify what Foucault means by the term "heroization of the present" as discussed before. As stated in Foucault's lecture on 5 January 1983, modernity, or the spirit of enlightenment, is the consciousness of what is happening at the present and the attitude of seeing the present as the carrier or indicator of a process (porteur ou significatif d'un processus), while the modernist—a thinker, an intellectual, or by extension, an artist—is the one who demonstrates that he plays a role in this process. Foucault says:

> Il faut qu'il [le moderniste] montre non seulement en quoi il fait partie de ce processus, mais comment, faisant partie de ce processus, il a, en tant que savant ou philosophe ou penseur, un certain rôle à jouer dans ce processus où il se trouvera donc à la fois élément et acteur.[67]
>
> (Not only should he [the modernist] demonstrate what he is part of in this process, but how, as part of this process, he, as an intellectual, philosopher, or thinker, has a certain role to play in this process where he thus finds himself element and actor at the same time.)

In Morand's invention, Chanel is certainly a female dandy who is highly conscious of the role she can play in the fashion industry during the two World Wars. Seeing that women are going into the workplace and want more freedom of movement, she discards the corset and creates a new silhouette for them. Sensing that they want to go out of doors and exercise, she invents women's sportswear. Knowing that the wars have shrunk the rich clientele, she invents fantasy jewelry affordable to the mass consumers. Morand has Chanel proudly declare: "J'ai crée la mode pendant un quart de siècle. Pourquoi? Parce que j'ai su exprimer mon temps . . . parce que j'ai, la première, vécu de la vie du siècle."[68] (I created fashion for a quarter of a century. Why? Because I knew how to express my times . . . because I was the first to live the life of the century.) Living the life of the century, she creates the clothes that walk into the street and revolutionizes the concept of haute couture—it is no longer the prestige of a few salon women, but the everyday necessity of the mass consumer.

In *L'allure de Chanel*, Morand has defined the essence of a female dandy. A modern girl/flâneuse pursuing the romantic spur of the moment to anywhere her lovers lead her, she is also a great fashion designer who roam the metropolises for the exhibition of her collections. Coco Chanel deserves a book-length treatment, because Morand the dandy, speaking through her, is declaring his treatise on dandyism. Is not Morand arrogantly saying here: "Chanel, c'est moi"?

Neo-sensation from Paris to Tokyo to Shanghai

For Japanese Neo-Sensation writers like Kawabata and Yokomitsu, Paul Morand (1888–1976) was a literary mentor. Chiba Kameo 千葉亀雄, the first Japanese critic to call attention to the uniqueness of the Neo-Sensation writers as a literary group, declares in "The Birth of the Neo-Sensation School" (Shinkankakuha no tanjō 新感覚派の誕生) in 1924:

> ... The new French writer Paul Morand with his art of "Neo-Sensation" was introduced into Japan and soon became widely acclaimed. It is hard to say that the birth of the Neo-Sensation School in our country was not to some extent swayed by him.[69]

In fact, Morand himself never used the term Neo-Sensation to refer to his own writing. According to Chiba, the English translation of Morand's collection of stories *Ouvert la nuit* (Open all night; 1922), with a preface by Marcel Proust, was available in Japan then.[70] The first person who translated Morand into Japanese was Horiguchi Daigaku, who was closely associated with the journals *Bright Star* (Myojō 明星) and *The Mask* (Kamen 仮面). His translation of Morand's story "La nuit nordique" (The Nordic Night), collected in *Tendres stocks* (Fancy Goods, 1921), appeared in *Bright Star*, a journal established by the literary couple Yosano Hiroshi 與謝野寛 and Akiko 晶子 in November 1922.[71]

To understand how contemporary Japanese react to the Neo-Sensation innovation of style, it would be interesting to look at Kataoka Teppei's article "Appeal to the Young Reader" (Wakaki dokusha ni uttawu 若き読者に訴ふ) published in 1924. In order to defend a beginner on the literary scene whose unusual style was attacked by many established writers, it takes more than four pages for Kataoka to analyze a single line from this young writer's work, as if it were a *haiku*:

> Ensen no koeki wa ishi no yō ni mokusatsusareta.
> 沿線の小駅は石のように黙殺された
> (The small stations along the route were ignored like stones.)[72]

This line describes the impression of a fast-moving train passing through small stations, which look like stones violently thrown out of sight, as if fired from a shotgun. Although the term "mokusatsu" 黙殺 means "to bypass," "to neglect," or "to disregard," the two *kanji* characters in the term, if read separately, could mean "silently" and "to kill" respectively. Therefore a sense of violence is conveyed. In Kataoka's view, although the line is describing the condition of a material object such as a fast-moving train, through the description of the sensations felt at the moment, the author's life is effectively transferred into the vivacity of the language. Or one can say directly that "the electric power of things real is sensation (kankaku)."[73] Though the identity of the young writer is never disclosed in the article, we know that the line

Kataoka explicates with so much enthusiasm is from Yokomitsu Riichi's "Heads and Bellies" (Atama narabi ni hara 頭並びに腹). The latter later became the foremost theorist of the Neo-Sensation School. A detailed analysis of his monumental article "On Neo-Sensation" will be discussed in Chapter 3.

While no evidence shows that the Japanese Neo-Sensation writers could read French or did any extensive study on Paul Morand's works, their Shanghai counterparts were certainly to the contrary. Liu Na'ou (1905–40) might have been exposed to Morand's works during the time he studied in Tokyo from 1920 to 1926. As I have mentioned in Chapter 1, after he graduated from Aoyama College, Liu and his later fellow Neo-Sensation writers Dai Wangshu, Shi Zhicun, and Du Heng studied French together at l'Université L'Aurore in Shanghai in summer 1926. Dai later even went to France and studied at l'Institut Franco-Chinois de Lyon from October 1932 to March 1935.[74] Their French proficiency enabled them to read and translate French writers such as Baudelaire, Verlaine, and Valéry, as well as Morand, directly from the original.

Liu started his literary career in 1928 and published in October that year his translation of Benjamin Crémieux's article "Paul Morand"[75] in *Trackless Train* (Wugui lieche), the journal he established with his own resources. This article, titled "On Paul Morand" (Baoluo Muhang lun 保羅·穆杭論), discusses Morand's early publications from poetry collections *Lampes à arc* (Arching Lamps; 1919) and *Feuilles de Température* (Leaves of temperature; 1920) to collections of short stories *Fancy Goods, Open All Night*, and *Fermé la nuit* (Closed All Night; 1923), with emphasis on the short stories. Judging from the French titles and terms in parentheses inserted in the Chinese text, one can infer that Liu translated directly from the French original.

One should note that Crémieux singles out *dandysme* (dandyism) as one of the characteristics of Paul Morand's writing: "Il y a plus encore de cruelle lucidité que de compassion, de narquoiserie ou de dandysme dans la manière de Morand." (There is still more cruel acuity than compassion, more malicious mockery or dandyism in Morand's way of writing.)[76] Notice that mockery and dandyism seemed to be synonyms for Crémieux. The interesting part is that, in his translation of Crémieux's article, Liu Na'ou keeps the original term "dandysme" in the text. The Chinese term he invents and puts in parentheses after the French word says *zhuangshipi* 裝飾癖, addiction to dress and refinery.[77] The fact that the French term *dandysme* is kept in the Chinese translation indicates that he is aware of the incommensurability of the Chinese term to convey the exact meaning of the original. More importantly, Liu's vague understanding of the ambiguities and rich implications of the French term discloses that the Shanghai Neo-Sensation writers' imitation of Morand is to a considerable extent at the subconscious level, internalized in the psyche without the imitators' own clear self-awareness.

The year 1928 was the French and Japanese year for the Shanghai Neo-Sensation School. In the same issue of *Trackless Train* in which Liu's translation of Crémieux's article on Morand appears there are also translations of "Vague de paresse" (Laziness) and "Les amis nouveaux" (New Friends), and two *contes* from Morand's *L'Europe galante* (Galant Europe; 1925). In the same year, besides the collected translations of Japanese stories, *Erotic Culture*, Liu Na'ou also published the translation of several collections of French short stories together with his Neo-Sensation friends. *Masterpieces of French Short Stories, Volume I* (Falanxi duanpian jiezuoji diyice 法蘭西短篇傑作集第一冊) includes Dai Wangshu's translation of Paul Morand's "La nuit des six-jours" (The Six-Day Night), one of the six stories in *Open All Night*. It is the story of Léa, a capricious Jewish girl, told by Eugène, the male narrator who ogles her quietly in a Paris dance hall for three nights and finally gets her into bed on the sixth night of the grand bicycle race. Beautiful and rebellious (Léa était toujours belle, et rebelle),[78] she has a baby fathered by an unknown person and a lover Petitmathieu, who is a bicyclist participating in the race. She drives him crazy by associating with the narrator, but hardly feels any real remorse. It is clear that she enjoys the dangerous game of *ménage-à-trois* and is used to her lover's jealousy.

Léa in "The Six-Day Night" is certainly the type of capricious modern girl that fascinates the Shanghai Neo-Sensation writers, whose stories are as a rule about Léas who drive men crazy and Eugènes who ogle them and tell about their treacherousness. Dance halls, cafés, and bicycle races are also familiar settings. The transcultural crossing is likewise similar: the Italian, Swiss, Corsican, Flemish and African bicyclists, the narrator from Paris, and the Jewish girl. Yet the most striking resemblance of all is probably the stylistic innovation. One paragraph in "The Six-Day Night" reads as follows:

> Coucher de soleil. Grenadine. L'heure était facile comme l'asphalte. Un apaisement tombait, malgré la brûlure des amers. J'attendais Léa à la brasserie de la Porte-Maillot. Elle descendit de Montmartre, en coupé de louage, vêtue d'un manteau de loutre, vers les apéritifs à l'eau.[79]
>
> (Sunset. Grenadine. Time was smooth as asphalt. Quiet descended, despite the scorching bitterness. I waited for Léa in a brasserie near Porte-Maillot. She came down from Montmartre in a hired coupé, clothed in an otter coat, toward the watered aperitifs.)[80]

The juxtaposition of nouns, the peculiar comparison equating time with the asphalt street, and to say "un apaisement tombait," testify to Marcel Proust's comment on Morand in his preface to *Fancy Goods*, "Il est certain que le style de Paul Morand est singulier." (It is certain that Paul Morand's style is unique.)[81] Benjamin Crémieux likewise points out Morand's innovation in diction, mode of expression, and style. This is a quality that both the Japanese and Shanghai Neo-Sensation writers share. One thing worth noting is that, in his 1928 translation of the story, Dai Wangshu made a mistake when he translated the phrase "vers les apéritifs à l'eau" into "towards the café-restaurant" in Chinese.⁸² The English translation by Vyvyan Beresford Holland had already been published in New York in 1923. It rendered the phrase correctly: "toward the watered aperitifs."⁸³ From this mistranslation on Dai's part, we can safely say that he translated directly from the French original, without consulting the English translation. The 1929 revised version remained the same, but in the revised version published in Hong Kong in 1945, when he was taking shelter there from the war in China, this mistake was corrected: "lai he bei danjiu" 來喝杯淡酒 (to drink a glass of watered liquor).⁸⁴

Not only do Dai's later versions contain corrections like this. Most often it is syntactical experiments: changing the Chinese word order without affecting the original meaning. For instance, the second sentence of the original story reads like this: "Elle était seule, sauf pour les danses, qu'elle ne manquait pas, mais avec les professeurs ou des copines." (She was alone save during the dances, all of which she danced, but with the instructors or with the girls.)⁸⁵ In the 1928 and 1929 Chinese versions the principal clause, "She was alone," appears at the end of the whole sentence, but in the 1945 one, it is moved to the beginning, following the word order of the original version, and the other parts of the sentence are rewritten to fit this major change. As a result, the Chinese of this version reads much more fluently than the previous ones. These three translated versions of a single story by the same translator show how Dai is more concerned with the possible renovation of Chinese lexicon and sentence structure than merely conveying the "original meaning." It indicates that while translating, he is a self-conscious actor on the transcultural site: He is testing the possibility of inventing a new language mode as well as his role as a mediator between two languages, and, by extension, between two cultures and worlds.

In addition to the stylistic innovation and the obsession with the love–hate relationship with the modern girl, the Shanghai and Japanese Neo-Sensation writers share with Paul Morand the passion for travel as well, as we will see in the next section.

Je n'aime que le movement (I like nothing but the movement)

> Otoko wa onna no kage ni suginai⁸⁶
> 男は女の影にすぎない
> (Man is nothing but woman's shadow)
> – Nishiwaki Junzaburō 西脇順三郎, *No Traveler Returns* (Tabibito kaerazu 旅人かへらず)

As I have pointed out at the beginning of this chapter, one of the major features of dandyism is the dandy's urge to travel and his stance as a woman watcher exercising the art of *flânerie*. We have already seen in Chapter 1 how the Shanghai Neo-Sensation writer Liu Na'ou is a compulsive traveler, the objective of his constant loitering being woman watching. In his 1927 diary, feeling that he and his Taiwanese friends, constantly traveling between Taiwan, Japan, and China, were losing their sense of home, he asks himself, "Where is my homeland?"[87] The feeling of homelessness is one of the major motifs in Neo-Sensation writings.

In *No Traveler Returns*, a 1947 poetry collection, Nishiwaki Junzaburō resorts to an exquisite trope: Man, as woman's shadow, follows her to eternity. Thus he is doomed to be the everlasting traveler (*yōgō no tabibito* 永劫の旅人) in search of the woman traveler (*onna no tabibito* 女の旅人).[88] This trope of Nishiwaki, who established the Japanese surrealist movement in 1926 at his home and at the Hakujūji 白十字 café,[89] is emblematic of a whole generation of Japanese literary men who found themselves suddenly homeless on the threshold of Japan's encounter with the West. In Japan, the Neo-Sensation writers were certainly not alone in their sense of homelessness and feeling of being compelled to travel during the World Wars.

In Kawabata Yasunari's story "The Izu Dancer" (Izu no odoriko 伊豆の踊り子; 1926), the male narrator who follows the *geisha* girls everywhere on their performance tours in the Izu Peninsula is as intriguing as the bewitching girls. It seems the lonely young student finds more than consolation in their company; watching their innocence and simple delight in life procures self-redemption for him. Turning himself into a *tabibito* 旅人 like the girls, he feels the encounter with the girls has become a trip to the depth of his heart. Practicing the art of *flânerie* while following the trails of women is the destiny, or "monopoly," of a dandy.

The theme of aimless wanderings is central to Kawabata's masterpiece *The Asakusa Crimson Gang* (Asakusa Kurenai Dan 淺草紅團, 1929–30), which he describes as "a tourist's notebook." The narrator, acting as an observer, never makes acquaintance with the people he observes, but contends himself with simply recording his sense impressions of them and the streets. Referring to how he walked in Asakusa, the working-class pleasure district in Tokyo, for weeks after the earthquake of 1923 in order to inspect the ruins and horrible sights, he says, "I desire to go not to Europe or America but to the ruined countries of the Orient. I am in large measure the citizen of a ruined country. . . . Perhaps it is because I was an orphan with nowhere I could call home that I have never lost my taste for melancholic wanderings."[90] The sense of being without home is also a dominant theme for Yokomitsu Riichi, whose family constantly moved from place to place during his childhood so that his father could find work as an engineering contractor for railway construction. According to Donald Keene, this "lack of a home" may "account for Yokomitsu's search in later years for roots not in a particular locality but in Japan itself, the ultimate 'home' of Japanese who despaired of ever coming to terms with a West they loved but could not make their own."[91]

Both the Japanese and Shanghai Neo-Sensation writers were deeply indebted to Paul Morand, a confirmed dandy, a man and writer of style as well as a woman watcher. He started to travel abroad in 1908, when he studied at Oxford for one year. In the following years until the end of his life he visited London, Rome, Madrid, Budapest, Germany, Scandinavia, Greece, Turkey, Lisbon, Belgium, the Netherlands, Mexico, Cuba, the United States, and the Middle East, among other places. In his capacity as diplomat he lived in London, Rome, Madrid, and Macao. After he had traveled through most countries of the West, in 1925 he started his grand tour of the Far East, believing in Balzac's prophesy: "Il n'y a que deux peuples, l'Orient et l'Occident" (There are only two nations, the East and the West).[92] This tour covered Japan, China, Singapore, Siam, Cambodia, and Vietnam.

He arrived in Yokohama in July 1925, when the aftermath of the 1923 earthquake was still being felt. Then he arrived in Beijing, "the middle of the earth." To him, China was "un monolithe compact, indifférent" (a compact monolith, indifferent). In Shanghai, he found the Shanghai Club "le plus grand bar du monde" (the largest bar in the world). With an eye for any sign that would indicate the recent history of East–West conflicts, he describes how "the pallid Chinese, who are tea-drinkers, serve their white enemies the cordial poison: Receiving opium from us, they retaliate with alcohol in this duel of toxics." He looks at the skyscrapers and the gardens on the top of grand plazas in the French concession, and cannot help noticing that "the largest hotels and brothels in Shanghai are owned by Spanish priests. The wives of the English officials from Weihaiwei 威海衛, the judges of the mixed Commission, and the Russian refugees are dancing on the deluxe floors. . . . What is the Asian epidemic side by side with these Western poisons?"[93]

Morand did not go to China solely to satisfy his Orientalist fantasy. He seemed to be seeking redemption for himself and the Westerners who had contaminated Chinese for more than a hundred years with the sale of opium, aided by guns and the Christian missions, and the foreign concessions that testified to the intrusion of the West. When he got off the ship in Yokohama in July that year, he describes his feelings thus:

> . . . je n'aime pas les voyages, que je n'aime que le mouvement. . . . Il faut enseigner au Français à accepter joyeusement le changement. . . . C'est un étroit assujettissement que la vie dans la maison, dit le Bouddha, un état d'impureté : la liberté est dans l'abandon de la maison.[94]
>
> (. . . I don't like travels, I like nothing but the movement. . . . Frenchmen should be taught to accept change joyfully. . . . Life in the home is a strict confinement, according to Buddha, an impure state: Liberty comes from abandoning the home.)

When the ideal of the Christian salvation of the East mocks itself in the opium and prostitution it helps to spread, maybe Buddha's words, uncontaminated by imperialism, convey more wisdom? Perhaps it is after abandoning the home that the quest for self and redemption begins? For travelers like Morand and the Neo-Sensation writers in China or Japan, to travel means not only to set off on the road, but also to engage in transcultural imaginings.

Furthermore, it is not travel itself that counts; it is the lost angels one collects on the roadside that makes travel a perpetual attraction. Crémieux's article on Morand discussed before stresses the cosmopolitanism and decadence represented by the modern girls roaming the streets, cabarets and dance halls of Paris, London, Rome, Finland, or Switzerland in his stories. These girls are not described for their souls, but are just collected in his stories as displaced human beings in the capitals worldwide:

> Déjà, le collectionneur d'épaves se fait jour chez Morand. Son cosmopolitisme ne va pas, comme celui d'un Giraudoux ou d'un Larbaud, jusqu'à l'âme des peuples. Ce qu'il recherche, c'est dans des capitals, les morceaux épars de l'Europe : ici c'est une Française perdue dans Londres, ailleurs, ce sera aussi bien une Catalane en Suisse et à Paris, une Russe à Constantinople, une Française à Rome, un Arménien à Londres, qu'une Parisienne à Paris ou une Finlandaise en Finlande.[95]

(Already Morand is aware that he is a collector of displaced human beings. His cosmopolitanism, unlike Giraudoux's or Larbaud's, does not go straight into the soul of people. What he is looking for in the capitals is the chunks and shards scattered in Europe: Here it is a French woman lost in London, there it can also be a Catalane in Switzerland or in Paris, a Russian woman in Constantinople, a French woman in Rome, an American man in London, as well as a Parisian woman in Paris or a Finnish woman in Finland.)

In this sense, the Neo-Sensation writers in Tokyo and Shanghai are perpetual travelers and "collectors of displaced human beings" as well. Kawabata Yasunari taking constant walks in the Asakusa district in Tokyo or on the Izu Island, Liu Na'ou lamenting the loss of the homeland in Shanghai, and so on, are all "everlasting travelers" in search of women travelers. Their art of *flânerie* manifests the circulation of Neo-Sensation, a traveling genre, as a transcultural aesthetic trend transcending the boundaries of nations and languages. What they intend to capture is not the "souls" of these modern girls, but their collective image inspiring the practice of transcultural modernity— the everlasting modern girl's image created by the dandy/artist's language marked by the macaronic. So exclaims Liu Na'ou, scrutinizing an unknown prostitute, "Ah, my hungry heart! Ah, the translucent eyes that I can hardly devour, the face of *Modernité!*"

In the Neo-Sensation writers' art of *flânerie*, these modern girls, scattered and lost in the metropolis, are described as types, each with only a face and a body to bewilder men. As we will see in Chapter 3, in Yokomitsu Riichi's *Shanghai*, his first novel and the last work of his Neo-Sensation phase, the flâneurs and flâneuses in the metropolis are types representing ideas, even though some of them seem to be endowed with a "soul." Yet, as will be discussed, it is not the soul *per se*, but the soul of one's lost country that each of them symbolizes.

3 The flâneur and the flâneuse
Yokomitsu Riichi's Shanghai

"You are here every night?"
"Yes."
"It seems you have no money."
"Money?"
"Um."
"I have neither money, nor country."
"Well, too bad."
"So it is."
– Yokomitsu Riichi[1]

This is the opening scene of Yokomitsu Riichi's *Shanghai*, serialized in the journal *Kaizō* 改造 in 1928–31. Sanki 参木, a Japanese young man seeking fortune in semicolonial Shanghai around the turbulent May 30th Movement in 1925,[2] wanders aimlessly to the Bund. When one of the Russian prostitutes, hanging around there night after night, catches sight of him and attempts to solicit, Sanki ends up exchanging these few terse lines in English with her. Both Sanki and the Russian prostitutes are, in a sense, flâneurs without money or country, displaced in the modern metropolis; we know that Sanki has not returned to Japan for the past ten years. The last scene of the novel, echoing the first, ends wonderfully well with the narrator's psycho-narration of Ōsugi お杉, a girl-next-door type falling into prostitution in the Chinese treaty port. One of the main themes of the novel is the fate of the flâneurs (represented by Sanki) and the flâneuses (represented by Ōsugi), expatriates of all nationalities in Shanghai. As characters who are victims of revolutions or followers of imperialist exploitations in the story, they are indeed described "through images of destitution and without any signs of agency."[3] On the other hand, as I will show in this chapter, cultural translators such as Yokomitsu who create their images are modernists consciously maneuvering on the transcultural site where linguistic, cultural, and political institutional powers meet.

Neo-sensation and symbolism

Shanghai was Yokomitsu Riichi's first novel, and he was very much aware of the technique he used in its composition, calling it "the last work of my so-called Neo-Sensation phase" in the preface to the 1939 Kaizō Bunko 改造文庫 edition.[4] He states that it was written during the time when Marxism was most prevalent in Japan, and that, using the May 30th Event as an opportunity, he intends to make known how Japanese were living in Shanghai when Jiang Jieshi 蔣介石 was beginning to extend his sphere of influence to the Orient. At the end of the preface he hopes that at a time when the Sino-Japanese war is raging unabated, his novel, with a theme connected with the ongoing war, will reflect "the fate of the Orient" (Tōyō no unmei 東洋の運命) to some extent.[5]

Shanghai as a modern metropolis with its international concession where "all nations have created a common city-state (toshi kokka 都市國家)" and formed a "microcosm of the world,"[6] as described in Yokomitsu's article titled "The China Sea" (Shinakai 支那海), was an inspiration to writers from East and West alike in the 1920s and 1930s.[7] Instead of an ordinary "city," it is the idea of a "toshi kokka" (city-state), a city equal to an independent state formed by many nations in China, to which Yokomitsu brings our attention. To Paul Morand, who in 1925 thought the Shanghai Club in the international concession "the largest bar in the world" and saw the Spanish priests and the Russian refugees mixed in the same hotel, Shanghai's attraction no doubt lies in its cosmopolitanism, as has been discussed in Chapter 2. One French writer who, like Yokomitsu, also wrote a novel about Shanghai was André Malraux (1901–76), whose *La condition humaine* (Man's Fate) in 1933 took Jiang Jieshi's 1927 purge of the Communists as theme.

Although both Yokomitsu and Malraux wrote about political movements, prostitutes, and people of all nationalities living in Shanghai, the latter's emphasis is on the political maneuvers and espionage activities that involve all the main characters in the story. We can tell this by comparing the opening scenes of the two novels. In contrast to *Shanghai*, *Man's Fate* opens with a prolonged murder scene where a Communist assassin, contemplating the sleeping victim he is about to kill, procrastinates for the narrative space of three and a half pages before eventually stabbing him with a dagger.[8] In *Shanghai*, on the other hand, all murders and deaths are reported; we never see a gruesome killing act taking place. In addition, the main character Sanki is occasionally drawn into the revolutionary movement mainly because he takes interest in the beautiful Chinese Communist activist and spy, Hō Shūran 芳秋蘭. She is often talked about in the story and observed by him, but her psychology remains opaque to him as well as the reader. As Yokomitsu says in the 1939 preface to the novel, the most noticeable part of the novel is the Neo-Sensation technique he resorts to in its composition. This can be made clear if we compare how the image of "the crowd," an important element in both novels, is treated by the two authors: Because of

Yokomitsu's Neo-Sensation language, it takes on a symbolic meaning in *Shanghai*, whereas in *Man's Fate*, it is simply and always "the crowd."

In the scene when the cabaret "The Black Cat" first appears in *Man's Fate*, the crowd of people inside is mentioned. The narrator says:

> "Le jazz était à bout de nerfs. . . . D'un coup il s'arrêta, et la foule se décomposa : au fond les clients, sur les côtés les danseuses professionnelles : Chinoises dans leur fourreau de soie brochée, Russes et métisses; un ticket par danse, ou par conversation."
>
> (The jazz was at the point of exhaustion. . . . Suddenly it stopped and the crowd broke up: at the depth of the hall the clients, on the sides the professional dancers: Chinese in their sheaths of brocaded silk, Russians, and half-breeds; a ticket per dance, or per conversation.)[9]

The crowd is simply "la foule" here, as is in other parts of the novel when mentioned. The descriptions of the Chinese, Russian girls or the half-breeds are succinct and to the point—their mixed nationalities are mentioned—but do not add any metaphoric aura to the image of the "crowd" at all. The delirious old man who is left in the middle of the empty floor, "flapping his elbows like a duck," may symbolize the craziness of the atmosphere, but, singled out from the crowd, he is a unique person who seems to warn people that they are all "on the brink of nihilism" (au bord du néant). Whatever symbolic meaning there may be, Malraux spells it out clearly, leaving little room for nuances.

By contrast, in Yokomitsu's *Shanghai*, the crowd, or the masses, is often described as a mysterious, collective entity, with the meaning quite ambiguous. One scene of a crowd of prostitutes is worth close reading. It occurs in Chapter 10, when Sanki walks into a teahouse, where "the women did not look like women" (onna ga onna ni mienu 女が女に見えぬ; Chapter 10, p. 65). When the crowd of hookers (shōhu no mure 笑婦の群れ) is approaching to accost him, he playfully puts some coins on the palm of his hand. Immediately the women throng round him to grab them:

> Women's hands groping for the coins struck each other on his chest. Earrings tangled up. Kicking away women's torsos with his knees, he stuck his head out of the shoes glittering in the air. When he finally struggled to his feet, the women, as if all jamming their heads into a single hole, were rattling around and clawing under the legs of the chair. He dropped the copper coins through the necks of the women thronging to get them. The waves of wasp waists began to surge more violently. Forsaking the women clinging to him, he made way to the exit. All at once a new crowd of hookers ambushed him from between the pillars and tables. Stiffening his neck ramrod straight, he made his way forward, pushing the women aside with the corners of his squared shoulders. His neck entwined by the arms of women front and back, he was as strong as

some sea creature cutting through waves. Sweating from the pressure of pulling women along, leaning his shoulders forward as though he were swimming, he made a dash and plunged into a gap among the women. But once shaken off from his body, the crowd of women would swarm over him again with newcomers added. He pushed and shoved in all directions with his elbows. The women, pushed aside by him, were staggering and soon carried off, clinging onto other men's necks.[10]

I am quoting this passage at length to show that the crowd of women described here is almost like a brood of water snakes, strongly suggested by phrases such as "hitotsu no ana e kubi o tsukkomu 一つの穴へ首を突っ込む" (jamming their heads into a single hole), "batabata shinagara ばたばたしながら" (rattling around), "isu no ashi o hikkaite ita 椅子の足をひっ抓いてゐた" (clawing under the legs of the chair), and "Mitsubachi no yō na koshi no nami ga issō hageshiku yuredashita 蜂のやうな腰の波が一層激しく揺れ出した" (The waves of wasp waists began to surge more violently). The waves of arms that keep coming and entwining his neck, and the bodies clinging onto him, deterring his movement and making him sweat, turn the whole scene of the crowd of hookers into a surrealist nightmare, as contrasted with the realistic description in *Man's Fate*. In this scene we are looking at the crowd of women through Sanki's eye, whose subjectivity transforms the hookers into snake-like creatures. It is highly symbolic, with all the metaphors evolving around prostitution, greed, and the commodification of women.

Symbolism as a major Neo-Sensation technique is repeatedly emphasized by Yokomitsu Riichi, as can be seen in his comment on Mu Shiying, the only Chinese Neo-Sensation writer who was known to have direct contact with the Japanese Neo-Sensation School. In addition to the common propensity for symbolism, Mu and Yokomitsu were connected through Japan's vision of the whole of East Asia sharing a common goal.[11] Yokomitsu wrote an essay on Mu for a special column in the journal *Literary World* (Bungakukai 文學界) in September 1940 to commemorate Mu's death on 28 June of that year. In this essay he mentions Mu's visit to Tokyo the winter before.[12] We should be aware that *Tōa Renmei* 東亞聯盟 (East Asian Union), the organization heralding the Pan-Asian Co-Prosperity Sphere, was established in Tokyo in October 1939. The establishment of the latter would be first announced by the Minister of Foreign Affairs Matsuoka Yōsuke 松岡洋右 on 2 August 1940.[13] It was not surprising that a Chinese Neo-Sensation writer like Mu, who was known to have followed the lead of his Japanese counterparts, became useful in Japan's all-out efforts to unite East Asian countries in the war against the West. We know that when Mu visited Tokyo in November 1939, he was with the diplomatic corps headed by Lin Bosheng 林柏生, the Minister of Public Relations of Wang Jingwei's puppet regime supported by Japan.[14] It is also known that in March 1940 Mu became the founding director of *National Subject Daily*, the puppet regime's news organ, and was later assassinated in that capacity, as mentioned in Chapter 1.

According to Yokomitsu's essay, one night during his visit Mu meets with Yokomitsu and other Japanese literary men (including Kataoka Teppei, Kikuchi Kan, Hayashi Husao 林房雄, Kume Masao 久米正雄, and Ozaki Shirō 尾崎士郎). In the conversation Mu mentions his brother-in-law (*gitei* 義弟), who was once Paul Valéry's student in Paris. (We know that Dai Wangshu studied in Paris from October 1932 to the spring of 1934, and that he married Mu's younger sister in 1936 and was then divorced in 1940.)[15] They also talk about Pearl Buck. (She won the Nobel Prize for literature in 1938.) By and by Mu asks Yokomitsu, "What is becoming of the Japanese Neo-Sensation School?" For the latter, this provides an opportunity for him to ruminate on the status of "modern East-Asian youth."

Mu's question was not easy to answer, of course. Yokomitsu writes first, "I finally told Mr Mu something in the vein that the Neo-Sensation School is now finding new meanings in the tradition of our country, trying to give it a new interpretation." Next he points out that he has not diverged from his original position when he started his career as a Neo-Sensation writer more than ten years ago, and the reason why he hesitated to answer Mu's question then was not because he felt ashamed to answer but because the difference between Chinese tradition and Japanese tradition made it difficult to explain. He claims further that Mu's assassination by gun was exactly caused by "the difference between the two countries' new traditions." Then he mentions the translation of Mu's story "Black Peony" (Ch. Hei mudan or Kuro bōtan 黒牡丹) published in the August issue of the magazine *Intellect* (Chisei 知性). In the story the young man, infatuated with a woman in the dance hall, follows her out into the night because of the carnation worn in her hair. When the woman, bitten by a dog, falls down on the road, he is dumbfounded to discover that the carnation he has been chasing is nowhere to be found. Yokomitsu praises it as "a Neo-Sensation story that contains symbolism" (shōchōsei wo hukunda shinkankakuha no tanhen de aru 象徴性を含んだ新感覚派の短篇である). From here he concludes:

> Neo-Sensation valorizes rationalism and scientism, which is a common practice assigned to all modern East Asian youths. Despite transformation anew due to each's own national tradition, this practice forms a congealing, not separating, force within East Asia.[16]

Nonetheless, Yokomitsu Riichi's attitudes towards Japan's pan-Asian policy may not be as clear-cut as it seems to be in this essay, apparently written for a propaganda purpose. In this chapter, I propose a close reading of *Shanghai*, which will shed light on his ambivalent attitudes towards the policy and the problem of writers' war responsibility. Before I delve into this, however, we should first try to understand the theoretical implications of the symbolic in

Yokomitsu's stories. To do this we need to examine in detail his essay "Shinkankakuron" (On Neo-Sensation) published in 1925.

"On Neo-Sensation" and the thing-in-itself

As Yokomitsu states in "On Neo-Sensation," all he recognizes as belonging to the Neo-Sensation school, including "Futurism, Cubism (rittaiha 立體派), Expressionism, Dadaism, Symbolism, Constructivism (kōseiha 構成派), and part of the Actuality School (nyojitsuha 如實派)," can be considered as a kind of symbolist literature (hitotsu no shōchōha bungaku toshite mireba mirareru 一つの象徴派文學として見れば見られる).[17] If this concept sounds vague, a more in-depth reading of this article may shed some light. According to him, through the vocabulary, poetry and rhythm of the constructed text (kōbun no goi to shi to rizumu 行文の語彙と詩とリズム) we can see how the sensations of these "Neo-Senstion schools" are activated. He says:

> Sometimes from the refractive angles of the theme, sometimes from the scale of the silent leaping from line to line, sometimes from the reversal, repetition, and speed of the advance and progression of the sinew of the text, and so on, the forms and shapes of the activated state are diverse.[18]

He especially points out how sensations are triggered through their effort to "synchronize the tempos of consciousness" (shinshō no tenpo ni dōjisei o ataeru 心象のテンポに同時性を與へる) and "to make the concept of time forgotten in the advance of the plot" (puloto no shinkō ni jikan kannen o bōkyakusase プロットの進行に時間観念を忘却させ), as do the Cubists, or "to directly hurl the interplay between consciousness and phenomena into the destruction of all forms" (issai no keishiki hakkai ni shinshō no kōgosayō o tanteki ni tōtekisuru 一切の形式破壊に心象の交互作用を端的に投擲する), as do the Expressionists and the Dadaists. He further states that

> all these various sensationist manifestations [kankaku hyōchō 感覺表徴] are basically something symbolized [shōchōkasareta mono 象徴化された物], therefore sensationist writing can be considered as a kind of symbolist literature.[19]

Yokomitsu demonstrates his familiarity with Western modernist literature and philosophical thinking in the essay "On Neo-Sensation."[20] He assesses the techniques of contemporary Japanese writers with the various European modernist schools mentioned above as benchmarks. For example, some of Akutagawa Ryūnoske's writings such as "The Bamboo Grove, or The Truth Unknown" (Yabu no naka 藪の中), because of their "intellectual sensations" (chiteki kankaku 知的感覺), are excellent as Constructivist works; The works by Inukai Takeru 犬養健 and Nakagawa Yoichi, due to the musical tone that brightens the senses and the delicate psychological effect on the troubled emotions, are akin to the Actuality School. Yet the most prominent feature of the aesthetic theory in "On Neo-Sensation" is its interaction with European philosophy. A close reading of the essay will disclose that Yokomitsu's concept of "Neo-Sensation" is very much a response to Kant's theory of the "thing-in-itself" (Ding an sich).[21] The term "monojitai," 物自體 the standard Japanese and Chinese translation of the Kantian "thing-in-itself," appears repeatedly in the essay when Yokomitsu explains what he means by "Neo-Sensation," as can be testified to by the following passage:

> The concept of what I call sensation, i.e., the sensationist manifestation [*kankakudeki hyōchō* 感覺的表徵] of Neo-Sensation, refers to the intuitive activating agency [*chokkan teki shokuhatsubutsu* 直感的觸發物] of subjectivity that strips away the phenomenon [*gaishō* 外相] of nature and leaps into the thing-in-itself [*monojitai* 物自體]. . . . Subjectivity refers to the active power to perceive the object as the thing-in-itself. Cognition [*ninshiki* 認識] is no doubt a synthesis of intellect and sensibility. During the process when subjectivity leaps into the thing-in-itself, both intellect and sensibility, which form the cognitive power to perceive the object, will take on the dynamic forms as the more powerful activating agents of sensation. It is very important to take this into account when explaining the fundamental concept of Neo-Sensation. The representation [*hyōshō* 表象, or *Vorstellung*] which functions to activate the symbolizing power [*hyōshō nōryoku* 表象能力] of pure external objectivity (not the objectivity as opposed to subjectivity) is sensation.[22]

The difficulty of translating "On Neo-Sensation" into English is to choose the right words to render the Japanese philosophical terms, which originated from German. Synonyms pose a problem, too. For instance, "hyōchō" 表徵 and "hyōshō" could mean manifestation and representation respectively, or they are synonyms meaning symbolization (same as shōchō 象徵). I choose to render the term "hyōshō nōryoku" as "symbolizing power" here, because Neo-Sensation as a kind of symbolist literature is a concept running throughout "On Neo-Sensation." Once the right diction is chosen, it is clear that this quoted passage is referring to Kant's theory of epistemology in *The Critique of Pure Reason*: how we come to know ourselves through knowledge of the world. But, as I explain below, while referring to Kant's theory of the thing-in-itself, Yokomitsu deliberately revises it at the same time.

Kant assigns man a three-fold cognitive power: sensibility, intellect, and reason. Phenomena stir sensibility to act and form empirical intuitions, which intellect takes in and conforms to their own inborn *a priori* forms. (Whether knowledge can be *a priori* is a problem. Aristotle, Thomas Aquinas, and the Scholastics believed that all knowledge is *a posteriori*, i.e., after experience and dependent on it.) The resultant piece of knowledge is called a "judgment." Then the resultant judgment stirs reason to act and produce reasoned knowledge, which conforms to the three innate *a priori* forms of knowledge: the idea of the self, the non-self (the world), and the super self (God). For Kant, while phenomenon is the object we perceive and understand through our five senses, the thing-in-itself is the conception of the thing as it is in itself, which, as opposed to phenomenon, is unknowable and indefinable. The phenomenon, or "appearance," is apprehended through sensibility, and its nature "is determined through its relation to the sensuous intuition and to the *a priori* forms of Sensibility. 'Things in-themselves,' on the other hand, are the objects of Reason."[23]

In contrast to Kant, here Yokomitsu is implicitly siding with Schopenhauer in the famous debate on epistemology and saying that, even though according to Kant human beings are unable to know or define the thing-in-itself, Neo-Sensation nonetheless strives to grasp the thing-in-itself by pushing subjectivity to outreach the limits of the sensuous intuition and sensibility, and "leaps into" the thing-in-itself. Neo-Sensation is feasible to Yokomitsu, because he believes that, with both intellect (gosei 悟性) and sensibility (kansei 感性) working together when subjectivity "leaps into the thing-in-itself" (monojitai ni odorikomu 物自體に躍りこむ), our cognitive power will reach the meaning of the thing-in-itself.

Another passage from "On Neo-Sensation" will show that one major source of Yokomitsu's concept of "Neo-Sensation" is Nietzsche's *Thus Spake Zarathustra*, and that he largely sides with Nietzsche in the debate with Kant on the concept of knowledge and cognition:

> Some works drive our subjectivity to arrive at deeper knowledge; the deeper they drive it, the richer they activate the sensation. The reason is that, this sort of sensation is activated by guiding our subjectivity from the known, empirical knowledge [keikenteki ninshiki 經驗的認識] to the cognitive activity yet unknown. I respect all works that contain sensations going after this kind of deeper knowledge. For instance, we can take the most commonplace works as examples, works such as Strindberg's *Inferno* and *A Blue Book*, the various works of Bashō 芭蕉 or one or two works of Shiga Naoya 志賀直哉, and Nietzsche's *Thus Spake Zarathustra*.[24]

So for Yokomitsu, the way to activate Neo-Sensation is to induce subjectivity to go beyond empirical knowledge (keikenteki ninshiki), which is perceived by the five senses, in order to arrive at deeper knowledge, or knowledge of the thing-in-itself.[25] In his mind, Nietzsche's *Thus Spake Zarathustra* (1883–85) is an example of works that contain what he calls "Neo-Sensation." Nietzsche in this book writes about the idea of the "superman" or "overman" (Übermensch) who has achieved his full power and self-mastery. What Nietzsche means by "the will to power" is the driving force of the human being in his journey to the ultimate goal of self-overcoming and self-enhancement. The central idea of *Thus Spake Zarathustra* is the overcoming of the self; human beings should go beyond the limits of empirical knowledge when trying to understand the world and themselves. Drawing on Kant's theory of the thing-in-itself for his conceptualization of Neo-Sensation, Yokomitsu as a trancultural modernist revises the Kantian theory and arrives at a new meaning through his art of creative transformation.

At the beginning of "On Neo-Sensation," Yokomitsu has already pointed out that, to understand the concept of Neo-Sensation, it is necessary to investigate the interplay (*kōshō sayō* 交渉作用) between the objective form and subjectivity, and that the achievement of this will set right an important basic concept in arts, and will no doubt be the "birth certificate of a fundamental revolution in arts" (*Geijutsujō ni okeru konponteki kakumei no tanjō hōkoku* 藝術上に於ける根本的革命の誕生報告).[26] He points out the result: Those who possess a powerful subjectivity will devastate old-fashioned aesthetics and habits, and will be "leaping more directly towards global concepts" (*yori tanteki ni sekai kannen e hiyakusen to shita* より端的に世界観念へ飛躍せんとした).[27]

We should be aware that Yokomitsu Riichi's "dialogue" with Kant was in fact imbedded in the philosophical thinking of his time. During the late Meiji and early Taishō periods the famous Kyōto School was emerging on the Japanese philosophical scene, when the assimilation of Western thought and the re-evaluation of Eastern philosophy took place at the same time. In 1911 the leader of the school, Nishida Kitarō 西田幾多郎 (1870–1945), already used the term *monojitai* to translate Kant's term "Ding an sich" in his article titled "On the Thesis of the School of Pure Rationalism in Epistemology" (Ninshikiron ni okeru junronriha no shuchō ni tsuite 認識論における純論理派の主張について).[28] He criticizes Kant's theory of the thing-in-itself in "Multitudes of World" (Shushu no sekai 種々の世界; 1917): "What connotation, what kind of relationship is there between the thing-in-itself and the world of our knowledge? If there is totally no connotation or relationship, the theory of the thing-it-self can be completely eliminated from Kant's philosophy."[29] Synthesizing Henri Bergson's theory and the neo-Kantian thought of Wilhelm Windelband and Heinrich Rickert, he states that the thing-in-itself is not "the origin of knowledge," as Kant thinks it to be, but the "direct experience" (*chokusetsu keiken* 直接經驗) before conceptual knowledge, as Windelband and the Biden School maintain.

According to Nishida, the so-called "direct experience" is equal to Bergson's concept of "pure durée" (*junsui jizoku* 純粹持續), as Rickert concedes. Nishida maintains that in the direct or pure experience, there can be no distinction between "subject" and "object," since they are the two sides of "reality" (*jitsuzai* 實在). To him this "direct reality" is what Kant calls the thing-in-itself, or "the world of absolute free will," from which are derived multitudes of phenomena (*shushu no taishōkai* 種々の對象界). In contrast to the absolute will, which is the direct reality, the phenomenal world in his conception is the world of indirect experience. As opposed to Kant's notion of the thing-in-itself, which is unknowable, Nishida's "direct reality" can be known. According to Nishida, when we project our will onto the phenomenal world, it is "life" itself, or the Bergsonian *élan vital*, while the will to life (*der Wille zum Leben*, German expression originally provided) is the will to cultural life (*der Wille zum Kulturleben*).³⁰

For Nishida the absolute will connects the direct experience of each human being and unites the universe in a whole stream of creative consciousness. This concept, however, seems to be a combination of Bergson's *evolution créatrice* (creative evolution) and the neo-Confucian theory of *shengsheng buxi* 生生不息 (unceasing creation). In addition, the concept of *shushu no sekai*, or multitudes of world derived from the individual being, is reminiscent of the Buddhist concept of *mandala* 曼荼羅 cosmology, in which a human being is the microcosm of the whole universe. Nishida practices Zen meditation and is well versed in Confucian studies. With all these philosophical traditions at his disposal he develops the philosophy of "the *topos* (place, or *basho* 場所) of absolute Nothingness," from which existence or life is generated. In this realm governed by intuitive agency, the dichotomy of subjectivity and objectivity is overcome.³¹ He says, "The absolute will is not anti-reason, but above reason."³²

With the above discussion of Nishida's theory in mind, it is clear that in the passage of "On Neo-Sensation" quoted before, the term "pure external objectivity," which Yokomitsu annotates with the parenthetical aside, "not the objectivity as opposed to subjectivity," refers to Nishida's concept of the realm of "direct reality" in which subjectivity and objectivity are indistinguishable; the term "intuitive activating agency" is reminiscent of Nishida's work *Intuition and Self-Reflexivity in Self-Consciousness* (Jikaku ni okeru chokkan to hansei 自覺における直観と反省, 1914–17), which is inspired by Bergson.³³ There is so much more to a word or a term than meets the eye. A single term such as "monojitai" can disclose an endless stream of transcultural concatenations. When translated simply as "object" as in Washburn's rendering,³⁴ the whole epistemological depth concerning the debate between Kant's "thing-in-itself" and Nishida's "direct reality" would be lost, while the fact that Yokomitsu is standing in the crisscrossing of Eastern and Western philosophical traditions would be ignored.

However the assimilation or appropriation of the Kantian term may seem to be a "superficial" borrowing, and however the "psychic excess" may go beyond his own consciousness, as a modernist who is striving to create a new concept among the flux of ideas available at each single moment of his invention, Yokomitsu certainly is making a distinct choice by referring to Nishida's critique of Kant, which invokes the streams of Eastern and Western philosophical thinking involved. There is no doubt that Yokomitsu is highly conscious of the role he is playing in the great divide between East and West, modern and traditional in contemporary Japanese literature and philosophical thinking. Acutely sensitive to his own transcultural practice, he deliberately resorts to the term *monojitai* and Nishida's theory of the absolute will critiquing the Kantian "Ding an sich" in order to lay out his own revolutionary concept of Neo-Sensation. A close look at how he criticizes traditional narrative mode will disclose the position he takes in the traditional/modern interplay: Instead of discarding the traditional, he advocates reinvention and moving forward with tradition as a point of departure. His assessment of Sei Shōnagon 清少納言, the Heian 平安 woman writer whose work *The Pillow Book* (Makura no sōshi 枕草子) has been considered on a par with *Genjimonogatari* 源氏物語, is most revealing in regard to what he considers as mere "sensuous manifestation" (*kannōteki hyōchō* 官能的表徵), which is without the intervention of intellect. By contrast, he advocates Neo-Sensation, which can only be arrived at through intellect.

In the section on "Sensuousness and Neo-Sensation" (Kannō to shinkankaku 官能と新感覺), he says the sensuous manifestation in Sei Shōnagon's work is by no means the Neo-Sensation he has in mind, but the sensuousness that is cool and vivid (*kannō ga seirei de senretsu deatta* 官能が静冷で鮮烈であつた). According to him, sensuous manifestation, being the part of sensationist manifestation that is most close to sensibility (*mottomo kanseiteki na kankaku hyōchō* 最も感性的な感覺表徵), is the category (*hanchū kōmoku* 範疇綱目) that is most difficult to distinguish from the latter. Diction such as *hanchū kōmoku* used here clearly indicates that Yokomitsu is working on philosophical or scientific terms (according to Kant, cognitive power works in four sets of triple judgments, called the twelve categories).[35]

For Yokomitsu, Sei Shōnagon's sensuous manifestation lacks the "sensationist Aufheben" (*kankakuteki na shiyōsei* 感覺的な止揚性; "Aufheben" means the synthesis both abolishing and preserving the thesis and antithesis, a central concept of the Hegelian dialectical method). He distinguishes between these two categories thus: The Neo-Sensation manifestation has to be the internal intuition (*naiteki chokkan* 内的直感) symbolized through the intervention of intellect, whereas sensuous manifestation, activated merely by pure objectivity, is the direct cognitive manifestation (*tanteki na ninshiki hyōchō* 端的な認識表徵) derived from empirical, external intuition (*keikenteki gaiteki chokkan* 經驗的外的直感). So sensuous manifestation, more prone to sensibility and prior to sensationist manifestation, is directly perceived and intuited. This is why, compared with sensationist manifestation, sensuous manifestation gives the impression that it is more straightforward and vivid. But it will not be able to possess the complex, synthetic unity (*hukugōteki sōgōteki tōitsutai* 複合的綜合的統一體) of the symbolizing power of sensationist manifestation.[36]

It is interesting to note how Yokomitsu assesses the traditional and the modern in terms of evolution. According to him, it is impossible to expect Sei Shōnagon's sensuousness to have "more complicated evolutionary ability" (*yori fukusatsu na shinka nōryoku* より複雑な進化能力), because it is "nothing but fresh, without any implication for sensationist growth" (*nan no anjiteki na kankakuteki seichō mo shinakatta* 何の暗示的な感覺的成長もしなかつた). Compared with Sei Shōnagon's sensuousness, which is like a civilized man free from the signifying confusion (*shōchōteki konmei* 象徴的混迷) and thus unable to evolve, Neo-Sensation is "as confounded as a barbarian" (*yabanjin no gotoku donjū ni kanjirareru* 野蠻人のごとく鈍重に感じられる) and thus is able to evolve. This is of course a vulgarized version of evolution, confusing it with the idea of progress as so many popular versions of evolution were wont to do in Europe and America as well as in Asia at the time.[37] Yokomitsu, definitely more adept in philosophical reasoning, is merely fiddling with the biological terrain.

A foremost theoretician and defender of the Neo-Sensation group, Yokomitsu is also the one most committed to putting theory into practice. *Shanghai*, his first novel, is an impressive work as far as the experiment with language is concerned. Read together with his theoretical work, the novel is the manifestation of a self-conscious writer who, at the historic crossroads where Japanese literary tradition and European modernist aesthetic concepts meet, chooses to invent a mode of expression that aims to transform the Japanese literary landscape. While carrying out the experiment with language, an indispensable element in Neo-Sensation writing, the novel is unique in his total Neo-Sensation output. The modern girl image constructed in the novel has a shade of nuances possible only in a full-length work. Yet even though we see more nuanced descriptions of the modern girls in this novel than in his short stories, the characters (female as well as male) are still types rather than round characters expected in realistic literature. In *Shanghai*, all characters are more or less representations of ideas, as we will see in the different types of women and men in the story. Sanki, who represents the lost soul of Japan, is the man to whom all the women in the story somehow are sexually attracted. As opposed to a modern boy like his friend Kōya 甲谷 who mourns for being tortured by women, Sunki is an anti-modern boy of sorts, always finding himself trapped in comic situations where women are angry with him because he will not have sex with them. The only one he eventually sleeps with is Ōsugi, who represents the lost body of Japan. Their sexual consummation symbolizes the union of the body and soul of Japan.

Miyako: the modern girl in the war of nations

At the turn of the twentieth century, European, American, and Japanese colonialisms were expanding their power of influence and vying for control over a turbulent Asia, where emergent nation-states such as China, Russia, and India were just undergoing birth throes marked by tremendous domestic unrest. Revolutions, civil wars, and imperialist invasions, aided by the developmental and entrepreneurial projects of the colonial powers, resulted in the great waves of global dislocation. Shanghai at the time, with its international concession, was a microcosm of the confluence of this global human flux. The men and women of all nationalities flocking to Yokomitsu Riichi's Shanghai are a reflection of this phenomenon, as is described in the dance hall scene in Chapter 20 of the novel: "An American holding a German, a

Spanish holding a Russian, Portuguese bumping into people of mixed blood."[38]

In the novel, in addition to the hordes of prostitutes always teeming in dance halls and teahouses who highlight the commodification of women as a whole, there are individual women characters representing different types of modern girls from various nations who end up in Shanghai for livelihood in the global wave of human dislocation. The Japanese taxi dancer Miyako 宮子 is a typical modern girl in the novel. Kōya, an employee of Muramatsu Steamship Company and very much a modern boy figure who thinks of nothing but finding a modern girl in Shanghai as a bride, is infatuated with her. As a modern boy should be, he speaks several languages, sings European songs, and is attracted to all beautiful girls in the novel. Miyako whets his appetite by flirting with him, the way she treats all other men, and enjoys torturing him. According to Yamaguchi 山口, an ex-architect who is now in the business of selling human skeletons for medical use, Miyako has never been known to be involved with any Japanese man; her customers are mainly white men, American or European. For Kōya, this is a war between him and white men over a Japanese woman. In Chapter 4, Yamaguchi, a self-proclaimed "authority on Asianism" (Ajiya shugi no ōsorichi アジヤ主義のオーソリチー), claims that she may be a spy and jokes about the way Europeans are vying for her attention: "Sometimes a war of European nations breaks out over her."[39] It is through Kōya's eye that we see how Western men surround her and worship her like a goddess, whose gaze could show mercy or kill: "Around her foreigners are vying, studying her tastes, searching the flow of her capricious gaze, silently counting how many times she dances with a rival, thus raising her higher and higher above their shoulders."[40]

Miyako's philosophy, "to live day to day as pleasantly as you can,"[41] epitomizes the *carpe diem* spirit of the quintessential modern girl. Kōya the modern boy prides himself on his fluency in German and French on a par with any foreigner, but feels that his Japanese skin color is his major disadvantage in the war of nations over her. When he complains that she is making him compete with all kinds of foreigners, she laughs and points out that what she has in mind is simply business and that she is not different from any Japanese businessman like himself: "Foreigners are customers. Doesn't someone like you need to conspire as much as we dance hall girls to take money from foreigners?"[42] In Chapter 21, she says at one point to Sanki, Kōya's close friend since elementary school, in a nonchalant way, "Right now I have collected five lovers. A Frenchman, a German, an Englishman, a Chinaman, an American. That doesn't mean there aren't others."[43] In addition, she is literally "collecting" (sorotte iru 揃っている) her lovers' pictures in an album, which she shows to Sanki in a matter-of-fact way. Apparently she treated them as nothing but her "gigolos."

When Kōya, frustrated by her, ruminates on how to beat foreigners in business as compensation for his loss in love, he feels that he is engaging in a global war over a Japanese woman as well as business opportunities in China. Just back from the headquarters of his company in Singapore, his business ambition is to become the manager of the branch office in Shanghai, try the gold market, and go into silk, currency, the cotton business in Bombay, and then the exchange market in Liverpool. In Chapter 17 Kōya's mind linking war over Miyako with international business competition is preposterous:

> The fact that he had lost Miyako to foreigners had been the main source of his melancholy agitation; and so at the core of these fantasies was a raging, heroic ambition aimed at attacking the very heart of the economic power of the foreigners who had taken her away from him.
> In the face of local Chinese products [Ch. *tuhuo* or *doka* 土貨], which were becoming the sources of the economic power of foreigners, he thought he had to disrupt as much as possible the fronts of the sharp vertical trusts they directed.[44]

Besides the comical effect, Kōya the modern boy is here assimilating the prevalent Japanese Asianist rhetoric at the time, with Westerners as Japan's competitors in the global imperialist expansion. As a contrast to a dandy whose main occupation is the creative transformation of information received on the transcultural site, a modern boy like Kōya, merely receiving it as it is, transmits it without much thinking.

Miyako is a capricious modern girl to the bone. Yamaguchi's comment that she has not been seen involved with Japanese could probably be revised, if only Sanki would succumb to her charms. Though she is not interested in Kōya and rejects him all the time, in Chapter 21 we see her, scantily dressed and lying on a sofa, trying to seduce Sanki, who accompanies the drunken Kōya to her apartment and is taking care of him. Her will to conquer him is probably all the more spurred simply because he shows no interest in her at all. Sanki, who is a Don Quixote in Kōya's mind, has always been longing for Kōya's sister who, now married, stays in Japan. This unrequited love constantly prevents him from getting involved with other women who come on to him, including Olga and Ōsugi.[45] In this scene of seduction, Sanki finally shows the sign that he is about to be tempted. Upon this, the whimsical Miyako taps on his face and intends to spur him on with her coy rejection, but Sanki, considering that "the danger to his heart (jibun no kokoro no kikensa 自分の心の危険さ) took priority over his flesh," backs out unexpectedly, much to her dismay.[46] This scene is hilarious, as are all the other scenes in which Sanki tries to shun women's sexual approaches. His success with women for whom he has absolutely no desire is just the opposite of Kōya's fate with women. A typical modern boy tortured by the modern girl, Kōya is always after women who talk with him about nothing but Sanki.

In the story the war of nations competing for Miyako's favor is paralleled with the global business war in Shanghai, emblematic of the international colonial warfare vying for gains in China. Chapter 30 (Chapter 29 in

Washburn's translation) is most revealing in this regard. The foreign men who always surround Miyako in the dance hall are discussing the strike at the Japanese cotton mill in Shanghai. According to Herman Pfilzer, a German from the A. E. G. branch, a loss for Japan is a gain for Germany, which used to enjoy big markets in the Far East before World War I until they were "grabbed" (ubatta 奪った) by other nations. When Harold Cleaver, an American from G. E., complains about how American companies suffer from the pressure of the German "superman power" (chōjinteki na seiryoku 超人的な勢力), a pun on Nietzsche's "superman," Pfilzer retorts that the Americans are monopolizing the broadcasting rights in China. While the mutual attacks are going on, Miyako, caught in the crossfire between the two, tries to intervene with joking remarks such as, "If the two of you are working for rival companies, from now on who should I side with?" (dochira e mikata shitara ii no kashira どちらへ味方したらいいのかしら).[47]

There is no doubt that Miyako represents Japan who flirts with all nations, trying to benefit from the international wars in China. In the next section, we are going to see how Russia is represented by Olga, the Russian aristocrat in distress.

Olga in a seizure: Russia's lost angel

Another striking modern girl type in the novel is Olga, a Russian girl of aristocratic origins who has become one of Yamaguchi's five kept women. Japanese men congregate in Shanghai for procuring either money or women, or both. Olga was sold to Yamaguchi by Kimura 木村, who used to keep six Russian women at the same time and sold them all at once when he happened to lose all his money on the horse track one day. As much as Kimura makes no distinction between women and "savings" (*chokin* 貯金; Chapter 4),[48] Olga, a typical modern girl, does not mind being sold from one man to another; even less does she care about how many women her man keeps at the same time (Chapter 12).[49]

As capricious and willful as a modern girl can be, Olga, feeling lonely, is sexually interested in Sanki. Having resigned from the Japanese bank because the boss's corruption disgusted him, Sanki, the only "high-minded man" (atama no takai hito 頭の高い人) in Shanghai in Olga's opinion,[50] stays in Yamaguchi's house while waiting for Yamaguchi to find him a new job. Like a typical modern girl, Olga turns on all her charm to lure him. Or one should say, she literally has her body and hands all over him: In Chapters 13 and 14, like a snake with long arms intertwining his neck and the body stubbornly clinging to him, she repeatedly plunges towards him and flings herself at him whenever she is pushed away, wrestling violently with him and chasing him from bed to floor and then to the stairway, where he eventually escapes.[51] The ridiculous scene is as graphically described and as astounding as that of the teahouse prostitutes discussed before.

Ready to burst into tears and laughter at any minute and feeling lonely all

114   *Dandyism and Transcultural Modernity*

the time, Olga is as dazzling as any modern girl and can be a handful for any man. In addition, she can plunge into seizures, whenever she talks about her past. As if to prepare the reader for the scene of her seizure, Yokomitsu carefully molds Olga's character to be in tune with her history to be disclosed later: She likes to talk about music and literature in Tsarist Russia; Chekov, Turgenev, and Tschaikovsky are her favorite topics. In fact, she likes any topic connected with Russia, including Bolsheviks and "sausages from the region of the Caspian Sea" (Kasubikai no chōtsumei no hanashi カスピ海の腸詰めの話).[52] When Sanki refuses to stay the night with her, she calls him a "Bolshevik."[53] Chapter 43, the climax of the Olga story line, turns her into a flâneuse and the symbol of White Russia in diaspora. She tells the story to Kōya, who was assigned by Yamaguchi to accompany her, of how, driven by the Bolshevik revolution, she and her parents fled from Moscow to Tomsk, a city in Southwestern Siberia where her father was caught by the revolutionaries and almost died in a public persecution, and then to Harbin, the Manchurian city connecting the Trans-Siberian Railroad and the Eastern Chinese Railway constructed by Russia. With their jewelry sold to a Chinese, they managed to live there for a while until the Soviets took over the city. Her father having died in Harbin, she and her mother finally escaped to Shanghai and found themselves without any means of livelihood. Then she became "debased" (asamashii 淺ましい),[54] sold from man to man. She says to Sanki, "Ah, I want to go home to Moscow" (Chapter 12).[55] But the Tsarist Russia she longs for is already *passé*, impossible to return to, as Kōya tells her.[56]

The seizure she suffers after telling her story is described vividly in the novel: the incontrollable contraction of her body, the chattering teeth, the head thrown up and back repeatedly, the arm clutching the neck of Kōya, who tries to help by holding her tightly in his arms. Her seizure, the physical sign of psychological trauma, symbolizes White Russia in suffering, whereas her body, through which memories of her life in diaspora flow in and out, epitomizes the transcultural site. Here we have one of the few moments of compassion in the novel. Kōya, who has wanted to marry Miyako but has been repeatedly rejected by her, looks at the gradually recovering Olga lying asleep in bed, as if he were looking at a bride (hanayome sugata 花嫁姿).[57] After saying, "Yes, this will do," he takes off his jacket and starts shaving with Yamaguchi's razor. Does this scene imply he will inherit Olga from Yamaguchi and really take care of her, or even marry her, after she has been treated like a subhuman by the other Japanese men in the story? The meaning is ambiguous, but there seems to be such a potential.

Hō Shūran: the mysterious Chinese woman revolutionary

> Then, suddenly, Yamaguchi saw an elegant Chinese woman among the dancers. He murmured,
> "Ah, that's Hō Shūran."[58]

When Hō Shūran first appears in Chapter 4, most of the main characters gather at Saracen, the dance hall where Miyako works as a taxi dancer. The scene of Hō Shūran's appearance is very much symbolic—an elegant, gorgeous Chinese woman whom all men ogle and crave, but none understands or manages to get hold of, just as China under the covetous scrutiny of all foreign nations is beyond their reach. It seems that no one in the story has ever had direct contact with her until the breakout of the riot in Chapter 23, when Sanki happens to be on the scene.

A Communist spy under cover, she seems to have multiple identities: a taxi dancer in this scene, a factory worker in another, and so on. When Kōya, the modern boy *par excellence* in the novel, catches sight of her, he is immediately enchanted, simply unable to take his eyes off her. In fact, she is the center of attention of all men in the dance hall, who turn their eyes towards the table where she sits. She is the only woman character in the story whose facial features and looks are described in detail, but this does not make her character penetrable. When she leaves and gets in a rickshaw, Kōya goes after her in another, trailing behind through the streets, all the way thinking of nothing but her beautiful image: "Compact lips. Big black eyes, swept-up bangs, butterfly necklace, light grey top and skirt" (Chapter 4).[59] He sticks behind until she gets out of the rickshaw and disappears, following a young man wearing a Western suit. It is a scene characteristic of the Neo-Sensation gender triad: the modern boy, like the dandy, is willing to follow the modern girl to eternity, even if he is doomed to be tortured by her.

A mystery that everyone talks about, Hō Shūran represents in many ways what China is to foreigners who intend to conquer her, especially to the Japanese. In Chapter 18 Kōya's brother Takashige 高重, conversing with Sanki, describes China as a country where no rules can apply. According to him, the Chinese would not depend on anything such as hopes or ideals; the only thing that works in China is money. He considers the Chinese wise in that they let foreigners who make money in China spend it all there, and kind in that they consider Japanese human at all. When Sanki asks, "Are you saying that Chinese aren't human? That they're gods?" Takashige replies, "They are avatars of men who aren't human."[60] He continues to say that to the Chinese, lies are not lies, but Chinese-style righteousness. He calls it the "inversion of their concept of righteousness," and declares that China is a "mysterious" or "weird" country (kaiki na kuni 怪奇な國), fascinating, but impenetrable.

In Chapter 23, when he first lays eyes on Hō Shūran among the women workers in the cotton factory, even Sanki, uninterested in any woman because of his unrequited love for Kyōko, "struggled with" her beauty.[61] Sanki has just learned that Kyōko's husband had died of tuberculosis, and his passion for her has been rekindled, but he cannot help feeling drawn by this "chillingly attractive woman" (sei'en na onna 凄艶な女). At this point Sanki has just quit his previous job at the Japanese bank, because he was angry with corruption in the office. He is now working in the factory of Takashige, who takes him to make rounds and tells him that Hō Shūran is a Communist and that "if she so much as raises her right hand, the machines in this factory will grind to a halt."[62] The reason why he keeps her in the factory is that "he takes pleasure in the competition with her," and he foresees that she will be killed in the end. He is right.

This scene, with Sanki carrying a pistol in hand while making rounds and the Indian policemen's turbans in a row portending violence, is the climax of the novel; the riot in the factory will lead to the May 30th Movement. As Sanki and Takashige come around from the drawing section to the scutching section, the description of the crowd of male workers working impassively at the roaring machines is highly symbolic, reminding one of the crowd of prostitutes likewise described as a horrific entity: "Among the crowd of handles (handoru no mure ハンドルの群れ) that formed an arc, the impassive faces of male workers flowed in and out. The high swell of cotton was a raging billow (dotō 怒濤) that bit at and shook the machines."[63] Here I am translating "han-do-ru no mure" into "the crowd of handles" in order to show the affinity of this scene with that of "the crowd of hookers" (shōhu no mure) discussed before. Yokomitsu uses the same word "mure" 群れ (crowd) to qualify both hookers and machines, while he equates the male workers with the latter. More important here is the image of a "raging billow," reminiscent of the hookers described as water snakes. The symbol of waves is consistently used to delineate the uprising of the workers in the May 30th Movement.

In the background of the uprising there are the competition of England's cotton business in India with Japan's in China, the workers' dissatisfaction with the wages earned, and "the rising tide of Marxism" (Marukishizumu no nami マルキシズムの波), again a symbol of sea waves. The riot breaks out when Sanki is making rounds with Takashige in the factory. At first a corridor is suddenly in flame, then the windows are shot through by a stream of bullets. The crowd of women workers (kōjo no mure 工女の群れ), becoming frantic, start to scream and rush round and round like a whirlpool (uzu wo maita 渦を巻いた), with the sound of the alarm whistle tearing the air.[64] In this chaotic turmoil, Sanki, catching a glimpse of Hō Shūran's face in the whirlpool of women workers, tries to rescue her from the commotion. The diction used and the image created in this scene is very much a reminder of the scene of Sanki caught in the crowd of the hookers in Chapter 10:

> From the edge of a wave that had collapsed in front of Sanki, Hō Shūran's face is adrift. He inched forward over slackened backs and stretched out toward her. His chin ended up on her shoulder. The overpowering tremors of the crowd caused his body to list like a ship. He could not resist the pressure coming from behind him and slipped diagonally between shoulders. Right after that Hō Shūran's body began to topple over. He held her up, trying to get on his feet. But someone fell on top of them. He was kicked in the head. Aiming for a space among the

oscillating bodies, he felt himself sinking. He took Shūran in his arms. But his arms were pinned in among feet. Shoes were thrust under his sides. Yet for Sanki, the riot behind his back had now passed. Like shellfish sunk to the bottom of the ocean, they had to wait until they could drift up from the depths of this ocean of people.[65]

To the theoretical framework of this study, the symbolic connotation of this scene is unmistakable: Sunki and Hō Shūran belong to the hordes of flâneurs and the flâneuses who float with the tide of the crowd. Although, given names as characters in the novel, they seem to be distinct, they are no different from the multitudes of ordinary people who flow in the ocean of life.

Finally Sanki manages to rescue Shūran from the crowd and escorts her to her home. Considering the danger for a Japanese walking alone in a Chinese district, she invites him to stay overnight so that she would not have to escort him out in the middle of the night with her leg injured. The next morning when she takes him to a nearby restaurant for breakfast, their conversation soon turns into a debate on Asianism and Proletarianism, a polemic moment when Sanki's and Shūran's symbolic roles are highlighted in the novel.

In the conversation, Shūran acts as the mouthpiece of Chinese Communism, and Sanki, from Shūran's point of view, of Japanese bourgeoisie. Shūran thinks that the Chinese Communists who attack the Japanese factory are attacking Japanese bourgeoisie, and thus helping to liberate Japanese Proletariats. But Sanki claims that unlike a Marxist, he is unable to consider himself a citizen of the world (sekai no ichiin 世界の一員). He declares, "You Marxists assume that the speed of cultural development is the same for both the East and the West. But I think that error will only result in a superior breed of victims."[66] When Shūran accuses him of being an Asianist, Sanki denies it and insists that he simply loves Japan, the way she loves China. To say that Sanki is a spokesman for Japanese bourgeoisie or Asianism may not be totally accurate, however. As I will discuss later in this chapter, Sanki at some moments in the novel actually represents *yamato tamashii* (the soul of Japan) in its purest form, as does Ōsugi the body of Japan. Yet even though Sanki is hardly an Asianist from head to toe, the influence of the prevalent Asianist discourse in Japan does find its way into his mouth when he debates with Shūran. Like a receptacle through which information flows in and out, he as a character in the story is certainly not fully aware of the historical significance of this discourse, or any other prevalent discourse, that is already deeply inscribed in his psyche.

We all know that during the Meiji period Fukuzawa Yukichi 福澤諭吉 advocated the famous concept "out of Asia, into Europe" in 1885,[67] thinking that Japan's future lies in secession with the backward Asia and catching up with European scientific achievements. This concept influenced Japan's policy making and a whole generation of Japanese intellectuals. But in Taishō Japan there were a newly established interest in Asia and the revival of Confucian studies which had been prevalent during the Edo period. The first to advocate the idea was Okakura Tenshin 岡倉天心 (or Okakura Kakuzō 岡倉覚三, 1863–1913), who in 1903, influenced by Ernest Fenollosa (1853–1908),[68] published an English book titled *The Ideals of the East with Special Reference to the Art of Japan*. He maintained that "Asia is one," in the sense that all Asian countries fall behind the West in modernization, and that the spiritual culture of the East is much superior to the material culture of the West. In this book, the primitive art of Japan, Buddhism in India, and Confucianism in northern China are listed among the epitome of Eastern civilization. Okakura believes that, with the onslaught of Western culture, Asia has to unite and revive its spiritual culture in order to prevail.[69] When Hamada Kōsaku 濱田耕作 published *The Dawn of East-Asian Civilization* (Tōa bunmei no reimei 東亜文明の黎明) in 1930, the term "Tōa" 東亞 (East Asia), as Okakura's term "Ajia" アジア (Asia), clearly marked an effort to downplay the leading role of China in East Asia. Both emphasized that all East Asian countries are an intimate cultural entity.[70] In other words, the so-called "East-Asian civilization" was now effacing "Chinese civilization." This was also, of course, an effort to sever Japan from the traditional concept of "ka'i chitsujo" 華夷秩序 (Sino-barbarian world order), a world order with imperial China as its center, and to enter into the global competition among modern imperial powers.[71] "Shibunkai" 斯文会 (The Confucian Society), active from 1918 to 1945, aimed at promoting Confucianism and cultural exchange among Asian countries that had shared a strong foundation in Confucian ideals. Both Okakura's thought and the Confucian Society's activities helped expedite the formation of the concept of Asianism and later the policies of The Asia Development Board in 1938 and Pan-Asian Co-Prosperity Sphere in 1940, as mentioned before.[72]

When Sanki says to Shūran that "You Marxists assume that the speed of cultural development is the same for both the East and the West" and declares that it is an error, he is certainly referring to Okakura's idea that all Asia falls behind the West in modernization. Yet, although he is bred in the Pan-East Asia Co-Prosperity discourse and is able to brandish its concepts in conversation, he often seems to be in doubt of its validity. If Yokomitsu Riichi intends to advocate Japan's Pan-East Asian movement, characters such as Sanki and Ōsugi in the novel do not seem to be strong advocates of this position. They are often seen wandering aimlessly in the streets, the lost children of Japan drifting in the semicolonial city of Shanghai in the wake of its economic as well as political and military warfare. Both represent the downside of imperial expansion; they drift along with Japan's political policy to the Chinese metropolis, hoping to make a living, but in the end are crushed to the bottom of society—both are unemployed and penniless in a foreign country. This will be discussed later in this chapter. The real Asianist in the novel is Yamaguchi, a human bones collector, as we will see in the following.

Yamaguchi: the Asianist and scavenger

As I have said at the beginning of this chapter, it is difficult to pinpoint what position the narrator, or Yokomitsu, takes in the Japanese Pan-Asian movement during the war. This is especially the case when we look at the characterization of Yamaguchi, the Asianist in the story. More a symbolic figure than a real human being, his character poses a problem of interpretation—although he is seen as an advocate of Asianism, he is also depicted as a businessman who profits from the war by selling human skeletons for medical use.

As a whole, racial discourse advocating the supremacy of yellow over white runs throughout the novel. Dialogues between Japanese and Chinese characters usually support this position. For instance, when Kōya tries to sell lumber to the rich businessman Qian Shishan 銭石山, who takes Oryū お柳, the woman who runs the Turkish bath, as mistress, he says to Qian, "The center of executive power (jikkōryoku 實行力) in the world lies with the yellow race. . . . The next world war won't be an economic war anymore. It'll be a race war. That's why if China and Japan keep quarreling with each other as they are now, the race that will benefit most is the white. India will be caught in the middle and will definitely never rise."[73] Ironically, Kōya's ideological propaganda of the yellow race in league to fight against the white seems to be wasted on Qian, an opium addict who loses interest in the conversation when it is time for him to get high.

Yamaguchi certainly has his own Asianist network in Shanghai, which encompasses the Indian jewelry shop owner Amuli, a revolutionary in exile and a follower of the Indian revolutionary Chittaranjan Das, and the Chinese Communist Li Yingpu 李英朴. For Amuli, independence from the British is the primary concern, and he does not mind the ascendance of Communism in India as long as the Communists are fighting the British as well. When Yamaguchi objects and says, "If the coastline from India to Shanghai will be utterly Communist, what will happen? We Asianists won't be fighting Europe, we'll be fighting the Communist army," Amuli replies that the situation of India caught in between Japan and Russia will be difficult to handle, if the Japanese Asianism excludes Communism.[74]

This dialogical approach to Asianism is complemented by Li Yingpu's letter to Yamaguchi in Chapter 43. Three days after the strike, Yamaguchi tells Kōya that he intends to go out and collect Hō Shūran's bones, though risking the danger to his own life. If he dies he wants Kōya to meet with Amuli and Li Yingpu, who will tell him what to do. Before he leaves, he shows Kōya Li's letter delivered by a messenger on the day of the strike without a return address. The whole scene implies that Yamaguchi is involved in international espionage activities with his Asianist cohort. In the letter Li states that the tragic incident was not simply an international dispute between China and Britain, but a key to the wax and wane of yellow and white (kōhaku shōchō no kanken 黄白消長の関鍵). He claims that yellow and white are the only races that matter in the world now, since white men have already subjugated the black and the red races: the American Indian, the Malay of Southeast Asia, and the "African Negro." He warns:

> The white men are expediting their racial extermination project; their imperialistic ambition will not stop until they control the whole world. ... We yellow race are on the verge of extinction. ... Japan and China share the same race and culture, fated to depend on each other like lips and teeth [Ch. *Chunchi xiangyi* or *shinshi sōi* 唇歯相依]. If China collapses, it will certainly do Japan no good. So how can we resign ourselves to raising high the national flags as we so often do?[75]

So in Yokomitsu's formulation, the Chinese Communists fully recognize the need to ally with the Japanese Asianism, and Li's purpose of writing this letter is to ask for a meeting with Yamaguchi to discuss how to "combine our efforts to save our nations" (waga minzoku わが民族). The message is clear: To fight against white, Asian nations should put their national differences aside and ally with each other.

Yokomitsu seems to be consistently straightforward in this line of development in the novel, and his stance in the Japanese Asianist movement would be clear and less nuanced, or less problematic, without the characterization of Yamaguchi the Asianist as a bone collector. Yamaguchi is a problem in the novel. He is a completely unsympathetic character, callously bragging to Kōya that one dead body is equal to seven Russian mistresses in value: "I bought dead bodies from Chinese and clean them up. One dead person can keep seven living Russian women, seven! And Russian nobility, too!" (Chapter 4).[76]

In Chapter 42, the most gruesome scene in the novel, we see the skeleton collector in an even more negative light, with graphic descriptions of him as a symbol of scavenger. At this point Yamaguchi shows Kōya the basement of his house, where his skeleton "workshop" (seisakusho 製作所) is situated. Lit by candle light, it is dark and stinky. Under the white ribcages dangling from the wall, a Chinese assistant is brushing severed human legs soaked in alcohol. In the meantime, a swarm of black rats are coming out of the corners and climbing onto the wall. They crawl into the white ribcages, climb out of their openings, and then descend along the wall. It is clear that Yamaguchi is using rats, scavengers since ancient times, to clean up the bones before the Chinese assistant performs the finishing touches. When Kōya is astonished that with the revolution on the street above, all he thinks of is his skeleton business, Yamaguchi retorts, "It's a Chinese revolution, isn't it? The ones who are put in disadvantage are the whites. If we don't screw the Europeans once in a while, we'll always be dismissed as nuisance. As of today, long live Asia!"[77]

The next scene, which ends this chapter, describes how Yamaguchi deliberately directs the rats to come to his and Kōya's way. The whole scene is graphically "realistic" and horrifying. If we compare this scene in the original version serialized in *Kaizō* in January 1931 with that in the 1935 Shomotsutenbōsha 書物展望社 edition, which was extensively revised by Yokomitsu himself,[78] some significant indication will be disclosed. In the 1935 revision, the scene is simply as follows:

> Yamaguchi went over to the rats and stuck out his hand. Immediately a swarm of rats hit the ground without even a sound and came flowing towards Kōya's way.
> Kōya already had had enough of it. Nauseous from the stench and filth, he climbed back up the ladder to the ground floor, his hands on his chest.[79]

In comparison, in both the original version serialized in *Kaizō* and the first single-volume edition published by Kaizōsha 改造社 in 1932, the whole scene is much more elaborated, with the graphic image of rats climbing over Yamaguchi's body, absolutely abhorrent:

> Yamaguchi went over to the rats and stuck out his hand. A swarm of rats suddenly clambered over him from his knees to his shoulders, gathering, climbing, rolling and falling, tumbling and crawling back up to his head. With rats stuck to his body like a suit of armor, he turned to Kōya,
> "What do you say? Want to give it a try?"
> Kōya closed the door and started back to the ladder alone.
> "Hey! Don't run away, Kōya! There's more inside! In here!" Yamaguchi yelled.
> But Kōya already had had enough of it. Nauseous from the stench and filth, he climbed back up the ladder to the ground floor, his hands on his chest. He tried imagining Yamaguchi's Russian women, who were in effect supported by the white bones [*hakukotsu* 白骨] he had seen just now. Those women, of course, had been driven from their mother country by revolution. What did their face look like? He could hardly wait to see them.[80]

When *Shanghai* was serialized in the journal *Kaizō*, two *kanji* characters, *hakukotsu* (white bones), were eliminated by the censor, with the omission indicated by two crosses. Such publication censorship was common in Japan and its colonies during the Shōwa and Taishō periods, when Japan, expanding its imperial powers, was tightening its control over cultural policies. In the 1932 version of the novel, the two eliminated characters were restored. The 1935 edition underwent a major revision. In the 1932 edition, all the *rubi* ルビ, or the *kana* indicating the pronunciation of *kanji*, were kept. But in the 1935 revision by Yokomitsu, most of the *rubi* were dropped; the original Chapter 44, in which the hungry Sanki arrives in Miyako's place looking for food in vain, is eliminated; and a lot of scenes become more or less simplified. The elimination of Chapter 44 does not seem to change the development of the story at all. Miyako's character as a capricious modern girl is underscored here: Because Sanki, whose gesture of gratitude leads her on, refrains from making love to her, Miyako gets angry and sweeps the bread out of his arms to the floor. The elimination of this scene is of no great significance. But eliminating the graphic scene of rats sticking on Yamaguchi's body "like a suit of armor," which makes the Asianist the symbol of the scavenger *par exellence*, is certainly toning down the negative side of Asianism.

Worthy of equal, if not more, attention is the deletion of the part where Kōya imagines that Yamaguchi's Russian women, "driven from their mother country by revolution," are being supported by the "white bones" of the dead bodies. So the revolutions in other countries are feeding Yamaguchi's skeleton business, which allows him to keep five aristocratic Russian mistresses at the same time. This echoes these lines from Chapter 4 discussed earlier: "One dead person can keep seven living Russian women, seven! And Russian nobility, too!" The image of Yamaguchi the Asianist, with an "armor" formed of rats, gloating over the white bones that allow him to exploit Russian women victimized by civil war, is certainly an accusation of Japan's Asianism that benefits from other countries' suffering. Why did Yokomitsu eliminate the whole symbolic scene all together in the 1935 edition?

Probably because the time of revision was close to the outbreak of the Sino-Japanese war in 1937, it was necessary to show full support of Japan's Pan-Asian policy by making it less equivocal in the novel. Or it was simply because Yokomitsu wanted to make the scene more succinct, to be in line with the full-scale revision of the novel. Whatever the reason for the elimination, more significant was the fact that the Asianist/scavenger symbol existed in his original conceptualization at all. In fact, if we talk about skeletal preparation on a "realistic" level, using rats to clean the bones is totally unfeasible, since it takes too long, and since rats eat not only flesh but also small and fragile bones. The standard procedure for skeletal preparation is removing the muscles after boiling the bones.[81] The rats-armor scene is no doubt from his own imagination. The questions that need to be asked are: Does the scavenger symbol indicate that he was only halfheartedly enthusiastic of Japan's Pan-Asian policy when he first wrote *Shanghai* from 1928 to 1931? Did he have any qualms about the war of invading Asian countries (*shinryaku sensō* 侵略戦争) at that time? Did he then change his attitude and become fully supportive of the policy during the 1935 revision of the novel? Or was it simply because he was obliged to demonstrate that he was fully supportive?

Writers' war responsibility was an issue that split the literary circle in postwar Japan. The June 1946 issue of the left-wing magazine *Shin Nihon Bungaku* 新日本文学, the organ of Shin Nihon Bungakukai 新日本文学會 (New Japanese Literary Society), published Odagiri Hideo's article titled "Pursuing War Responsibility in Literature" (Bungaku ni okeru sensō sekinin no tsuikyū 文学における戦争責任の追求). The article denounced Yokomitsu Riichi as one of the 25 famous writers believed to be guilty of war responsibility during the society's inaugural meeting on 29 March of the same year.[82] It says,

> Literary men who should have been the soul of the people [*jinmin no tamashii* 人民の魂] became instead the megaphones of the aggressive power, driving the people into war. Resorting to deception and sycophancy, they became the shameless maids of the dominators. . . .[83]

The writers listed as guilty in the article included Kikuchi Kan, Kobayashi Hideo 小林秀雄, Hayashi Husao, Mushanokōji Saneatsu, Nakagawa Yoichi, Satō Haruo, and so on, almost all the high-profile writers at the time.

Writers' sudden reversal of position in wartime is a complex issue. Yokomitsu was certainly not alone in making such a significant turnabout during Japan's escalating colonial expansion in the 1930s and 1940s. We can take Mushanokōji, one of the Shirakaba School 白樺派 leaders, as another prominent example. As an anti-war, anti-state writer, he had inspired many anarchists in both Japan and China with the publication of his 1916 play *A Young Man's Dream* (Aru seinen no yume ある青年の夢), which was translated into Chinese by Lu Xun in 1919.[84] Influenced by Tolstoy's ideal of a classless utopian society, Mushanokōji established the "Atarashiki Mura" 新しき村 (New Village) in Hyūga 日向, Miyazaki 宮崎 Prefecture, in 1918, advocating a farm commune where all members participated in daily labor and cultural creation. The division of labor, based on each person's aptitude and mutual aide, was designed to ensure individual independence and freedom. He believed that if this lifestyle prevailed, nations would be reformed and war would be avoided.[85] Zhou Zuoren 周作人, Lu Xun's brother, wrote in March 1919 an article titled "The Japanese New Village" (Riben de xincun 日本的新村) to introduce its ideal into China, citing extensively from Mushanokōji's article "Life in the New Village" (Atarashiki Mura no seikatsu 新しき村の生活).[86] Mao Zedong 毛澤東, before becoming a Communist, read Zhou's article and responded with an article in December 1919, advocating the construction of a New Village in Hunan 湖南 County.[87] Although the plan did not come to fruition, it is believed that the People's Commune during the Cultural Revolution was based on the idea of the New Village. All this being said, it is surprising that an anti-state humanist like Mushanokōji would write a play titled *Three Laughs* (Sanshō 三笑) in 1943 to support Japan's Pan-Asian war.[88] "Three laughs," pronounced as "sanshō" and thus a pun for "three victories," implies the Japanese all-scale victories in sea, land, and air.

Three Laughs was written right after the Second Meeting of the Dai Tōa Bungakusha Taikai 大東亜文学者大会 (Association of Pan-Asian Literature) took place in Tokyo from 25 to 27 August 1943. It was convened by the Bungaku Hōkokukai 文学報国会 (Literary Society for Patriotism), a society under the aegis of the Intelligence Bureau. The purpose of the society, established on 26 May 1942, was to "unite the forces of all Japanese literary men, to advocate the imperial ideal and traditional Japanese literature, and to help promote the imperial culture."[89] In the composition of *Three Laughs*, Mushanokōji, as chief of the society's dramatic literature section, did fully express the spirit of "hakkō ichiu" 八紘一宇 (the eight corners of the world becoming one family), the main slogan of Pan-Asia Co-Prosperity Sphere during the Pacific war. The purpose of the Co-Prosperity Sphere was to organize East-Asian countries under the leadership of Japan in a united front against the West, as the hunchback artist Nakano says to the blind poet Nakamura in Act 3 of *Three Laughs*:

> In fact, if Asia doesn't cooperate as a unity, it will lose in the global competition for survival. In contrast, if all of Asia is working as a team, it will become the strongest nation in the world. Therefore England and America are deeply afraid of it. Exactly because of their fear, we need to fulfill this ideal.[90]

Since Yokomitsu Riichi was once critical of Asianism in the original characterization of Yamaguchi the Asianist as a bone collector and scavenger, and since Mushanokōji was once an anti-war humanist when he wrote *A Young Man's Dream*, shall we give them both the benefit of doubt before we judge them to be guilty of war responsibility? Maybe during the Pan-Asia Co-Prosperity Movement, writers had to cooperate. Maybe subconsciously they internalized the propaganda and enthusiasm for Japanese military expansion. Did they succumb to the Asianist rhetoric out of free will, pride, or fear? In a way, it is like asking why a religious person chooses to become a martyr. One can never assess how much state power can twist humanity, or what hideous collective crimes can be committed in the name of patriotism. Perhaps, as Tsurumi Shunsuke 鶴見俊輔 says about *tenkō* 転向 (turnabout or conversion) as a subject of study in Japanese intellectual history, the term suggests "humiliation" on the part of the individuals who "volunteer" to convert:

> Indeed, since the term "tenkō" is mainly used from the viewpoint of the institutional power that directed the turnabout phenomenon, for the individuals who are implicated in it, a sense of humiliation [*kutsujoku* 屈辱] is accompanied, however voluntary [*jihatsuteki* 自発的] each of them can be.[91]

If Yokomitsu could not help feeling "a sense of humiliation" when he converted to Japan's imperialist rhetoric, did he somehow try to vindicate himself by disclosing the downside of imperialism through characters such as Yamaguchi, Sanki, and Ōsugi in *Shanghai*? His conscience as an intellectual facing institutional powers, or contemporary Japanese writers' conscience for that matter, is the heart of darkness that could never see full light. Yet, if he was unable to directly confront the ideological arena, at least in art he managed to bring about the subtle creative transformation that puts ideology into question.

Sanki and Ōsugi: Japan's lost children

All the Japanese characters in the novel, either exploiting Chinese or Europeans for money or pleasure, seem more or less "in place" in Shanghai, except for Sanki and Ōsugi. They are often seen wandering aimlessly in the streets, most of the time lost, with no idea where they are going. When Sanki appears in Chapter 1, the reader is told about his longing for the homeland, a sentiment symbolized by the memories of two women: He misses his mother, who from time to time writes him tender letters from his home village, and Kyōko, whose news he can hear only from her brothers, Kōya and Takashige. Sanki and Ōsugi are the only two Japanese characters in the story who suffer in Japan's imperialist project and whose psychological connections with Japan are ever mentioned at all, though always in a tokenistic fashion. They are the two characters in the novel whose suffering defeats Japan's Pan-Asian rhetoric.

In Chapter 1 we know that Sanki has not been back to Japan for ten years, and that his life in Shanghai has been far from ideal: He has been forced to cover up the embezzlements of the manager of his bank. Sanki is repeatedly described by Kōya, though in a tongue-in-cheek fashion, as still believing in the traditional Japanese virtue, or *Yamato tamashii* (Chapter 17).[92] The split between ideal and reality drives him to constant thoughts of suicide, even though he has never attempted it, nor does it seem he will ever commit it. The only thing urging him to go on living is the image of his mother that floats up in his mind all the time. He says to himself: "I am still alive because I'm a filial son. My body is my parents' body, my parents" (Chapter 1).[93] But in Chapter 9 he would further see his body as an extension of his homeland. After he finally resigns from the bank out of indignation, in that chapter he is at a restaurant with Ōsugi. At this moment he realizes that both he and Ōsugi, unemployed in the colonial space in China, would fare worse in their homeland, because there is no way that they could make a living in Japan. Staying in China, they represent at least "an expression of patriotism" (aikokushin no araware to natte iru 愛國心の現れとなつている):

> Another way to look at it was that each representative of people made their living here as suckers on the tentacles of a giant octopus, pulling in a huge amount of local products for their home countries. Thus, with the exception of the Russians, even people who were idle, unemployed, or simply aimless could be thought of as an expression of patriotism simply by their mere presence in Shanghai.[94]

The image here is certainly negative: Foreign people in Shanghai seen as the "suckers on the tentacles of a giant octopus" intent on grabbing China's local products to enrich their own countries. But it curiously convinces Sanki that he is serving his mother country by simply staying in Shanghai. He thinks that "because he was in Shanghai, the space his body took up was always a territory of Japan, floating around" (taezu Nihon no ryōdo to natte nagarete iru 絶えず日本の領土となって流れてゐる): "My body is a territory. This body of mine. And Ōsugi's body."[95] Here the body in diaspora as an extension of one's homeland wonderfully sums up the concept of the character as a transcultural site: The moving body is the carrier of memories formed by all the diverse voices and discourses converging on and flow through it. Sanki, though upright and with a tender heart by nature, inevitably absorbs Japan's colonial ideology subconsciously, hardly ever questioning the injustice and human suffering it entails. In contrast, the narrator is able to point out Sanki's deficiency, or blindness, in this regard. Seeing Russian men begging and women selling their bodies on the streets of Shanghai, Sanki thinks to himself, "They (the Russians in Russia) were the ones at fault, since they were the ones to force their compatriots in a foreign land to lie under men, or to become beggars."[96] But, for his own misfortune, Sanki blames his boss. The omniscient narrator, who is certainly better informed, points out the irony of the situation:

> Yet he had forgotten that hating his boss was the same thing as hating his mother country. Once the mother country was rejected, the only activities left for a Japanese in Shanghai were begging and prostitution.[97]

One could read this passage as a circuitous critique of Japan's colonialism that drags its people into destitution in a foreign land. It will never occur to Sanki, who considers his presence in Shanghai as service to his country, that his country's colonial expansion is to blame for his misfortune. Being a man and more resourceful than Ōsugi, he soon manages to find a job in Takashige's factory. But Ōsugi, the most pitiable character in the novel, has no option but fall into prostitution.

Before she follows Sanki to the restaurant, Ōsugi was fired by Oryū, the Turkish bath owner, because Sanki had jokingly shown sexual interest in her when the latter was seducing him. Not knowing why she was fired nor where to go, she wandered in the streets and then ended up in Sanki's place, hoping to see him once more, but he was not home. Kōya came to visit him and let her into the apartment. At night she was ravished by Kōya, but in the morning when she saw that Sanki was sleeping in the bed with the former, she could not tell who of the two had done it. At this moment in Chapter 5 of the novel, as she looks out at the canal, a sort of huge sewer system in Shanghai, she sees floating on the water a barge loaded with coal and iron pipes sticking out of the road, with scraps of straw, stockings, fruit peels, and what not, which flow into the muddied sewers lining the back of the streets.[98] Characterized as a helpless woman who does not understand what is happening to or around her, she is the quintessential symbol of the unconscious body as the transcultural site, floating with the tide of historical events and discourses without understanding them. The parallel between her and the useless floating objects in the canal is apparent.

Sanki, sensing the "danger" of being sexually drawn to Ōsugi, refrains from returning to the apartment again. Neither does Kōya go back. In Chapter 15, Ōsugi, without food and waiting for them in vain for three days, thinks that the two men must dislike her. Feeling more confused than angry, she takes to the street and walks all the way to the riverbank. While roaming the streets like a flâneuse on her trip without direction, the image of the aimlessly floating objects appears again, all the more depressing than ever: Besides the motionless cranes over the mud and stacks of lumber, there is a broken boat covered with white fungus and the body of a baby with a foot floating up in the stagnant bubbles. She begins to think of prostituting herself, and before she finally does that, we see her wandering through the bridge, onto the riverbank, into the back alleys, where she turns corner after corner, until she is totally lost: "She stumbled like a trembling stick across the paving stones and got lost farther and farther in the labyrinth of walls. Lights gradually disappeared."[99] At last she loses consciousness and, dragged by unknown men, she was "sucked" into the dark (suikomarete mienaku natta 吸ひ込まれて見えなくなつた).

In Chapter 45 the novel ends with Sanki, hungry and penniless during the riot, looking for Ōsugi for shelter and food. Like Ōsugi who wandered on the riverbank and looked at the dirty canal before falling into prostitution, he is now walking along a canal in the "dangerous part of town," meaning the Chinese district. Suddenly he is attacked by a group of men, and is physically "falling" into the heaps of excrement (haisetsubutsu 排泄物) in the sewage. This is, of course, the ultimate symbol in the novel: The unconscious flâneur driven by the colonialist ideal literally ends up in the gutters. Sanki laughs hysterically at his own misfortune at the moment, but the experienced reader would know better: His present misfortune is caused by Japan's colonial ambition. The "fertilizer smell" of the sewage reminds Sanki of that of his "home village in Japan" (kono hiryō no nioi—kore wa Nihon no kokyō no nioi da この肥料の匂ひ—此れは日本の故郷の匂ひだ), conjuring up the thought of his mother. This association seems to imply the humility a Japanese needs to go through in order to find redemption amidst the suffering caused by colonialism.

In the previous chapter, Sanki, begging for food at Miyako's place, left her because she got angry at his lack of sexual interest in her. His continual rejection of women's constant sexual approaches due to his memories of Kyōko is getting more and more ridiculous as the narrative unravels. Finally in the last scene of the novel, he makes love to Ōsugi. The sexual consummation of the two indicates his acknowledgement of their common predicament and the ultimate redemption: Feeling that he is becoming no better than the Russian beggars whom he has despised all along, he realizes that he and Ōsugi, who has become a prostitute because of his as well as other men's continual "mistreatment" (ichime tsutsukete ikareru 虐め續けていかれる), are intertwined by an uncontrollable fate—even though, unlike the reader, he is unable to name it as the fate of Japan's colonialism.

The whole scene in which Sanki makes love to Ōsugi takes place in pitch-darkness, because the electricity has been cut, probably due to the uprising. But even though he asks her to light a match, she refuses. The reason is that she does not want him to see her face, which is now covered with the heavy makeup of a hooker. The lovemaking in the dark also reminds the reader of the night when she was ravished: Because of the darkness, she could not tell whether it was Kōya or Sanki. But now from comparison she is sure that it was Kōya the other night. The most unsettling reading is that the darkness suggests the hopelessness of her situation. She knows that Sanki will not come back; her brief happiness at this moment will not be repeated. If the next day the Japanese naval brigade comes and restores order to Shanghai, it will be safe for him to leave, while her days of satisfying Chinese men's dirty lust will continue: "Reflecting on these things, she stretched out like a patient who has given up and stared into the darkness spread across the ceiling."[100] The novel ends on that gloomy note.

From the masses to the flâneur and the flâneuse

If Sanki and Ōsugi can be seen as the quintessential flâneur and flâneuse in Yokomitsu Riichi's *Shanghai*, their affinities and contrasts to the crowd in the novel, or the masses, always faceless and unknown, are manifold and disconcerting. As a group, the masses are monolithic and fearful, representing either the forces of revolution or the commodification of women. Yet each individual of the masses, if singled out, could be a flâneur and a flâneuse, instantly losing the gigantic anonymity that makes the masses a horrific entity. As helpless individuals, they are the forlorn spirits devastated by social injustice and displacement caused by either colonial expansion or revolution, homeless and alone in a foreign land. In a way Sanki, having lost his job and begging for food from Myako and then Ōsugi, is no different from a Chinese or Russian beggar in the story, who is a common sight in the streets of Shanghai. Ōsugi, falling into prostitution, is just another hooker among the crowd of prostitutes the novel is so fascinated with. Foreign characters in the novel are reflective of the numerous foreigners who thronged into Shanghai for the sake of trade, livelihood, taking refuge, missionary work, revolutionary cause, or other reasons. They came either to escape from revolutions at their homelands like Olga, to connect their own revolutionary cause with that of China like Amuli, to seek their fortunes following imperialist invasions like Yamaguchi and the European and American businessmen. This was certainly true for people in real life as well; in Chapter 1 of this study we have already seen how Liu Na'ou saw Shanghai as the promised land, because there were limited opportunities for him to develop a literary career in colonial Taiwan.

Here I want to ask one question: Were the flows of people in and out of Shanghai and China at the time made possible by the Nationalist regime's "open governance," as Frank Dikötter maintains in his 2008 book, *The Age of Openness: China Before Mao*?[101] Whereas the late Qing was forced to open its borders by international treaties, the Republican government, basically an authoritarian regime, simply had no power to exercise effective border control, mainly due to its weakness aggravated by civil wars and international power struggles in China. It would take a strong central government such as that of the early Nationalist regime in Taiwan to maintain strict border control before 1987, and the Mao regime to close up China's borders all of a sudden after the "liberation." A weak central government such as the Republican regime in modern China could at best maintain the status quo, thanks to the sound administrative structure it had inherited from the late Qing.

As a treaty port, Shanghai since the late Qing had been forced open to the flux of Europeans, American, Indians, Japanese, and so on. This influx (and outflow) continued during the Republican era. While Dikötter categorically brushes aside the causes of Republican China's "openness"—weak governance, revolution, and imperialism, his rosy vision of "open borders" and "open governance" tells only half of the story—the flows of ideas, people, and goods into and out of Republican China, which are historical facts no literary critics, in China or the rest of the world, are ignorant of. Apparently Dikötter's position is revisionist;[102] he intends to contest the "common wisdom" and "unitary understanding" that the Republican period was "a weak and corrupt central government." His own unitary vision of the "open governance" of the Nationalist regime inclined towards "democracy," however, falls into the trap of tailoring archival findings for a preconceived agenda. He is neglecting facts such as the assassinations by secret agents, executions of Communists without trials, and censorships controlled by the central government at the time. We all know that open borders and open governance are by no means synonyms.

Open borders brought in people like the flâneurs or flâneuses in Yokomitsu's novel. If we use the metaphor of the transcultural site as the body of a character on the stage, their bodies are the site where cross-cultural memories are inscribed.[103] It is merely a receptacle where information and communication converge and flow out, as the bodies of Olga, Ōsugi, and Sanki are depicted in the story. Picture their bodily images: Olga is searching her memory in vain for the meaning of the Soviet revolution and her cross-continental journey from Moscow to Siberia, Harbin, and then to Shanghai; her body, overburdened with tragic recollections, is always crushed in a seizure. Ōsugi, compared to the floating objects in the canal, is wandering along the canal while getting lost in the labyrinth of the back alleys; she eventually ends up with her body dragged into darkness. Sunki, who considers his body to be "always a territory of Japan, floating around," literally winds up falling face up into the sewage in the Chinese district. They are simply floating with the tide of the crisscross of discourses and events, without the agency to effect any changes.

In contrast, in the next two chapters the cultural translators discussed, like Liu Na'ou, Mu Shiying, and Yokomitsu Riichi whom we have analyzed so far, can be compared to actors who are consciously working on the transcultural site. We will see how they are aware of their own positions at the frontiers, always ready to challenge the limits of the various institutions that contend with each other. Through the transcultural space between institutions where layers on layers of information are available to them, they manage to bring about creative transformation and invent the trend.

4 A traveling text
Souvenirs entomologiques

> The male praying mantis, grabbed and engulfed by the female, never tries to free itself even if its life is in imminent jeopardy.
> This is how the sense of touch generates pleasure for the two sexes.
> —Ōgai Kamome

Personal agency in translation

This chapter starts with a palm-of-the-hand story published by a Shanghai Neo-Sensation writer in September 1934. Through this story, I would like to demonstrate how a literary subgenre, having crossed the borders of nations from Europe to Asia, was used in China to ridicule the trend of scientism and modernist pursuits, while taking on aspects quite different from its original Japanese and French models.

The topic of the palm-of-the-hand story is usually about a male narrator ogling a seductive girl, as we have already seen in Chapter 2. The particular story I am going to analyze here, written by the Hong Kong poet Ōgai Kamome (1911–95), elaborates on this classic topic, while equating human behavior with insect behavior. Titled "The Three Who Study Antennas" (Yanjiu chujiao de sangeren 研究觸角的三個人), it uses the science of insect behavior to interpret man-and-woman love in a playful fashion, typical of Neo-Sensation stories. But the meaning of the story goes beyond pleasantry. Although no names or books are ever mentioned, it implies Lu Xun's (1881–1936) advocacy of Jean-Henri Fabre's (1823–1915) 10-volume work *Souvenirs entomologiques: étude sur l'instinct et les mœurs des insectes* (Memories of Insects: Study on the Instinct and Manners of Insects; 1879–1907) during the 1920s. Lu Xun, who did not know French, read the Japanese translation, titled *Book of Insects* (Konchūki 昆蟲記, 1922–31), by Ōsugi Sakae 大杉榮 (1885–1923) and Shiina Sonoji 椎名其二 (1887–1962), two anarchists during the Taishō period.

The intriguing questions this chapter addresses include: Why were anarchists attracted to Fabre's work? Did it ever occur to Lu Xun, who used Fabre's work to comment on the Chinese national character, that science carried special meanings for anarchism? Was Ōgai Kamome, intending to ridicule intellectuals like Lu Xun, aware of the complex implications of Fabre's work, including his famous disputes with Charles Darwin on the theory of evolution? Did they choose Fabre because he seemed to be helping promote their own cultural agenda? This chapter will explore how texts and ideas traveled in the Euro-Asian context during the 1920s and 1930s, and how certain values were lost during the transaction, while others were accrued during the process. Most importantly, whatever "mistranslation" or "misunderstanding" there was during the transmitting process, it shows how people and ideas, originally unrelated at all, were connected by the traveling of a single text, *Souvenirs entomologiques*. Ōgai Kamome's ridicule of the insect-worship phenomenon may not indicate his grasp of the whole conglomeration of the connections involved, but it shows how as a cultural translator and transcultural modernist he captured vividly the popular memories reflecting the phenomenon, and transformed it into a literary work that was part of the concatenation of events.

As Walter Benjamin tells us in "The Task of a Translator," meaning "is in a constant state of flux—until it is able to emerge as the pure language"; a text, having transcended language boundaries, reaches its "afterlife" or "the age of its fame" in a new language and culture.[1] Yet, absorbed in the metaphysical concept of the pure language, he never directly addresses the issue as to why the text is transformed after it crosses the borders of languages. Poststructuralist translation theories, following Benjamin, often emphasize the untranslatability or incommensurability of languages, while addressing this issue from the epistemological perspective. The dissemination of knowledge cannot transcend the limitations and traditions of cultures; the needs and limits of the receiving culture complicate the transaction and often force a transformation in the meaning of a foreign text. In examining the travel of *Souvenirs entomologiques* in the Euro-Asian context during the early decades of the twentieth century, I would like to explore the following issues related to this: Why is a certain text favored and introduced into a new language and culture at a particular historical moment? A translator or a conscious transmitter of knowledge, with a view to using foreign concepts to reform the domestic cultural tradition, may choose particular texts that meet this goal. But when foreign knowledge enters into a new language and culture, it may have to transform because of the translator's or the transmitter's own cultural agenda. Therefore this study emphasizes the agency of the translator and the receiving culture, which play key roles in the selection, interpretation, and transmission of a foreign text.

The three modern boys and the science of love

Scientific concepts or terms, taken at their face value, were often debunked in a tongue-in-cheek fashion in Shanghai Neo-Sensation stories when they used these terms to describe man-and-woman relationships. To illustrate my point, I will analyze "The Three Who Study Antennas," Ōgai Kamome's palm-of-the-hand story published in *The Women's Pictorial* in 1934. Originally named Li Zongda 李宗大, he moved from Hong Kong to Canton in 1925. He went back to work in Hong Kong during the 1930s,[2] and later, with a penname suggestive of the Japanese writer Mori Ōgai 森鴎外, became one of the first-generation New Literature writers on the island. Besides contributing to Hong Kong literary journals, he also wrote for journals in Shanghai such as *Les contemporains* and *The Women's Pictorial*. In 1941 when Hong Kong fell under the Japanese occupation, he went to Guilin 桂林 and did not come back until 1988. It is said that he was deeply influenced by Horiguchi Daigaku,[3] a Japanese poet during the Taishō period. Renowned as the first person to translate Paul Morand's works into Japanese, as we have seen in Chapter 2, Horiguchi belonged to the coteries of the Japanese literary journals *Bright Star* and *The Mask*.

A regular contributor to *The Women's Pictorial*, the organ of the Shanghai Neo-Sensation School during the 1930s, Ōgai Kamome attracted a lot of attention from the literary circle in Shanghai with his dandyish didacticism towards women, eclectic style, extraordinary syntactic structure, and free borrowings of Japanese *kanji* in his stories. In "The Three Who Study Antennas," the science of insect behavior is used to interpret human behavior in amorous acts. At first it might seem that it is the human behavior that is being mocked. At closer reading, one cannot help asking the following question: Why does the author draw our attention to insect behavior in this connection? Or rather, is it the insect behavior that is important in the story, or is the human being who compares it with human behavior that is at issue?

All these questions cannot be answered before we know how the story proceeds. According to the narrator, the three protagonists of the story, A, B, and C, are *Daxue shengtu* 大學生徒, university students. The term *shengtu* is a direct borrowing from *kanji*. In Japanese it is pronounced as *seito* 生徒, meaning high school students. In fact, the Japanese term for university students is *gakusei* 學生, pronounced as *xuesheng* in Chinese. *Xuesheng*, however, can refer to elementary school pupils, high school students, or university students. It is unclear whether the combination of *daigaku seito* is an unconscious mistake on the part of the narrator, or a deliberate ridicule of the three progressive Casanovas, who, overenthusiastic about science and sex, have unfortunately only limited knowledge of both. They are the typical modern boys in Neo-Sensation stories, eager to pursue whatever is *à la mode*. Scientific knowledge, a sign of progress, is certainly on their list of priorities.

The narrator tells us that the three modern boys are studying on their own the significance of the sense of touch in the relationship between the two sexes. The beginning of the story discloses clearly that science is the target of ridicule. Similar to a proposition in a scientific treatise, the story starts with a common-sense expression: *tongxing xiangchi, yixing xiangxi* 同性相斥，異性相吸, meaning "members of the same sex repel each other, while those of the opposite sex attract each other." Then, to describe the fatal attraction between male and female, the narrator uses a semiscientific metaphor serving as an exposition: When passing by a mountain of magnetic stones, the steel ship, despite its responsibility for the lives of the people aboard, will be sucked into the bottom of the sea and become a submarine forever. Images such as the steel ship, the submarine, and the magnet seem to be out of place in a story about human love. Nevertheless, they call to mind the magnificent power of Western science and excite the sense of awe. Of course, these images are connected with daily experiences in Shanghai, where gigantic foreign ocean liners enter and leave the Huangpu harbor day in and day out. It is no wonder the Shanghai Neo-Sensation writers like to use ships or ocean liners as the setting for their stories.

The narrator of the story further elaborates on the notion of fatal attraction between the opposite sexes with examples taken from insect behavior:

> The claws of the male diving beetle, equipped with suction cups, snatch relentlessly at the female body for days on end.
> The male praying mantis, grabbed and engulfed by the female, never tries to free itself even if its life is in imminent jeopardy.
> This is how the sense of touch generates pleasure for the two sexes.[4]

Using the female praying mantis as a metaphor for *la femme fatale* seems to be a recurrent figure of speech in Shanghai during the 1930s. As indicated in Guo Jianying's cartoon published in *Modern Sketch* in January 1934, "Black, Red, Cruelty, and Women" (Hei, hong, canrenxing yu nüxing 黑、紅、殘忍性與女性), we see the female mantis eating the male juxtaposed with the half-naked modern girl in the center. On the left is the facsimile of the photograph of the black American revue dancer Josephine Baker (1906–75), who made her name with the banana skirt that highlights her nudity in 1920s Paris.[5] The figure on the right is an Indian woman. All the women—black, yellow, or red—are connected with the female mantis because of their cruelty towards men, after having sex with them (Figure 4.1).[6]

Returning to Ōgai's story, I would say that all the descriptions about the mating habits of the diving beetle and the praying mantis are true; one can easily find such descriptions in natural science textbooks. But, the question is, how does one know that "the sense of touch generates pleasure" in insect behavior? This is no doubt projecting human psychology on insect behavior, a practice most noticeable in Fabre's *Souvenirs entomologiques*.

It is well known that natural history became popular in Japan and China after Darwin's evolutionary theory was introduced into both countries.[7] The establishment of natural history as a discipline in China is a topic worth pursuing, but it is not what this study is concerned with. Rather, I am interested in how this new branch of science inspired ordinary people's imaginations, and how it both conditioned the understanding of their lives and led to fresh interpretations of the world they lived in—in this case, love between the opposite sexes. Using examples from natural history, the narrator of the

Figure 4.1 Black, Red, Cruelty, and Women.

palm-of-the-hand story is telling us how the three modern boys are connecting insect and human behavior through the sense of touch.

Judging from human beings' closely intertwined bodies in lovemaking, the three modern boys imagine that humans are also born with "suction cups," though "metaphysical" (*xing er shang* 形而上, or imaginative) rather than realistic ones. In addition, they think humans have suction cups all over their bodies, unlike insects, endowed with this equipment on their "claws" only. But, of course, the suction cups on the hands and mouths of a human being have the strongest sucking power than those on other parts of the body. The three modern boys, taking evidence from insect behavior, believe that the attraction between the two sexes comes mainly from the sense of touch, which, because of its independent value, deserves to be treated as a scientific subject.

The narrator takes every opportunity to demonstrate his (and the three modern boys') erudition in scientific jargon. When referring to the sucking power of the mouth, he says "the mouth which the disciples of Freud call the oral erotic," with "Freud" and "oral erotic" written in English, exhibiting the macaronic style typical of the Neo-Sensation mode of writing. He emphasizes the various "experiments" the three modern boys carry on in order to confirm their theory of "the metaphysical sucking cups" in human bodies: How female nurses taking male patients' temperature are reluctant to let go of their pulses; and how lovers embracing and kissing each other are unwilling to release each other's hands or lips. According to the narrator, the three modern boys' understanding of the sense of touch is "informed by the knowledge of anatomy." Here anatomy is *jiepo* 解剖 in Chinese, a term borrowed from *kaibō*, a Japanese term.

Finally, during the movement to prevent the epidemic of smallpox, the three modern boys have a chance to put their theory into practice. The school authorities ask male students to go to male doctors for vaccinations, and female students to female doctors, because it is feared that the sense of touch between the opposite sexes may lead to dangerous liaisons. A, B, and C, telling the male doctor the school assigned to them to "get lost," decide to look for a woman doctor in the neighborhood instead. After searching quite a few streets, they find at last a clinic displaying a beautiful name on the sign Mifeishite 糜非時特 (Decadence-No-Time-Unique), which seems to be a Western name transcribed into Chinese. But when the doctor with the beautiful name finally appears, the three modern boys sitting patiently in the waiting room are stupefied—her entire face is pitted by smallpox.

Upon leaving the clinic after the vaccination, they ask one another, "How did it feel?" The fact is that, during the injection, none of them felt the tactile pleasures supposedly inherent in the physical contact with the opposite sex. So they come to the conclusion that tactile pleasure is possible only when reinforced by visual pleasure:

> If there is no visual pleasure, there is no way for tactile pleasure to spring into being, and as a result, the suction cups on human beings' bodies lose their sucking power.
>
> Therefore the sense of touch for the two sexes has no independent value. Even though it is the most sensitive among the five senses, it cannot but ally itself by treaty with the sense of sight.[8]

Thus by way of a "scientific experiment," the three modern boys overturn their previous assumption and arrive at a new scientific theory: The value of the sense of touch lies in its combination with the sense of sight.

Souvenirs entomologiques and Ōsugi Sakae

The palm-of-the-hand story analyzed above has connotations deeper than a mere entertaining story. It tells how, after texts and ideas travel in the Euro-Asian context, certain values are lost, or, more exactly, creatively transformed, along the way. It also tells how people from different cultures are connected through the circulation of texts and ideas. Although no names or books are ever mentioned in the story, it is clear that the parody of the comparison of human behavior with insect behavior and the ridicule of scientific experimentation point to the vogue of entomology since Lu Xun's advocacy of Fabre's *Souvenirs entomologiques* during the 1920s. Lu Xun, without knowledge of French, read the Japanese translation by two famous anarchists, Ōsugi Sakae and Shiina Sonoji, and four other translators.[9] Since it is the argument of this study that the translator's agency plays a key role in the practice of cultural translation, it is crucial that we examine the lives and thoughts of Ōsugi and Shiina as anarchists. What is the connection of anarchism with science and entomology? Was it simply coincidence that the two anarchists, who did not know each other in person, chose the same text to translate? Or, did their identity as anarchists play a decisive role for both to select this particular text to translate: *Souvenir entomologiques*?

Ōsugi was murdered with his wife Ito Noe 伊藤野枝 and seven-year-old nephew in the wake of the Great Tokyo Earthquake in September 1923, when the Japanese government cracked down on anarchists, union workers, Chinese, and Koreans. His story illustrates the transnational/transcultural characteristic of anarchism. He was closely connected with Chinese anarchists such as Liu Shipei 劉師培 (1884–1919) and Zhang Ji 張繼 (1882–1947), who learned Esperanto with him while studying and participating in anarchist activities in Tokyo in 1907 and 1908. Advocating the organization of "the alliance of Great East-Asian anarchists," Ōsugi was looked upon as mentor by many Chinese anarchists.[10] It is known that he went to Shanghai twice. In 1920, in order to participate in the Convention of Far-Eastern Socialists, he left Japan clandestinely. Arriving in Shanghai in October, he stayed there for a month before he returned secretly to Japan. On 20 November 1922, Ōsugi received a letter from a French anarchist, who invited him to participate in the international anarchist convention to be held in Berlin from 25 December to 2 January 1923. In December 1922, he stole out of Japan again. He arrived first in Shanghai and then moved on to Paris in February 1923. In St. Denis, a suburban area close to Paris, he participated and spoke in a May Day demonstration and was arrested. In June 1923 he was deported back to Japan. His second trip to Shanghai is recorded in detail in his 1923 autobiography, titled "Escapes from Japan" (Nihon dasshutsuki 日本脱出記), with his first trip constantly mentioned in passing as a comparison.[11] The complicated maneuvers and quick shifts he made in both trips in order to dodge the policemen tailing him, and the intricate connections of the international anarchists, including French, German, Russian, Chinese, Korean, and Japanese ones, are as dazzling as scenes and plots in espionage movies.

When news of Ōsugi's violent death was brought to China, it aroused a great deal of attention among Chinese anarchists. Ba Jin, the famous anarchist and novelist, published a series of works in an anarchist journal *Chunlei* 春雷 (Spring Thunder) in 1924, commemorating him as a great martyr.[12] In a poem dedicated to Ōsugi, "The Great Martyr: To the Spirit of Our Comrade Ōsugi Sakae" (Weida de xundaozhe: cheng tongzhi Dashan Rung jun zhi ling 偉大的殉道者—呈同志大杉榮君之靈), the last words of Adolph Fischer (1858–87), the American anarchist executed after the Haymarket riot in Chicago on 4 May 1886, are quoted in Chinese translation, "Hurrah for Anarchy! This is the happiest moment of my life."[13] An article in the Shanghai anarchist journal *Ziyouren* 自由人 (Free People) in May 1925 mentions that during his trip to Shanghai two years before, Ōsugi urged Chinese anarchists to keep close connections with international anarchist organizations.

Placing great value in education, anarchists believed science to be the most effective means to overthrow the feudalist past. The value of scientific education is taught by the Russian Anarchist leader Peter Kropotkin (1842–1921) in his 1912 book *Anarchism and Modern Science*, and embraced by anarchists all over the world. If the connection of anarchism and science is a given, why did anarchists such as Ōsugi and Shiina choose to translate *Souvenirs entomologiques* out of the numerous Western texts in natural science? As I will explain a little later, Ōsugi could have chosen at the time to buy the books of either Wallace, Elisée Reclus, or even Darwin, which he found in the same bookstore where he discovered Fabre's work. Why did he choose Fabre over the others? One of the initial questions raised in the beginning of this chapter is why in the practice of cultural translation a certain text is chosen in a particular historical moment. Lydia Liu, analyzing Talal Asad's study of cultural translation, describes the relationship between individual free choice and institutional practices as follows:

> Asad's critique of the notion of cultural translation has major implications for comparative scholarship and for cross-cultural studies such as this one. It warns us that the business of translating a culture into another language has little, if anything, to do with individual free choice or linguistic competence. If we have learned anything useful from Foucault, it should be clear that we must confront forms of institutional practices and the knowledge/power relationships that authorize certain ways of knowing while discouraging others.[14]

Lydia Liu here is obviously referring to Foucault in the early period, before the time of *Les mots et les choses* (The Order of Things, 1966). To complicate this issue, I think it necessary to bring in the later Foucault and re-examine his ideas concerning institutional practices and power relations, and his concept of "a state of domination" (un état de domination). For the later

Foucault, the discourse of power is not about clear-cut domination/subjugation, but about a whole network of power relations (un faisceau de relations de pouvoir) among individuals, in the family, in a pedagogical relation, or in a political entity, that are mobile and allow the participants to adopt strategies to modify these relations. It is only when power relations lose their mobility and become fixed that a state of domination is found.[15] For Foucault, the essence of knowledge/power relations is the mobility that leaves room for individuals to engage in what he calls "practices of freedom" (les pratiques de liberté), which constantly test the limits of power relations and open up grounds for new relationships. I would say, to him power relations are regulated by practices of freedom, which allow domination/subjugation relationships to be a game of continuing checks and balances, or ongoing negotiations.

Here I would like to argue that, in the case of cultural translation, the translating agency or individual free choice, though inevitably defined or conditioned by "forms of institutional practices and the knowledge/power relationships," plays a key role in the selection of a particular text. Such a translating agency, though characterized by an ambivalent nature, is, nevertheless, a decisive factor in the mediating process of cultural translation. In the case of Ōsugi and Sonoji, anarchism, as an anti-institutional trend that believed in science as a panacea for curing the mistakes of human organizations, certainly directed their attention to scientific masterpieces when they were searching for texts to translate. Yet which text in the category of science to choose from was a result of personal choice complicated by historical contingency. I will try to demonstrate this in the following discussion.

Like most anarchists who resorted to their linguistic competence to promote or learn about anarchism, Ōsugi was a talented linguist. He began studying French at school when he was 17 years old. Later, as an active anarchist, he was in and out of prison all his life. According to his 1921 autobiography, titled *Autobiography* (Jijoden 自叙伝), each time he was jailed, he managed to learn one language. That was how he learned Esperanto, Italian, Russian, and Spanish. It was in prison that he read the major works of Kropotkin and Bakunin. In the preface to *Jijoden*, he discloses that he read Fabre's *Souvenirs entomologiques* when he was serving time in Toyotama 豊多摩 Prison in Nakano from December 1919 to March 1920.[16] He was a diligent translator. In addition to anarchist treatises such as Kropotkin's *Mutual Aid* and *Memoirs of a Revolutionist*, he translated quite a few masterpieces in science, including Charles Darwin's *Origin of Species* in 1914 and the first volume of Fabre's 10-volume *Souvenirs entomologiques* in 1922. Entitled *Konchūki*, the ten volumes of the Japanese translation were published by Sōbunkaku 叢文閣 between 1922 and 1931.

According to the "Translator's Preface" (Yakusha no jo 譯者の序) included in the first volume of the Sōbunkaku translation, how Ōsugi ended up bringing *Souvenirs entomologiques* with him into Toyotama prison was partly due to his intention to read Fabre's work, and partly a result of luck. In the episode he recounts in the preface, one is able to glimpse how the working of individual agency is complicated by historical contingency. For years he had wanted to read *Souvenirs entomologiques*, but since he had been out of prison for a while, he did not have the leisure to do it. When he was detained in the temporary prison (miketsukan 未決監) in Ichigaya 市ヶ谷 before entering Toyotama prison, he remembered that he had seen three volumes of Fabre's work in the Sansaisha bookstore 三才社 in Kanda 神田, a district famous for used-books stores. So he wrote to Sansaisha from prison asking for those volumes, but they were sold out. During his bail, the day just before he entered Toyotama prison, he went to the Maruzen 丸善 district to look for travelogues to bring with him to prison to while away the time. He found *La nouvelle géographie universelle* (1892) by Elisée Reclus (1830–1905), a friend of Kropotkin's and fellow anarchist, Darwin's *What Mr. Darwin Saw in His Voyage Around the World In the ship "Beagle,"* and Alfred Russel Wallace's *Island Life: Or, the Phenomena and Causes of Insular Faunas and Floras, Including a Revision and Attempted Solution of the Problem of Geological Climates.* Then, out of pure chance, he spotted Fabre's *Souvenirs entomologiques*.[17] That was how he managed to bring this work to read in prison.

The choice of the edition to translate is where individual freedom is most clearly shown. The edition of *Souvenirs entomologiques* Ōsugi Sakae translated was the 1914 illustrated edition (Édition definitive illustré). While mainly using the first volume of this illustrated edition, he consulted at the same time the English translation by Alexander Teixeira de Mattos that had been in print since 1912. By the time Ōsugi began his translation, de Mattos had already published 12 volumes of his translation of Fabre. Ōsugi's original plan was to use his English translation, which collected in one volume insects of the same species originally dispersed in different volumes of Fabre's work. He thought this special arrangement might be more convenient and useful to the reader. But when he saw the definitive illustrated edition in French, he liked the illustrations so much that he abandoned the original plan.[18] The first volume of the illustrated edition he translated corresponds to de Mattos' *The Hunting Wasps* in 1915 in its entirety,[19] plus part of *The Mason-Bees* (les Chalicodomes) in 1916 and *The Sacred Beetle and Others* (le Scarabée sacrée) in 1918. Ōsugi mentions in the same preface that before he translated the first volume of Fabre's work, he had written an unpublished article titled "The Poet of Science" (Kagaku no shijin 科學の詩人), which is the key element we should take into consideration when discussing Ōsugi's predilection for Fabre's work over other scientific works.

After Ōsugi was murdered, Shiina Sonoji, an anarchist in spirit, continued to translate volumes 2 to 4. A Waseda 早稲田 University teacher from 1923 to 1927, he was favorably inclined towards anarchism. A native of Akida 秋田, he attended Waseda University but quit and went to the United States to study journalism at the University of Missouri, Columbia in 1908. After graduation he became a journalist, studied agriculture at Amherst College, and then cultivated a farm near St. Louis. In 1916, longing to understand the agricultural problem in France, the country of Romain Roland, he moved to Paris. He met his future wife Marie Ravaillot at a farm in the Pyrénées, where he found a job through the help of the English poet Edward Carpenter. In 1922 he brought his wife and son back to his hometown in Japan. The following year he taught in the French department recently established by Yoshie Takamatsu 吉江喬松 (1880–1940) at Waseda University. In the meantime he started a free seminar at home, teaching peasants' literature, French literature, and philosophy with his friends Yoshie and Ishikawa Sanshirō 石川三四郎 (1876–1956). During the chaos of the Great Earthquake, when the authorities arrested dissidents such as anarchists and union workers, both Shiina Sonoji and Ishikawa Sanshirō were temporarily detained by the police.[20]

Shiina started translating the second volume of *Souvenirs entomologiques* in 1924. He managed to finish translating three volumes in three years, but eventually gave up translation as well as teaching in 1927 in order to return to France, because Marie, unbearably homesick, had already gone back with their son the previous year. In Paris, working as a clerk at the Japanese Association, he also wrote articles on French agriculture and social history for journals in Japan. When Paris fell under the German occupation, he worked in the Japanese Naval Service at the Japanese embassy. During World War II he worked for the Vichy Government, but was sympathetic towards the Jews. Responding to the radio broadcasting of La France Libre, he secretly helped French Jews escape from the Nazis. After the war was over, he was held as an enemy in the Drancy detention center in 1945. As a result of the intervention of Paul Langevin (1872–1946), director of l'École de Physique et de Chimie Industrielles, who testified that he had been a friend of the Resistance and saved many lives during the war, he was released, with his health severely impaired by life in the detention center.[21] Estranged from his family, he returned to Japan once more in 1957, and then died alone in a hospital in Paris in 1962.[22]

Besides *Konchūki*, in 1925 Shiina Sonoji also translated Fabre's 1913 biography by Georges Victor Legros, titled *La Vie de J.-H. Fabre, naturaliste, par un disciple* (Life of J.-H. Fabre, naturalist, by a disciple).[23] The title of Shiina's translation is *Life of Fabre, Poet of Science* (Fāburu no shōgai, kagaku no shijin ファブルの生涯科學の詩人),[24] combining the original French title with the title of the 1913 English translation by Bernard Miall, *Fabre, Poet of Science*.[25] It is likely that when Shiina translated, he consulted both the English and the French versions. In the first chapter titled "Intuition de la nature" (intuition of nature), Legros describes how for Fabre "poetry" (la poésie) can be found everywhere in nature, and declares that Fabre was born above all a poet, a poet by instinct and vocation (il est né surtout poète ; il l'est d'instinct et de vocation).[26] Hence the English title of the book: *Poet of Science*.

To the Japanese anarchists, followers of the Russian Anarchist leader Peter Kropotkin, both Charles Darwin and Jean-Henri Fabre were great scientists. Ōsugi Sakae translated the works of both. But to Kropotkin, Fabre, because of his cosmological orientation, would not be a "scientist" in the strictest sense. I will talk about this in the last section of this chapter.

Lu Xun and Konchūki

The Japanese have had an unusual liking for Fabre's work. Besides the Sōbunkaku edition, publication of two other complete translations began in 1930. One was the 20-volume Iwanami Bunko 岩波文庫 edition (1930–52) translated by Yamada Yoshihiko 山田吉彦 and Hayashi Tatsuo 林達夫, and the other, the 10-volume ARS (Arusu) edition in 1931, translated by Iwata Toyoo 岩田豊雄 (1893–1969). After World War II, the Iwanami edition was revised twice into modern Japanese, in 1958 and 1993. In November 2005, a 20-volume edition began to be published by Shueisha 集英社, with Okumoto Daisabrō 奥本大三郎 as translator. One cannot overlook the uniqueness of the Japanese infatuation with *Souvenirs entomologiques*, considering that there is not even one complete edition in English to date. The first complete edition in Chinese did not appear until 2001.[27] What lies behind the attraction of Fabre's account of insect behavior for the Japanese? The tradition of natural history in Japan no doubt played a major role here. Because of the limited space of this study, I will not dwell on the topic here. Let us ask the same question about Lu Xun, who managed to collect the whole set of the Sōbunkaku edition one volume after another within a long period of seven years, a period long enough for anyone to give up a passing fancy. What sustained his unwavering interest in Fabre's work?

The history of how Lu Xun managed to collect the complete set is amazing in itself. He bought the sixth Sōbunkaku edition that came out in Japan in 1924. As recorded in his diary, he bought Ōsugi's translation in bookstores in both Beijing and Shanghai. The first purchases were made in Dongya Bookstore 東亞書店 in Beijing on 28 November and 16 December 1924. In 1926, the year before the Nationalist government's party purge broke out, Lu Xun moved from Beijing to Amoy 廈門, and then left Amoy in early 1927 for Canton and on to Shanghai in October. The rest of the set were bought in Uchiyama Bookstore 內山書店 in Shanghai starting in October 1927. The purchases were made on 5 and 31 October 1927, 15 February, 2 May, and 23 December 1930, and 17 January, 3 February, 5 September, 29 September, 4 November, and 19 November 1931.[28] Even during the last year of his life, he bought the English translation of *Souvenirs entomologiques* consecutively by mail from England, planning to translate it with his brother Zhou Jianren 周建人.[29] But the plan never saw light before he died of tuberculosis in 1936.

Uchiyama Bookstore, in business between 1917 and 1945, served as a bridge between Chinese and Japanese intellectuals at the time. Japan as a vector of Western thought for China is best illustrated when we examine the history of the bookstore. Its owner Uchiyama Kanzō 內山完造 (1885–1959), with recommendations from Japanese missionaries, first came to China in

1913 and worked as a salesman at the Shanghai branch of the Osaka-based Santendō 参天堂, a pharmaceutical company in business since 1890.[30] The company was famous for the eye-lotion called "College Eye-Lotion" (Daigaku Megusuri 大學目薬) it launched in 1899 to cure the various eye diseases rampant in Meiji Japan.[31] Uchiyama went back to Japan to marry Inoue Mikiko 井上美喜子 in 1916. The newlyweds returned together to Shanghai and established the Uchiyama Bookstore in the Japanese concession the following year. Starting in 1920, with the help of the Shanghai Association of Christian Youth, the bookstore sponsored a summer seminar for years, inviting professors from Japanese universities to give talks. In 1923 Uchiyama established the journal *Mirror of Ten Thousand Flowers,* or *Kaleidoscope* (Mangekyō or Bankakyō万華鏡). With the regular "mantankai" (random talk meetings 漫談會), the bookstore had already become a salon for Chinese and Japanese intellectuals. After Lu Xun moved to Shanghai in 1927, he and Uchiyama became friends instantly, and their friendship lasted until Lu Xun's death.[32]

During the 1930s, when the Nationalist government tightened its control and cracked down on Communist activities, Uchiyama Bookstore became a haven for leftist intellectuals. Lu Xun and his family took refuge there several times, once hiding out for more than a month in March 1930. When Lu Xun's brother Zhou Jianren and his family were arrested by the Japanese navy in March 1932, it was Uchiyama who intervened and effected their release. Because his constant intervention for the sake of his Chinese friends aroused strong suspicion from the Japanese military, he had to return temporarily to Japan for his own safety in April 1932. Uchiyama's wife died in Shanghai in January 1945, and the bookstore was confiscated by the Nationalist government on 23 October 1945, following the end of World War II. But Uchiyama stayed on and opened a second-hand bookstore in February 1947, selling books he had bought from the Japanese planning to return home. At the end of that year he was deported to Japan with other Japanese. But Uchiyama's love of China did not end there. During the 1950s, he visited China three times. The third time, invited to participate in the celebration of the 10th anniversary of the People's Republic of China, he died of a stroke in Beijing on 20 September 1959. In accordance with his will, he was buried in the International Cemetery in Shanghai, where his wife Mikiko as well as Lu Xun rested in peace.

The books Lu Xun bought at Uchiyama Bookstore cover vastly diverse topics, including the complete works of Japanese authors such as Kuriyagawa Hakuson 厨川白村 and Akutagawa Ryūnosuke, the 12-volume *Complete Works of World Arts* (Sekai bijutsu zenshū 世界美術全集) published by Heibonsha 平凡社, and Japanese translations of Marxist literature. His collection of books, more than 4,000 titles and altogether more than 14,000 volumes, are mostly housed in the Lu Xun Museum in Beijing today. A true book lover, Lu Xun's particular liking for *Konchūki* can be witnessed by the article he wrote on the subject.

In his 1925 essay "Random Talks in the Late Spring" (Chunmo xiantan 春末閑談), Lu Xun talks about Fabre's *Souvenirs entomologiques*, but he does not seem to be aware that the translator of the Japanese version, *Konchūki*, was a famous anarchist. In the beginning of the essay, Lu Xun compares a legend about the digger wasp recounted by elderly people in his hometown with a passage in Fabre's work. According to Lu Xun, the elders believed that "since digger wasps are all females, they need to catch beetles to be their foster children. One wasp would seal a beetle in her hive, while she herself would flap her wings and strike at the outside of the hive, wishing at the same time, 'Grow like me, grow like me.' After a few days—I don't remember how many, maybe seven times seven, or 49 days—the beetle eventually becomes a wasp."[33] This is, in fact, an imaginative elaboration on "The beetle's son is raised by the digger wasp" (mingling you zi, guoluo fu zhi 螟蛉有子，果蠃負之), a simple sentence in *Classic of Poetry* (Shijing 詩經), which was later recorded in a slightly more complicated form in *Book of Gods* (Soushenji 搜神記).

In the same article Lu Xun continues to say that, even if some experts of ancient texts have already pointed out that digger wasps are able to lay eggs, and that the beetles are kept in the beehives to feed the wasp's larvae, Chinese people would rather believe the foster-children version, which sounds legendary and more interesting than reality. He then compares this version with the scientific finding in Fabre's work, not without his usual touch of sarcasm on Chinese national character:

> Foreigners are so annoying, with their scientific crap and all that. Even though science does bring many surprises, it disturbs our fond dreams as well. Since the great French entomologist Fabre's close observation, the fact of the beetle serving as feed for the larvae has been proved. In addition, the digger wasp is not just an ordinary killer, but a cruel one—an anatomist with great knowledge and skill. She knows the organization and function of the beetle's nerve system. With a magic, poisonous sting, she gives its motor nucleus simply one thrust, leaving it in a paralyzed state, neither living nor dead. She then lays eggs on its body, and seals it in the beehive. Because the beetle is in a state neither living nor dead, it can neither move nor decompose. Therefore all the time her children are hatching, the feed remains as fresh as the day when it was caught.[34]

Thus Lu Xun, as he is always wont to do, takes this opportunity to comment on the national character of Chinese people as shown in the juxtaposition of these two versions of the story of the digger wasp: Chinese, so complacent in rural pleasure and traditional interpretation of nature, stubbornly turn their backs on science, unaware of the progress foreigners have made in scientific studies beyond their imagination.

In addition, Lu Xun dwells on the digger wasp's art of anesthesia and further turns it into an attack on the relentless control of the ruling class. He recounts a dialogue between himself and a Russian gentleman M. E concerning the possibility of a medicine invented by scientists for the government to control its people:

> Three years ago I became acquainted with M. E from Russia, who was hypersensitive. One day out of the blue he said with great concern, "I hope future scientists will not go so far as to invent some magic medicine, which, if injected into a person, will make him content to do service and to be a war machine forever." ... He didn't know that the great emperors, courtiers, and saints and their disciples in our country had already shared this golden world ideal long ago. ... The thing to regret is that, even though the theory was excellent, no good method had been invented. In order to make them obey the emperor's will, the people have to be kept as if dead; in order to make them contribute food to feed the rulers, they have to be kept alive. If you want them to be ruled, they should be like dead people; if you want them to feed you, they have to be living. As the most gifted of all living creatures, man should be congratulated, of course. But, without the poisonous sting of the digger wasp, it has encumbered our great emperors, courtiers, and saints and disciples of yore, and rich men, scholars and educators of present days. We don't know about the future yet. As to the past, even though rulers had tried their best with all kinds of paralyzing methods on the people, no method has been as effective as that of the digger wasp.[35]

"Random Talks in the Late Spring" was published in April 1925. The "M. E from Russia" referred to in this passage was no doubt Vasilii Eroshenko (1890–1952), the Russian Esperantist who had been off and on in China from 1921 to 1923, probably staying a year altogether. Before he came to China, he had lived in Japan from April 1914 to 1916 and then from July 1919 to 1921, and was known there as "the blind Russian poet."[36] He became associated with the labor movement led by people such as Ōsugi Sakae and was deported because of his socialist activities.[37]

During Eroshenko's stay in China, he lived with Zhou Zuoren's family in Beijing for four months, while teaching Esperanto at Beijing University.[38] Eroshenko had published children's stories and three collections of poems in Japanese.[39] Lu Xun published translations of some of his stories into Chinese, for instance, "A Spring Night's Dream" (Chunye de meng 春夜的夢) in October 1921[40] and "The Tragedy of a Chicken" (Xiaoji de beiju 小雞的悲劇) in September 1922. The latter was the only story that Eroshenko wrote in Beijing. After Eroshenko left China in 1922, Lu Xun published an article titled "The Comedy of Ducks" (Ya de xiju 鴨的喜劇) in December of that year, describing Eroshenko as a man who "maintained that each person should labor to feed himself; while women could raise animals, men should work in the field."[41] In "Random Talks in the Late Spring," the hypersensitive "M. E from Russia," who worries about the ruling class wanting to paralyze the people in order to have a total control over them, does fit the image of Eroshenko as a socialist activist who often participated in May Day activities.

After the "M. E from Russia" episode in the essay, Lu Xun continues to criticize "a special intellectual class," namely people with degrees from abroad, who are also feeding on the people. He concludes that the Chinese government, or any other government, can deprive people of the freedom of gathering and speech, but cannot prohibit them from thinking. If the rulers could cut off people's heads and still keep them at service and use them as war machines, Lu Xun says, it would be easy to distinguish rulers from slaves, officials from people, and noblemen from underdogs. The result would be that no revolution is possible, and "a lot of telegrams would be saved."[42] From Fabre's *Souvenirs entomologiques* to ruminations on the Chinese national character, and then to the critique of the ruling class, Lu Xun does not seem to be particularly interested in science *per se*, but rather in science as a weapon of cultural critique.

Jean-Henri Fabre and Charles Darwin

Lu Xun's account of the episode of the digger wasp paralyzing the beetle is taken from Chapter 5, Volume 1 of *Souvenirs entomologiques*, where Fabre refers to the digger wasp by its scientific names, *Cerceris* and *Hyménoptère* (*guêpe* in common French). This chapter, titled "Un savant tueur" (A Master Killer) in the original, is titled "Koroshi no meijin" 殺しの名人 in Ōsugi Sakae's translation.[43] It recounts how the wasp subjects the beetle (Coléoptère in French) to anesthesia with a scientific skill far surpassing what an anatomist is able to do in a laboratory.

According to Fabre, the digger wasp needs to stock in an underground cell a certain amount of beetles for its larvae to feed on, which are hatched from the eggs laid on the heap of feed.[44] To accomplish this, there are three major tasks for the digger wasp: (1) Since the larvae eat only the viscera of a living insect, how can one paralyze the beetle for an extended period of time, from three weeks to one or even two months, without killing it? (2) How is the nerve apparatus of the beetle constructed, and above all, where is the nodal point to inject the paralyzing agent so that the effect will be instant and prolonged? (3) Out of the numerous kinds of beetle, which kinds are easy victims of the digger wasp's poison? Fabre's comment is that this is an art beyond human capability:

> Devant pareil problème alimentaire, l'homme du monde, possédât-il la plus large instruction, resterait impuissant ; l'entomologiste pratique lui-même s'avouerait inhabile. Le garde-manger du Cerceris défierait leur raison.[45]
>
> (Facing the same alimentary problem, a human being with the best education would be powerless; even the sensible entomologist would have

to admit that he is inept. The digger wasp's art of food preservation would challenge their reasoning.)

To compare humans with insects, while maintaining that the instinct upon which insects behave is far superior to the most advanced human technical know-how, is one of the prevailing agendas throughout Fabre's work. He proves this by imagining a group of anatomists and physiologists as renowned as Marie-Jean Pierre Florens (1794–1867), François Magendie (1783–1855), and Claude Bernard (1813–78), gathering together to solve the problem. The easiest way that comes to their mind is the use of food preservatives. But it is a gratuitous assumption, since food preservatives will never be able to conserve a living animal. Then it dawns on the learned group that paralysis is the issue here—one should paralyze the insect without killing it. The questions that immediately follow are these: How is the nerve apparatus of the insect constructed, and above all, where is the nodal point to inject the paralyzing agent? No doubt it should be in the brain and along the spinal marrow, as is with superior animals. But our learned group of anatomists and physiologists will tell you that this is a serious mistake. Fabre informs us, " . . . l'insecte est comme un animal renversé, qui marcherait sur le dos ; c'est-à-dire qu'au lieu d'avoir la moelle épinière en haut, il l'a en bas, le long de la poitrine et du ventre."[46] (An insect is like an animal reversed, which walks on its back; that is to say, instead of having the spinal marrow on top, it has it at the bottom, along the chest and the abdomen.)

After the position of the nodal point is decided, there arises the following problem: Unlike a well-controlled situation in a laboratory, where the anatomist uses a scalpel to treat his patient, with all obstacles removed at ease, the digger wasp's delicate sting, on the other hand, is dealing with the beetle equipped with solid breast armor. Although the joints of the beetle are vulnerable, they are not where it should be operated on, because a sting on them would induce only local paralysis. It is crucial to direct the sting to the nerve-centers in order to bring about an instant general paralysis. Fabre explains to us in great detail the construction of the nerve-centers of "les insectes à l'état parfait" (well-grown insects), in order to show what complicated procedures are involved in the seemingly simple operation, and to eulogize the digger wasp for accomplishing it with such precision and dexterity through the guidance of "instinct" alone. The fact is that the nerve-centers of all mature insects consist of three ganglions, to which two passages are possible for the beetle's delicate sting to get through. One passage is located in the joint between the neck and the prothorax, bearing the first pair of legs, while the other is in the joint between the prothorax and the thorax, or between the first and second pairs of legs. The former will not do, because it is too far away from the ganglions; it is the latter where the digger wasp should plunge its dart. Fabre marvels by uttering a rhetorical question: "Par quelle docte intelligence est-il donc inspiré ?" (By what learned intelligence is it thus inspired?)

The difficulty is not only where to plunge the sting, but also which kinds of beetle to choose. For all kinds of beetle, the ganglions are more or less grouped together. The ganglions of some kinds are almost contiguous, while those of some other kinds are completely welded together. The more blended the ganglions are, the more animated the beetles are, and therefore, the more vulnerable. These are the kinds that should be the digger wasp's easy prey. With a single plunge of its sting, these kinds of beetle will be paralyzed instantly. But which are they? Will the high science of a physiologist like Claude Bernard teach us the right choices? No. Without looking into the archives in his library, it is impossible for him to find which kinds of beetle have ganglions blended together; even if he looked in the library, he would not know instantly where to find the information he wants.

Fabre finds the answer in Emile Blancard's (1816–1900) article published in the journal *Annales des sciences naturelles*.[47] According to his analysis, the *Scarabéiens* are too big for the wasp to attack or carry to the cell for storage. Some other kinds of beetle such as the *Histérien* live in filth and will never be sought by the digger wasp, which is always neat and clean. The *Scolytien* is too small in size. Among the numerous kinds of beetle, only the jewel beetle (Bupreste) and the snout beetle (Charançon) fit the need of all eight kinds of digger wasp. To Fabre, one should be amazed by the fact that these two kinds, so different in their appearances, resemble each other only in the structure of their nerve-centers, something unobservable from their looks:

> Une certaine ressemblance intérieure, c'est-à-dire la centralisation de l'appareil nerveux, telle serait donc la cause qui, dans les repaires des divers Cerceris, fait entasser des victimes ne se ressemblant en rien pour le dehors.[48]
>
> (A certain inner resemblance, that is to say the centralization of the nerve structure, is therefore the cause for the victims, so unalike in appearances, to be heaped in diverse digger wasps' dens.)

So how does the digger wasp manage to discern at an instant the right kinds of beetle as the easy victims of the paralyzing agent, a mystery that may take a scientist years of observation and study to resolve? Fabre attributes the digger wasp's marvelous ability to "un savoir transcendant" (a transcendent wisdom), saying it can be proved that "[L]'Hyménoptère a, dans les inspirations inconscientes de son instinct, les ressources d'une sublime science." (The digger wasp has, in the unconscious inspiration of its instinct, the resources of a sublime science.)[49] His method to prove this is by way of an experiment, injecting drops of ammonia with the sharp point of a metal pen into the beetles' nerve-centers. The effects of experimenting with the kinds equipped with welded ganglions and those with ganglions grown apart differ enormously. With the first group, the effect is instant, with all movements suddenly ceased. The paralysis can last from three weeks to two months, while the beetle is alive, its viscera as fresh as that of a living insect. With the second group, on the other hand, the inoculation causes violent convulsions and struggles before the insect slowly calms down. But after a few hours or one or two days of rest, it resumes its usual movements and vitality, as energetic as before. Fabre's conclusion is that the digger wasp's instinct of choosing the right beetles for feed is equal to what the wisest physiologist and the best anatomist can teach. He closes the chapter with the following remarks: "Vainement on s'efforcerait de ne voir là que des concordances fortuites : ce n'est pas avec le hasard que s'expliquent de telles harmonies."[50] (In vain does one try hard to see nothing but fortuitous concord here; such great harmony cannot be explained away by chance.)

I have tried to analyze this chapter in such great length and detail in order to show that, despite all his meticulous scientific observation and careful experiments, Fabre's interpretation of the digger wasp's instinct is limited by his presumption that everything with such harmony and perfection has to have a designer—God. This presumption, known as "natural theology," had been prevalent since the eighteenth century. The famous historian Peter J. Bowler explains in the following words the implications of this theory:

> Traditional accounts of Darwin's discovery tend to imply that little attention was being paid to the idea of evolution by other biologists during the decades leading up to 1859 [the year Darwin's *On the Origin of Species* was published]. It is assumed that almost everyone accepted a fairly straightforward creationism and that the vast majority of biologists went out of their way to argue that the adaptation of each species to its environment proved the existence of a wise and benevolent Creator. William Paley's *Natural Theology* of 1802 is seen as a classic exposition of this 'argument from design'—the claim that species are designed by an intelligent Creator in the way that a watch is designed and built by a watchmaker.[51]

Fabre was very much in the tradition of "natural theology," believing in the superiority of animal instinct, the manifestation of divine wisdom, to reason, created by the human brain. According to him, the lower animals' instinct of survival, seemingly guided by reason, is in fact the illumination of divine spirit. With the first volume of *Souvenirs entomologiques* written in 1879, the one biologist he ridicules often for attributing reason to animal behavior is Erasmus Darwin (1731–1802), Charles Darwin's grandfather. For instance, in Chapter 9 of Volume 1, titled "Les hautes théories" (The High Theories), Fabre recounts an episode in Lacordaire's "Introduction à l'entomologie" in which Erasmas Darwin, witnessing a sphex (digger wasp) cutting off the head, the abdomen, and then the wings of a fly before it manages to carry the victim to its nest, concludes that the sphex dismembers its victim so that the unnecessary parts will not hamper it during its flight, and that nothing but reason can explain the series of activities engaging the efforts of the sphex. Fabre comments, "Darwin a vu ce qu'il nous dit, seulement il s'est mépris sur le héros du drame, sur le drame lui-même et sa signification. Il s'est profondément mépris, et je le prouve" (Darwin saw what he tells us, but he was mistaken about the hero of the drama, about the drama itself and its significance. He is seriously mistaken, and I will prove it).[52] First, he criticizes "le vieux savant anglais" (the old English scientist) for his laxity in naming the insects. Since all the members in the species of the sphex capture only the praying mantis (*mante religieuse* in French, or Orthoptère), how could the sphex in England be so aberrant as to catch the fly, which is the same size as the sphex? Erasmus Darwin was certainly not looking at a sphex. Then, what exactly did he see?[53] There is the same ambiguity with the term "fly" (*mouche* in French), which could indicate thousands of species, according to Fabre. He thought the hero must have been a wasp (*guêpe* in French) rather than a sphex. Then, after elaborate, graphic descriptions, which I will not repeat here, of how he observes several species of wasp, including the common wasp (*la guêpe commune*, or *vespa vulgaris*) and the hornet (*la guêpe frelon*, or *vespa crabo*), kill and dismember their victims, he concludes it was a common wasp attacking a big fly (*Elistalis tenax*) that Erasmus Darwin describes in his book.

So Fabre has solved the mystery of the "hero of the drama." The remaining question is about the "significance" of the "drama": Why does the common wasp dismember the big fly before it carries the victim to its nest? Fabre's answer is simple: Because the discarded parts have no nutrition value for the common wasp's larvae; only the thorax of the big fly is useful for feeding. Is the common wasp, in its ingenious act, guided by reason, as Erasmas Darwin so believes? Of course not, according to Fabre. He maintains, "Loin d'y voir le moindre indice de raisonnement, je n'y trouve qu'un acte d'instinct, si élémentaire qu'il ne vaut vraiment pas la peine de s'y arrêter" (Far from seeing the least sign of reason, I find it nothing but an act of instinct, so elementary that it is really not worth dwelling on).[54] One can easily see that Fabre and Erasmas Darwin, observing the same natural phenomenon, arrive at different interpretations. It is the position of natural theology to maintain that science alone cannot arrive at "truth"; it is revealed in divine providence that shines through the surface phenomenon.

Natural theology, prevalent from the eighteenth century to the mid nineteenth century, was based on the beliefs that God's existence can be proved by observing nature and through personal interpretation rather than theological definition. These notions carried through to theosophy, a new religious trend that emerged in the mid nineteenth century. Madame H. P. Blavatsky (1831–91), the founder of the Theosophical Society which was based in New York and later spread to India, Ceylon, London, and Paris, constantly argued against scientists such as Charles Darwin, Thomas Huxley (1825–95), and John Tyndall (1820–1893). She says in her 1877 book *Isis Unveiled*:

> Reason being a faculty of our physical brain, one which is justly defined as that of deducting inferences from premises, and being wholly dependent on the evidence of other senses, cannot be a quality pertaining to our

divine spirit. The latter *knows*—hence all reasoning which implies discussion and argument would be useless. . . .

Reason, the outgrowth of the physical brain, develops at the expense of instinct—the flickering reminiscence of a once divine omniscience—spirit. . . . Reason is the clumsy weapon of scientists—intuition the unerring guide of the seer.[55]

Madame Blavatsky, likewise born of Russian aristocratic parents, shared the religious views of Count Leo Tolstoy (1828–1910), who spurned Voltaire's *la raison* and embraced Rousseau's *le Coeur*.[56] Tolstoy believed that the inner spirit of man, or conscience, alone "constitutes the link between man and God,"[57] and militated against the notion of the Church as the mediator and only authority of God's knowledge. He did not believe that Christianity was the sole possessor of the truth and that other religions such as Buddhism, Islam, and Confucianism were in error. Neither did he believe that the state is a legitimate institution, going so far as to say that "The law of man is nonsense. . . . I will never serve any state anywhere. . . . All governments are equal with regard to good and evil. The highest ideal is anarchy."[58] He was against the Hegelian theory of historical progress, observing that "Nothing so impedes freedom of thought like faith in progress."[59] Madame Blavatsky's theosophical teachings borrowed a great deal from Tolstoy's views. She defends his position in the article titled "Is Theosophy a Religion?" published in *Lucifer*, a journal she established in London from 1887 to 1891:

> Count Leo N. Tolstoy does not believe in the Bible, the Church, or the divinity of Christ; and yet no Christian surpasses him in the practical bearing out of the principles alleged to have been preached on the Mount. And these principles are those of Theosophy; not because they were uttered by the Christian Christ, but because they are universal ethics, and were preached by Buddha and Confucius, Krishna, and all the great Sages, thousands of years before the Sermon on the Mount was written. . . .
>
> The modern Materialist insists on an impassable chasm between the two [religion and science], pointing out that the "Conflict between Religion and Science" has ended in the triumph of the latter and the defeat of the first. The modern Theosophist refuses to see, on the contrary, any such chasm at all. . . . Theosophy claims to reconcile the two foes. It premises by saying that the *true* spiritual and primitive Christian religion is, as much as the other great and still older philosophies that preceded it—*the light of Truth*—"the life and the light of men."[60] [Original italics]

On the one hand, both Tolstoy and Madame Blavatsky distrusted the Church as an institution and believed in the inner light of man and universal brotherhood. On the other, both embraced "primitivism" in religion and disliked the crass materialism represented by science. Although there is no explicit record of Fabre's attitude towards the Church, we know that he and his family were once evicted from their home in Avignon because the Church was displeased with his free courses taught to young girls (more will be said about this later in this chapter). We also know that he was critical of contemporary scientists and scientific theories. Evolution, one of the "hautes théories" Fabre mocked and associated with "progress," and the idea of transmutation are criticized throughout *Souvenirs entomologiques*. In Chapter 9 of Volume 2, titled "Les fourmis rousses" (The Redhead Ants), discussing why the pigeon transported to a long distance knows where to regain its columbary, and the swallow where to find its nest across the ocean when returning from its winter quarters in Africa, Fabre challenges the opinions currently among "les évolutionnistes." He asks a key question: Whatever guides this special sense possessed by animals and insects, be it the eyesight, the meteorology, or magnetism, why are human beings deprived of such a unique quality? After all, "C'était une belle arme et de grande utilité pour le *struggle for life*" (it would be a beautiful weapon and of great service to the struggle for life). The sarcastic tone here is unmistakable. If human beings were endowed with such a unique quality, wouldn't it be great progress? According to evolutionists such as Charles Darwin and his grandfather before him, Fabre says, all animal life, including the human being, originates from a unique cell and has been transmutating throughout the ages, with the better gifted favored and the less gifted perishing. Then how does it happen that this marvelous sense, shared by the lower species, has not left a single trace in the human being, the culminating point of "la série zoologique" (the zoological scale)? He says:

> Si la transmission ne s'est pas faite, ne serait-ce pas faute d'une parenté suffisante ? Je soumets le petit problème aux évolutionnistes, et suis très désireux de savoir ce qu'en dissent le protoplasme et le nucléus.[61]
>
> (If the transmission [of such a great quality] is not made, wouldn't it be the lapse of sufficient parentage? I submit this small problem to evolutionists, and desire to know what the protoplasm and the nucleus would say about this.)

In Chapter 6, Volume 2 titled "Les odynères" (Beetles), after praising the insect's instinct, Fabre explicitly criticizes the theory of evolution while confirming the "Intelligence" of the maker of the universe:

> Le monde est-il soumis aux fatalités d'évolution du premier atome albumineux qui se coagula en cellule ; ou bien est-il régi par une Intelligence ? Plus je vois, plus j'observe, et plus cette Intelligence rayonne derrière le mystère des choses.[62]
>
> (Is the world subjected to the fatality of the evolution of the first albuminous atom which coagulated into a cell, or is it rather governed by

an Intelligence? The more I look, the more I observe, the more this Intelligence shines through the mystery of things.)

In writing his book on instinct and insect behavior, Fabre was no doubt responding to the theory of evolution, which, denying the existence of a miraculous maker, was heresy to many learned men like him at the time. Indeed, in *On the Origin of Species*, Darwin takes up the position of a defender of science, constantly reminding the reader not "to enter into the realms of miracle, and to leave those of Science."[63] He addresses the issue of instinct, habit, and natural selection in Chapter 8, titled "Instinct." For instinctive actions performed by animals or people without knowing for what purposes they were performed, Darwin believes that "A little dose of judgment or reason, as Pierre Huber expresses it, often comes into play, even with animals low in the scale of nature."[64] Admitting instinct to be inherited, Darwin emphasizes that it can be lost with disuse, and can be generated and acquired as a habit because of selection, as is the case with domestic animals. He maintains that because there are variations in the same species in nature, "natural selection might have secured and fixed any advantageous variation."[65] His conclusion is that what seem to be instincts in animals may be interpreted as the results of natural selection:

> Finally, it may not be a logical deduction, but to my imagination it is far more satisfactory to look at such instincts as the young cuckoo ejecting its foster-brothers,—ants making slaves,—the larvae of ichneumonidae feeding within the live bodies of caterpillars,—not as specially endowed or created instincts, but as small consequences of one general law leading to the advancement of all organic beings,—namely, multiply, vary, let the strongest live and the weakest die.[66]

In contrast, Fabre believed that insect behavior is constant and formulaic, not subject to change and variation. When put in a different situation, the instinct that guides an insect unerringly to accomplish its daily routine may lead to its death. He thought he was objective, but did not realize that his conclusion was in fact guided by his theory, or preconceptions.[67]

Fabre and Darwin were different not only in their scientific views, but in origin. Unlike Darwin—a gentleman naturalist born into a wealthy gentry family—Fabre was a self-made man, born into a family without means in Saint-Léons-du-Lévezou, a small village in Provence. He managed to get a solid training in Latin, Greek, history, and literature at the university chapel in Rodez, where his parents moved in 1833 to make a living by establishing a café. He won the scholarship of l'École Normale (Normal School), passed the *baccalauréat* examinations by learning algebra and analytic geometry on his own, and received the licence in sciences, mathematics, and physics.[68] While teaching at the Lycée d'Avignon (Avignon High School) in 1855, he presented a thesis for the doctorate in sciences in Paris.[69] With the income of a high school teacher and honoraria from private lessons, Fabre, raising a family of five children (there would be eight altogether), was struggling to make ends meet. It was the writing of textbooks, such as *Leçons élémentaires de chimie agricole* (Elementary Lessons of Agricultural Chemistry, 1862), and popular science books, such as *La terre et le ciel* (Earth and Heaven, 1865), that increased his income. In 1866 he received from the Academy of Sciences the Thore Prize with a 3000 francs award, which, almost twice his annual salary, finally relieved him from financial strain, at least temporarily.[70] From 1866 to 1873, he served as curator of the Requien Museum. In 1879, with the copyright from *Souvenirs entomologiques*, he managed to purchase l'Harmas, the house and garden in Sérignan du Comtat, where he would live from the following year to the end of his life.[71]

Fabre was raised in the countryside in the center of France. Yves Delange, his biographer, calling him "ce provincial, paysan et erudit" (this provincial, peasant and erudite), points out that all his life Fabre maintained his Languedoc accent and dressed like a peasant from Provence. Two famous incidents in his life illustrate well how much at odds he was with Parisian ways of thinking and manners. In June of 1865, in order to solve the problem of the silkworm diseases that were ravaging le Midi (southern Europe) and the Mediterranean countries, Louis Pasteur (1822–95), the administrator and director of scientific studies of l'École Normale Supérieure in Paris, came to le Midi, and was advised to visit the great entomologist in the region to learn about the life of the silkworm. During this encounter, first of all, Fabre was shocked that Pasteur, whose mission was to battle the silkworm diseases, knew nothing about the cocoon, the chrysalis, and the metamorphosis of the caterpillar. Next, when Pasteur, an expert on fermentation and wine-making, said to Fabre, "Montrez-moi votre cave" (Show me your wine cellar), the latter was embarrassed beyond measure. His "cave" was nothing but a demijohn of a dozen liters put on a shabby kitchen chair![72] Of course, after this unfortunate encounter, there was no further communication between the two scientists.

Another incident revealing Fabre's simple modesty was his meeting in 1867 with Victor Duruy (1811–94), the Minister of Public Instruction. The latter came to visit him for his research on garancine, a pigment extracted from the plant called *la garance*, which was a rich source of income for both agriculture and industry in Vaucluse and Provence. When the minister asked him if he needed financial aide to buy better equipment for his laboratory, Fabre asked simply for "une poignée de main" (a handshake) with the minister.[73] In 1868 Duruy appointed him *chevalier de la légion d'honneur* (Knight of the Legion of Honor). After the decoration, he was brought to the Tuileries to have an audience with the Emperor. But to him, the entourage of the society of distinguished scientists tending the Emperor, with so much attention and acuity, was like "le monde des insectes" (a world of insects). The "chambellans" (gentlemen in charge of services in the Emperor's chamber), in their shorts and shoes with silvery buckles, were "des scarabées" (the beetles) in his eye.[74] This sarcasm towards high society in fact carries through to *Souvenirs entomologiques*, in which great physiologists and anatomists of the time are often mocked.

For any man who aspired to make his way in the scientific world, the first place to go would be Paris, where the scientists associated with each other and formed a network. But all his life Fabre kept a discreet distance from Paris and the scientific circles, satisfied in his idyllic world in Provence. Those he had close ties with were people of the same origin and mind, for instance, the poet and prose writer Joseph Roumanille (1818–91), who was the initiator in the renaissance movement of the provençal language and literature. Another long-term friend he cherished was the British philosopher and economist John Stuart Mill (1806–73), who spoke for the rights of peasants, workers, and women in Parliament.[75] Besides sympathizing with peasants and workers, Fabre himself took an interest in women's education. In 1871 the Fabres were evicted from their home in Avignon, because the free night courses Fabre taught to young girls infringed the interests of the Church—up to then the education of young girls had been the exclusive prerogative of the Church. The whole issue was connected with Victor Duruy's reform of the educational system starting in 1867. The innovation of adult education and popular instruction was thwarted when Duruy stepped down from the Ministry of Public Instruction two years later.[76]

Fabre's mockery of contemporary scientists in the Parisian establishment was in line with his stance as a provençal in the idyllic tradition. Charles Darwin, a gentlemen naturalist in the British establishment and a member of the Academy of Sciences, was certainly the representative of the "high society" that Fabre was highly suspicious of. In addition, Fabre's opposition to the theory of transmutation was deep-rooted. He was totally averse to Darwinian theories, referring to them as "l'inanité des brutales théories darwiniennes" (the inanity of the brutal Darwinian theories).[77] The thing to note is that, even though Fabre was critical of evolutionists such as Erasmus and Charles Darwin, the latter showed great respect for the French master's keen observation of insects, referring to him as "that inimitable observer M. Fabre" in Chapter 4 of the fourth edition of *On the Origin of Species* in 1866.[78] The two of them in fact carried on a correspondence for some time. On 3 January 1880 Fabre sent Darwin a copy of the first volume of *Souvenirs entomologiques*, published in the previous year, no doubt hoping to know the opinion of the renowned English evolutionist, who was his senior by fourteen years, while the latter thanked him in a letter dated 6 January. After reading it, Darwin wrote on 31 January, telling Fabre that Erasmus Darwin, his grandfather, instead of talking about a sphex, was referring to a wasp cutting off the wings of a fly. Fabre immediately made remedy by putting in a note in Chapter 10, Volume 2 of *Souvenirs entomologiques*, apologizing for his previous mistake resulting from reading a French translation, which renders "wasp" (*la guêpe* in French) into "sphex." On 18 February Fabre wrote to Darwin about French peasants' custom of putting a cat into a bag while rotating it, in order to prevent the cat, thrown away in another part of the town, from finding its way home. In a letter dated 20 February 1880, Darwin expresses his interest in Fabre's "experiment of rotation." On 21 January 1881, Darwin wrote to Fabre on the latter's experiments with the sense of direction of animals, while suggesting an experiment involving magnetism. Fabre had sent Darwin his essay on Haclitus, and the latter thanked him.[79] Their correspondence did not continue since Darwin died in 1882.

The "dialogue" between Fabre and Darwin, two scientists separate in their ways of interpreting the same natural phenomena, discloses a fundamental issue concerning the antagonism between science and religion since the eighteenth century in Europe. To the Japanese anarchists who translated both Fabre and Darwin, and to the Chinese literary men who took both to be champions of science, the opposition between the two probably never entered their minds.

A traveling text

This chapter is about the story of a traveling text, *Souvenirs entomologiques*. Originating in the countryside of France at the turn of the last century, it traveled to the great metropolis in Japan during the early 1920s when anarchists were persecuted in the Taishō period, and then through Japan to the Chinese treaty port in the turbulent years of civil strife aggravated by Japanese invasion in the late 1920s and early 1930s. At a time of international political turmoil, it traveled across the boundaries of nations and languages, connecting the minds of men who did not know each other in person. Most important, it exemplifies how European concepts and ideas traveled to China with Japan as the vector, a topic yet insufficiently researched.

Not only did this text travel across the borders of nations, but it also traveled across the boundaries of disciplines: from natural sciences in France to social sciences (anarchism) in Japan, and then to literature in China. The interdisciplinary movement of this particular text was made possible because of the concept of science as progress, prevalent in Europe, America, and Asia during the late nineteenth and early twentieth centuries. But a concept or an idea, as it moves from a certain culture of a particular historical period to another culture and period, will inevitably be transformed or take on new meanings, as Edward Said says in "Traveling Theory":

> There are particularly interesting cases of ideas and theories that move from one culture to another, as when so-called Eastern ideas about transcendence were imported into Europe during the early nineteenth century, or when certain European ideas about society were translated into traditional Eastern societies during the later nineteenth century. Such movement into a new environment is never unimpeded. It necessarily involves processes of representation and institutionalization different from those at the point of origin. This complicates any account of the

transplantation, transference, circulation, and commerce of theories and ideas.[80]

For a concept such as science as progress, the "point of origin" is hard to pinpoint. But if we consult Kropotkin's words in *Modern Science and Anarchism*, it would be clear that, to him, this concept originates from the mid nineteenth century, when both natural and social sciences began a revolutionary phase. He believes that the inductive method of science (developed by the French Encyclopaedists in the eighteenth century) alone is sufficient in the study of religions, the moral sense, and history of thought, while "metaphysical conceptions" such as the "immortal soul," "imperative and categorical laws" inspired by a superior being, meaning Kantian theory, together with the "purely dialectic method," meaning Hegelian theory, are losing their grip to "mechanical facts." In Kropotkin's mind, the thinkers of the eighteenth century such as the Encyclopaedists "endeavored to explain the whole of the universe and all its phenomena in the same way as naturalists," forerunners of Charles Darwin. According to him, even though science met with a temporary setback "when the reactionaries [meaning 'keepers of tradition'] got the upper hand" during the early half of the nineteenth century, it finally flourished after "the revolutionary year of 1848."[81]

Kropotkin, against all political, social, and religious organizations, maintains that it is impossible for science and religion to coexist. He says in Chapter 3 of his book:

> In science ... We can already read the book of Nature, which comprises that of the development of both inorganic and organic life and of mankind, without resorting to a Creator, or to a mystical vital force, or to an immortal soul; and without consulting the trilogy of Hegel, or hiding our ignorance behind any metaphysical symbols whatever, endowed with a real existence by the writer. *Mechanical* phenomena, becoming more and more complicated as we pass from physics to the facts of life, are sufficient to explain Nature and all the intellectual and social organic life on our planet.[82] [Original italics]

Written while he was in exile in London in 1912, *Modern Science and Anarchism* expresses Kropotkin's view of Anarchism as a branch of modern science, using the inductive/deductive method of science to study human society and therefore concordant with the idea of progress. To him the ultimate development of modern science is Darwin's theory of evolution. There seems to be a contradiction between his theory of "mutual aid" among animals and Darwin's "struggle for existence." But Kroptkin himself did not think so, because he believed that Darwin changed his position twelve years after he wrote *On the Origin of Species*. In his 1902 book *Mutual Aid: a Factor of Evolution*, Kroptkin addresses this issue in the introduction. He acknowledges the severe struggle for existence most animals carry on against "an inclement Nature" in eastern Siberia and northern Manchuria, but he claims that he fails to find "that bitter struggle for the means of existence, *among animals belonging to the same species*, which was considered by most Darwinists (though not always by Darwin himself) as the dominant characteristic of struggle for life, and the main factor of evolution" (original italics).[83] In his mind, Darwin, when he was writing *Descent of Man* twelve years after *On the Origin of Species*:

> ... already took a far broader and a more metaphorical conception of the struggle for existence than that of a hard struggle between all the individuals within each species, which he had taken in his first great work in order to prove the importance of natural selection for the origin of new species. In his second great work, "The Descent of Man," he wrote, on the contrary, that those species which contain the greatest number of mutually sympathetic individuals have the greatest chance of surviving and of leaving a numerous progeny, and thus he entirely upset his first conception of the struggle for life. And nevertheless, Spencer maintained it in full.[84]

Convinced that Darwin was on his side when he wrote *Descent of Man*, Kropotkin in fact constructs a revision of the theory of the struggle for existence when he said, "Among animals, mutual aid is, in fact, not only the most efficacious weapon in the struggle for existence against the hostile forces of Nature and against other inimical species, but *it is also the principal instrument of progressive evolution*" (original italics).[85] He praises Darwin as "the most renowned naturalist of our own times," and claims that "the whole science of organic beings (biology) felt the effect of his work." The most important contribution of Darwin, according to him, is to have worked out his theory of natural selection in the struggle for life "on a scientific basis," and to "account for the wonderful accommodation of most of them [the existing species of plants and animals] to their surroundings from the action alone of natural causes, without the intervention of a guiding power."[86]

A scientist himself who made valuable contributions to geology, geography, chemistry, and economics, Kropotkin appreciated Darwin's work, especially for his position as a scientist who endeavored to find natural causes for natural phenomena, "without the intervention of a guiding power." An entomologist such as Jean-Henri Fabre, who attributes animal instinct to "divine illumination," would certainly not be his choice of a true scientist. The fact that he never talked about Fabre when he discussed the scientific development in the nineteenth century is ample proof of that.

Kropotkin's anarchist followers Ōsugi Sakae and Shiina Sonoji, sharing his faith in science and education, were social activists and writers with no scientific training. They seemed to see no distinction between Darwin and Fabre as scientists. But I would venture to say that their interests in Fabre probably went beyond scientific enquiry. Fabre's position as a writer from

Provence and his constant emphasis on his status as a peasant no doubt appealed to Sakae and his anarchist friend Yoshie Takamatsu, who were looking for anti-mainstream thinking to fill the spiritual vacuum during the tumultuous years of the Taishō period. Yoshie wrote several articles from 1920 to 1923 on le Midi and the Félibrige Movement led by Federick Mistral and Joseph Roumanille to revive the provençal language and literature.[87] He later wrote articles to promote peasants' literature in Japan during the 1920s.[88] Fabre was not the only counter-Darwinian intellectual that Sakae and his generation of Japanese intellectuals were attracted to. Ōsugi Sakae also favored Henri Bergson's theory of *élan vital* (vitalism) over Darwinism.

Ōsugi wrote in 1913 a series of articles on the development of evolution theories, including "*Evolution créatrice*: On Henri Bergson" (Sōzōteki shinka—Anri Beruguson ron 創造的進化—アンリ・ベルグソン論). In the article, he mentions Lamarck's adaptation theory, Theodor Eimer's (1843–98) orthogenesis, August Wiesmann's (1834–1914) germ plasma theory, and so on. Quoting Sir Charles Wyville Thomson (1830–1822) near the end of the article, he compares Darwinism with capitalism, "Comparing Darwin's theory and the capitalists' mindset, one can find many shocking similarities between them."[89] This may not come as a surprise if we consider Engels's famous oration at Marx's funeral in 1883: "Just as Darwin discovered the law of evolution in organic nature, so Marx discovered the law of evolution in human history."[90] In fact Marx himself had acknowledged the similarity, as he wrote to Engels in 1862, "It is remarkable how Darwin has discerned anew among beasts and plants his English society with its division of labor, competition, elucidation of new markets, 'discoveries' and Malthusian 'struggle for existence.' . . . in Darwin the animal kingdom figures as bourgeois society."[91] Thus it is understandable for Ōsugi to favor Bergson's creative evolution, a critique of Darwinian evolution. In addition to Bergson, Ōsugi also looked up to Tolstoy as spiritual mentor. That in another article he called Tolstoy "a spirit wrestler" (reikon no tame no senshi 霊魂のための戦士) and connected him with peasants, religious dissidents, and the Doukhobors (Dōhaboru ドゥハボル; spirit wrestlers) Movement in Russia, bespeaks his longing for spiritual guidance and hope for the future of the underclass.[92]

Let us look at Lu Xun again, who advocated Fabre. Though once a medical student in Japan, Lu Xun seemed to be more concerned with Chinese people's national character and the injustice of the ruling class than with science when reading Ōsugi Sakae's translation. He was a sincere proponent of popular science writing, writing in 1925 that "at least there should be a magazine for popular science, easy to read and interesting. It is a shame that scientists in China nowadays don't write much. When they do, it is too deep, thus too boring. Right now we need a Brehm (1829–84) to describe lives of animals, a Fabre to tell stories of insects, with a lot of images and pictures, too."[93] It is no wonder that he was especially interested in Fabre's work.

Lu Xun's brother Zhou Zuoren, on the other hand, was impressed by Fabre's writing style, which manages to combine "poetry and science." In his

1923 article, Zhou refers to the chapter titled "L'Harmas"[94] (荒地 Ch. "Huangdi" or "Arachi," meaning an uncultivated land) in the first volume, in which Fabre describes how people criticize the fluency of his writing that, according to them, indicates the shallowness of his thought and the lack of scientific value of his book. Fabre retorts that he is writing not only for scholars and philosophers interested in the problem of instinct, but for teenagers, so that they will learn to love natural history. That is why, while tightly guarding the truth, he has discarded the "scientific prose" (*prose scientifique*) of scholarly writing, which is most often as incomprehensible as one of the North American Indian dialects (*quelque idiome de Hurons*).[95] Zhou says, "Even though we are not in a position to downplay the usual scholarly style, when we read his writing combining poetry and science in such a harmonious way, we cannot help respecting and loving him more."[96] Zhou confesses that he has read a few volumes of *Souvenirs entomologiques* in English translation and the Japanese translation of the first volume. He is mostly thrilled by the affinity between human beings and insects:

> Looking at the fate of our own kind in novels and plays, we are deeply moved. Now seeing the tragic-comedy in the entomological world, as if listening to the news of our distant relatives—indeed very distant relatives—we are equally moved, and are inspired to many thoughts.[97]

Zhou's words represent the typical reaction of Chinese literary men faced with science books at the time. Like his brother Lu Xun, he is inspired to humanitarian concerns rather than with scientific curiosity. Given this, Ōgai Kamome's ridicule of the three enthusiastic modern boys in his story, intending to promote scientific studies by comparing insect behavior and human behavior in amorous acts, does not seem particularly out of line.

When we consider the fate of *On the Origin of Species* in China, the picture may be clearer. Yan Fu 嚴復 (1853–1921), who translated Thomas Huxley's *Evolution and Ethics* into *On Evolution* (Tianyanlun 天演論) in 1898, represented evolution as a warning to Chinese people that China should reform, otherwise she will perish in the struggle for existence among nations. It is no exaggeration to say that the whole of China, already beset by foreign invasions and constant failures in diplomatic negotiations, was immediately shaken by this gloomy prospect. *Wujing tianze shizhe shengcun* 物競天擇, 適者生存, the Chinese terms Yan coined to translate the Darwinian scenario "struggle for existence, natural selection, and survival of the fittest," became catchwords indicating China's perilous situation in world politics in the generations to come. In contrast, when Ma Junwu's 馬君武 (1881–1940) translation of Darwin's *On the Origin of Species* was published in 1919, the impact was nowhere near that of Yan Fu's *Tianyanlun*. It was as if, since the Chinese Darwinists had already said so much about him, what Darwin himself had to say did not matter much any more.

We should not forget that as in Japan, Bergson was also admired as a spiritual mentor in China during the 1920s, a fact that complicated the view of science as the panacea for China's problems since the late Qing. This will require looking into the science and metaphysics debate,[98] which involved almost all famous intellectuals at the time, as rooted in the opposition between Darwin's evolutionism (representing Western science) and Bergson's vitalism (representing Eastern wisdom in alliance with Confucianism, Buddhism, and Daoism). But it will take a full-length study to explore the topic.

What Lu Xun would think of Dandyism

Had he known that he were the target of satire in "The Three Who Study Antennas," Lu Xun would certainly retaliate with articles attacking dandies like Ogai Kamome, whose nonchalance and playfulness turns him into a laughing stock. It is not difficult to imagine what he would write in return.

A dexterous delineator of types of people in his time, Lu Xun ws a physiognomist of sorts. He wrote several articles on *bexiang*, which means "to play" in Shanghai dialect, ridiculing the decadent lifestyle of good-for-nothing characters whose only occupation was amusement. When the Neo-Sensation writers were relentlessly attacked during the Shanghai types debate in 1933, as discussed in Chapter 1, he published an article titled "Living on *Bexiang*" (Chi bexiang fan 吃白相飯) under the penname "Ruogu":

> To translate into Mandarin the so-called "bexiang" in Shanghai, probably "playing" [wanshua 玩耍] is the only choice. As to the expression "living on *bexiang*," I am afraid it would be clearer for people from other places if we use classical Chinese to translate it: "Without a commendable occupation, living a life of fun and frolic" [buwu zhengye youdang weisheng 不務正業，遊蕩為生]."[99]

The sarcasm towards fun-seekers like the Neo-Sensation writers is beyond doubt. We remember that once in a moment of self-criticism, Liu Na'ou wrote about himself in his diary: "These few weeks have been spent in *bexiang*," as discussed in Chapter 1. But, however much Lu Xun despised people—laymen or literati—living dandyish lives, he is practicing the macaronic like the Neo-Sensation writers: He is combining Shanghai dialect and classical Chinese expressions with his vernacular. In another article, also written in 1933, he comments on the "bad habits" (Ch. *opi* or *akuheki* 惡癖) of Japanese writers, resorting to Japanese *kanji* terms as well as classical Chinese to express himself. In addition to fully disclosing his sarcastic attitudes towards the living style that dandyism connotes, the article demonstrates the macaronic as freely employed as that found in the Neo-Sensation mode:

> Every modern Japanese literary man has a strange bad habit in addition to smoking tobacco and drinking coffee. Maedakō Hiroichirō

> 前田河廣一郎 loves alcohol like life, howling ceaselessly when drunk; Tanizaki Junichirō likes to smell women's body odor [Ch. *tichou* or *taishū* 體臭] and taste their spit and tears; . . . Hosoda Genkichi 細田源吉 loves sex talks [*weitan* or *waidan* 猥談] and sleeps two hours after breakfast. . . .
>
> Modern Japanese literary men's bad habits are as disgusting as that of Gu Hongming 辜鴻銘, a literary man in ancient China, who liked to smell women's golden lotus [classical Ch. jinlian 金蓮, meaning bound feet]. I ask promising young men as well as literary debutants in modern China to maintain a healthy spirit [Ch. *jianquan de jingshen* or *kenzenteki seishin* 健全的精神]. Never use the proverb "literary men have no code of conduct" [classical Ch. *wenren wuxing* 文人無行] as a pretext to fall into the same detestable bad habits as those of Japanese literati.[100]

It is unlikely that in 1933 Lu Xun wrote these two articles purely by chance. Targeting the Japanese dandies' "bad habits" and cautioning young Chinese writers against them, this article could well be a criticism of the Shanghai Neo-Sensation writers as well.

Whatever their differences in attitudes towards life, if we pay attention to the macaronic used by Lu Xun and his contemporary writers in general, we would be astonished by the amount of foreign text and classical expressions dispersed in their writings. The macaronic was by no means exclusive to the Neo-Sensation writers at all. Even though Lu Xun was averse to dandyish behavior in literary men, he himself was engaging in transcultural practice like the Neo-Sensation writers. We should say that transcultural practice is an integral part of dandyism, but certainly not its equal. One needs to be a dandy to practice dandyism.

The following chapter will continue to explore the concept of dandyism by drawing attention to the image of the modern boy, who leads a dandyish lifestyle but is intellectually inferior to the dandy. As the dandy's same-sex other self, the modern boy manages only to parrot information received on the transcultural site—unlike the dandy who devotes himself to artistic excellence, the modern boy, nevertheless, has no power for creative transformation.

5 A traveling disease

The "malady of the heart" and the modern boy

His (Bain's) theory involving pure philosophy is sometimes erroneous. In addition, his book is so wide-ranging that it is inconvenient for beginners. Therefore, after selection, deletion, and compromise (Ch. *qushe zhezhong* or *shusha secchū* 取捨折衷), I grasped its essence and made this book.

—Inoue Tetsujirō 井上哲次郎

Translation and transcultural modernity

This chapter analyzes the scientific jargon incorporated into Mu Shiying's 1933 story "A Man Taken as a Plaything" (Bei dangzuo xiaoqianpin de nanzi 被當作消遣品的男子). Medical and psychological terms, such as "misogyny," "autopsy," "neurasthenia," "indigestion," "germ," and so on, abound in the story. Typical of Neo-Sensation stories, these terms, borrowed from Japanese translations of Western scientific lexicon, are used in a flippant fashion to ridicule a fickle modern girl who enjoys torturing her suitors. My ultimate goal is to indicate that loanwords from modern Japanese scientific terminology transformed not only the lexicon of modern Chinese literature, but also that of our everyday language—in speech, newspapers, textbooks, and so on—conditioning the way we understand our own body and mind as well as others'. The loanwords, scientific or non-scientific, we use in our daily life are so copious and so ingrained in the psyche that it seldom occurs to us that they are not originally "Chinese." As Lydia Liu says in her book *Translingual Practice*, the lists of loanwords in the appendix of her book is by no means exhaustive;[1] in fact, however comprehensive a loanword dictionary tries to be, it will not be able to list all the loanwords we use on a day-to-day basis. Loanwords have changed our sensibilities, perception of the self and personal relationships as well as worldview.

I will first trace the introduction of psychology as a discipline in Japan and China and use the translation of a few key terms as examples to demonstrate that it is through translation that we learn to name our perceptions and mental illnesses. After the discourse of the "sick man of Asia" (*dongya bingfu* 東亞病夫) prevalent in China since the late Qing,[2] writers in the 1920s and 1930s were telling us that Chinese were now suffering from the "malady of the heart." It is a modern disease that we are talking about, a disease that is discovered together with modernity, the transformation of man-and-woman relationships, and the onslaught of civil wars and colonial invasions.

At the end of this chapter I will show that not only scientific terms, but also the vocabulary we use to express our passionate attachment for each other today is a modern invention. Love and desire, heterosexual and homosexual, has been an indispensable topic in any book on psychology since the nineteenth century. In a book that traces the origin of the Western concept of "love" and Japanese translation for the word, Yanabu Akira 柳父章 claims that the *kanji* word *ai* 愛 (love) used to translate "love" came from classical Chinese, but the word *koi* 戀 (Ch. *lian*, attachment) in *ren'ai* 戀愛 (Ch. *lian'ai*) was originally *yamato kotoba* 大和言葉 (native Japanese language). I do not agree. I intend to point out that the traveling and cross-borrowing of words have been so pervasive, and that we are so familiar with our daily language, that it is hardly obvious which word is "native" and which is not. After words, by the same token ideas and books, cross borders, linguistic or national, they take on lives of their own. The "origin" of the word is less meaningful than the process of its transformation and its taking roots in another culture and renewing it.

During the process of cultural translation, are translators passive responders who are so dominated by "institutional practices" that they are deprived of "individual free choice," as Lydia Liu believes them to be, or conscious actors who study and calculate every word they use to translate key concepts? Chapter 4 has already tackled this theoretical problem concerning knowledge and power. Drawing on Foucault's concepts of "practices of the self" and "practices of freedom" which allow individuals to modify power relations, I have shown that in the choice and interpretation of texts, the translator's agency plays a key role. In this chapter I will further emphasize that no institutional power ever exists without other contending powers vying for supremacy. During translation translators resort to all possible resources—or divergent institutional practices—available to them at the moment and make the choices they consider most appropriate: drawing inspiration from classical, Buddhist, or medical texts, from another national language, or even from indigenous vulgar expressions. It is a process of negotiating and, most of the time, compromising, with the translator constantly testing the limits of standard practices in order to find possible breakthroughs, as Inoue Tetsujirō's term *"shusha secchū"* suggests. The result is often the creation of a new form of expression.

The so-called "translated modernity," which Lydia Liu describes so well, in fact results from the translator's personal agency and creative energy released when crossing borders on the transcultural site; once conventional divides are consciously challenged, eventually both sides of the divides would be transformed. This is the concept of creative transformation and transcultural modernity. During the complex process of creative transformation, personal agency, constantly testing the checks and balances among institutional powers, plays a key role. Men and women always live under the constraints of all sorts of institutional powers; even emperors and presidents are no exception. Without personal agency, how could creativity be possible? How could there be revolution, or even reform, in history?

We are all indebted to the European linguist Federico Masini and Lydia Liu for their study of loanwords.[3] Yet neither of them tells us how loanwords were transmitted from one culture to another. One purpose of this chapter is to use the Japanese and Chinese translation of "neurasthenia," what I call the malady of the heart, as a case study to show how this modern disease traveled from the West to the East, and then from Japan to China at the turn of the twentieth century. This kind of traveling process points to the fact that national or linguistic borders have no power to obstruct the global circulation of concepts and ideas; during the process cultural translators' agency challenges institutions, creating modes of expression while introducing new way of thinking. They are the propellers of transcultural modernity; the transcultural site is where they perform creative transformation.

"You have cured me of misogyny, but given me neurasthenia"

When psychological jargon becomes the target of ridicule in a literary work, we are looking at the vernacularization, or popularization, of the knowledge imbedded in psychology as a discipline. First let us look at Mu Shiying's story and see how the new scientific terms are employed, and how the boundaries between literary and non-literary are blurred in his ironic attitudes towards science, the pinnacle of what constitutes the "modern."

The narrator of the story, a college boy enamored of a capricious college girl from head to toe, is constantly tortured by her infidelity. Called by her "Alexy," his English name, he is a modern boy *par excellence*. He reads pictorials, smokes foreign cigarettes, frequents dance halls, enjoys partying and "Afternoon Tea" (original in English), likes jazz and "Saxophone," and even quotes an English poem by Louise Gilmore and sings "Rio Rita," the theme song in Florenz Ziegfeld's 1927 musical with the same title.[4]

Scrutinized by the modern boy and compared to the American movie star "Clara Bow" (Kelailabao 克萊拉寶, Ch. transliteration), the modern girl in the story is certainly on a par with him in every way. In his description, she has "a body like a snake, a brain like a cat," and is a "mixture of tenderness and danger." She likes to wear a long red silk *qipao*, with the edges flying in the wind. Her feet in high-heeled shoes made of red satin "looked like a pair of feet for dancing."[5] She has a Japanese name, Yōko, and loves Nescafé chocolates, *Sunkist* (original in English), Shanghai beer, and the wild flower she calls "Forget-me-not" in English.[6] To the narrator, her facial features are a composite of Hollywood movie stars: Vilma Banky's (1903–91) eyes, Nancy Carrol's (1904–65) smile, and Norma Shearer's (1902–83) nose. She sings in English "Kiss Me Again," and hums "Minuet in G." She wants "a lovable lover, an ugly husband, and playthings not too hateful," so that her life will not be "lonely."⁷ The narrator comments, "What a girl living on sensations and speed! Yōko! A composite of *Jazz* (original in English), machine, speed, urban culture, American taste, and the beauty of our age (*shidai mei* 時代美)!"⁸ In a word, our modern boy and modern girl in the story are actively engaged in everything that can be dubbed "modern" in the metropolis. They are the types of characters Neo-Sensation stories are as a rule concerned with.

The relationship of the two shows how a modern girl enjoys torturing a modern boy, who is completely at her mercy. Professing to love him only, the girl demands that he allow her to be admired by other men as well, who, according to her, are only her playthings. "One can love only one person, but there can be many playthings," says the fickle girl. The narrator, overpowered by her, succumbs, considering himself "a lamb enjoying the bliss of being loved by a lion."⁹ But every time he turns his back, she goes out with other men. She lies about everyone she dates; it is a match either her father or brother has picked for her, always with a Ph.D. or M.A. degree. When he confronts her with her lies, she refuses to see him, and in the end it is always he who apologizes for his "misbehavior." Images of war and hunting abound in the story to describe their relationship. For instance, he describes their relationship as "a war more drastic than the European war,"¹⁰ meaning World War I. In this war of love, he is doomed to lose, calling himself a "moron" (*dineng'er* 低能兒) in the game of love.¹¹

During the whole losing battle, the narrator constantly engages in self-analysis, with the narrative studded with psychological and medical jargon, typical of Neo-Sensation stories. In the beginning when the modern girl seduces him by proposing a date, he warns himself against women's treachery, with which he has been quite experienced. Every time he feels tempted by her, he lies in bed and begins self-"autopsy" (*jiepo*).¹² Telling himself to resort to "misogyny" (*nüxing xian'ezheng* 女性嫌惡症), he deliberately views her as a "dangerous animal" (*weixian de dongwu* 危險的動物) who devours the hunter as a piece of chocolate in her mouth: "Gosh, I am worried. I am already in her mouth, like chocolate (*zhugulitang* 朱古力糖) under her tongue. I immediately urged the germs (*bingjun* 病菌) of misogyny to multiply speedily in my veins."¹³ That is to say, he is trying very hard to hate her so that he will be protected from her charms before being devoured by her. The lovers' talk between the two elaborates on the metaphor of germs and illness time and again, for instance:

> "What a misogynist you are!"
> Through the smoke of Gentleman [*Jishipai* 吉士牌, cigarette], I saw her proud nose, mocking eyes, and disappointed mouth [because the chocolate refuses to get under her tongue].
> "Tell me where the germs of your misogyny originated from."
> "They were gifts from a girl who knew how to lie."[meaning: He hates women because he was once betrayed by a girl]

"So you have been spreading your germs in magazines? [meaning: His stories about misogyny are published in magazines] What a hateful man!"

"My germs are prescriptions for girls' indigestion [*xiaohua buliangzheng* 消化不良症, caused by devouring too much chocolate, or too many men]."

"You are certainly a man girls cannot hate!"[14]

When she says she cannot see him, he begins to look for her wherever she might be, her dormitory room, her school gate, the dance halls in town, her aunt's house for which she has given him a fake address, and so on. He even gets in a fight with one of her suitors. The poor doting lover says he gradually develops "neurasthenia" (*shenjing shuairuozheng* 神經衰弱症), or, as I call it, the "malady of the heart." In a letter to the girl, he writes: "You have cured me of misogyny, but given me neurasthenia."[15] He complains of this disorder at least thrice again in the story.[16]

Fully displaying the macaronic nature of their language, the modern boy and modern girl can be viewed as the quintessence of hybridity that challenges the stability and consistence of a unified "nation," the borders of which are constantly infiltrated by foreign cultures. While disclosing the ambivalence of the concept of what is "national," the story also epitomizes the shaping of the Chinese vernacular in the early decades of the twentieth century. During its process of formation, the new vernacular is in a state of constant flux, which should be in fact the essence of any living language in any period. When a language becomes enclosed and rejects change, it will die out; it is hybridity, challenging the stasis of a language, that keeps it living. What is most prominent here is the Neo-Sensation experiment with language. As always, *kanji* loanwords abound: autopsy, *jiepo* in Chinese or *kaibō* in Japanese *kanji*; misogyny, *nüxing xian'ezheng* or *josei ken'oshō*; moron, *dineng'er* or *teinōji*; germ, *bingjun* or *byōkin*; indigestion, *xiaohua buliangzheng* or *shōka huryōshō*; and neurasthenia, *shenjing shuairuozheng* or *shinkei suijyakushō*. All these are psychological and medical terms indicative of modern scientific development. Bantered between the modern boy and the modern girl, their frequent appearances in the story show how these new scientific terms have found their way into everyday life and become the vocabulary of middle-class educated laymen.

In addition to transcriptions of foreign texts or words inserted into the narrative, as we have seen above, transliteration using Chinese words to represent the sound of foreign words can be found throughout the story: *zhugulitang* (Cantonese dialect) for chocolate, *pijiu* 啤酒 for beer, and so on. Neologisms in the form of compound terms to translate the meaning are plenty as well, e.g., *Quechaopai* 雀巢牌 for the brand name Nescafé. There are also neologisms created by adding the suffix *pin* 品 (item) to a noun to indicate an item with a certain function: *xiaoqian-pin* 消遣品 (pleasure-item) for plaything and *ciji-pin* 刺激品 (stimulation-item) for stimulant. The word *pin* is pronounced as *hin* in Japanese, meaning "work," "product," or "quality," as in classical Chinese. The combination use of the word *pin* has become a standard practice in Chinese today, for instance, *xiaofei-pin* 消費品 (consumption-item) for commodity, *jing-pin* 精品 (quintessence-item) for deluxe product, *jue-pin* 絕品 (limited-item) for rare, highest-class product, and so on. Two other suffixes often used in the period which caught on and are still in use today are *xing* (*sei* 性 in *kanji*), meaning "quality" or "nature," and *wu* (*butsu* 物 in *kanji*), indicating a thing or a person with a distinct quality. Take for example *nanxing* (*dansē* 男性 in *kanji*), meaning man, and *nüxing* (*josē* 女性 in *kanji*), meaning woman, which can be found in the story. For the suffix *wu*, *hunhe-wu* (*kongōbutsu* 混合物 in *kanji*), meaning "mixture," is used when the narrator calls the modern girl "a mixture of tenderness and danger." The term *dongwu* (animal), or *dōbutsu* 動物 in *kanji*, is used when the narrator calls her "a dangerous animal." In today's usage, terms with *wu* as suffix abound, for example, *shengwu* (*sēbutsu* 生物), meaning "animate being," or *wushengwu* (*museibutsu* 無生物), meaning "inanimate being." Most often terms with these suffixes concern biological, psychological, and commercial usages, connected with scientific knowledge or the idea of modern capitalist circulation. It goes without saying that modern knowledge needs new language to convey meanings.

Mu Shiying is highly conscious of the roles the Neo-Sensation writers play in their search for a new literary language and narrative mode, and of the position they take in the ongoing process of literary transformation. A passage in the story, in addition to prescribing readings for a modern girl's intellectual formation, discloses what Mu Shiying considers as *passé* and, in contrast, the new mode he embraces in literature. The narrator, "trying very hard to build the bases of friendship under love," asks Yōko:

"Have you read *La dame aux camélias*?"
"It should have been what our grandmothers read."
"Do you like realistic writings? For example, Zola's *Nana*, Dostoevsky's *Crime and Punishment*. . . . "
"When I am sleepy, they are effective sleeping pills for me. I like to read Paul Morand, Yokomitsu Riichi, Horiguchi Daigaku, and C. S. Lewis—Yes, Lewis is my favorite."
"What about Chinese writers?"
"I like Liu Na'ou's new language skills [Ch. *huashu* or *wajutsu* 話術], Guo Jianying's cartoons [*manhua* or *manga* 漫画], and your violent vocabulary [*cubao de wenzi*, or *sobōteki moji* 粗暴的文字], the smell of wilderness [kuangye or *kōya* 曠野] . . . "[17]

Masked as random conversation between a modern girl and a modern boy, this dialogue is in fact a moment of literary criticism and self-reflexivity on the part of the author. It points to his extreme self-consciousness as an artist, who is positioning himself and his fellow Neo-Sensation writers with their

Japanese counterparts and is highly aware of the affinity of both groups with Paul Morand. According to this dialogue, great nineteenth-century European realistic masters such as Alexander Dumas, Zola, and Dostoevsky are already out-dated and fail to interest young people, while the Neo-Sensation mode of writing is an intentional breakaway from that grand realistic tradition. Deliberately putting the Neo-Sensation writers on a par with C. S. Lewis, the Irish popular writer of science fiction and children's books, Mu Shiying is declaring, as it were, that the Neo-Sensation mode aims to narrow the gaps between elite and popular literatures—there is no reason why literature should not be understood and liked by college boys and girls. As discussed in Chapter 1, contemporary writers such as Lu Xun and Shen Congwen criticized him and his fellow Neo-Sensation writers in 1933 and 1934 for their catering to college girls' taste and commercialism,[18] just around the time "A Man Taken as a Plaything" was published. The valorization through the modern girl's voice, "Liu Na'ou's new language skills, Guo Jianying's cartoons, and your violent words, the smell of wilderness . . . ," indicates beyond doubt that Mu was highly aware of his fellow Neo-Sensation writers' language experimentation as a counter trend against the realistic mode prevalent at the time, and that he was proud of the modern sensations, marked by "the smell of wilderness" or "primitivism," they were trying to convey. Furthermore, among the texts the modern girl rejects, *La dame aux camélias* was not just an old-fashioned novel, but an old-fashioned translation; it was the first translation by Lin Shu 林紓, written in classical Chinese and highly assimilationist, as opposed to the macaronic highlighting the foreign and the hybrid the Neo-Sensation writers were trying to create.

On the one hand, the story reflects the mentality and speech habits of college students in the metropolis who were well versed in the macaronic practice of language; it is a demonstration of characters as the transcultural site, where heterogeneous information flows in and then flows out. On the other, the loose usage of scientific terms demonstrates how, since Hu Shi in 1917 maintained that vernacular literature should abandon classical expressions and allusions, the new vernacular awkwardly evolving in the 1930s resorted to vocabulary bantering with modern scientific knowledge instead. Most important, the scientific jargon used freely by characters in Mu's story discloses how medical knowledge formulated people's understanding of each other's mind and body when disciplines such as psychology were beginning to be established in China. The formation of psychology as a discipline in China was inseparable from that in Japan, which we will see in the next section.

Psychology as a discipline in Japan and China

The person whose seminal work influenced the development of psychology in Japan is Nishi Amane 西周 (1829–97). Arriving in Holland in 1867, he was the first Japanese student sent by the Eidō Bakuhu who studied philosophy and psychology in Europe. It is obvious from his class notes that he had to resort to the Confusion concepts he had been trained in to interpret Western learning: The natural world was *qi* 氣 (air) for him, while what is inside a person's mind was *ri* 理 (reason or logic). Thus science became *qika* 氣科 (subjects on air), and the humanities, *rika* 理科 (subjects on reason). The term he used to indicate "psychology" in his class notes was *seirigaku* 性理學 (*xinglixue* in Chinese, study of the logic of human nature), which was the learning of the Confucian school of the Song Dynasty. It is interesting to read in his class notes the quotations from *The Practice of the Mean* (Zhongyong 中庸), *The Analects* (Lunyu 論語), and *Mencius* (Mengzi 孟子) in his handwriting (Figure 5.1).[19] If we could say Confucian training was part of the institutional practices in Eidō Japan, these quotations disclose beyond doubt a Confucian scholar consciously striving to search in traditional scholarship for equivalents of the major concepts he is now learning in a Western classroom. Apparently he was not satisfied with the Confucian term, *seirigaku*, since we know that later in his 1875–76 translation of Joseph Haven's (1816–74) *Mental Philosophy: Including the Intellect, Sensibilities and Will* (Boston: Gould and Lincoln, 1857), he would coin the term *shinrigaku* 心理學 (*xinlixue* in Chinese) by combining the two words *shin* 心 (the heart) and *ri* (reason) to translate the main title.[20] It is clear that for him, to talk about new knowledge, brand new terms were needed, and the coinage of this new term would take him years of deliberation long after his student days in Holland. This neologism soon became the standard translation of "psychology" in Meiji Japan and later in China.

After the Meiji Reform began, psychology was considered a required

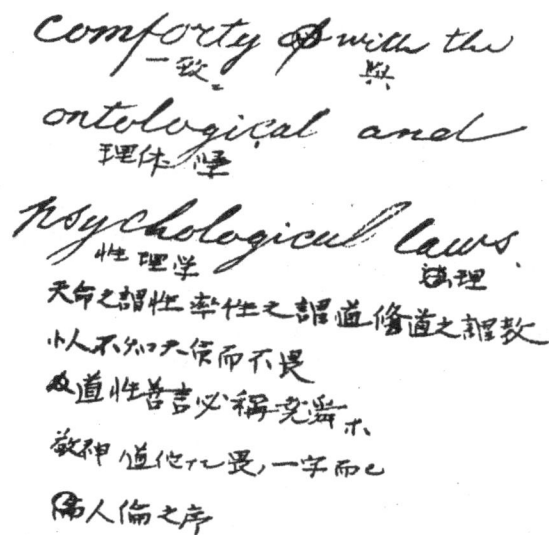

Figure 5.1 Nishi Amane's handwriting.

course for teachers' training. Tokyo Normal College (present-day University of Tsukuba 筑波大學) reformed its curriculum and added the course on psychology in 1879, using Nishi Amane's translation of Haven's book as the textbook. Isawa shūji 伊澤修二 (1851–1917), who had studied at Bridgewater Normal School (present-day Bridgewater State College) in Massachusettes, and Takamine Hideo 高嶺秀夫 (1854–1910), at Oswego Normal School (present-day Oswego) in New York, were the masterminds behind the curriculum reform. Tokyo Imperial University offered the course on psychology in 1873. Motora Yūjirō 元良勇次郎 (1858–1912), who had studied at Boston University and the Johns Hopkins University, became Japan's first professor specializing in psychology at Tokyo Imperial University in 1890.[21] Without further ado on the Japanese side, I am now moving on to psychology as a discipline in China.

Even though the first book on psychology translated into Chinese in 1889 was also Joseph Haven's book *Mental Philosophy*, there seemed to be no connection with Nishi Amane's translation.[22] Yan Yongjing 顔永京 was an Anglican Church priest and Dean of Saint John's College (Saint John's University from 1905–52) in Shanghai for eight years. An orphan, he was taken to America at the age of 14, and received a B.A. degree from Kenyon College in Ohio in 1861.[23] The title of his translation was *Study of the Heart and Soul* (Xinlingxue 心靈書). It was in classical Chinese and only the first volume, consisting of the introduction and the part on intellect, was published.[24] It did not seem to have much impact on later translations or studies on psychology. In the following I am going to review Japan's role in helping shape the modern education system in China. Taught and used in schools, Japanese neologisms introducing modern knowledge began to prevail in China in the early twentieth century, while most of those coined by the European missionaries since the late sixteenth century were gradually eclipsed.[25]

The first school in China to include the subject of psychology in its curriculum was the forerunner of Beijing Normal University, Jingshi Daxuetang Shifanguan 京師大學堂師範館 (Normal College of Beijing University), which was founded in 1902. Beijing University itself had been established in 1898. The establishment of Beijing University's Medical School would follow in 1903. The modern Chinese education system, established after China's defeat in the 1895 Sino-Japanese war, took Japan's as its model, as did the curriculum of the Normal College. Textbooks and handouts for the courses were mostly translated from Japanese.[26] Critics so far have not paid enough attention to the role of Japan in the establishment of psychology as a discipline in China, or other disciplines, for that matter.[27]

After Japan established the Tōa Dōbunkai 東亞同文會 (East Asia Common Culture Association) in 1898, Sino-Japanese scholarly exchange accelerated. When the Normal College of Beijing University was first established, Hattori Unokichi 服部宇之吉 (1867–1939), the famous Japanese Neo-Confucian scholar and an assistant professor at Tokyo Imperial University, was invited to help build a teacher training program. He had studied in China for one year in 1899 and then in Germany for three years. This time he stayed in Beijing from 1902 to 1909 and offered courses on education, psychology, and logic.[28] His handout for the course on psychology is still kept in the libraries of Beijing University and Nanjing University today. According to Gao Juefu (ed.), *History of Psychology in China* (Zhongguo xinlixue shi 中國心理學史), among the 30 textbooks or course handouts used during the period from 1900 to 1918 that can still be seen today, 20 were either translated or adapted from Japanese textbooks based on Western originals, or transcribed from a Japanese teacher's class notes.[29] With the pedagogical advantage, it does not come as a surprise that the Japanese lexicon of this brand of new knowledge became widely used in China from the outset.

In the 1910s and 1920s more and more Chinese students went to study in Europe or America instead of Japan, while psychology as a discipline in China likewise began to take a Euro-American turn. Cai Yuanpei (1868–1940), the president of Beijing University who had studied psychology, history, and culture at Leipzig University, established the Department of Psychology in 1926. But Chen Daqi 陳大齊 (1886–1983), the first chairman appointed, was still Japan-trained. He had a degree from Tokyo Imperial University. Qinghua University also established its Department of Educational Psychology in 1926, aiming to study how humans learn in educational settings. It was changed to the Department of Psychology in 1930.[30] Because of the influence of Freud, abnormal psychology was part of the curriculum of most departments of psychology in China.[31]

To glimpse how the new discipline of psychology attracted attention at the time, one can look at one work by the famous eugenicist and psychologist Pan Guangdan 潘光旦, who entered Columbia University in 1924.[32] He wrote in 1922 "On Feng Xiaoqing" (Feng Xiaoqing Kao 馮小青考), a term paper for the great scholar-journalist Liang Qichao's 梁啟超 (1873–1929) course on "Methodology of Chinese History" at Tsinghua University,[33] using Freud's theory of psychoanalysis to analyze the "abnormal psychology" (*bingtai xinli* 變態心理) of a young woman living during the Ming Dynasty. Liang praised Pan's talent highly, and later the revised version was published in *Women's Magazine* (Funu zazhi 婦女雜誌) in 1924.[34]

Feng Xiaoqing 馮小青 (1595–1612), becoming a man's concubine at the age of 16, died of tuberculosis two years later. Contemporary and later critics generally believed that she died of a broken heart, because she had been prevented from seeing her husband for half a year by his extremely jealous wife. But Pan, finding evidence from her poetry and her deathbed letter to an intimate woman friend, maintains that the abundant mirror and water imageries in her poetry and, before her death, her portrait which she commissioned an artist to paint several times until perfection indicate that she suffered from "Narcissism" (Original in English).[35] Pan coins the Chinese term "yinglian" 影戀 (shadow-love), to translate Narcissism. His thesis is that she was a typical case of "psychoneurosis" (original in English, sometimes *jingshen aoli* 精神拗戾 in Pan's translation), showing her endowed with character traits of a person with a Narcissist complex: self-admiration, self-centeredness, and self-regard. Terms such as "Narcissism, psychoneurosis, abnormal psychology, subconscious" (*qianyishi* 潛意識, a term adapted from the Japanese translation *senzai ishiki* 潛在意識), "sexual inversion" (*xing xinli zhi biantai* 性心理之變態), "hypochondria" (*youyu zheng* 憂鬱症), and "neurasthenia" (*jingxie shuairuo* 精血衰弱), all point to Freud's 1914 article "On Narcissism."

Pan Guangdan in fact refers to Freud as his main source of inspiration when writing on Feng Xiaoqing. One should note that the term Pan used for "neurasthenia" is *jingxie shuairuo* instead of *shenjing shuairuo* 神經衰弱. Pan's coinage combines *shuairuo* (weakness) with the term *jingxie*, a traditional medical concept denoting the essence of life, as described in the line, "When *jingxie* is insufficient, the marrow is sapped."[36] As I will point out later in this chapter, the term *shenjing shuairuo* to render "neurasthenia" would not be commonly used in China until the mid 1920s, even though it had already been employed in Chinese medical texts in the 1910s. But from 1939 to 1941 when Pan translated Havelock Ellis's *Psychology of Sex: A Manual for Students*, he would use *shenjing shuairuo* to translate "neurasthenia."[37] In China during the late 1920s and later decades the term became so widely known that Pan chose to use it instead of his own earlier coinage. More will be said about this later in this chapter.

Another European psychologist who figured prominently in the early development of psychology in China was the British psychologist Havelock Ellis (1859–1939), who invented the terms sexual inversion, auto-eroticism, and Narcissism before Freud. His works were well known among Japanese and Chinese intellectuals. *Studies in the Psychology of Sex* (1897–1928), published by F. A. Davis Company from 1905 to 1928 in seven volumes, collects his works of more than two decades.[38] As early as 1913, Zhou Zuoren wrote, "Havelock Ellis is the thinker I admire most."[39] He translated a few passages from Ellis's *Impressions and Comments* (1914–24) in 1925,[40] and in 1944 he was still writing about Ellis, praising him for his ideas that were "neither conservative, nor radical," i.e., conforming to "the practice of the mean."[41] Except for a few introductory articles like these, Zhou Zuoren did not really engage too much with Ellis's theories. The one who made an effort to make use of them in building up a preliminary sexology was the famous Dr. Sex, Zhang Jingsheng, whose *Sex Histories* (Xingshi) in 1926 took the form of case histories like those in Ellis's *Sexual Inversion*. Since I have already written on this topic elsewhere, I will not delve into it now.[42] I would like only to mention that Pan Guangdan's translation (1939–41) of Havelock Ellis's work was based on the 1933 single volume *Psychology of Sex: A Manual for Students*, which was an abridged version of the seven-volume *Studies in the Psychology of Sex*.[43]

In Japan in 1921 and 1922 alone, Washio Hiroshi 鷲尾浩 published translations of seven of Havelock Ellis's works, among which was *Sexual Selection*

174 *Dandyism and Transcultural Modernity*

in Man (1905).⁴⁴ In the following I will use the translation of a few key concepts in his translation to provide a glimpse into how Japanese translations of Western scientific terms have transformed both modern Japanese and Chinese lexicons. One of the key concepts is "neurasthenia," indicating the "malady of the heart."

How to name the five senses and the malady of the heart

Translations of scientific terms have provided us with the terminology to talk about our body, mind or heart, and sensibilities. Two examples will suffice for the sake of this study. One of the theses of Ellis's *Sexual Selection in Man* is the key roles that "touch, smell, hearing, and vision" play in human sexual selection.⁴⁵ In Washio's translation, they are rendered as *shokkaku* 觸覺, *shūkaku* 嗅覺, *chōkaku* 聽覺, and *shikaku* 視覺.⁴⁶ To use the suffix *kaku* as a noun to indicate the function of the five senses was in fact an invention by Inoue Tetsujirō (1855–1903), a professor of Tokyo Imperial University who studied in Germany from 1884 to 1890. In his 1882 translation titled *New Psychology* (Shinri shinsetsu 心理新說), originally *Mental Science* by Alexander Bain (1818–1903), he used these terms with the *kaku* suffix.⁴⁷ Although in his translation of *Mental Philosophy* Nishi Amane had invented the term *gokan* 五官 (*wuguan* in Chinese) for the "five senses" and used *shokkaku* (*chujue* in Chinese) for "touch," he used *kiku koto* 聞くこと for "hearing" and *miru koto* 見ること for "sight," adding *koto* to the infinitive being the way for Japanese to derive nouns from verbs.⁴⁸ It is to Inoue's translation that we owe the terms indicating the function of the four other senses in addition to *shokkaku* invented by Nishi Amane.

Later, in a textbook edited in 1898 for students of normal schools, titled *Essence of Psychology* (Shinri sazuyō 心理撮要), Nakajima Rikizō (1858–1918) used the word *kan* 感(feeling) as the suffix and coined the terms *shokkan* 觸感, *shūkan* 嗅感, *chōkan* 聽感, *mikan* 味感, and *shikan* 視感 for the five senses.⁴⁹ But history tells us that Inoue's coinages with the suffix *kaku* would prevail in Japan and then in China, while Nakajima's with *kan* would be forgotten. It is interesting to note that Nakajima, translating the term "mental life" into *shinteki seikatsu* 心的生活 (life of the heart) instead of *nōteki seikatsu* 腦的生活 (life of the mind), clearly followed Nishi Amane's interpretation of psychology as a subject.⁵⁰ We know that in 1914 when Ōse Jintarō 大瀬甚太郎 edited another textbook for students of normal schools, also titled *Shinri satsuyō*, he followed Inoue in using *kaku* as the suffix.⁵¹

In the preface to his translation written in *kanbun* (Chinese writing), Inoue Tetsujirō demonstrates his erudition in Confucianism as well as Western philosophy, giving a brief history of both traditions. Juxtaposing the East and the West, he praises Bain, John Stuart Mill, and Spencer as the leading experimental psychologists who represent the pinnacle of Western science and philosophy, and regrets the vacuum of Chinese philosophy since Wang Yangming 王陽明 in the Ming Dynasty: "China did not lack philosophy, but since there was no one to carry on the tradition, it did not flourish."⁵² Bain's original text in fact covered psychology, physiology, and philosophy, but Inoue, intending to propagate psychology as the essence of Western science, eliminates the parts not directly concerned with psychology. He gives another reason for abridging the text:

> His [Bain's] theory involving pure philosophy is sometimes erroneous. In addition, his book is so wide-ranging that it is inconvenient for beginners. Therefore, after selection, deletion, and compromise [*shusha secchū*], I grasped its essence and made this book.⁵³

Inoue is highly aware of his own agency in the translating act, honestly laying bare his intervention. Given the incommensurability of languages, "selection, deletion, and compromise," at least to a certain degree, is indeed what any translator has to resort to, however "faithful" one may intend to be.

The terms *shokkaku*, *shūkaku*, *chōkaku*, *mikaku*, and *shikaku* Inoue used to render the five senses have a distinct Buddhist flavor. Since among his publications was *Biography of Buddha* (Shakāmuni ten 釋迦牟尼傳) in 1902,⁵⁴ we can be sure that Inoue was familiar with Buddhism, and that these terms he used in his translation were influenced by Buddhist scriptures. In Chinese Buddhist or medical texts the same character as *kaku* in Japanese, pronounced as *jue* in Chinese, sometimes follows the characters indicating "touch" and "taste," but is always used as a verb. For instance, in a medical text titled *The Dongyuan Collection of Medicines: Amomum Cotatum Pills* (Dongyuan yiji. Caodoukouwan 東垣醫集.草豆蔻丸): "When triggered, a swollen tumor grows, which is the mass formed of tapeworms and can be felt by touch (*keyi chu jue* 可以觸覺)."⁵⁵ Or in Volume 25 of Feng Menglong's 馮夢龍 *General Stories to Alarm the World* (Jingshi tongyan 警世通言), a Ming Dynasty text: "When licked with the tongue, its taste feels sweet (*wei jue ganmei* 味覺甘美). The only regret is that there is too little to eat."⁵⁶ In both cases *jue* means "to feel." Modern Chinese borrowed the expressions back from Japanese *kanji* to indicate the functions of the five senses as nouns. If we look at Chen Daqi's *Outlines of Psychology* (Xinlixue dagang 心理學大綱) in 1918, these terms are already rendered as *chujue* 觸覺, *xiujue* 嗅覺, *tingjue* 聽覺, and *shijue* 視覺.⁵⁷ Considering Chen's degree from Tokyo Imperial University in 1912, it does not seem surprising at all.⁵⁸ In Pan Guangdan's translation of Chapter 2 of *Psychology of Sex*, titled "Biology of Sex," these Japanese loanwords are also used.⁵⁹ It was through Japanese translation that modern Chinese learned to name the five senses.

Another example we can look at is Washio Hiroshi's translation of the term "neurasthenia" in Chapter 3 of the part on "Smell" in Ellis's *Sexual Selection in Man*.⁶⁰ Washio used the term *shinkei suijyaku* to translate "neurasthenia,"⁶¹ which Miura Kinnosuke 三浦謹之助 had already used in his 1894 book, *A List of Diagnoses for Diseases of the Nerves* (Shinkeibyō shindanhyō 神經病診斷表).⁶² Giving the German terms for the disorders he discusses, he lists the following under the diseases diagnosed as *kannōteki shikkan* (官能的疾患 in *kanji*, no German term is provided; functional diseases; "diseases stimulated by sexual desire" in Japanese dictionaries): *hipokondori* (ヒポコンドリー in *katakana*, or *Hypochondrie* in German), *shinkei suijyaku* (神經衰弱 in *kanji*, or *Neurasthenie*), and *hisuteri* (ヒステリー in *katakana*, or *Hysterie*). *Kannōteki*, meaning "functional," was a neologism in Japanese during the period when psychology was appropriated into the country. In Miura's book "hysteria" is sometimes transliterated into *kanji*. The author says: "Neurasthenia is the cause of 'hypochondria.' In addition, neurasthenia more or less mixes the dispositions of hypochondria. It is often caused by overworking the sexual organs. That the spirit is easily excited is similar to 'hysteria.'"[63] Although the author does not give any source of his work, the German terms he provides for major concepts indicate that he is German-trained. The German term he provides for the title of the book is "Diagnostiche [Diangnostische]Tabellen für Nervenkrankheiten."

In China the term *shenjing shuairuo* appeared in the 1910s. The earliest title I can discover in the National Bibliographic Information Network of National Central Library in Taipei is *Shenjing Shuairuo san da yanjiu* 神經衰弱三大研究 (Three Great Studies on Neurasthenia) published by Yixue Shuju 醫學書局 (Medical Bookstore) in Shanghai in 1910, edited by Ding Fubao 丁福保 and Hua Wenqi 華文祺.[64] This book is unavailable, but from the terms such as *guannengzheng* 官能症 and *shenjing shuairuo* used to describe it by the library, one can assume that it is based on Japanese sources.

The earliest book on the subject I have seen is Lu Shoujian's 盧壽籛 *A Treatment for Neurasthenia* (Shenjing shuairuo liaoyangfa 神經衰弱療養法) in 1917, written in classical Chinese. It is based on Inoue Masayoshi's 井上正賀 1915 *A Nutritional Treatment for Neurasthenia* (Shinkei suijyaku eiyō ryōhō 神經衰弱病營養療法).[65] Lu in the preface of the book blames neurasthenia on "global civilization" (*shijie wenming* 世界文明) and "struggle for existence" (*shengcun jingzheng* 生存競爭), a term ringing with evolution theory. Erotic indulgence in Europe and America, sexual repression in China particularly, and stomach diseases are also listed as the major causes of neurasthenia.[66] Contesting overemphasis on theory and medicinal-physiological cures, he thinks that nutrition and sleep as advised by Inoue are the best cures. Opposing the excessive intake of milk, meat, and eggs, the essence of Inoue's nutritional treatment is the sufficient intake of rice and whole grains, a traditional Japanese and Chinese diet, which, Lu maintains, can be an effective method of self-treatment.[67] This seems to be an "Eastern" cure for neurasthenia, apparently aiming to refute the American neurologist George Beard's (1839–83) theory of "the diet of the nervous," as I will explain below. Lu's diction itself suggests his heavy reliance on the classical Chinese medicinal lexicon, e.g., *liaoyangfa* for rendering *eiyō ryōhō* 營養療法 in the title. *Liaoyang* is a concept in traditional Chinese medicine for maintaining the body in balance, whereas *eiyō* is a Japanese invention for rendering "nutrition." But in the text he uses Japanese *kanji* terms such as *eiyō* 營養 (*yingyang* in Chinese), *kanzen eiyō* 完全營養 (*wanquan yingyang* in Chinese, full nutrition), *nikkōyoku* 日光浴 (*riguangyu* in Chinese, meaning "sun bath"), *onsenyoku* 溫泉浴 (*wenquanyu* in Chinese, meaning "spa") and so on. The Japanese term *onsen* is derived from classical Chinese, of course.

In comparison, Wang Xiho's 王羲和 translation published in 1919, *A Self-Treatment for Neurasthenia* (Shenjing shuairuo ziliaofa 神經衰弱自療法), was written in vernacular Chinese. It is based on the theories of Beard,[68] to whom is generally attributed the invention of the disease in 1869 with the famous article "Neurasthenia, or Nervous Exhaustion," although some, including Freud, believed that it was a new label describing an old disease which had had a history in Britain since the mid seventeenth century.[69] Beard's 1871 book *The Medical and Surgical Use of Electricity* was translated into German and led to "a wide vogue" in Europe.[70] In *American Nervousness*, published in 1881, he stated that neurasthenia was especially an American disease, caused by modern civilization, i.e., industrialization and urbanization, exhausting climate (extreme heat, cold, or dryness), or excessive indulgence of appetites or passions.[71] In *Sexual Neurasthenia*, published posthumously in 1884, he lists varieties of neurasthenia, including cerebral, spinal, digestive, sexual, traumatic, and hysterical neurasthenia, and "hemi-neurasthenia," which affects one side, usually the left side, of the body.[72] He calls the brain, the stomach, and the genital system "a trinity"; when one is attacked by illness, all are touched. He advises a combination of cures, including electrotherapy, water therapy, injection, and so on, but considers food without any other medicine better than all other medicines without food.[73] Reading about this, it suddenly dawns on me why the male protagonist of Mu Shiying's "A Man Taken as a Plaything" plays so much with the term "indigestion" resulted from eating too much chocolate (or men) in connection with neurasthenia.

Beard is very much into the theory of evolution, or his own interpretation of evolution, maintaining that "The functions of the human body that are last in order of development are the reproductive and productive—the power to reproduce the species, and the power of abstract thought, including memory.... Therefore, when the nervous system is attacked by enfeebling disease, these latest evolved functions... should suffer."[74] In Chapter 8, "The Diet of the Nervous," he resorts to his own notions of evolution again: "The theory of evolution is that the universe is a growth in a series, from the simple to the complex."[75] He believes that the best food for man is that which is nearest to him on the scale of biological development, according to his own concept of evolution, namely animal food such as meat, eggs, milk, and fish. He advises against fruits, vegetables, cereals (except wheat), and fat (except butter). For the extremely delicate constitution, butter and even bread are not recommended. This is totally the reverse of what we consider health food today. In this respect, Inoue Masayoshi's book discussed above, *The Nutritional Treatment for Neurasthenia*, could well be viewed as a counter-theory to Beard's.

However naïve Beard's theories of neurasthenia may have seemed, it was he who popularized it as a notion of pathological psychology. His cultural and social etiology differs from Freud's psychotherapy, which concentrates on neurosis and its roots in sexual repression. According to Philip Wiener, Freud took Beard seriously in his 1895 article "Über die Berechtigung, von der Neurasthenie einen bestimmten Symptomenkomplex als 'Angstneurose' abzutrennen" (The Justification for Detaching from Neurasthenia a Particular Syndrome: The Anxiety Neurosis).[76] In this article, even though Freud disagrees that the so-called neurasthenia is an American disease in particular, and that one should distinguish all the neurotic symptoms from those of neurasthenia, he admires Beard for being the first American physician to perceive and maintain the particular symptoms of this disorder and their connection with the modern way of life.

Nerasthenia as a mental disorder traveled in modern times from Europe to America, where it was dubbed a modern disease, and then back to Europe, where new interests in the disease were revived, and then to Japan and China, where traditional Eastern medicine was enlisted to fight it. We have seen how the concept and the treatment of the disease underwent creative transformation along the way, which is the inevitable process characteristic of transcultural modernity. The disease gradually found its way into modern Chinese literature around the mid 1920s. As I have discussed earlier in this chapter, in Mu Shiying's story "A Man Taken as a Plaything," the modern boy tortured by the modern girl claims repeatedly that he is developing "neurasthenia." He says so in a playful fashion, very much in line with the usual Neo-Sensation sarcasm against modernism and scientism. Mu was not alone in using psychological terms like this in his story, and the way he ridiculed such terms indicates that the real targets were literary men who took them seriously and made them the central motifs in their works. In other words, literary men who were easy prey to scientism were under attack.

During the 1920s, terms like "neurasthenia," "hypochondria," and "hysteria" appeared frequently in works by Creation Society writers such as Zhang Ziping and Yu Dafu, but in a matter-of-fact manner. They usually wrote about the sexual psychology of the characters in their stories and could well be considered predecessors of the Neo-Sensation writers such as Liu Na'ou, Mu Shiying, and Shi Zhicun in the predilection for the erotic. That these two groups of writers were familiar with these medical terms does not come as a surprise at all, since Zhang, Yu, and Liu studied in Japan when they were young. In the Creation writers' works there is a strong suggestion that neurasthenia is connected with sexual indulgence, which, according to Chinese folk belief, may lead to tuberculosis.[77] For instance, in Zhang Ziping's novel *Taili* (1926), the male protagonist says of Taili, his cousin's wife with whom he is having an affair, "She fell ill with hysteria (*xiesidilibing* 血斯得利病), while I, with neurasthenia (*shenjing shuairuo*) and early-stage tuberculosis (*laobing* 癆病). Both of us sacrificed our health for love and desire."[78] In Yu Dafu's *Sinking* (Chenlun 沈淪, 1921), the term *youyuzheng* repeatedly appears. When it first appears in Chapter 2 of the novel, the English word "hypochondria" is given.[79] It seems that without this term accompanied by its English original, it would be impossible for him to describe the male character's psychological condition.

If we trace its etymological origin, the Chinese term *youyu*, pronounced as *yūutsu* in Japanese *kanji*, can be found in classical texts such as *Anecdotes of the Xuanhe Period of the Great Song, Newly Reprinted* (Xinkan Dasong Xuanhe yishi 新刊大宋宣和遺事) and *Manuscript of Qing History* (Qingshi-gao 清史稿). It was usually used as a verb in sentences such as *youyu cheng bing* 憂鬱成病 (suffered unvented anxiety and became ill), or *youyu sui jiubing* 憂鬱遂久病 (suffered unvented anxiety and developed a chronic illness).[80] In classical medical texts, the term *youyu*, again used as a verb, is well documented, usually connected with an illness of the lung, as in the phrase *youyu shangfei* 憂鬱傷肺 (suffered unvented anxiety and hurt the lung).[81] The combination of *youyu* (*yūutsu*) with the suffix *zheng* (*shō*) to indicate an illness is a Japanese invention.

The contemporary writer and critic Su Xuelin (1897–1999), discussing Yu Dafu's works in 1934, wrote:

> "Egotism" [*Ziwo zhuyi* 自我主義] and "Sentimentalism" [*ganshang zhuyi* 感傷主義] are also the basic elements in Yu's works.... Both "sentimentalism" and "egotism" are the characteristics of modern thought, a kind of abnormal "Hysteria" [*xiesidili* 歇私的里] with which the malady of the century [Ch. *shijibing* or *seikibyō* 世紀病] endowed the modern literati ... The protagonist in *Sinking* (Chenlun 沈淪) ... fell ill with hypochondria in Japan.... Because of the inability to contain his sexual desire, he was self-destructive and became emaciated with neurasthenia, committing suicide by jumping into the sea in the end.[82] [English words in quotation marks originally provided by the author]

The point is, for modern writers such as members of the Creation Society and the Neo-Sensation School, to describe the sensations, feelings, psyche, and malady of the heart of the modern person, they needed to use translated vocabulary. As a result, contemporary critics had to use terms of psychoanalysis to discuss their works.[83] In addition, these writers' public images became connected with the disorder known as neurasthenia.[84] In the February and March entries of his 1927 diary, Liu Na'ou writes about his symptoms of neurasthenia, for which he is treated as an inpatient at Shinakawa Hospital 品川醫院, a Japanese hospital in Shanghai:

> I felt a splitting pain in half of my head. Two or three swollen masses grew on my face. It's really neurasthenia again! [7 February]
>
> My head and face were more swollen. My left eye was so miserably thin that I looked awful. They [doctors and nurses] said it's migraine caused by extreme neurasthenia. [11 February]

I hate human beings, feeling like committing suicide.[85] [16 March, in Japanese]

私は人間嫌い自殺するかもしれない

The diary writer is telling us that he is suffering from the "malady of the heart." After Akutagawa Rūnosuku's suicide on 24 July 1927, Liu, visiting Japan at the time, was haunted by the thoughts of suicide and madness and wrote on the following day:

> When my nerves were pricking because of insomnia, another shock came. Didn't Akutagawa Rūnosuku commit suicide? . . . he was an unfortunate guy claimed by the devil of nerves. . . . The extremities of the nerves are avenues to madness. Didn't Uno Kōji 宇野浩二 go mad? [My ellipses]

Liu Na'ou, Mu Shiying, Zhang Ziping, and Yu Dafu belonged to a generation of writers who sought to understand people's body and mind, including their own, through translated knowledge. But had not the generation or generations before them done the same? We certainly still do today. If we think the Creation and Neo-Sensation writers were the only groups of intellectuals who were afflicted by the malady of the heart in the 1920s and 1930s, we will be underestimating the pervasiveness of the new disease. With the courtship dramas enacted in modern cities complicated by traditional practices of arranged marriages back in rural hometowns; with the elimination of the imperial examinations and the intelligentsia thrown into the everyone-for-his-own-livelihood condition; with the large-scale human displacements and suffering caused by civil wars and imperial invasions, and so on, China in the early decades of the twentieth century was the incubatory bed for psychological illnesses.

Even Lu Xun and Shen Congwen, two of the most outright critics of these two groups of writers for their decadence, were not free from the crippling affliction of the nerves.

As early as 1912 Lu Xun already recorded a Japanese doctor's diagnosis of his chronic disease in the 12 August entry of his diary: "I have been coughing for a few days, and I suspected it to be bronchitis. In the morning I went to Ikeda Hospital 池田醫院 (a Japanese hospital in Beijing) to see a doctor, who said it was nothing serious, but the symptoms indicated neurasthenia."[86] His literary works also disclosed traces of obsession with this modern disorder. "Diary of a Madman" (Kuangren riji 狂人日記, 1918) depicted a man suffering from the malady of the heart caused by splitting values. The deranged narrative voice in his prose poetry collection, *Wild Grass* (Yecao 野草, 1927), called by critics the "window to Lu Xun's soul," induces a reading that identifies the narrator with the author. Suffering from unknown pains and illnesses all his life and eventually dying of tuberculosis, his suicidal impulses were made known in only a recent study in China.[87]

If we read Shen Congwen's highly autobiographical work, "Letters from a Genius" (Yige tiancai de tongxin 一個天才的通信, 1929), fictional letters written by a writer to an editor begging for the speedy payments of his honorariums and complaining about the chronic illnesses that make writing extremely exhausting for him, we see an intellectual verging on a nervous breakdown. Afflicted with splitting headaches, lowness of spirit, unspecified pains, insomnia, nose bleeding, tuberculosis, and so on, he is haunted by hallucinations of executions, genocide, people dying of war and famine. With suicidal thoughts and thinking about killing people, he is emaciated, pale, and reduced to a human wreck.[88] Written after the civil war which drove him to flee from Beijing to take shelter in Shanghai, this piece is telling us in every way that the narrator-author is suffering from neurasthenia, the malady of the heart to which intellectuals became easy prey because of their oversensitivity. Shen says:

> Unless one lives in Nanjing or the concessions in Shanghai, isn't killing a daily phenomenon? War is also absurd. Everybody having been living in this new war for years, talking about it would be boring. As to famine, the headlines in the newspapers are about the two thousand people dying of famine in Shanxi and Gansu every day. In the same newspaper is printed in extra large characters the cure effects of Bailingji. But on the reverse side, people are urged to go to meetings "in a ceremonious way," manifesting peace under the sky.[89]

"A Hundred-Year-Old Machine" (Bailingji 百齡機) is a tonic for anemia and neurasthenia. In the 1930s the newly adopted medical jargon such as neurasthenia and hypochondria indicating the malady of the heart was commonly employed in daily usage. In the newspapers and magazines all kinds of advertisements for medicines and vitamins curing this kind of disorder abounded. In *Shanghai Post* (Shenbao) in 1930 alone, more than ten advertisements devoted to such tonics could be found. For instance, on 12 August there was an ad for "Bailingji." It uses the metaphor of a machine to describe the human body. As a machine needs oil, so does a body energy. When the machine is covered with dust and rust, it needs to be replenished with oil; when the heart is attacked by hypochondria, it needs "Bailingji" (Figure 5.2).

On 13 May the *Shanghai Post* carried an ad for "Doan's Pills for Strengthening the Nerves" (Dou'anshi bushen yaopian 兜安氏補神藥片), with the English name "Doan's Nerve Tonic Tablets" printed on the box of the medicine. To promote the nerve tonic, the Chinese name of the medicine uses the term *bushen*, literally meaning "spirit-strengthening," a concept in traditional medicine. In the ad, in addition to images of the pine tree and the crane representing longevity, and the box of Doan's nerve tonic tablets hanging down from the tree branch, the caption boasts that the medicine is a comprehensive cure-all: "This medicine especially cures men and women of neurasthenia, lack of energy, neurological pains, forgetfulness, insomnia,

182 *Dandyism and Transcultural Modernity*

Figure 5.2 A Hundred-Year-Old Machine.

dyspepsia, weakness after illnesses, and so on, with fantastic effects. For literary men and scholars who suffer from neurasthenia in mid life due to overworking, this medicine is a wonder cure for strengthening the nerves, with speedy effect" (Figure 5.3).[90] On the bottom of the ad is printed "Doan's Medical Company of Western medicine." This company sold medicines such as "Doan's Backache Kidney Pills" in Victorian England and Sydney. On 13 December 1900 one ad for this medicine could be seen in *The Bulletin*, published in Sydney (Figure 5.4).[91]

There is an ad in *Shanghai Post* on 8 November for "Blutose" (Bu'erduoshou 補爾多壽), a blood-fortifying tonic with the English description, "new iron tonic," and the German name of the tonic, "Blutose." The caption again states that the medicine will cure any ailment, with a mysterious German name in transliteration: "This medicine is an effective blood-fortifying and spermatozoon-strengthening tonic (*buxie qiangjing lingyao* 補血強精靈藥) invented by Humi Teubal, Ph.D., from Germany. Fragrant and delicious, it ... specializes in curing all kinds of weaknesses, including anemia, neurasthenia, lack of stamina, lowness of spirit, back pain, feeble feet, tuberculosis, coughs, ... "[92] (Figure 5.5). Though it boasts of a German inventor, probably because a European name would add to its credibility and authority, this medicine was in fact sold by Fujisawa Medical Company. After its initial founding as Fujisawa Shōten (store) in Ōsaka by Fujisawa Tomokichi 藤澤友吉 in 1894, it functioned as Fujisawa Tomokichi Shōten from 1930 to 1943. Then it gradually expanded to Taiwan, Sweden, London, America,

Figure 5.3 Doan's Nerve Tonic Tablets.

France, and Germany.[93] A color poster for Blutose in Shōwa Japan shows a smiling woman holding a bottle of the medicine, with the caption on the upper-left saying, "*tadashiki hoketsu kyōsō zōshinzai*" 正しき補血強壯増進劑 (the true blood- and strength-fortifying tonic). The name "Burutōze" ブルトーゼ is printed on the upper right. At the bottom of the ad is the name of the seller: Fujisawa Tomokichi Shōten (Figure 5.6).[94] 藤澤友吉商店

Comparing the two Blutose ads, we seem to be witnessing the tonic for curing neurasthenia becoming a household medicine in both China and

184 *Dandyism and Transcultural Modernity*

Figure 5.4 Doan's Backache Kidney Pills.

Japan during the 1930s. While knowledge of the new disease was transmitted from the West to Japan and then to China through translated texts and the establishment of psychology as a discipline, those who diagnosed Lu Xun and Liu Na'ou as having neurasthenia were Japanese doctors who came to China with the Japanese imperialist invasion. Furthermore, in these ads Japanese and Westerners were now telling Chinese that, simply by buying the medicines they produced, neurasthenia, the malady of the heart, could be cured. So the traveling of this modern disease was facilitated not only by the transmission of scientific knowledge through translation, but by commercialism that went hand in hand with the expansion of Western and Japanese imperial powers.

A traveling disease 185

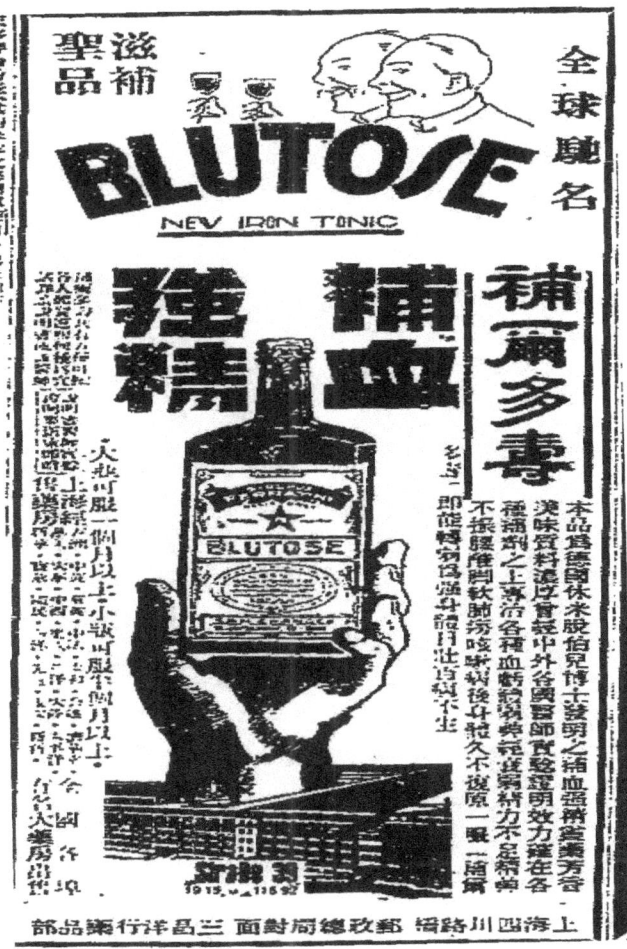

Figure 5.5 Blutose.

How to say "I love you"

"Yōko, you do love me, don't you?"
"Yes."
This mouth would never lie. I kissed this mouth that didn't lie.
"Yōko, what about those playthings?"
"Playthings are still playthings."
"Aren't you also saying you love them in front of those playthings?"
. . .
"Actually you don't need to say whether you love someone; all you need to know is the other party's heart. I do love you. Do you believe that? . . ."[95]

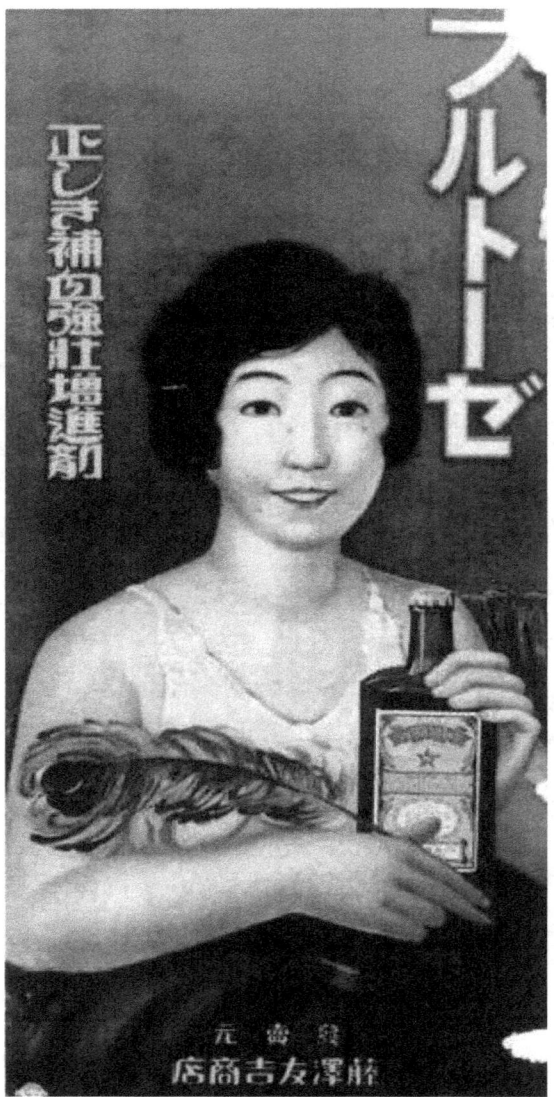

Figure 5.6 Burutōze.

In Mu Shiying's story "A Man Taken as a Plaything," the much frustrated modern boy, thinking he is developing neurasthenia, is so uncertain of the fickle modern girl's heart that he repeatedly asks her if she loves him, if she will stop loving him someday, and if she loves someone else. The "malady of the heart" is caused by the uncertainty of love, of course. It is no doubt a jealous lover that we are looking at. However, it is not a traditional Chinese lover we are talking about, but one in modern China. On the other hand, the capricious modern girl reassures her tortured lover by repeatedly saying, "I love you," an expression that would never appear in classical Chinese. Love became a big issue in May Fourth literature. Haiyan Lee's 2007 book, *Revolution of the Heart: A Genealogy of Love in China*, is devoted to the transformation of the concept of love in China in the first half of the twentieth century, tracing the "genealogy" of love from the Confucian concept of "qing" to the May Fourth concept of "free love." As a way of concluding this chapter, I am going to look at this issue from a slightly different angle: How the term "I love you" came into Chinese because of the missionary translations of Christian scriptures, and how Japanese adopted the word "love" in translating Western texts and then influenced the discourse of love in May Fourth literature.

Translated vocabulary has transformed not only the way we feel about ourselves and each other, but how we express our feelings for each other in modern China and Japan—without translation, Japanese and Chinese would not even know how to say "I love you." This we owe to the Protestant missionaries in their translations of the sacred scriptures, in which the word *ai* (love) used as a verb abounds, indicating God's love for men and vice versa, and the love between parents and children, between men and women, and between friends. We all know that in the *Book of Exodus* God explicitly tells his people, "I, the LORD thy God, am a jealous God," guarding them strictly from worshiping idols and demanding exclusive love from them.[96] A few passages from the Book of John, where "love" is most frequently used in the Bible, will show how persistently God demands the pledge of his people's love. *The Holy Bible* (Shentian shengshu 神天聖書, 1813), the first printed Chinese Bible, has these translated passages, in classical Chinese:

14:15 Erdeng ruo ai wo, ze shou wo jie. 爾等若愛我則守我戒 (If ye love me, keep my commandments.)
14:28 Er ruo ai wo ze huanxi. 爾若愛我則歡喜 (If ye loved me, ye would rejoice.)
15:9 Ru fu ai wo, wo ru shi ai er, qie ju yu wo ai ye. 如父愛我, 我如是愛爾, 且居于我愛也 (As the Father hath loved me, so have I loved ye; continue ye in my love.)[97]

The most revealing example is in Verses 15–17, Chapter 21, in which Jesus asks Simon, son of Jonas, three times, "Lovest thou me?" Simon, having to pledge his love three times, becomes distressed in the end and says: "Lord, thou knowest all things; thou knowest that I love thee." God, in extracting promises of love and fidelity from his loved one, is as pestering as any jealous lover could be, in real life or in fictional works in any literature.

If we pay enough attention to the prominent Christian motifs in the stories of Zhang Ziping, Yu Dafu, and Mu Shiying, among their contemporaries, we will not downplay the significance of Christian influences on the discourse of love in May Fourth literature. Christian influences on modern Japanese literature cannot be overemphasized, either.[98]

Until the nineteenth century no versions of the Bible in Chinese had been printed and distributed, although translations existed in private hands among the Catholic churches. It was the Protestant missionaries who began to publish the Chinese Bible. Robert Morrison (1772–1834), a Presbyterian minister from Scotland, became the first Protestant missionary in China, stationed in Guangzhou. He stayed in China for 27 years, pioneering the translation of the whole Bible into Chinese with a delegation of missionaries. The result was *The Holy Bible* (Shentian Shengshu), published in Malacca, Malay in 1813.[99] Walter Henry Medhurst (1796–1857), the English Congregationalist missionary, stayed in China for 16 years and revised the existing Chinese versions of the Bible with other missionaries. The New Testament was published in Shanghai in 1852, and the Old Testament, in Shanghai in 1856.[100] Both Morrison and Medhurst also compiled dictionaries that are most helpful to this study.

Robert Morrison's *A Dictionary of the Chinese Language* (1815–23) used the word *ai* (pronounced as *gae* in Cantonese) to translate "love."[101] That the Chinese words listed in Parts 2 and 3 of the dictionary, in three parts divided into six volumes, are given Cantonese pronunciation is consistent with the fact that Morrison and his missionary collaborators were based in either Guangzhou or Macao, the only two cities in China where missionary activities were allowed.[102] If we move on to the *Dictionary of Meiji Vocabulary* (Meiji no kotoba jiten 明治のことば辞典, 1986), we will see that the word *ai*, a Chinese loanword used in Meiji Japan to translate "love" or "to love," is listed as the first entry.[103] According to this dictionary, Suematsu Kenchō 末松謙澄 (1855–1920) used the word *ai* to render "love" in 1889 (the twenty-second year of Meiji) when translating *A Lily of the Valley* (Tanima no himeyuri 谷間の姫百合; original title *Dora Thorne*, 1877) by the British popular writer Charlotte Mary Brame (pseudonym Bertha M. Clay, 1836–84). He explains why he uses the word *ai* in a footnote:

> For me the original word *rābu* [love] has no equivalent in our language, therefore in this book when I translate it, I use *ai*, *bō* [慕 admiration], *ren* [戀 attachment], *shi* [思 miss], *kō* [好 favor], and so on. In principle I follow the mood and textual flow to decide on the proper word to translate it, without any set rules. The word "to like" in the original is less serious than "to love." Since it is also difficult for me to find the right word to show the difference in degree, its translation is often mixed with "to love." So I have no choice but to proffer the word [*ai*].[104]

Here we see a highly self-conscious translator weighing every possible equivalent available within his linguistic ability, simply to render a word properly. This is where personal agency comes in: In the choice of diction, which determines the correctness (as if "correctness" were possible) of the knowledge or the feeling transferred, a translator has to exhaust his linguistic learning to find the word he is most comfortable with. In this case, the word *ai* taken from classical Chinese is what he thinks is closer to the English word "to love."

As far as I know, the translation of "to love" as *lian'ai* (*lwân gnaé* in Cantonese pronunciation) in Chinese first appeared in Walter Henry Medhurst's *English and Chinese Dictionary* (Ying Hua zidian, 1847–48), under the phrase "to love tenderly." The other Cantonese equivalents under the item "to love" include *gnaé* (*ai* in Mandarin pronunciation) *haóu* (favor, *hao* in Mandarin), *pung* (to dote on, or *peng* in Mandarin as in "holding preciously in the palm of the hand"), *teĭh teĭh* (to be tender to, or *tengxi* in Mandarin), and so on.[105] In Japan "love" was first translated as *ren'ai* (*lian'ai* in Chinese) in 1870, when Nakamura Masanao 中村正直 (Nakamura Keiu 中村敬宇; 1832–91) translated Samuel Smiles's *Self-Help* (Saikoku risshihen 西國立志編 *Stories of Success in the West*, 1859) into Japanese. It was used as a verb by Nakamura, but later became a noun.[106] According to Yanabu Akira's study, Nakamura might have adopted the term from Medhurst's dictionary, which was widely read in Japan at the time.[107] Iwamoto Yoshiharu, 岩本善治 the editor of *Magazine of Women's Education* (Jogaku zasshi 女學雜誌), in a book review on a translated novel in 1890 points out that the word *koi* 戀 (pronounced as *ren* when used in the combination *ren'ai*), originally taken from vulgar Japanese, is transformed into something pure when used in the compound term *ren'ai*:

> The translator [in using the term *ren'ai*] has most purely and correctly rendered the feelings of *rābu* [love], while this vulgar Japanese word [*koi*] filled with unclean associations is dexterously used in the cleanest way possible.[108]

Kitamura Tōkoku's 北村透谷 (1868–94) 1892 article titled "The Unworldly Poet and Women" (Ensei shika to josei 厭世詩家と女性), published in the same magazine, opens with this statement: "Love (*ren'ai*) is the secret key to life—with love there is an afterlife; without love life is totally colorless." It is well known that this article heralded the romantic era in Japan.[109] Yanabu Akira's book *Love* (Ai) traces the etymology of "love" and the evolution of its meaning: as *eros* (love between man and woman) and *agape* (God's love for men) in Greek philosophy; as *caritas* and *cupiditas* in Christian theorists' Latin translation; as *amour* (man-woman love sublimated) sung by the troubadours combining both meanings; as *Liebe* in German and "love" in English after the Protestant reform; and as *ai* in modern Chinese and Japanese. For him, "It is a matter of the translated word" (*mondai wa honyakugo da* 問題は翻訳語だ).[110]

When we study the evolution of the concept of love in China, it would be limiting our perspective if we failed to look at what was happening at the same time in Japan, our close neighbor. The genre of "revolution + romance," which was prevalent in May Fourth China, had been a prominent genre in Taishō Japan when Anarchists such as Osugi Sakae advocated "free love" (Ch. *ziyiu lian'ai* or *jiyū ren'ai*) as an ideology against feudalism. As I have mentioned in Chapter 4, the Chinese anarchists Liu Shipei and Zhang Ji learned Esperanto with him when studying and participating in anarchist activities in Tokyo in 1907 and 1908. To contrast the "love + revolution" concept with the tradition of *qing* in China is not that meaningful; the key is why the discourse of *qing* that had lasted hundreds of years since the late Ming period seemed to be transformed overnight in modern China. Haiyan Lee's book *Revolution of the Heart* would have been more satisfying and illuminating if she had included Japan, our cultural *doppelgänger*, in the loop of the trajectory of this concept traveling from the West to May Fourth China.[111] If she had allowed the "genealogy" of the word "love" to cross the borders, both national and linguistic, between Japan and China, her book would have been a real eye-opener.

According to Yanabu, in *Manyōshū* 萬葉集 (625–750s), the collection of songs during the late Nara period, the word *ai* was borrowed from classical Chinese, while *koi* (*lian* in Chinese) was *yamato kotoba*, or the native Japanese language. He states that the word *ai* appears only in the "*daishi*" 題詞 (thematic statement) usually elaborating on Buddhist teachings, but never in the songs themselves, which are in native Japanese. According to him, the native words equivalent to *ai* were *omohoyu* and *shinubayu*.[112] But his notion that the word *koi* (*lian*) in *ren'ai* was of Japanese origin should be contested.

I have no problem that *koi* itself, if written in *kana*, was Yamato kotoba. But *ren'ai* as a term, always pronounced in *onyomi* (Chinese pronunciation) instead of *kunyomi* (Japanese pronunciation), is definitely the combination of the characters *lian* and *ai* in Chinese, which were both abundantly used in classical Chinese texts.[113] For instance, in the biography of Zhang Qian in *Book of Han* (Hanshu), by the great historian Ban Gu (32–92 AD), the words *lian* and *ai* appear in terms such as *manyi lian gudi* 蠻夷戀故地 (the barbarians were deeply attached to their homeland), *manyi ai zhi* 蠻夷愛之 (the barbarians loved him [Zhang Qian]), and *Chanyu aiyang zhi* 單于愛養之 ([the barbarian general] Chanyu loved and raised him [the baby orphan]).[114] Both *lian* and *ai* in the beginning were written instead of spoken language. Nearly ten centuries later in the *ci* poetry of the Song Dynasty, the word *lian* was already close to spoken language. For instance, Huang Tingjian 黃庭堅 (1045–1105) wrote in his *ci* poem, "*Yuan ni you lian ni, hen ni xi ni, bijing jiaoren zen sheng shi.*" 怨你又戀你。恨你惜你。畢竟教人怎生是。(Discontent with you but attached to you, hating you but holding you precious, how can one cope with this after all?)[115] But the usage *lian ni* (I am attached to you) never caught on.

Like us today, people living in classical China or before Meiji Japan knew how to love, of course. The poetess Wei Furen 魏夫人 (Madame Wei, 1040–1103) of the Song Dynasty wrote a *ci* poem in which a woman narrator, suffering from the long absence of her loved one, speaks her mind. The concluding stanza, rather explicit by the classical standard, reads like this: "I hate you, I miss you, how could you know?" (*Wo hen ni, wo yi ni, ni zhengzhi?* 我恨你，我憶你，你爭知？)[116] She intended to say "I love you," but simply couldn't find the word to say it.

The crucial expression that escaped Madame Wei in the eleventh century was made possible through the missionaries' translation of the sacred texts into Chinese in early nineteenth century. At the time when Chinese were facing the crisis of inventing a new language, it was through cultural translation that they learned to express the heart's desire, as they learned to name the malady of the heart; it was an "acquired" modern disease and sensibility. The eclectic language used by the modern boy and the modern girl in Mu Shiying's story highlights their fake affect, putting into relief the popularization, or vulgarization of acquired knowledge. In this story we see how a Neo-Sensation writer dexterously combines language experimentation, literary criticism, and critique of modernist pursuit of scientific knowledge in the delightful hodgepodge of the macaronic as a transcultural practice.

The subtle parallel between "a traveling disease" and traveling jargon in this chapter is aiming at defining transcultural modernity. This concept denotes more the mindset of an actor than that of a character in a play, if we use performativity as a metaphor. The making of a character as a site where different voices, languages, and discourses converge is fascinating, just as in Diana Taylor's description of a character called Intermediary, a mestiza woman, in a Mexican play in her book, *The Archive and the Repertoire*.[117] It is indeed the transcultural site, indicating a largely unconscious character who is drifting with the flux of ongoing currents, which flow in and out of her heart and body and inscribe cultural memory there. Our modern boy and modern girl are exactly such characters.

What this book is trying to get at, however, are self-conscious actors who find the intermediary or interstitial space a site for creative transformation. It is a space of the possible transformation of meanings, intents, and utterances where cultural translators—artists, thinkers, literary men, and intellectuals—work. In other words, an artist or writer in cultural translation is more an actor who acts upon the transcultural site than a character who is the site itself. He is not merely a "receptor/transmitter within that network of communication," as Taylor puts it, but one who finds "an agency of initiation" in that network, as Homi Bhabha says in *Location of Culture* when discussing minority communities,[118] or one who finds a mode of performative agency, as when Judith Butler talks about the representation of lesbian sexuality.[119] For Bhabha, agency is always created "through incommensurable (not simply multiple) positions."[120] It goes without saying that men all work under constraints, but those who are able to exercise agency despite the limits of institutional powers are those who stand out among the unconscious multitudes in the flux of voices and discourses. They are Foucault's modernists who are always at the frontiers and take upon themselves the task of the "heroization of the present," or the creative transformation of the present reality. Acting as propellers of transcultural modernity, they are trendsetters of all times.

Conclusion
To connect

The concept of transcultural modernity proposed in this book aims to bring into light the receptiveness of literature and the creative transformation practiced on the transcultural site. The macaronic, the term I use to highlight the transcultural hybridity of the Chinese new vernacular, can in fact be applied to modern Japanese during the early decades of the last century as well. With just a quick browse through the works of Nishiwaki Junzaburō, one would be amazed by the copious foreign (including Latin, French, and English) names, vocabulary, and sentences freely inserted into his poetry and theoretical writings. A line taken from the preface to his 1929 collection of articles, *Poetics of Surrealism*, exemplifies the not unusual practice in Japanese (and Chinese) literature during the modern era, when European culture represented the civilization of progress:

> Especially, this book simply records my thoughts surrounding *Ch. Baudelaire* . . . The influence of *Baudelaire*'s *Surnaturalisme* reached *Surréalisme* in the twentieth century.[1] [italicized words originally in French]

He emphasizes "simply," because, according to him, the works collected in this book are not governed by any theoretical or systematical guideline, but simply center around his thoughts on Baudelaire. The title of the poetry collection, "Ambarvalia," refers to a Roman agricultural fertility rite held in the end of May in honor of the goddess Ceres. The first section of this poetry collection is titled "LE MONDE ANCIEN" (original in French), and the second, "LE MONDE MODERNE." Like the writings of many of his avant-garde contemporaries, foreign words are freely inserted into his works without being transcribed into *katakana*. A lot of long passages of foreign text are not translated at all.

The susceptibility to the foreign and the experiment with the Japanese language in the beginning decades of the twentieth century was by no means exclusive to the Neo-Sensation School alone. Critics such as Miriam Sas and Steven Snyder have already pointed out how European influences spurred the invention of a new literary language and mode of writing among writers such as Nagai Kafū 永井荷風 and the surrealists at the time. Sas sees Japanese surrealism as an avant-garde encounter of Japan with France in which "creative intersections between distant realities, distant cultures" are possible. To him, both French and Japanese surrealists "investigated in their new use of language and in breaking apart and challenging notions of poetic meaningfulness."[2] The concept of dandyism, though not named as such, can be found in Nagai as well. To Snyder, "Nagai Kafū was a flâneur, that urban 'prowler' immortalized by the 'first modernist,' Baudelaire, in *Le Spleen de Paris*."[3]

Not only does Snyder point out that Nagai was a Baudelairean-style flâneur, but he quotes from Edward Seidensticker's translation of Nagai Kafū's 1919 essay, "The Fireworks" (Hanabi 花火), in which Nagai is literally turned into an "old-style dandy":

> I concluded that I could do no better than drag myself down to the level of the Tokugawa writer of frivolous and amatory fiction. Arming myself with the tobacco pouch that was the mark of the old-style dandy, I set out to collect Ukiyoe 浮世絵 prints, and I began to learn the samisen. . . .[4]

Here Seidensticker's translation is in fact an interpretative rendering. In Nagai's original, the word "dandy" does not exist at all. It says simply, "From then on with the tobacco pouch hanging on my side, I set out to collect Ukiyoe prints and learn the samisen."[5] But even though the word "dandy" is not there, Nagai's text unmistakably conveys the idea of dandyism, which both Seidensticker's translation and Snyder's discussion imply: the highly self-conscious dandy/artist on the threshold of the historical divide, looking for self-invention. Fascinated by Western literary models and obsessed with his own artistic perfection, Nagai searches in Edo and Tokugawa traditions for his own literary connection with the past and the possibilities for a new literary language and narrative mode. The outward or behavioral indicators of a dandy's leisurely life are of course there, too: the tobacco pouch, Ukiyoe prints collecting, samisen learning, and the patronage of demimonde women. Here we see tradition and the foreign mixed in his self-styled dandyish image: the foreign tobacco combined with the traditional art form and musical instrument. Underneath this seemingly leisurely lifestyle is the dandy's highly self-conscious artistic pursuit and endless toil for self-invention. Nagai Kafū was certainly not alone in this attitude towards testing the limits and exploring possibilities for transgression. Even though the term "dandyism" might not have existed, writers of the period in Japan were certainly practicing it.

Likewise, the practice of the macaronic and dandyism in China was not restricted to the Shanghai Neo-Sensation writers alone. As early as 1901, Liang Qichao wrote an essay titled "Inspiration" (Yanshipilichun 煙士披里純), which can be seen as a perfect demonstration of the macaronic. The Chinese characters in the title, literally meaning "smoke-scholar-drape-homeland-pure," are used to transcribe the sound of the original English word. Only a little longer than one page, the essay, resorting to episodes in Western history to illustrate the concept of inspiration, contains transliterated foreign names such as Moses, Alexander Hamilton, Martin Luther, Rousseau, Washington, Napoleon, Cromwell, Joan of Arc, and so on. Names enlisted from classical Chinese texts abound, too: Mencius 孟子, the poet and scholar-historian Zhao Oubei 趙甌北 (1727–1814), and characters from *Romance of the Three Kingdoms* such as Zhuge Liang 諸葛亮, Guangong 關公, Zhang Fei 張飛, Zhao Yun 趙雲, Liu Bei 劉備, Caocao 曹操, and Sun Quan 孫權. Titles of Western and classical Chinese texts such as Rousseau's *The Confessions* and *Records of the Grand Historian* (Shiji 史記) are not lacking. The essay is written in classical Chinese, with transliterations of foreign names and original foreign text inserted into the narrative. The English word "INSPIRATION," appears twice in parenthesis. The sentence "WOMAN IS WEAK, BUT MOTHER IS STRONG" appears in parenthesis after the Chinese translation.[6] Liang's macaronic style, combining classical Chinese, traditional vernacular, transliterations of foreign names and diction, and foreign text, had a great influence on later literary men. On the threshold of a new era, the macaronic as a free composite of various linguistic elements met the increasing demand for speedily conveying new concepts and new ideas. When he was in exile in Yokohama as a reformist against the corrupted Qing regime, Liang established a magazine titled *The New People Biweekly* (*Xinmin congbao* 新民叢報), which lasted from 1902 to 1907. His specific writing style, venerated as The New People style (*xinminti* 新民體) at the time, could be considered as a forerunner of the new vernacular in China.

Take for instance the poet Xu Zhimo (1897–1931), leader of the Crescent Moon Society and famous for translating Baudelaire's poem "Une Chargone" (A Carcass).[7] Son of a well-to-do businessman, he was endowed with all the material qualities of a dandy. He was known to be handsome in early youth, with fine features and delicate skin. Particular about his clothing, he usually wore a traditional silk gown (*changpao* 長袍) with a short vest, decorated with buttons made of precious stones or jade. Even his footwear was special. Between the cotton socks and black satin shoes, each of his feet was always wrapped with a square cloth in the shape of a fan. It is also known that all his life he wore glasses with golden frames.[8] Driven by the will for self-perfection, he was a compulsive traveler as well, intending to learn from famous men in the world. A disciple of Liang Qichao, he studied sociology and political science at Columbia University and Cambridge University. It is said that before he was 24, he was more interested in relativism and Rousseau's Social Contract than in poetry. When he was in England in 1921, he began to write poetry, because he fell in love for the first time, unfortunately with the talented Lin Huiyin 林徽音, who was engaged to be Liang Qichao's future daughter-in-law through the arrangement between Liang and her father.

Xu himself was not free, either. His 20-year-old wife, married to him for five years, also through an arranged marriage, had once been adored by him. Lin Huiyin was taken back to China by her father to avoid a scandal, while Xu cruelly divorced his beautiful and virtuous wife, when she was about to give birth to their second son. He stubbornly destroyed his own marriage, but could never get the woman he wanted. Like a typical dandy, complex relationships with women seemed to be his destiny. Before he returned to China in 1922, he traveled in England and visited Berlin, Paris, Singapore, Hong Kong, and Japan. In each place he encountered numerous modern girls whose enchanting beauty was recorded in his writings, for instance, the short-lived, New Zealand-born writer Katherine Mansfield, whom he once met in London.[9] Intending to introduce her works to the Chinese, he became a translator. His relationship with his second wife, Lu Xiaoman 陆小曼, a typical modern girl who spoke English and French, turned out to be disastrous. She divorced her first husband, who was also Liang Qichao's disciple, to marry him. After marriage, he tolerated her affair with another man who was always at her bed where she smoked opium all day long, and taught courses at universities from Shanghai to Beijing to support her extravagant lifestyle. In the end, he accepted Hu Shi's invitation to teach full-time at Beijing University, but was summoned back to Shanghai by her. On his way back to Beijing, he died in a plane crash.

The story of Xu Zhimo, known as the Chinese Byron, and the three women in his life has inspired numerous stories and adaptations, including a popular television drama series in 2006. The driving force behind his cruelty towards an innocent wife (he even asked her to have an abortion), his longing for a woman he cannot get, and his infatuation with an opium addict has aroused different interpretations, since the poet was known for his unusual generosity and kindness towards friends and students. From my point of view, the story reflects a dandy's relentless search for his perfect other self in the modern girl. The first wife, a paragon of virtue but intellectually inferior, was certainly not a modern girl. We know that he tried to educate her: Before he went to study in the States, he arranged for his old school teacher to give her lessons in classical Chinese.[10] Lin Huiyin, on the other hand, represented his ideal other self. She wrote poems as well, and they shared the same views on the prosody, musicality, and emotional power of the new poetry as a revolutionary literary medium. In a 1923 letter responding to Liang Qichao, who advised him to be cautious in man-and-woman relationships (implying his relation with Lin), Xu wrote, "I will look for my only soul mate in the sea of human beings."[11] In his everlasting search for his perfect other self, he saw the potential of the dazzling modern girl, Lu Xiaoman, to become his soul mate (he encouraged her to write), but was tortured by her and died for her.

Xu Zhimo's literature was a perfect example of how dandyism brings about transcultural modernity on the threshold of a new era. His works as a whole are a demonstration of the macaronic and his efforts in negotiating between traditional and modern verse forms, standard Mandarin and dialects. He translates the poems of Keats, Elizabeth Browning, and Maurice

Thomson in the form of the *Book of Poetry* (*Shijing* 詩經).¹² For instance, the opening line of Browning's "Inclusions," "Wilt thou have my hand, dear, to lie along in thine?" is turned into *"Xujie wo ai! He wo yu shou?"* 「吁嗟我愛！盍握予手？」 (Ah, my love! Why don't you hold my hand?), with "*xujie*," onomatopoeia indicating sighs, recurring throughout the poem like a refrain, typical of *Book of Poetry*. It is truly soothing and delightful to the Chinese ear. The poem "A Shaft of Golden Light: Monologue in the Xiashi Dialect" (Yitiao jinse de guanghen: Xiashi tubai 一條金色的光痕：陝石土白), combines monologue, a newly introduced Western literary form, with the dialect of Xiashi, his hometown in Zhejiang Province.¹³ With the monologue form, he successfully practices the May Fourth slogan of turning folk language into poetry. His essays fully illustrate the concept of the macaronic as well. Transliterations of foreign names and terms, foreign text quoted without translation, translations of foreign concepts, these all constitute an integral part of Xu's as well as other literary men's writing since the late Qing throughout the May Fourth period.

In fact, the macaronic can be considered as the essence of any literature and language in formation. Indeed, are not all living languages and literatures marked by this kind of receptiveness, and thus in a constant state of flux? A Japanese friend of mine told me that, returning to Tokyo after a year of visit at Harvard University, she was totally unable to understand the new *katakana* terms that had emerged during her absence. It is the same with Mandarin Chinese. I cannot even understand the currently emerging student slang terms without my son explaining them to me.

After recapitulating the essence of dandyism and the macaronic as practiced by modern Japanese and Chinese literary men other than the Neo-Sensation writers, by way of conclusion I would venture another aspect of the concept of transcultural modernity: to connect. One major intention of this book is to highlight this aspect: What is happening in one place is connected with occurrences in another place, maybe on the other side of the globe, most often through seemingly unrelated events, as is so powerfully shown in Alejandro González Iñárritu's 2006 movie *Babel*. In the movie, a gunshot in the desert connects the two Moroccan teenage brothers with the American tourist couple, the Japanese who sold the gun to the Moroccan hunter, his unhappy daughter Chieko 千惠子 who witnessed her mother's suicide, the Japanese detective investigating the gunshot incident, and the Mexican nanny of the couple's children for 16 years who is deported from the United States due to the stringent border control. This movie inspires thinking over the difficult conundrum: connecting or border control? We are all familiar with the downside of open borders such as exposure to terrorism and drug trafficking and the threat to domestic labor force, but relentless control results in tragedies such as family separation and xenophobia. The point is, however tightly the borders are guarded, there is no way to stop the illegal moving of people and goods. When we are talking about literature, what would be at stake if we "legalize" all the circulation of people, texts,

Conclusion 197

concepts, and so on, beyond national borders, since it is unstoppable in any case?

To further develop the concept of "to connect," I would like to mention an event in modern Japanese literature. It is known that Japanese modernist poetry did not begin in Japan proper. In 1924 the poetry magazine *A* (亞 Asia) was published in Dairen (Dalian 大連 in Chinese), Manchuria by Anzai Fuyue 安西冬衛 (1898–1965) and Kitagawa Fuyuhiko 北川冬彦 (1900–990), poets in diaspora. Anzai came to Dairen as an employee of the South Manchurian Railway Company, run by the Japanese colonial government, whereas Kitagawa came with his father who worked for the same company. Together the two poets advocated a new kind of prose poetry intended to reform the new poetry developed since the early Meiji period, which was already becoming stylized and losing vitality. Later the British-trained Nishiwaki Junzaburō, who established the Surrealist School in Tokyo in 1926, would recognize their creative talent and express his admiration of their poetry. In 1928 he invited Anzai to join him in establishing the magazine *Shi to Shiron* (Poetry and Poetics), an event that marked the convergence of modernist poetics from both Japan's colony and its mainland.[14]

The beginning of Japanese modernism connected with Japan's empire building and Manchuria has drawn sporadic critical attention so far, while Manchuria studies itself, one that brings in perspective China, Japan, Korea, Russia, among other nations, has become a most fascinating field.[15] The example of the beginning of Japanese modernism in Manchuria indicates at least two aspects to me.

First, what we deem to be "Japanese" or "Chinese" has never been as exclusive as the words themselves seem to suggest. When we study literature, the concept of "national literature" is perhaps less stimulating than literature that moves across national borders and connects different nations. Terms such as Chinese literature, Japanese literature, English literature, and so on, are, of course, still legitimate. But we need to note that the so-called national literatures are never enclosed entities; they are fluid, with their borders, like national borders, constantly infiltrated by foreign literary, cultural, and philosophical concepts and ideas. A certain magazine in Manchuria might start the Japanese modernist movement. A certain literary genre and style like the Neo-Sensation mode originated in 1920s Paris might find its way to Tokyo and Shanghai and transform what is traditional and native to the two countries. Similar situations can certainly be claimed with other literatures.

Second, Japanese modernism in Manchuria indicates that interdisciplinary studies is inevitable: Literature, politics, economics, and colonialism are intertwined. As no literature is so purely "national" to the extent that it is xenophobic, so is no literature completely exclusive to non-literary elements. As is often the case, to understand a literary phenomenon we sometimes need to investigate gender relations, philosophical concepts, missionary activities, political maneuverings, ideological beliefs, social mores, economic developments, scientific concepts, and so on. Insistence on "pure" literary studies would fail to present the richness and complexity of literature as not only the receptacle, but the creative transformer, of non-literary elements, as it were.

In this book while drawing attention to the traveling of people, genres, texts, concepts, and thoughts, what I am interested in is how they are connected by seemingly unrelated factors. While transcultural modernity is marked by the hybridity that accompanies literary and linguistic invention, the concept also indicates possible routes of connection. Connecting various cultures and disciplines with our own necessitates, on the one hand, multilingual and multicultural competence, and on the other, interdisciplinary investigation.

It has become a common sense that May Fourth literature was marked by the "obsession with China," as C. T. Hsia's 夏志清 famous 1961 phrase goes.[16] In fact, we can say the same about scholarship on modern Chinese literature. Today we are still not free from the obsession with the "national," as far as political sovereignty or literary studies are concerned. In the Sinophone communities, people in the Chinese Department seldom associate with those in the Japanese, and vice versa. This mutual exclusion does not improve much with departments of East Asian studies or Oriental studies in the United States, England, France, or elsewhere. Furthermore, the East–West divide in scholarship also seems insurmountable, however consistently comparative literature departments have been encouraging East–West comparison. The main reason is that somehow studies of non-European literatures fail to interest people in European studies. The real improvement for comparative literature would probably be to transgress the boundaries of departments and languages—not in the sense of denying the existence of boundaries, but of knowing where the limits are. Only when we are aware of our limits can we transform the status quo. Learning another language in or, better still, outside your own region, familiarizing yourself with another culture, would be the beginning of a new direction.

In recent years the untranslatability of languages and cultures has engaged quite a few literary theorists. Despite the fact of untranslatability, we still translate; comparative studies as a discipline still hangs on.[17] Is not the motivation behind this conundrum the will to relate, and to connect, with the Other? I agree that regional studies has limits; East–West or European and non-European comparison is not satisfying, either. Do we need to renew the concept of world literature and find "universal values" or a "poetic universalism" on which to base comparative studies?[18] This would be going back to the old paradigm of parallel study. Rather, I suggest that we disregard for the moment the overburdened concept of "comparison," and propose instead the idea of "to connect"—to connect with languages/cultures and disciplines other than our own—as an alternative approach. It is when we are able to connect with what is not ours that we understand better our own reality in the crisscross of heterogeneous information in the global context. The point is to know that "our reality," forever indeterminable, always contains something that is not ours.

Notes

Preface

1 Cf. Silvia Spitta, *Between Two Waters: Narratives of Transculturation in Latin America* (Houston, TX: Rice University Press, 1995), pp. 3–4. For a detailed discussion of the evolvement of the Latin American concept of "transculturation" (a "two-way give and take), from that of "acculturation" (the one-way imposition of the dominant culture), see pp. 1–28.
2 For her inspiring concep of "translingual practice," see Lydia Liu, *Translingual Practice: Literature, National Culture, and Translated Modernity—China, 1900–1937* (Stanford, CA: Stanford University Press, 1995).
3 Mary Louise Pratt, *Imperial Eyes: Travel Writing and Transculturation* (London and New York: Routledge, 2000), pp. 4–11. First published in 1992. Also Emily Aptor, *The Translation Zone: A New Comparative Literature* (Princeton: Princeton University Press, 2006). Pratt's concept of the "contact zone," emphasizing the "colonial frontier" where subjects previously separated by geographic and historical disjunctures are related, is similar to Emily Apter's concept of the "translation zone."
4 Cf. Lydia Liu, *The Clash of Empires: The Invention of China in Modern World Making* (Cambridge, MA: Harvard University Press, 2004). Shu-mei Shih also sees East-West relations as confrontational. See note 8 in the following.
5 Mary Louise Pratt, *Imperial Eyes: Travel Writing and Transculturation*, pp. 4–11.
6 Diana Taylor, *The Archive and the Repertoire: Performing Cultural Memory in the Americas* (Durham: Duke University Press, 2003), pp. 79–86. Taylor uses the body of a mestiza woman in a play as a metaphor for the transcultural site: "The Intermediary looks to her body as the receptor, storehouse, and transmitter of knowledge that comes from the archive ("I know texts, pages, illusions") and from the repertoire of embodied knowledge ("I also retain memories that belonged in my grandmother, my mother, or my friends") (pp. 81–82).
7 Judith Butler, "Imitation and Gender Insubordination," in Aiana Fuss, ed., *Inside/Out: Lesbian Theories, Gay Theories* (New York: Routledge, 1990), pp. 13–31.
8 Shu-mei Shih, *The Lure of the Modern: Writing Modernism in Semicolonial China, 1917–1937* (Berkeley: University of California Press, 2001), pp. 3–5. Shih proposes to discuss the "difference and similarity" of non-Western modernisms with their Western model. She says, "Where similarity is emphasized, we perceive a transnational and deterritorialized modernism that promises the possibility of a cosmopolitan cultural politics, even as it necessarily hides a fundamentally hierarchical notion of center and periphery. When concerns over cultural domination are projected onto similarity, however, non-Western modernisms become sites of anxiety and paranoia. All of these modes of seeing non-Western modernisms acknowledge a *necessary* confrontation with the West. It is from the perspective of

this necessity that Chinese modernism must also be understood." (Original italic) She further maintains that "Debunking the myths of Eurocentric modernism and the binary model of cultural confrontation is thereby a central task in any discussion of Chinese modernism."
9 See Chapters 4 and 5 of this study.
10 Diana Taylor, *The Archive and the Repertoire: Performing Cultural Memory in the Americas*, p. 7. Taylor says, "From the wing commonly referred to as the 'dramaturgical,' anthropologists such as Turner, Milton Singer, Erving Goffman, and Clifford Geertz began to write of individuals as agents in their own dramas. Norms, they argued, are contested, not merely applied. Analyzing enactment became crucial in establishing claims to cultural agency. Humans do not simply adapt to systems. They shape them. How do we recognize elements such as choice, timing, and self-presentation except through the ways in which individuals and groups perform them?"
11 Cf. Alexis de Tocqueville, *De la démocratie en Amerique* (Paris : Librarie Philosophique, 1990), an annotated and revised edition, 2 volumes. The two volumes were originally published in 1835 and 1840 respectively. This book is a criticism of American democracy. For Tocqueville, equality and freedom are antithetical. According to him, the blind belief in equality results in the "tyranny of democracy" in the United States. Joseph Epstein points out that Tocqueville realizes that the major issue for modern societies under democracy is the "necessary and continuing rivalry between equality and liberty." See his *Alexis de Tocqueville: Democracy's guide* (New York: HarperCollins/Atlas Books, 2006), p. 119.

Introduction

1 The caption of the portrait reads: "Rigaud was the favorite court painter of Louis XIV, the Sun King. The monarch, interested in conveying power and status in his state portraits, was pleased with this composition and commissioned several copies from Rigaud and his workshop. In this third version of a 1701 composition, the king's elegant pose, his haughty expressions, and the luxurious rendition of his satin and ermine coronation robes work together to glorify the monarch."
2 Peter Burke, *The Fabrication of Louis XIV* (New Haven and London: Yale University Press, 1992), p. 16.
3 Ibid., p. 184. The so-called formality is marked by "the stiff Spanish manner" of Spanish royal portraits, and the informality, "the more demoted style of other seventeenth-century kings, notably Christian IV of Denmark and Gustav Adolf of Sweden, who liked to speak to his subjects in the market-place."
4 Ibid., p. 33.
5 Ibid., p. 192.
6 Joan DeJean, *The Essence of Style: How the French Invented High Fashion, Fine Food, Chic Cafés, Style, Sophistication, and Glamour* (New York: Free Press, 2005), pp. 83–103. DeJean points out that until the seventeenth century footwear was almost identical for both sexes, while women's shoes, hidden by long skirts, were often less decorated than men's.
7 For an English account of the story of Lestage, see DeJean, pp. 86–90. What DeJean fails to mention is that the 1677 poetry collection acclaiming Lestage's achievement, *Poésies nouvelles sur le sujet des bottes sans couture présentées au Roy par le sieur Nicolas Lestage, maître Cordonnier de Sa Majesté* [New Poems on the Subject of the Boots without Seams Presented to the King by Lord Nicolas Lestage, His Majesty's Master Shoemaker], was probably compiled under the shoemaker's own commission, since Lestage himself dedicated the poetry collection to the Duke of Roquelaure. One passage in his dedication mentions how the portrait was hung in the king's gallery with the label, "Il est miracle de son âge."

For a French account on the topic, see Paul Lacroix, Alphonse Duchesne, and Ferdinand Seré, *Histoire des cordonniers et des artisans dont la profession se rattache à la cordonnerie* [History of Shoemakers and Craftsmen Whose Profession Is Attached to Shoemaking] (Paris : Librairies Historique, Archéologique et Scientifique de Seré, 1852), pp. 189–97. The authors imply that the portrait with the label was probably the arrogant shoemaker's own fabrication.

8 Julia Prest, *Theatre Under Louis XIV: Cross-Casting and the Performance of Gender in Drama, Ballet and Opera* (New York: Palgrave Macmillan, 2006).

9 Homosexuality was a common practice in Louis's court, even though he had to impose a law prohibiting it under the pressure from the Church. Louis's father (Louis XIII), uncle (César de Vendôme), brother (Philippe d'Orléons), a son (the comte de Vermandois), and top generals (duke de Luxembourg, duke de Vendôme, Charles Louis Hector de Villars) were known to be gay, who more or less hid their homosexual pleasures from public. Cf. Louis Crompton, *Homosexuality & Civilization* (Cambridge, MA: Harvard University Press, 2003), pp. 339–60.

10 Plato, *The Symposium*, trans. Christopher Gill and Desmond Lee (New York: Penguin, 1999), pp. 26–31.

11 Joshua Goldstein, *Drama Kings: Players and Publics in the Re-creation of Peiking Opera, 1870–1937* (Berkeley: University of California Press, 2007).

12 Ibid., 77–101.

13 Notably, Louis's court and the salon culture of the day provided women with a social space where they were able to act nearly as freely as men, while women in Spain and Italy were still segregated from men in social life. State intervention in universal basic education conducted by the Church also began during Louis's reign; it was regulated by law that girls had the same right as boys to receive both religious education and basic education. Cf. Roger Duchêne, *Être femme au temps de Louis XIV* [Being Woman at the Time of Louis XIV] (Paris : Perrin, 2004).

14 Cf. Maureen Needham, "Louis XIV and the Académie Royale de Danse, 1661: A Commentary and Translation," *Dance Chronicle*, 20.2 (1997): 173–90.

15 One of the Japanese pioneers of the translation of French literature is the poet Horiguchi Daigaku 堀口大学, whose 1925 collection *Gekka no ichigun* 月下の一群 [Gathering in Moonlight] includes 340 poems by 66 modern French poets. According to his preface to this edition, almost half of the total output of his poetry translation in the past 10 years were French poems, which constitute the present collection. Among the French poets included were Charles Baudelaire, Paul Verlaine, Guillaume Apollinaire, and Stéphane Malarmé. See Horiguchi Daigaku, "Jo" 序 [Preface], in *Horiguchi Daigaku zenshū* 堀口大学全集 (Tokyo: Ozawa Shoten, 1981), vol. 2, p. 7.

16 See, e.g., Yiu-man Ma 馬耀民, "Baudelaire in China" (Ph. D. dissertation, National Taiwan University, 1997); Shibusawa Takesuke 澀澤孝輔, *Shi no kongen wo motomete – Bōdorēru, Ranbō, Hagiwara Sakutarō sono ta* 詩の根源を求めて—ボードレール・ランボー・萩原朔太郎その他 [Searching for Poetic Origins: Baudelaire, Rimbaud, Hagiwara Sakutarō, and others] (Tokyo: Shichōsha, 1970); Fukuda Mitsuharu 福田光治 et al., eds., *Ōbē sakka to Nihon kindai bungaku* 歐米作家と日本近代文學 [European authors and modern Japanese literature] (Tokyo: Kyōiku Shuppan Sentā, 1974), 5 volumes. For a translation and discussion of Xu Zhimo's translation of Baudelaire's poem "Le charogne" [A Carcass] into Chinese see Haun Saussey, "Death and Translation," *Representations*, 94.1 (Spring 2006): 112–30.

17 Cf. Rhonda K. Garelick, *Rising Star: Dandyism, Gender, and Performance in the Fin de Siècle* (Princeton, NJ: Princeton University Press, 1998). Garelick discusses four famous treatises of dandyism: Balzac's "Traité de la vie élégante" [Treatise on the Elegant Life] (1830), Barbey d'Aurevilly's "Du Dandysme et de George Brummell" [On Dandyism and George Brummell]; (1843), Baudelaire's *The*

Painter of Modern Life (1863), and Jean Lorrain's *Une Femme par jour* [A Woman during Daytime] (1890). While Garelick's definition of dandyism centers on the dandy's urge for aesthetic or social reproduction (how originality can be replicated to create a whole movement), my definition emphasizes the dandy's self-consciousness of being at the frontiers and readiness for transcultural practices to effect change. Unlike Balzac, who divides humanity into three categories and assigns the dandy to the category of "those who do nothing," I think the dandy, though seeming to be a flâneur doing nothing serious, belongs to the other two categories in his division: "those who work" and "those who think."

18. Walter Benjamin, "The Paris of the Second Empire in Baudelaire," in *The Writer of Modern Life: Essays on Charles Baudelaire*, ed. Michael W. Jennings (Cambridge, MA: Harvard University Press, 2006), p. 85. This convenient collection gathers Benjamin's essays on Baudelaire in one volume, with the editor's annotations added to Benjamin's original notes. The article, never published in his lifetime, was written in 1938. The passage quoted here is translated by Harry Zohn.
19. Ibid., p. 40.
20. Ibid., p. 72.
21. Ibid., p. 10.
22. Ibid., p. 40.
23. Ibid., p. 54.
24. Ibid., p. 41.
25. Ibid., p. 89. Benjamin says here," "On the scale we are dealing with here, this class (the bourgeois) was only at the beginning of its decline. Inevitably, many of its members would one day become aware of the commodity nature of their labor power."
26. Ibid., p. 139.
27. Kant's "Was ist Aufklärung" [What Is Enlightenment] was published in the journal *Berlinischen Monatsschrift* [Berlin Monthly] in December 1784. It is a text Foucault repeatedly lectures on in his courses at Collège de France. In addition to "Qu'est-ce que les lumières ?", see Michel Foucault, "Leçon du 5 Janvier 1983," in Frédéric Gros, ed., *Le gouvernement de soi et des autres : Cours au Collège de France, 1982–1983* [The Government of Self and Others: Courses at Collège de France, 1982–1983] (Paris : Le Seuil, 2008), pp. 3–39. In the first hour of this lecture Foucault points out that in Kant's text we see for the first time in philosophical history when a philosopher asks this crucial question about his age: What is the present? Or what is happening today? (la question de actualité, c'est la question de : qu'est-ce qui se passe aujourd'hui ?) This question is also the major concern in "Que'est-ce que les lumières ?". In the second hour of the 5 January lecture, Foucault points out that Kant's text clarifies the distinction between the absolute freedom of speech in the public sphere—e.g., public criticism of the tax policies of the state—and the obedience and subjugation of the self in the private sphere—e.g., paying taxes as demanded by law. According to Foucault, this distinction is the true spirit of enlightenment, which is the moment we proceed from the state of minority (l'état de minorité) to become mature human beings (majeurs). I am grateful to Fabien Heubal for calling my attention to this lecture and letting me use this text when it was still unpublished. A shorter version of this lecture appears as "Qu'est-ce que les lumières ?" (L'Art du dire vrai), in *Magazine Littéraire*, 207 (May 1984), pp. 34–9. This shorter version is included in *Dits et écrits, 1976–1988* (Paris : Gallimard, 2001), vol. 2, pp. 1498–507.
28. See Michel Foucault, "What Is Enlightenment?" trans. Catherine Porter, in Paul Rabinow, ed., *The Foucault Reader* (New York: Pantheon Books, 1984), pp. 32–50. This quote is on p. 41.
29. Michel Foucault, "Qu'est-ce que les lumières ?", in *Dits et écrits, 1976–1988*, vol. 2,

pp. 1381–397. This is originally a lecture at Collège de France around 1983. This quote is on p. 1389.
30 Foucault, "Qu'est-ce que les lumières ?", p. 1390; Porter, "What Is Enlightenment," p. 42.
31 Foucault, "Qu'est-ce que les lumières ?", p. 1388, Porter, "What Is Enlightenment," p. 39.
32 Walter Benjamin, "Das Paris des Second Empire bei Baudelaire," in Rolf Tiedemann and Hermann Schweppenhäuser, eds., *Gesammelte Schriften* (Collected Works; Frankfurt am Main : Suhrkamp, 1980), vol. 1, p. 558.
33 Foucault, "Qu'est-ce que les lumières ?", p. 1387, Porter, "What Is Enlightenment," p. 39.
34 Foucault, "Qu'est-ce que les lumières ?", p. 1390.
35 Ibid., p. 1389.
36 Ibid., p. 1390.
37 Porter, "Qu'est-ce que les lumières ?", p. 42.
38 Foucault, "Qu'est-ce que les lumières ?", p. 1588; Porter, "What Is Enlightenment," p. 40.
39 Foucault, "Qu'est-ce que les lumières ?", p. 1388–389; Porter, "What Is Enlightenment," p. 40.
40 Porter, "What Is Enlightenment," p. 40.
41 Ibid., p. 41.
42 Foucault, "Qu'est-ce que les lumières ?", p. 1393; Porter, "What Is Enlightenment," p. 45, with modifications.
43 At the end of the lecture, Foucault concludes that "the critical task still entails faith in Enlightenment; I continue to think that this task requires work on our limits, that is, a patient labor giving form to our impatience for liberty" (le travail sur nos limites, c'est-à-dire un labeur patient qui donne forme à l'impatience de la liberté). See Porter, p. 50, Foucault, p. 1397.
44 Foucault, "Qu'est-ce que les lumières ?", p. 1394; Porter, "What Is Enlightenment," p. 47.
45 Foucault, "Qu'est-ce que les lumières ?", p. 1393.
46 Donald Keene's use of "Neo-Sensationalism," referring to the Japanese group, is a little misleading, because "sensationalism" is associated in our time with the negative effect caused by the media craving public attention. "Neo-Sensation," on the other hand, is about new sensations, which for Yokomitsu Riichi has epistemological connotations. Shu-mei Shih in *The Lure of the Modern: Writing Modernism in Semicolonial China, 1917–1937* calls this genre "new sensationism." Isabelle Rabut and Angel Pino use the term "Neo-Sensationnisme" in their book *Le fox-trot in Shanghai, et autres nouvelles chinoises* [The Fox-Trot in Shanghai, and Other Chinese Stories] (Paris : Albin Michel, 1996).
47 Recent studies of the modern girl have taken on transnational perspectives, as is shown in "Higashi-Ajia ni okeru shokuminchideki kindai to modan gāru" 東アジアにおける植民地的近代とモダンガール [Colonial Modernity and the Modern Girl in East Asia], the 2005 mid-term report of an international modern girl project sponsored by Ochanomizu University in Tokyo. The countries covered in this report include Japan, Okinawa, Taiwan, China, Korea, South Africa, and so on, while the image of the modern girl is connected with the international circulation of material culture. See also Jina Kim, "The Circulation of Urban Literary Modernity in Colonial Korea and Taiwan" (Ph.D. dissertation, University of Washington, 2006).
48 Miriam Silverberg, *Erotic Groteque Nonsense: the Mass Culture of Japanese Modern Times* (Berkeley: University of California Press, 2006), p. 51.
49 Cf. Mary Louise Roberts, *Civilization without Sexes: Reconstructing Gender in Postwar France, 1917–1927* (Chicago and London: The University of Chicago

Press, 1994), p. 11. Roberts sees the modern girl as the production of World War I, and investigates "how moral and gender trauma became confused during wartime" (p. 215). Jina Kim distinguishes the modern girl from the new woman in Korea in the introductory chapter of her dissertation. See her "The Circulation of Urban Literary Modernity in Colonial Korea and Taiwan," pp. 1–50.

50 Cf. Go Haichin 吳佩珍, "1910 nendai no Nihon ni okeru rezubianizumu: 'Seitō dōjin wo chūshin ni" 一九一〇年代の日本におけるレズビアニズム：「青鞜」同人を中心に [Lesbianism in 1910s Japan: On the "Blue Stocking Society" Coterie], *Kōhon Kindai Bungaku* 稿本近代文学 [Modern Literature] 26 (December 2001); Dina Lowy, *The Japanese "New Woman": Images of Gender and Modernity* (New Brunswisk, NJ: Rutgers University Press, 2007).

51 Cf. Peng Hsiao-yen, "The New Woman: May Fourth Women's Struggle for Self-Liberation," *Bulletin of Chinese Literature and Philosophy, Academia Sincia*, 6 (March 1995): 259–337; Sarah E. Stevens, "Figuring Modernity: The New Woman and the Modern Girl in Republican China, *NWSA Journal* (Fall 2003), 15.3: 82–103.

52 Louis Icart, "Dessin de Icart" [Sketch by Icart], *A coups de Baïonnete* [At the Thrust of the Spear], 4.40 (6 April 1916): 252.

53 See Ōya Sōichi 大宅壯一, "Hyaku pasento moga" 百パーセント.モガ [One Hundred Percent Modern Girl] (1929), in *Ōya Sōichi zenshū* 大宅壯一全集 [Complete Works of Ōya Sōichi] (Tokyo: Sōyōsha, 1980), vol. 2, pp. 10–17: "Madame A was the first modern girl in Japan, or her original model. To say the least, the term 'modan gāru' was invented by my friend Mr N to describe her" (p. 11). It is widely known that Mr N mentioned here is Nii Itaru. See Suzuki Sadami 鈴木貞美, ed., *Modan gāru no yūwaku* モダンガールの誘惑 [The Modern Girl's Charm] (1989), in Suzuki Sadami et al., eds., *Modan toshi bungaku* モダン都市文学 [Modern City Literature] (Tokyo: Heibonsha, vol. 2, p. 397: "'My friend Mr N' refers to Nii Itaru." See also Kaji Ryūichi 嘉治隆一, "Nii Itaru to Okaue Morimichi: dokusōteki bunka kisha, kosumoporitan kisha" 新居格と岡上守道：独創的文化記者、コスモポリタン記者 [Nii Itaru and Okaue Morimichi: A Creative Cultural Journalist and a Cosmopolitan Journalist], in Asahi Shinbunsha, ed., *Oriori no hito* 折り折りの人 [Men of All Walks in Life], vol. 2 (Tokyo: Asahi Shinbunsha, 1967), pp. 190–4. According to this article, Nii was the inventor of neologisms such as *moga*, *mobo*, *Marukusu boi*, and *Engurusu gāru*.

54 Tanaka Hisara, "Mogako to moborō" [Miss Modern Girl and Master Modern Boy], in *Tanaka Hisara gashū* 田中比左良画集 [Collected Paintings of Tanaka Hisara] (Tokyo: Kōdansha, 1978), pp. 129–44. Originally published in *Gendai Yumoa Zenshū Kankōkai* 現代ユウモア全集刊行會, ed., *Namita no neuchi* 涙の値打 [Values of Tears], 1929.

55 Ibid., p. 129.

56 Katō Hidetoshi et al. 加藤秀俊等, *Meiji Taishō Shōwa sesōshi* [Social History of the Meiji, Taishō, and Shōwa Periods] (Tokyo: Shakai Shisōsha, 1967), p. 107.

57 Zhang Wenyuan 張文元, "Weilai de Shanghai fengguang de kuangce" [Wild Prophesy of the Future Cityscape of Shanghai], in Shen Jianzhong 沈建中, ed., *Shidai manhua, 1934–1937* 時代漫畫 *1934–1937* [Modern Sketch, *1934–1937*] (Shanghai: Shanghai Shehui Kexueyuan Chubanshe, 2004), vol. 2, pp. 404–7. Originally published in the magazine *Modern Sketch*, 30 (20 September 1936).

58 Ibid., p. 406.

59 Cf. Peng Hsiao-yen, "Sex Histories: Zhang Jingsheng's Sexual Revolution," in Peng-hsiang Chen and Whitney Crothers Dilley, eds., *Critical Studies: Feminism/ Femininity in Chinese Literature* (Amsterdam: Editions Rodopi B.V., 2002), pp. 159–77; Peng Hsiao-yen 彭小妍, "Xing qimeng yu ziwuo de jiefang: 'Xing boshi' Zhang Jingshing yu wusi de seyu xiaoshuo" 性啟蒙與自我的解放：

「性博士」張競生與五四的色慾小說 [Sexual Enlightenment and Self-Liberation: "Dr. Sex" and May Fourth Erotic Fiction], in *Chaoyue xieshi* 超越寫實 [Beyond Realism] (Taipei: Lianjing Chuban Gongsi, 1994), pp. 117–37.
60 Zhang Wenyuan, "Weilai de Shanghai fengguang de kuangce," p. 406.
61 Walter Benjamin, *The Writer of Modern Life: Essays on Charles Baudelaire*, p. 84.
62 Walter Benjamin, *The Arcades Project*, trans. Howard Eiland and Kevin McLaughlin (Cambridge, MA: Harvard University Press, 2003), 4th edn, p. 106. Here Benjamin writes, "Existence in these spaces (the arcades) flows then without accent, like the events in dreams. Flânerie is the rhythmics of this slumber. In 1839, a rage for tortoises overcame Paris. One can well imagine the elegant set mimicking the pace of this creature more easily in the arcades than on the boulevards."

1 A dandy, traveler, and woman watcher: Liu Na'ou from Taiwan

1 Liu Na'ou's diary written in 1927 was found by his grandson in a closet at his home in Tainan and handed to me in the mid 1990s. It was published with annotations and translations in two volumes in 2001. For the French quotation, see Liu Na'ou, *Rijiji* 日記集 [Diary], ed. and trans. Peng Hsiao-yen and Huang Yingzhe 黃英哲, in *Liu Na'ou quanji* 劉吶鷗全集 [Complete Works of Liu Na'ou], ed. Kang Laixin 康來新 and Xu Zhenzhen 許秦蓁 (Tainan: Tainanxian Wenhuaju, 2001), Part 1, p. 296. For Liu's family background and education in Taiwan and Japan, see Peng Hsiao-yen, "Langdang tianya: Liu Na'ou yijiuerqi nian riji" 浪蕩天涯：劉吶鷗一九二七年日記 [Flâneur of the World: Liu Na'ou's 1927 Diary], *Bulletin of Chinese Literature and Philosphy, Academia Sinica*, 12 (March 1998): 1–40; collected in Peng Hsiao-yen, *Haishang shuo qingyu: cong Zhang Ziping dao Liu Na'ou* 海上說情慾：從張資平到劉吶鷗 [Desire in Shanghai: From Zhang Ziping to Liu Na'ou] (Taipei: Institute of Chinese Literature and Philosophy, Academia Sinica, 2001), pp. 105–44.
2 Cf. Charles Baudelaire, "Au lecteur" (To the Reader), in *Oeuvres complètes* [Complete Works] (Paris : Gallimard, 1990), vol. 1, pp. 5–6. In Baudelaire's *Les fleurs du mal*, sea voyage always connotes freedom of spirit and elevation of mind as opposed to the mediocrity of the world, as can be seen in this poem. See also "L'homme et la mer" [Man and the Sea], in *Oeuvres complètes*, vol. 1, p. 18. Praising man and the sea as two eternal fighters, the poem ends with the line "O lutteurs éternels, o frères implacable !" [O eternal fighters, o implacable brothers!]
3 Huang Tianzuo 黃天佐 (Suichu 隨初), "Wuo suo renshi de liu na'ou xiansheng" 我所認識的劉吶鷗先生 [The Mr Liu Na'ou I Knew], in *Osaka mainichi shinbun* 大阪每日新聞 [Osaka Daily], *Chinese Edition*, 5.9 (1 November 1940), p. 69. I will discuss Liu's murder later in this chapter.
4 Under the Japanese colonial policy Taiwanese were not entitled to the same education system as the Japanese. For elementary education, Japanese children went to the six-year *shōgakō* 小学校, while Taiwanese children went to *kōgako* 公学校, which required four to six years. For high school education, it took young Japanese five years to graduate, and young Taiwanese, three to five years. As a result it was difficult for the latter to catch up with the former when they went to study in Japan. The only exceptions were the private Tamsui School in Taipei and the Presbyterian School in Tainan, which had the same system as the Japanese schools. Cf. Qin Xianci 秦賢次, "Zhang Wuojun ji qi tongshidai de Beijing Taiwan liuxuesheng" 張我軍及其同時代的北京臺灣留學生 [Zhang Wuojun and Contemporary Taiwanese Studying in Beijing], in Peng Hsiao-yen, ed., *Piaobo yu xiangtu: Zhang Wuojun shishi sishi zhounian jinian lunwenji* 漂泊與鄉土— 張我軍逝世四十週年紀念論文集 [Diaspora and Homeland: Commemorating the 40th Anniversary of Zhang Wuojun's Demise] (Taipei: Council of Cultural Affairs, 1996), pp. 57–81.

5 See the list of Taiwanese who graduated in March 1926 from schools in Tokyo as recorded in "Liujing zuyesheng songbiehui" 留京卒業生送別會 [Farewell Party for Taiwanese Students Graduating from Schools in Tokyo], in *Taiwan minbao* 臺灣民報 [Taiwan People's Daily], 99 (4 April 1926): 8.
6 Shi Zhicun, *Zhendan er nian* 震旦二年 [Two Years at L'Aurore] (Shanghai: Wenyi Chubanshe, 1996), pp. 289–90.
7 See especially entries of 18 January and 19 January of the diary.
8 For articles on Zhang Wuojun's life and work, see Peng Hsiao-yen, *Diaspora and Homeland*.
9 Huang Tianzuo, "The Mr. Liu Na'ou I knew."
10 See Shu-mei Shih, "Gender, Race, and Semicolonialism: Liu Na'ou's Urban Shanghai Landscape," in *The Lure of the Modern: Writing Modernism in Semicolonial China, 1917–1937*, p. 276.
11 *Shenbao* 申報 [Shanghai Post], "Fuzhoulu zuori xie'an/Liu Na'ou bei jisi" 福州路昨日血案 / 劉吶鷗被擊死 [Bloody Murder Yesterday at Fuzhou Road /Liu Na'ou Shot to Death] (4 September 1940), p. 9.
12 Huang Tianzuo, "The Mr Liu Na'ou I Knew." "Kōa'in" was a Japanese intelligence agency established on 16 December 1938 to take charge of the day-to-day running in the fast expanding occupied areas and the controlling of entrepreneurial development there.
13 Huang Tianzuo, "The Mr Liu Na'ou I Knew."
14 Ibid. For the news coverage of the murders of Mu Shiying and Liu Na'ou, see *Guomin xinwen* [National Subjects' Daily], from 29 June to late September 1940. See also *Shanghai Post*, "Fuzhoulu zuowan xie'an/Mu Shiying zao qiangsha" 福州路昨日血案 / 穆時英遭槍殺 [Bloody Murder Last Night at Fuzhou Road / Mu Shiying Gunned Down] (29 June 1940), p. 9. According to Shu-mei Shih, Liu Na'ou died in 1939. It is a mistake inherited from Yan Jiayan 嚴家炎. See Yan Jiayan, *Zhongguo xiandai xiaoshuo liupai shi* 中國現代小說流派史 [Schools of Modern Chinese Fiction] (Beijing: Renmin Wenxue Chubanshe, 1989), pp. 131–41; Shu-mei Shih, *The Lure of the Modern: Writing Modernism in Semicolonial China, 1917–1937*, p. 276.
15 Yan Jiayan, *Schools of Modern Chinese Fiction*, pp. 131–41.
16 During one of the interviews in Shanghai in October 1998, Shi Zhicun told me so.
17 Huang Tianzuo, "The Mr Liu Na'ou I Knew."
18 Ibid.
19 Lou Shiyi, "Zuopin yu zuojia: Shi Zhicun de xinganjue zhuyi – du le 'Zai Bari Daxiyuan' yu 'Modao' zhi hou" 作品與作家：施蟄存的新感覺主義—讀了〈在巴黎大戲院〉與〈魔道〉之後 [Literary Works and Writers: The Neo-Sensationism of Shi Zhicun – After Reading 'In the Grand Paris Movie Theater' and 'The Enchanter'], *Wenyi xinwen* [Literary News] 33 (26 October 1931): 4. Lou was the editor-in-chief of *Literary News* at the time.
20 "Bianji yutan" 編輯餘談 [Editor's Afterwords], *Furen huabao* [The Women's Pictorial] 17 (April 1934): 32.
21 I quote the definition of "acculturation" from *Webster's Third International Dictionary*.
22 Cf. Silvia Spitta, *Between Two Waters: Narratives of Transculturation in Latin America* (Houston, Tex: Rice University Press, 1995), pp. 3–4. For a detailed discussion of the evolvement of the Latin American concept of "transculturation" from that of "acculturation," see pp. 1–28 of this book.
23 Cf. Terry Eagleton, "Nationalism: Irony and Commitment," in Seamus Deane, ed., *Nationalism, Colonialism, and Literature* (Minneapolis: University of Minnesota Press, 1990), pp. 23–42.
24 Seamus Deane, "Introduction," in *Nationalism, Colonialism, and Literature*, pp. 3–19.

25 See Liu Na'ou, *Diary*, Part 1, p. 232; Part 2, p. 762 and p. 770.
26 The movie has another English title, *The Man with a Hat*. Judging by the approximate age of Liu's children at the time of the movie, I presume that it was made in the mid 1930s. Around 1934 Liu's family, including his wife, two sons and a daughter, moved to Shanghai. One daughter was born in Shanghai in 1936, and one son, in 1938. The titile of Liu's documentary is, of course, an echo to *Living Russia, or the Man with a Camera*, a Russian documentary released in 1929. The original title is "Cheloveks kino-apparatom." See the discussion later in this chapter.
27 See Liu Na'ou, *Diary*, Part 1, p. 102.
28 In Liu's 1927 diary there is a reading list at the end of each month. See Liu Na'ou, *Diary*, Part 2, pp. 486 and 553.
29 Charles Baudelaire (1863) *Le Peintre de la vie moderne* [The Painter of Modern Life], in *Oeuvres complètes*, vol. 2, p. 710.
30 Ibid.
31 See Liu Na'ou, "18 May," in *Diary*, Part 1, p. 322.
32 See Liu Na'ou, "19 May," in *Diary*, Part 1, p. 324.
33 Charles Baudelaire, "Le Vampire", in *Oeuvres complètes*, vol. 1, p. 33.
34 Baudelaire, verse 5, "Spleen et idéal", in *Oeuvres complètes*, vol. 1, p. 12.
35 Baudelaire, "I Love to Think of Those Naked Epochs," in *The Flowers of Evil*, trans. William Aggeler (Fresno, CA: Academy Library Guild, 1954), p. 27.
36 Liu Na'ou, *Diary*, vol. 1, pp. 308–27.
37 Walter Benjamin, *The Arcades Project*, trans. Howard Eiland and Kevin McLaughlin (Cambridge, MA: Harvard University Press, 2003), 4th edn, pp. 21–2.
38 Michel Foucault, "What is Enlightenment?" ["Qu'est-ce que les lumières?"] (1983), trans. Catherine Porter, in Paul Rabinow, ed., *The Foucault Reader* (New York: Pantheon Books, 1984), p. 40.
39 Liu Na'ou, "24 October," in *Diary*, Part 2, pp. 664–5. In the diary entry, the French word "fugitive" is spelled as "fugatif," obviously a typo.
40 Charles Baudelaire, "To a Passer-by," in *The Flowers of Evil*, trans. William Aggeler, p. 311.
41 Liu Na'ou, "17 November," in *Diary*, Part 2, pp. 716–17.
42 Liu Na'ou, "27 November," in *Diary*, Part 2, pp. 736–7.
43 Michel Foucault, "What is Enlightenment?" p. 40.
44 Charles Baudelaire, *The Painter of Modern Life*, pp. 683–724. This quote is on p. 694.
45 Cf. Water Benjamin, *Charles Baudelaire: A Lyric Poet in the Era of High Capitalism*, trans. Harry Zohn (London: Biddles Ltd., Guildford and King's Lynn, 1989), pp. 11–66.
46 Baudelaire, *The Painter of Modern Life*, pp. 713–14.
47 Liu Na'ou, *Diary*, Part 2, p. 702. In Liu's diary, Apollinaire is misspelled as "Anapollinaire."
48 See Shu-mei Shih, *The Lure of the Modern*, p. 370: "As for the new sensationists, there was neither a passionate call to denounce tradition nor a qualified recuperation of it. One may argue that, with the exception of Shi Zhecun's writings after his modernist phase, tradition did not even constitute a problematic which one needed to take a stand one way or the other: Capitalist modernity was the only reality to reckon with . . . Indeed, what we witness is the physical and psychic consequences to those who have absorbed the May Fourth ideology of total Westernization."
49 Liu Na'ou, *Diary*, Part 2, p. 702.
50 For the annual accounts of Mu Shiying's life, see Li Jin 李今, "Mu Shiying nianpu jianbian" 穆時英年譜簡編 [Concise Annual Accounts of Mu Shiying's Life],

Zhongguo xiandai wenxue yanjiu congkan 中國現代文學研究叢刊 [Studies of Modern Chinese Literature], 6 (2005): 237–68. Li's study corrects mistakes in Shu-mei Shih's accounts of Mu's life such as his alleged birth in Zhejiang 浙江 province and his alleged major in Chinese literature. See Shu-mei Shih, *The Lure of the Modern*, p. 307.

51 See Shu-mei Shih, *The Lure of the Modern*, pp. 305–6.
52 Mu Shiying, "Craven 'A,'" in Yueqi 樂齊, ed., *Zhongguo xinganjuepai shengshou: Mu Shiying xiaoshuo quanji* 中國新感覺派聖手：穆時英小說全集 [A Chinese Neo-Sensation Writer of Genius: Complete Collection of Mu Shiying's Stories] (Beijing: Zhongguo Wenlian Chuban Gongsi, 1996), pp. 205–20. Originally published in *Gongmu* 公墓 [Public Cemetery] (Shanghai: Xiandai Shuju, 1933).
53 Ibid., p. 211.
54 Guo Jianying, "Yijiusansannian de ganchu: ai zhi fangshi" 一九三三年的感觸：愛之方式 [The Touch of 1933: The Way of Love], in Chen Zishan 陳子善, *Modeng Shanghai* 摩登上海 [Modern Shanghai] (Guangxi: Guangxi Shifan Daxue Chubanshe, 2001), p. 44. Originally published as *Jianying manhuaji* 建英漫畫集 [Collection of Cartoons by Jianying] (Shanghai: Liangyou Tushu Gongsi, 1934), which collects Guo's cartoons from 1931 to 1934.
55 Ibid.
56 Heiner Frühauf wrote about the Creation writers when they studied in Tokyo during the 1910s and early 1920s. According to him, they indulged in "the exotic mood of French symbolism, café ambience, and find de siècle decadence." Cf., Heiner Frühauf, "Urban Exoticism and its Sino-Japanese Scenery, 1910–23," in *Asian and African Studies* 6.2 (1997): 126–69.
57 Guo Jianying, "The Touch of 1933: The Enchantment of a Machine," p. 42.
58 See Baudelaire, "Éloge du maquillage" [Elogy of Make-up], in *The Painter of Modern Life*, pp. 714–18.
59 For the theory of psycho-narration, see Dorrit Cohn, *Transparent Minds: Narrative Modes for Presenting Consciousness in Fiction* (Princeton, NJ: Princeton University Press, 1983).
60 See Baudelaire, "Elogy of Make-up," p. 716.
61 Mu Shiying, "Shouzhi" [Fingers], in Yueqi, ed., *A Chinese Neo-Sensation Writer of Genius: Complete Collection of Mu Shiying's Stories*, pp. 30–3. First published in *Qingnienjie* 青年界 [The World of Youths], 1.3 (1931).
62 Huang Chaoqin, "Hanwen gaige lun" 漢文改革論 [On the Reform of Classical Chinese], *Taiwan* 台灣 (January and February 1923), Hanwen zhi bu (Classical Chinese Section): 25–31, 21–7.
63 See the entries written from September to December in Liu Na'ou's 1927 diary.
64 Cf. Liu Na'ou, *Diary*, part 2, p. 628.
65 Cf. Heiner Frühauf, "Urban Exoticism in Modern and Contemporary Chinese Literature"; Leo Lee, *Shanghai Modern* (Cambridge, MA: Harvard University Press, 1999), pp. 241–50. Although Leo Lee does not use the term dandyism, he describes Shao Xunmei as a "flamboyant literary dandy," who was handsome, openly cohabiting with his American mistress, "took great pride in his Greek nose," and drove "a long brown Nash."
66 "Wentan xiaoxi" 文壇消息 [News of the Literary Circle], in *Xin shidai* 新時代 [New Age], 1.1 (1 August 1931): 7.
67 This is Shi Zhicun's opinion during an interview with me in October 1998.
68 Cf. Peng Hsiao-yen, *Desire in Shanghai*, pp. 145–88.
69 For example, Yan Jiayan, Shu-mei Shih, and Zhang Yingjin, to name just a few. I agree that for the sake of analysis it is necessary to divide writers into categories, but concerning the division between the Shanghai School (allegedly experimental in their penchant) and the Beijing School (allegedly traditional in style), we should

be aware that Chinese tradition was never totally removed from the psyche of the writers labeled as "the Shanghai School," while the so-called Beijing School writers were by no means less experimental in literary style.
70 Cf. Peng Hsiao-yen, *Desire in Shanghai*, pp. 95–103.
71 Shen Congwen (Jiachen 甲辰), "Yu Dafu, Zhang Ziping ji qi yingxiang" 郁達夫、張資平及其影響 [Yu Dafu, Zhang Ziping, and their Influences], in *Xinyue* 新月 [Crescent Moon], 3.1 (March 1930): 1–8.
72 Shen Congwen, "On Mu Shiying," in *Shen Congwen wenji* 沈從文文集 [Works of Shen Congwen] (Hong Kong: Sanlian Shudian, 1982–3), vol. 11, pp. 203–5. Originally published in 1934.
73 Yingjin Zhang, *The City in Modern Chinese Literature and Film: Configurations of Space, Time & Gender* (Stanford, CA: Stanford University Press), pp. 23–4; see Lu Xun (Luan Tingshi 欒廷石), "Jingpai yu haipai" 京派與海派 [Beijing Types and Shanghai Types], *Shanghai Post* (3 February 1934): 17. For an account of the *Haipai* controversy *per se*, the emergence of "Beijing School," and the redefinition of "Shanghai School," see Yingjin Zhang, pp. 21–7.
74 Hu Shi, trans. "Bolin zhi wei" 柏林之圍 [The Siege of Berlin], *The Young Companion*, 64 (December 1931): 10. Originally published in 1914. Cai Yuanpei, "Ti *Liangyou* sheyingtu" 題良友攝影圖 [on the photographs of *The Young Companion*], 69 (September 1932), inside cover.
75 *The Young Companion*, 73 (January 1933), inside cover advertisement.
76 Cf. Katherine Huiling Chou, "Representing 'New Woman': Actresses & the *Xin Nüxing* Movement in Chinese Spoken Drama & Films, 1918–49" (New York: New York University Ph.D. dissertation, 1996), pp. 132–3.
77 Huang Jiamou, "'Xiandai dianying' yu Zhongguo dianyingjie—benkan de chuangli yu jinhou de zeren—yubei geiyu duzhe de jidian gongxian" 現代電影與中國電影界 – 本刊的成立與今後的責任 – 預備給予讀者的幾點貢獻 [*Modern Screen* and Chinese Movies—The Establishment of This Journal and Its Responsibility from Now on—A Few Contributions Intended for the Reader], in *Xiandai dianying* 現代電影 [Modern screen], inaugural issue (1 March 1933): 1.
78 Shen Xiling 沈西苓, "Yijiusan'er nian Zhongguo dianyingjie de zong jiezhang yu yijiusansan nian de xin qiwang" 一九三二年中國電影界的總結帳與一九三三年的新期望 [A Summing Up of the Chinese Movie Industry in 1932 and New Hopes for the Year 1933], in *Modern Screen*, inaugural issue (1March 1933): 7–9.
79 Liu Na'ou, "Ecranesque" [About the Screen; Liu's own French title], in *Modern Screen*, 2 (1 April 1933): 1.
80 Liu Na'ou, "Lun ticai" 論題材 [On Subject Matter], in *Modern Screen*, 4 (1 July 1933): 2–3.
81 Liu Na'ou, "Dianying jiezou jianlun" [A Brief Essay on the Rhythm of the Camera], in *Modern Screen*, 6 (1 December, 1933): 1–2; "Kaimaila jigou—weizhi jiaodu jineng lun" [On the Mechanism of the Camera—The Function of Angle and Position], in *Modern Screen*, 7 (1 June 1934): 1–5.
82 Cf. David Bordwell, *The Cinema of Eisenstein* (Cambridge, MA: Harvard University Press, 1993), p. 10.
83 Liu Na'ou, "Yingpian yishulun" [On Cinematic Art], in *Dianyingji* 電影集 [Film], collected in *Complete Works of Liu Na'ou*, pp. 256–80. In this collection foreign words and names in Liu Na'ou's works are often misspelled, for instance in the article under investigation, "cinématographique" is turned into "cinegraphique," "ciné-oeuil" becomes "cin'e-oeil," and so on. It is unnecessary to name them all. This article was originally published in *Dianying zhoubao* (Cinéma Weekly), nos. 2, 3, 6–10, and 15 (1 July to 8 October 1932).
84 Ibid., p. 264.

85 Ibid., pp. 264–5.
86 Cf. Richard M. Barsam, *Nonfiction Film: A Critical History* (Bloomington and Indianapolis: Indiana University Press, 1992), p. 68. First published in 1973.
87 Vlada Petric, *Constructivism in Film: "The Man with the Movie Camera," A Cinematic Analysis* (Cambridge: Cambridge University Press, 1987), p. 4.
88 Liu Na'ou, "On Cinematic Art," p. 267.
89 Petric, *Constructivism in Film*, pp. 1–3.
90 Barsam, *Nonfiction Film*, p. 76.
91 Liu Na'ou, "On Cinematic Art," p. 267.
92 Ibid., p. 269.
93 Cf. Barsam, *Nonfiction Film*, p. 73; Petric, *Constructivism in Film*, pp. 82–4. While Barsam uses the term "self-reflexivity," Petric uses "self-referentiality."
94 For a discussion comparing Liu's family film and Vertov's *The Man with a Movie Camera*, see Kwok Sze-wing 郭詩詠, "Chi sheyingji de ren: shilun Liu Na'ou de jilupian" 持攝影機的人：試論劉吶鷗的紀錄片 [The Man with a Movie Camera: On Liu Na'ou's Documentary], *Shiji wenxue* 世紀文學 [Century Literature] 2.7 (July 2007): 28–32.
95 Cf. Barsam, *Nonfiction Film*, pp. 71–2.
96 Peng Hsiao-yen, *Desire in Shanghai*, pp. 121 and 176–7.
97 For a collection of articles on film theory in twentieth-century China, see Ding Yaping 丁亞平, ed., *Bainian Zhongguo dianying lilun wenxuan, 1897–2001* 百年中國電影理論文選 [Collection of Chinese Film Theories in the Past One Hundred Years] (Beijing: Wenhua Yishu Chubanshe, 2002), 2 volumes.
98 Huang Jiamou, "Yingxing yingpian yu ruanxing yingpian" [Hard Films and Soft Films], in *Modern Screen*, 6 (1 December 1933): 3.
99 Tang Na, "Qingsuan ruanxing dianying lun—ruanxing lunzhe de quwei zhuyi" [Purging the Soft-Film Theory—The Entertainment Theory of Soft-Film Theorists], in *Chenbao* [Morning Post] (19 June 1934): 10.
100 Liu Na'ou, *Diary*, Part 1, p. 234.
101 Liu Na'ou, *Diary*, Part 2, p. 450.
102 See entries of 21 March, 3 April, 6 April, and 9 April, in Liu Na'ou, *Diary*, vol. 1, pages 198, 228, 234, and 240.
103 Liu Na'ou, *Diary*, Part 2, p. 744.
104 For a book on the connotations of the term in Japan, see Miriam Silverberg, *Erotic Grotesque Nonsense: The Mass Culture of Japanese Modern Times* (Berkeley: University of California Press, 2007).
105 Liu Na'ou, *Diary*, Part 2, p. 662.
106 Liu Na'ou, *Diary*, Part 1, p. 288.
107 Richard Eaton, *The Best French Short Stories of. . . . and the Yearbook of the French Short Story* (Boston: Small, Maynard & Co., 1924–7).
108 Liu Na'ou, "12 January," *Diary*, Part 1, p. 52.
109 Liu Na'ou, "19 January," *Diary*, Part 1, p. 66.
110 Liu Na'ou, "25 June," *Diary*, Part 1, p. 402.
111 Liu Na'ou, *Diary*, "17 June," Part 1, p. 386.
112 Cf. Peng Hsiao-yen, *Desire in Shanghai*, pp. 1–40.
113 Cf. Yan Jiayan, *Schools of Modern Chinese Fiction*, pp. 131–41.
114 Edward Gunn, *Rewriting Chinese: Style Innovation in Twentieth-Century Chinese Prose* (Stanford, CA: Stanford University Press, 1991), pp. 31–7.
115 For a table listing Shanghai Neo-Sensation writers' high-brow journals and a detailed description of them see Shu-mei Shih, *The Lure of the Modern*, pp. 241–57.

2 A traveling subgenre: the palm-of-the-hand story

1. See Chen Zishan, ed., *Modern Shanghai*, p. iii.
2. Guo Jianying, "Zui shimao de nanzhuang xiasi le gonggong cesuo de gu'niang" 最時髦的男裝嚇死了公共廁所的姑娘 [The Most Fashionable Man's Dress Startles a Girl in the Public Toilet], in Chen Zishan, ed., *Modern Shanghai*, pp. 132–3.
3. Ibid., p. 21.
4. The Japanese *kanji* for "tenohira" 掌 can also be read as "tanagokoro," meaning "the heart of the hand." Donald Keene's transcription for the name of this subgenre is "tanagokoro no shōsetsu." See Donald Keene, *Dawn to the West: Japanese Literature of the Modern Era* (New York: Henry Holt and Company, 1984), p. 800. The 2001 Shinchōsha edition of Kawabata's palm-of-the-hand stories gives the pronunciation "tenohira no shōsetsu."
5. Kawabata Yasunari, "Shōhen shōsetsu no ryūkō" 掌篇小説の流行 [The Booming of Palm-of-the-Hand Stories], in *Kawabata Yasunari zenshū* 川端康成全集 [Complete Works of Kawabata Yasunari], vol. 30 (Tokyo: Shinchōsha, 1982), pp. 230–4.
6. Ibid.
7. Kawabata Yasunari, *Kanjō sōshoku* [Decoration of Emotions] (Tokyo: Kinseidō, 1926).
8. Yoshimura Teiji, "Kaisetsu" [Exposition], in Kawabata Yasunari, *Tenohira no shōsetsu* [Palm-of-the-Hand Stories] (Tokyo: Shinchōsha, 2001), pp. 553–9.
9. Kawabata Yasunari, "Shōhen shōsetsu ni tsuite" [On Palm-of-the-Hand Stories], in *Complete Works of Kawabata Yasunari*, 1982, vol. 32, pp. 543–7.
10. Kawabata Yasunari, "Atogaki" [Postscript], in *Kawabata Yasunari senshū*, vol. 1 [Selected Works of Kawabata Yasunari] (Tokyo: Kaizōsha, 1938), pp. 405–11.
11. Kawabata Yasunari, "Atogaki" [Postscript], in *Kawabata Yasunari zenshū* [Complete Works of Kawabata Yasunari] (Tokyo: Shinchōsha, 1948), vol. 11, pp. 401–23.
12. Kawabata Yasunari, "Yukigunishō" [The Snow Country Sketch], in *Sandei mainichi* [Sunday Everyday] (13 August 1972), pp. 50–59.
13. Kawabata Yasunari, "Hinata" [Toward the Sun], in *Tenohira no shōsetsu*, pp. 24–6. For an English translation of this story, see "A Sunny Place," in Lane Dunlop and J. Martin Holman, *Palm-of-the-Hand Stories* (San Francisco: North Point Press, 1988), pp. 3–4. I prefer to translate the title as "Toward the Sun," since the original title suggests a sense of direction; the blind man in the story is turning his face towards the sun by moving his head every five minutes.
14. Kawabata Yasunari, "Watashi no seikatsu 私の生活 (3): kibō" 希望 [My Life, part 3: Hopes], in *Shinbungei nikki* 新文藝日記 [(New Literary Diary], 1930. In *Complete Works of Kawabata Yasunari*, 1982, vol. 33, p. 58.
15. Shi Yan, "Hangxianshang de yinyue" [Music on the Cruising Route], in *The Women's Pictorial*, 21 (September 1934): 7–8.
16. [Qing 清] Xizhousheng 西周生, *Xingshi yinyuan* 醒世姻緣 [Marriages That Awaken the World] (Taipei, Lianjing Chubanshe, 1986), Chapter 28, p. 370.
17. "Zhongguo nüxingmei zanli" [Odes to Chinese Women's Beauty], in *The Women's Pictorial*, Special Issue, 17 (April 1934): 9–29.
18. Philippe Collas, *Maurice Dekobra : gentleman entre deux mondes* [Maurice Dekobra: Gentleman between Two Worlds] (Paris : Séguier, 2002).
19. Mo Ran, "Zhongguo nanren budong lian'ai yishu" 中國男人不懂戀愛藝術 [Chinese Men Do Not Know the Art of Love], in *The Women's Pictorial*, 16 (March 1934): 9–13.
20. Ibid.
21. Mo Ran, "Wairen muzhong zhi Zhongguo nüxingmei' [Chinese Women's Beauty in a foreigner's eye], in *The Women's Pictorial*, 17 (April 1934): 10–12.
22. Ibid.

23 Hu Kao, "Zhongguo nüxing de zhizhuomei" [Chinese Women's Innocent and Ignorant Beauty], in *The Women's Pictorial*, 17 (April 1934): 10.
24 Ōgai Kamome, "Zhonghua ernümei zhi gebie shenpan" 中華兒女美之個別審判 [A Personal Critique of Chinese Daughters' Beauty], *The Women's Pictorial*, 17 (April 1934): 12–15.
25 Hu Kao, "Chinese Women's Innocent and Ignorant Beauty," p. 10.
26 Yokomitsu Riichi, "Nanakai no undō" [The Exercise of Seven Floors], in *Yokomitsu Riichi zenchū* 横光利一全集 (Tokyo: Kawade Shobo, 1981), vol. 2, pp. 447–59.
27 Liu Na'ou (pen-name Nanaou 呐呐鷗), trans. "Qilou de yundong" 七樓的運動 [The Exercise of Seven Floors], in *Seqing wenhua* 色情文化 [Erotic Culture] (Shanghai: Diixian Shudian, 1928), pp. 37–53.
28 Ibid., p. 449.
29 Ibid., p. 452.
30 Ibid., p. 453.
31 Ibid., p. 452.
32 Ibid., p. 459.
33 Shangbanyu 上半魚, "Wu linghun de routi" [A Body without Soul], in Shen Jianzhong, ed., *Shidai manhua, 1934–1937* [Modern Sketch, *1934–1937*] (Shanghai: Shanghai Shehui Kexueyuan Chubanshe, 2004, vol. 2, p. 400. Originally published in *Modern Sketch*, 29 (20 August 1936).
34 Guo Jianying, "Xiandai nüxing de moxing" [A Model of Modern Women], in Chen Zishan, ed., *Modern Shanghai*, p. 1.
35 Ibid.
36 Cf. Miriam Silverberg, *Erotic Grotesque Nonsense: The Mass Culture of Japanese Modern Times*.
37 Chen Zishan, *Modern Shanghai*, p. 60.
38 Ibid., p. 61.
39 Paul Morand, "Préface", *L'allure de Chanel* (Paris : Hermann, 1999), p. 8. First published in 1976.
40 Chanel's lovers included a wealthy military officer, an English industrialist, a business partner, and a Nazi officer during World War II. Morand never mentions her Nazi lover in the book, probably due to the sensitiveness of the matter, since he himself was also accused of being a collaborator during the war. In fact the war and the occupation of Paris are only carefully implied in the book, for instance, "[J]e verrai entrer dans ma boutique des officiers américains en uniforme" (I saw American officers in uniform coming into my boutique, p. 204). The book ends with her leaving Paris for Switzerland after the war.
41 Morand, *L'allure de Chanel*, p. 64.
42 Ibid., pp. 63–4.
43 Ibid., p. 194.
44 Ibid., p. 194.
45 Ibid., p. 49.
46 Ibid., p. 47.
47 Ibid., p. 49.
48 Ibid., p. 200. At this point of the story Chanel is ready to leave Paris for her exile in Switzerland because of the accusation of collaborating with the Germans during World War II, and it is implied that she will stage a comeback and start all over again. In true life, Chanel had a liaison with the German diplomat Hans Gunther von Dincklage. Later biographers have found that Chanel's twelve-year romantic liaison with him started because she resorted to him for the rescue of her nephew André Palasse, who was imprisoned by the Germans in 1940. She was nearly 60 years old then. See Henry Gidel, *Coco Chanel* (Paris : Flammarion, 2000), pp. 350–70. According to Gidel, in November 1943 Chanel even tried to effect a

negotiation between the Germans and Winston Churchill, whom she knew personally, to end the war earlier. But due to his illness she did not get a chance to see him in Madrid, and the mission failed (pp. 358–64).
49 Morand, *L'allure de Chanel*, p. 11.
50 Ibid., p. 10.
51 Ibid.
52 In Morand's book Chanel was born in Puy-de-Dôme and her mother died when she was six, leaving two other daughters who were sent to a convent, while she was sent to her aunts by her father. This version of her childhood was what she herself dictated to Louise de Vilmorin in 1947, to whom she committed to write her unfinished memoir. In Morand's account the aunts play a key role in the formulation of Coco Chanel's "puritanical taste" that conquers the fashion world in Paris. However, it is known today that Chanel in fact was born in the small city of Saumur, Maine-et-Loire, her mother died when she was 12, and she had five siblings. She stayed in an orphanage of the Catholic monastery of Obazine for seven years, where she learned to be a seamstress. Later biographers of Chanel, though correct about facts in her life, mostly follow Morand in her characterization. Cf. Henry Gidel, *Coco Chanel* (Paris : Flammarion, 2000); Louise de Vilmorin, *Mémoire de Coco, le promeneur* [Memoirs of Coco, the flâneur] (Paris : Gallimard, 1999).
53 Morand, *L'allure de Chanel*, p. 54.
54 Ibid., p. 176.
55 Ibid., p. 183.
56 "Marie Bell in *La garçonne* (1936)" online posting <http://en.wikipedia.org/wiki/La Garçonne (1936 film)> (accessed 15 April 2010).
57 For Josephine Baker's life and performance art, see Bennetta Jules-Rosette, *Josephine Baker in Art and Life: The Icon and the Image* (Urbana and Chicago: University of Illinois Press, 2007).
58 Cf. Edmonde Charles-Roux, *Le temps Chanel* (Paris : Éditions de La Martinière, 2004), pp. 224–5.
59 Paul Morand, *L'allure de Chanel*, p. 54.
60 Ibid., p. 171.
61 Ibid., p. 175.
62 Ibid., p. 176.
63 Ibid.
64 Ibid., pp. 175–6.
65 Ibid., pp. 171–2.
66 Ibid., p. 174.
67 Michel Foucault, "Leçon du 5 Janvier 1983", in Frédéric Gros, ed., *Le gouvernment de soi et des autres: Cours au Collège de France, 1982–1983* [The Government of Self and Others: Courses at Collège de France, 1982–83] (Paris : Le Seuil, 2008), pp. 14.
68 Ibid., p. 172.
69 Chiba Kameo, "Shinkankakuha no tanjō" [The Birth of the Neo-Sensation School], in *Seiki* 世紀 [Century] (November 1924). Collected in Itō Sei 伊藤整 et al., ed., *Nihon gendai bungaku zenshū* 日本現代文学全集 [Complete Works of Modern Japanese Literature] (Tokyo: Kōdansha, 1968), vol. 67, pp. 357–60.
70 Marcel Proust wrote a preface for the 1921 Gallimard edition of *Tendres stocks* (Fancy Goods). The English translation Chiba mentions was probably an edition that mixes stories from *Fancy Goods* and *Open all Night*, with Proust's preface to the former attached. Japanese translations of European writers such as Paul Morand, Marcel Proust, and James Joyce were published in avant-garde journals like *The Star*, *The Mask*, and *Shi to shiron* [Poetry and Poetics].

71 Horiguchi Daigaku, "Hokuō no yo" 北歐の夜 [The Nordic Night], in *Myōjō* [Bright Star] (November 1922): 177–88.
72 Kataoka Teppei, "Wakaki dokusha ni uttawu" [Appeal to the Young Reader], in *Bungei jidai* [Literary Age] (December 1924). Collected in *Complete Works of Modern Japanese Literature*, vol. 67, pp. 360–4.
73 Ibid., p. 361.
74 Cf. Wang Wenbin 王文彬, "Dai Wangshu nianbiao" 戴望舒年表 [Annual Accounts of Dai Wangshu's Life], in *Xin wenxue shiliao* 新文學史料 [Historical Documents on New Literature], 106 (January 2005): 95–105.
75 Benjamin Crémieux, *XXe Siècle* (Paris : Librairie Gallilmard, 1924), 9th edn, pp. 211–21.
76 Ibid.
77 Liu Na'ou, "Baoluo Muhang lun" [On Paul Morand], in *Wugui lieche* [Trackless Train], 4 (25 October 1928): 147–60.
78 Paul Morand, "La nuit des six-jours" [The Six-Day Night], in *Paul Morand : Nouvelles complètes* [Paul Morand: Complete Short Stories] (Paris : Gallimard, 1992), p. 145; trans. Dai Wangshu (pen-name Lang Fang), "Liuri zhi yeh" 六日之夜 [The Six-Day Night], in *Falanxi duanpian jiezuoji diyice* [Masterpieces of French Short Stories] (Shanghai: Xiandai Shudian, 1928), vol. 1, p. 16. I have seen two later revised versions of this translation, each with slightly different Chinese titles. See Dai Wangshu, "Liuri jingzou zhi yeh" 六日競走之夜 [The Night of the Six-Day Race], in *Tiannü Yuli* 天女玉麗 [Yuli the Daughter of Heaven] (Shanghai: Shangzhi Shuwu, 1929), pp. 53–80; "Liuri jingsai zhi yeh" 六日競賽之夜 [The Night of the Six-Day Competition], in *Xiangdao ribao.zongho* [Hong Kong Island Daily. Miscellany] (28–30 June and 2–12 July 1945): 2.
79 Morand, "The Six-Day Night," p. 144; trans. Dai Wangshu, "The Six-Day Night," p. 15.
80 Vyvyan Beresford Holland, trans. "The Six-Day Night," in *Open All Night* (New York: T. Seltzer, 1923), pp. 118–29.
81 Marcel Proust, "Preface," in *Fancy Goods*, in *Paul Morand: Complete Short Stories*, pp. 3–12.
82 Dai Wangshu, trans. "The Six-Day Night," p. 15.
83 Vyvyan Beresford Holland, trans. "The Six-Day Night," p. 124.
84 Dai Wangshu, trans. "The Night of the Six-Day Competition," Part 6, in *Hong Kong Island Daily* (4 July 1945). Dai moved to Hong Kong in 1938 and stayed on until 1949.
85 Morand, "La nuit des six-jours," p. 137; Vyvyan Beresford Holland, trans. "The Six-Day Night," p. 118.
86 Nishiwaki Junzaburō, *Tabibito kaerazu* [No Traveler Returns](1947), in *Teihon Nishiwaki Junzaburō zenshū* [Complete Works of Nishiwaki Junzaburō: Definitive Texts] (Tokyo: Chikuma Shobō, 1993), vol. 1, verse 147, p. 286.
87 Liu Na'ou, *Diary*, vol. 2, pp. 446–7. Cf. Peng Hsiao-yen, *Desire in Shanghai*, p. 115.
88 Nishiwaki Junzaburō, *No Traveler Returns*, in the *Complete Works of Nishiwaki Junzaburō: Definitive Texts*, vol. 1, pp. 209–308. In the preface to the collection titled *Gen'ei no hito to onna* 幻影の人と女 [The Man of Shadow and Woman], Nishiwaki explains that he views himself as "a man of shadow" or "the everlasting traveler," who follows woman to eternity. To him, the female sex is the center of the natural world, in which the aim of life is the survival of the species; the male sex is the stamen and the bee that go after the pistil, which will bear seeds and fruits. The term "onna no tabibito" 女の旅人 [the woman traveler] appears in Verse 156, p. 291.
89 Miryam Sas, *Fault Lines: Cultural Memory and Japanese Surrealism* (Stanford, CA: Stanford University Press, 1999), p. 201. This book has a useful selected

chronology at the end, juxtaposing events of the surrealist movements in Japan and Europe, with global historical events mentioned.
90 Donald Keene, *Dawn to the West: Japanese Literature of the Modern Era* (New York: Henry Holt and Company, 1984), p. 796. *Complete Works of Kawabata Yasunari*, vol. 33, p. 96.
91 Keene, *Dawn to the West*, p. 645.
92 Paul Morand, "Epoques d'une vie" [Epochs of a Life], in Michel Bulteau, ed., *Paul Morand : au seul souci de voyager* [Paul Morand: For the Sake of Travel Only] (Paris : Louis Vuitton, 2001), p. 8.
93 Ibid., p. 35.
94 "Yokohama," in Bulteau, ed., *Paul Morand*, p. 31.
95 Crémieux, *XXe Siècle*, p. 212.

3 The flâneur and the flâneuse: Yokomitsu Riichi's Shanghai

1 Yokomitsu Riichi, *Shanghai* (Tokyo: Kaizō Bunko, 1932), p. 4. This is the first edition of the novel published as a volume. I am using this edition and indicate the chapter numbers, because later editions, more or less revised, may have different chapter numbers. For an English translation, see Dennis Washburn, *Shanghai: A Novel* (Ann Arbor, MI: University of Michigan Press, 2001), p. 3. Washburn's translation is based on Kōdansha's 講談社 Bungei Bunko 文芸文庫 edition in 1991, which is an edited version, as is the text in *Teihon Yokomitsu Riichi zenshū* 定本横光利一全集 [Complete Works of Yokomitsu Riichi: Definitive Texts] (Tokyo: Kawade Shobō, 1981). He translates "teihon" into "original texts." See Dennis Washburn, *Shanghai: A Novel*, p. 239. In fact "teihon" 定本 here, pronounced like "an original text" 底本, means a definitive text revised by comparing different editions. The Kaizō Bunko first edition I use retains the pre-war *kana* usage and the *rubi* (*kana* alongside *kanji* characters to indicate their pronunciation) as serialized in *Kaizō*. Chapters 29 and 32 are reversed in the Bungei Bunko edition. For a further account of the different editions of the novel, see later discussion in this chapter. I am using Dennis Washburn's translation, but with modifications when necessary.
2 For an account of the May 30th Movement, see Odagiri Hiroko 小田桐弘子, *Yokomitsu Riichi: hikaku bungakuteki kenkyū* 横光利一：比較文学的研究 [Yokomitsu Riichi: A Comparative Literary Study] (Tokyo: Nansōsha, 1980), pp. 116–34.
3 Cf. Seiji Lippit, *Topographies of Japanese Modernism* (New York: Columbia University Press, 2002), p. 75. Here Lippi analyzes Yokomitsu Riichi's story "Aoi taii" 青い大尉 [The Pale Captain] (1927), in which Korean and Chinese drug addicts in Korea are described as destitute human beings "without any signs of agency." But in *Shanghai*, not only are the Chinese underclass in the semicolony deprived of human agency, but all in the lower social stratum, Japanese as well as foreigners of other nationalities, are characters without agency, who drift with the tide of colonialist expansion and transcultural flux.
4 Yokomitsu Riichi, *Shanghai*, p. 1.
5 Ibid.
6 Yokomitsu Riichi, "Shinakai" [The China Sea], in *Complete Works of Yokomitsu Riichi: Definitive Texts*, vol. 13, p. 439. Washburn translates "toshi kokka" into "city." See Dennis Washburn, *Shanghai: A Novel*, p. 228. I think the idea of a "city-state" is important in Yokomitsu's conception of Shanghai as an independent modern metropolis dominated by other nations in China.
7 Japanese works about China during the period includes Akutagawa Ryūnosuke's 芥川龍之介 *Shina yūki* 支那游記 [Travels in China]. He was the one who encouraged Yokomitsu to visit Shanghai in 1928. Yokomitsu had direct contact with Mu

Shiying and wrote about him after his death in June1939. See his "Mu Ji'ei shi no shi" 穆時英氏の死 [The Death of Mr Mu Shiying], in *Bungakukai*, 7 (September 1940): 174–5. For a discussion of this see later in this chapter and Shu-mei Shih, *The Lure of the Modern: Writing Modernism in Semicolonial China, 1917–1937*, pp. 16–30.
8 André Malraux, *La Condition Humaine* (Paris : Gallimard, 1933), 209th edn, pp. 9–12. For an English translation, see Kaakon M. Chevalier, *Man's Fate* (New York: The Modern Library, 1961), pp. 1–3.
9 Malraux, *La Condition Humaine*, pp. 32–3; Chevalier, *Man's Fate*, pp. 28–9. I am consulting Chevalier's translation, but make changes when necessary.
10 Yokomitsu Riichi, *Shanghai*, pp. 65–6; Dennis Washburn, *Shanghai: A Novel*, p. 48.
11 Cf. Shu-mei Shih, *The Lure of the Modern*, p. 29. Shih discusses Yokomitsu Riichi's essay on Mu Shiying after his death. According to her, from this essay "we can glimpse how the two new sensationisms diverged, the Japanese one shifting to serve the imperialist state." But a closer reading of the essay in its historical context may tell us otherwise – Mu himself was not so engrossed in the autonomy of art as to be insulated from the entanglement of nationalism, imperialism, and colonial politics; his visit to Japan the year before was part of Japan's Pan-Asian mobilization movement.
12 "The Death of Mr. Mu Shiying," in *Complete Works of Yokomitsu Riich: Definitive Texts*, vol. 14, pp. 250–1.
13 As mentioned in note 12 of Chapter 1, the Japanese government established the Asia Development Board in December 1938 to administer the occupied territory in China. See "Dai Tōa Kyōeiken kakuritsu" 大東亜共栄圏確立 [Pan-Asia Co-Prosperity Sphere Established], in *Tōkyō Asahi, Yūkan* 東京朝日夕刊 [Tokyo Morning Sun, Evening Paper] (2 August 1940).
14 For details of these facts in Mu Shiying's life, see Li Jin, "Mu Shiying nianpu jianbian" [Concise Annual Accounts of Mu Shiying's Life], *Zhongguo xiandai wenxue yanjiu congkan* [Studies of Modern Chinese Literature], 6 (2005): 237–68.
15 Ibid.
16 Shu-mei Shih's translation with modifications. See her *The Lure of the Modern*, p. 29.
17 Yokomitsu Riichi, "Shinkankakuron"[(On Neo-Sensation], in *Complete Works of Yokomitsu Riichi: Definitive Texts*, vol. 13, pp. 75–82. Washburn translates part of this essay in "Translator's Postscript," in *Shanghai: A Novel*, pp. 222–3. He renders "Kōseiha" into "Structuralism," which is in fact "Kōzōha" 構造派 in Japanese, while "Nyojitsuha" [The Actuality School] is rendered as "Surrealism," which in Japanese should be "chōgenjitsuha" 超現実派. Constructivism was a movement in art and architecture in Russia and Germany roughly from 1919 to 1934, and was later replaced by social realism. Discarding "pure art" for an art devoted to the service of the revolution or for social purposes, it advocated the defamiliarization of art and was famous for techniques such as photomontage and the graphic design for mass production. Practitioners include Vladimir Tatlin, Vladimire Mayakovsky, Lyubov Popova, Vavara Stepanova, George Grosz, and John Heartfield. I have not been able to find any reference to "nyojitsuha" so far. I think it might refer to the actuality film created by the Lumière brothers, Auguste Marie Louis Nicholas and Louis Jean Lumière, in 1895. Making the effect of motion pictures more real than reality, it had an immediate and significant influence on popular culture. For instance, the train running towards the viewers in *Arrival of A Train in a Station* would make them scream out of terror. The precursor of documentary film, actuality film is generally considered to be the beginning of film as a commercial medium.
18 Yokomitsu Riichi, "On Neo-Sensation," p. 80.

19 Ibid.
20 For an account and a table of the foreign writers mentioned in Yokomitsu's writings see Odagiri Hiroko, *Yokomitsu Riichi: A Comparative Literary Study*, pp. 7–21.
21 As early as 1889, Nakajima Rikizō 中島力造 wrote a Ph.D. dissertation for Yale University titled "Kant's Doctrine of the 'Thing-in-Itself.'" After studying briefly in England and Germany, he returned to Japan the following year, and later taught ethics at Tokyo Imperial University.
22 For another translation of this passage, see Washburn, *Shanghai: A Novel*, p. 223. He translates the term *monojitai* into "object."
23 Cf. Oscar W. Miller, *The Kantian Thing-in-Itself or the Creative Mind* (New York: Philosophical Library, 1956), p. 20. This is a rich, thorough critical review of how the Kantian thing-in-itself evolves from early Greek philosophers, Plato and Locke, and how it was criticized by contemporary philosophers such as Schopenhauer, and then critiqued and transformed by later philosophers such as Henri Bergson in *Evolution créatrice*.
24 Yokomitsu Riichi, "On Neo-Sensation," p. 81.
25 According to Lippit, "As their name indicates, the works of the New Sensation writers emphasized the depiction of corporeal sensations rather than contemplation or intellectual grasp of phenomena." But as shown here, my analysis of Yokomitsu's theory on Neo-Sensation indicates otherwise. Cf. Seiji M. Lippit, "A Melancholic Nationalism: Yokomitsu Riichi and the Aesthetic of Cultural Mourning," in Dick Stegewerns, ed., *Nationalism and Internationalism in Imperial Japan* (London and New York: Routledge Curzon, 2003), pp. 228–46.
26 Yokomitsu Riichi, "On Neo-Sensation," p. 76.
27 Ibid., p. 80.
28 Cf. Nishida Kitarō, "Ninshikiron ni okeru junronriha no shuchō ni tsuite" [On the Thesis of the School of Pure Reason in Epistemology] (1911), in Ueyama Shunpei 上山春平 ed., *Nishida Kitarō* 西田幾多郎 (Tokyo: Chūō Kōronsha, 1970), pp. 234–51.
29 Nishida Kitarō, "Shushu no sekai" [Multitudes of World] (1917), in Ueyama Shunpei, ed., *Nishida Kitarō*, pp. 264–73.
30 Ibid., p. 272.
31 For a discussion of Nishida's philosophy of "direct reality" and the *topos* of Nothingness, see Ueyama Shunpei, "Zettai bu no kenkyū" 絶対無の研究 [Study of the Absolute Nothingness], in *Nishida Kitarō*, pp. 7–85. For discussions in Chinese, see Yu-kwan Ng 吳汝鈞, *Jingdu xuepai zhexue qijiang* 京都學派哲學七講 [Seven Lectures on the Philosophy of the Kyōto School] (Taipei: Wenjin Chubanshe, 1998); Wen-hong Huang 黃文宏, "Xitian Jiduolang lun 'shizai' yu 'jingyan,'" 西田幾多郎論「實在」與「經驗」 [Nishida Kitarō on "Reality" and "Experience"], *Taiwan Journal of East Asian Studies*, 3.2 (December 2006): 61–90.
32 Nishida Kitarō, "Shushu no sekai," p. 272.
33 Cf. Nishida Kitarō, *Jikaku ni okeru chokkan to hansei* [Intuition and Self-Reflexivity in Self-Consciousness] (1914–17), in *Nishida Kitarō*, pp. 276–82.
34 See Washburn, *Shanghai: A Novel*, p. 223.
35 The four master categories are quantity, quality, relation, and modality. Each of these master categories has three branches.
36 Yokomitsu Riichi, "On Neo-Sensation," p. 77.
37 Cf. Michael Ruse, *The Evolution-Creation Struggle* (Cambridge, MA: Harvard University Press, 2005).
38 Yokomitsu Riichi, *Shanghai*, p. 110; Washburn, *Shanghai: A Novel*, p. 80.
39 Yokomitsu Riichi, *Shanghai*, p. 29; Washburn, *Shanghai: A Novel*, p. 22.
40 Ibid.
41 Yokomitsu Riichi, *Shanghai*, p. 69; Washburn, *Shanghai: A Novel*, p. 50.

42 Ibid.
43 Yokomitsu Riichi, *Shanghai*, p. 115; Washburn, *Shanghai: A Novel*, p. 84.
44 Yokomitsu Riichi, *Shanghai*, pp. 95–6; Washburn, *Shanghai: A Novel*, p. 69.
45 Lippit has a fine analysis of Sanki as a Don Quixote figure in the novel, who "inhabits his own phantasmal world" in the beginning, but later "becomes conscious of a split in his identity." See, Seiji Lippit, *Topographies of Japanese Modernism*, p. 100. But my analysis differs from his in that I don't think Sanki, as a character through which all discourses converge, is conscious of that split, as is indicated by the narrator's psycho-narration: "Yet he had forgotten that hating his boss was the same thing as hating his mother country."
46 Yokomitsu Riichi, *Shanghai*, p. 120; Washburn, *Shanghai: A Novel*, p. 87.
47 Yokomitsu Riichi, *Shanghai*, p. 172; Washburn, *Shanghai: A Novel*, p. 123.
48 Yokomitsu Riichi, *Shanghai*, p. 22.
49 Yokomitsu Riichi, *Shanghai*, p. 78; Washburn, *Shanghai: A Novel*, p. 56.
50 Yokomitsu Riichi, *Shanghai*, p. 261; Washburn, *Shanghai: A Novel*, p. 197.
51 Yokomitsu Riichi, *Shanghai*, pp. 79–86.
52 Yokomitsu Riichi, *Shanghai*, p. 76; Washburn, *Shanghai: A Novel*, p. 55.
53 Yokomitsu Riichi, *Shanghai*, p. 81; Washburn, *Shanghai: A Novel*, p. 58.
54 Yokomitsu Riichi, *Shanghai*, p. 278; Washburn, *Shanghai: A Novel*, p. 197.
55 Yokomitsu Riichi, *Shanghai*, p. 79; Washburn, *Shanghai: A Novel*, p. 57.
56 Yokomitsu Riichi, *Shanghai*, p. 279; Washburn, *Shanghai: A Novel*, p. 198.
57 Yokomitsu Riichi, *Shanghai*, p. 283; Washburn, *Shanghai: A Novel*, p. 200.
58 Yokomitsu Riichi, *Shanghai*, p. 23. In the 1932 Kaizō edition, the woman revolutionary's name is pronounced as "Hō Shūran," as indicated by the *rubi* for the pronunciation of the *kanji* characters. Washburn, however, uses the Chinese pronunciation of her name, Fang Qiulan.
59 Yokomitsu Riichi, *Shanghai*, p. 32; Washburn, *Shanghai: A Novel*, p. 22.
60 Yokomitsu Riichi, *Shanghai*, p. 104; Washburn, *Shanghai: A Novel*, p. 76.
61 Yokomitsu Riichi, *Shanghai*, p. 126.
62 Yokomitsu Riichi, *Shanghai*, p. 126; Washburn, *Shanghai: A Novel*, pp. 91–2.
63 Yokomitsu Riichi, *Shanghai*, p. 127; Washburn, *Shanghai: A Novel*, p. 92.
64 Yokomitsu Riichi, *Shanghai*, pp. 129–30.
65 Yokomitsu Riichi, *Shanghai*, p. 132; Washburn, *Shanghai: A Novel*, p. 96.
66 Yokomitsu Riichi, *Shanghai*, p. 140; Washburn, *Shanghai: A Novel*, p. 101.
67 Fukuzawa Yukichi, "Datsuaron" 脱亜論 [On Severing with Asia], *Jiji shinpō* 時事新報 [Current News Daily] (16 March 1885).
68 Ernest Fenollosa, born in the American town Salem, was invited to Tokyo Imperial University in 1879. Originally invited to teach philosophy, he became an expert in Japanese art and taught the Japanese to value their traditional art at a time when Westernization was in full swing in Japan. In 1882 at the inaugural ceremony of the Art Club of Nobles he gave a speech, denouncing the upper class for abandoning their own national treasures. He was later appointed the Commissioner of Fine Arts for the Emperor. From 1890 to 1896 he was the curator of the Department of Oriental Art at Boston Museum of Fine Arts. His articles were posthumously collected in a volume, *The Epoch of Chinese and Japanese Art* (London: William Heinemann, 1913). The Japanese edition was published in 1921. Cf. Van Wyck Brooks, "Earnest Fenollosa and Japan," *Proceedings of the American Philosophical Society* 106.2 (30 April 1962): 106–10.
69 Okakura Kakuzō, *The Ideals of the East with Special Reference to the Art of Japan* (London: John Murray, 1904), 2nd edn.
70 Koyasu Nobukuni 子安宣邦, "*Ajia" wa dō katararete kita ka: kindai Nihon no orientarizumu* アジアはどう語られてきたか：近代日本のオリエンタリズム [How "Asia" Was Formulated in Discourse: Modern Japan's Orientalism] (Tokyo: Fujihara Shoten, 2003), pp. 83–147.

71 CF. Kōketsu Atsushi 纐纈厚, "Taiwan Shuppei no ichi to teikokku Nipon no seiritsu" 台湾出兵の位置と帝国日本の成立 [Invasion of Taiwan and the Establishment of Imperial Japan], *Shokuminchi bunka kenkyū: shiryo to bunseki* 植民地文化研究：資料と分析 [Studies of Colonial Cultures: Materials and Analysis], 4 (July 2005): 25–33. According to the author, Japan's invasion of Taiwan and colonial expansion in general were carried out in the framework of "ka'i chitsujo kara no dakkyaku to bankoku kōhō chitsujo e no sannyū" 華夷秩序からの脱却と万国公法秩序への参入 [Secession from the Sinobarbarian Order and Entry into the Order of International Law].
72 For a concise account of the establishment and goal of the Pan-Asia Co-Prosperity Sphere, see Fujii Yūsuke 藤井祐介, "Tōji no mippō—bunka kensetsu to wa nani ka?" 統治の秘法 - 文化建設とは何か？ [The Secret of State Rule—What Is Cultural Construction?], in Ikeda Hiroshi 池田浩士, *Dai Tōa Kyōeiken no bunka kensetsu* 大東亜共栄圏の文化建設 [The Cultural Construction of the Pan-Asia Co-Prosperity Sphere] (Kyoto: Jinbun shoin, 2007), pp. 11–73.
73 Yokomitsu Riichi, *Shanghai*, p. 167; Washburn, *Shanghai: A Novel*, p. 119.
74 Yokomitsu Riichi, *Shanghai*, p. 191; Washburn, *Shanghai: A Novel*, p. 135.
75 Yokomitsu Riichi, *Shanghai*, p. 270; Washburn, *Shanghai: A Novel*, p. 192.
76 Yokomitsu Riichi, *Shanghai*, p. 23; Washburn, *Shanghai: A Novel*, p. 17.
77 Yokomitsu Riichi, *Shanghai*, p. 263; Washburn, *Shanghai: A Novel*, p. 188.
78 The many editions and revisions of *Shanghai* have been pointed out by critics. It was first published by Kaizōsha in one volume in 1932, comprising 45 chapters. Chapter 32, added and inserted into the chapters originally serialized in *Kaizō*, was first published in the journal *Bungaku Kuotarii* 文学クォータリー [Literary Quarterly] in June 1932, a month before the Kaizōsha volume came out. The 1932 edition was later revised by Yokomitsu and published by Shomotsutenbōsha in 1935, with Chapter 44 eliminated. Cf. Inoue Ken 井上謙, *Yokomitsu Riichi: hyōden to kenkyū* 横光利一：評伝と研究 (Yokomitsu Riichi: A Biographic Study and Research; Tokyo: Ōfū, 1994), pp. 227–47. For a facsimile reprinting of the eight parts serialized in *Kaizō* and *Literary Quarterly*, see Inoue Satoshi 井上聡, *Yokomitsu Riichi to Chūgoku: "Shanhai" no kōsei to 5.30 jiken* 横光利一と中国：『上海』の構成と五・三〇事件 [Yokomitsu Riichi and China: The Structure of *Shanghai* and the May 30th Incident] (Tokyo: Kanrin Shobō, 2006), pp. 14–164. Inoue Satoshi's study opens with the preface written by Yokomitsu Yūten 横光佑典, Yokomitsu Riichi's son, and includes a comparison of the May 30th Incident described in the serialized edition with that in the 1935 revised edition. According to Seiji Lippit, "The 1935 edition has value mainly as a testament to the end of Yokomitsu's modernist project." See Lippit, *Topographies of Japanese Modernism*, p. 248. But as I show in this chapter, some of the revisions found in the 1935 edition are significant as to Yokomitsu's ambiguous attitudes towards Japanese imperialism.
79 Yokomitsu Riichi, *Shanghai* (Tokyo: Shomotsutenbōsha, 1935), pp. 297–8.
80 Yokomitsu Riichi, *Shanghai* (Tokyo: Kaizō Bunko, 1932), pp. 263–4; Washburn, *Shanghai: A Novel*, p. 188. This scene in the 1932 single-volume version is the same as that in the 1931 serialized version. For the latter, see Inoue Satoshi, *Yokomitsu Riichi and China: The Structure of "Shanghai" and the May 30th Incident*, pp. 134–5.
81 See the section titled "Skeletal Preparation" in Stanley Rhine, *Bone Voyage: A Journey in Forensic Anthropology* (Albuquerque: University of Mexico Press, 1998), pp. 204–9. Although forensic anthropologists usually say "boil," what they really mean is "simmer": "Bringing the bones to a boil is good for making soup, but bad for making skeletons" (p. 206).
82 Victor Koschmann, "Victimization and the Writerly Subject: Writers' War Responsibility in Early Postwar Japan," *Tamkang Review*, 26.1–2: 61–75. Odagiri's

article is reprinted in Usui Yoshimi 臼井吉見 and Ōkubo Tsuneo 大久保典夫, eds., *Sengo bungaku ronsō* 戦後文学論争 [Postwar Literary Debate] (Tokyo: Banchō Shobō, 1972), vol. 1, pp. 115–17.

83 Odagiri Hideo 小田切秀雄, "Bungaku ni okeru sensō sekinin no tsuikyū" [Pursuing War Responsibility in Literature], in Usui Yoshimi and Ōkubo Tsuneo, eds., *Postwar Literary Debate*, p. 115.

84 It inspired the Chinese writer Sun Lianggong 孫俍工 to write a play titled *Xu ige qingnian de meng* 續一個青年的夢 [A Sequel to *A Young Man's Dream*], right after the Japanese army attacked the Chinese army in Manchuria on 18 September 1931.

85 Although Mushanokōji left the village in 1924 to pursue a literary career, he remained a "songai kaiin" 村外会員 [external member] and continued to pay membership fees. The village moved to Moroyamamachi 毛呂山町, Saitama 埼玉 County, in 1939 because of the construction of a dam in Kijōchō 木城町, and it still exists today. For the philosophy of the New Village, see Mushanokōji Saneatsu, *Atarashiki Mura no seikatsu* [Life of New Village] and other works, in *Mushanokōji Saneatsu zenshū* 武者小路実篤全集 [Complete Works of Mushanokōji] (Tokyo: Shōgakukan, 1987–91), vol. 4.

86 Zhou Zuoren, "Riben de xincun" [Japanese New Village], in *Xin qingnian* 新青年 [New Youth], 6.3: 265–77.

87 Mao Zedong published an article titled "Xuesheng zhi gongzuo" 學生之工作 [The Work of Students] in *Hunan jiaoyu yuekan* 湖南教育月刊 [Hunan Education Monthly] 1.2 (1 December 1919). He advocates building a "new village" in Yuelu 嶽麓 Mountain in Changsha 長沙, where the reforms of family life, education, and society can be carried out simultaneously. He writes, "Many Russian youths live with farmers in villages. Recently the New Village movement is popular with Japanese youths. The principle of 'Work-study' is welcome in America and her colony the Philippines. The Chinese students in America follow the vogue and establish work-study groups; in France they form the societies of *les étudiants-ouvriers*." Cf. Mao Zedong, "Xuesheng zhi gongzuo" [The Work of Students], in *Mao Zedong zaoqi wengao* 毛澤東早期文稿 [Mao Zedong's Early Writings] (Changsha: Hunan Chubanshe, 1995), pp. 449–57.

88 For a detailed analysis of Mushanokōji's political turnabout, see Dong Bingyue 董炳月, *"Guomin zuojia" de lichang: Zhong-ri xiandai wenxue guanxi yanjiu* "國民作家"的立場：中日現代文學關係研究 [Writers' Position as National Subjects: The Relationships between Modern Chinese and Japanese Literatures] (Beijing: Sanlian Shudian, 2006), pp. 77–122.

89 Ibid., p. 114.

90 Mushanokōji Saneatsu, *Sanshō* [Three Laughs], in *Complete Works of Mushanokōji Saneatsu*, vol. 14, p. 331.

91 Tsurumi Shunsuke, "Tenkō no kyōdō kenkyū ni tsuite" 転向の共同研究について [The Joint Research on Turnabout], in Shisō no Kagaku Kenkyūkai 思想の科学研究会, ed., *Tenkō* [Turnabout] (Tokyo: Heibonsha, 1967), vol. 1, pp. 1–27. For a concise account of the history of "tenkō" during the war, see his *Senjiki Nihon no seishinshi* 戦時期日本の精神史, 1931–45 [Mental History in Wartime Japan, 1931–45] (Tokyo: Iwanami Shoten, 1991). First published in 1982.

92 Yokomitsu Riichi, *Shanghai*, p. 98; Washburn, *Shanghai: A Novel*, p. 71.

93 Yokomitsu Riichi, *Shanghai*, p. 7; Washburn, *Shanghai: A Novel*, p. 5.

94 Yokomitsu Riichi, *Shanghai*, p. 61; Washburn, *Shanghai: A Novel*, p. 44, with modifications.

95 Yokomitsu Riichi, *Shanghai*, p. 61; Washburn, *Shanghai: A Novel*, p. 45.

96 Yokomitsu Riichi, *Shanghai*, pp. 61–2; Washburn, *Shanghai: A Novel*, p. 45.

97 Yokomitsu Riichi, *Shanghai*, p. 62; Washburn, *Shanghai: A Novel*, p. 45.

Notes   221

98   Yokomitsu Riichi, *Shanghai*, p. 44; Washburn, *Shanghai: A Novel*, pp. 30–31.
99   Yokomitsu Riichi, *Shanghai*, p. 89; Dennis Washburn, *Shanghai: A Novel*, p. 64.
100 Yokomitsu Riichi, *Shanghai*, p. 310; Washburn, *Shanghai: A Novel*, p. 217.
101 Frank Dikötter, *The Age of Openness: China Before Mao* (Hong Kong: Hong Kong University Press, 2008).
102 Cf. Elizabeth J. Perry, "Reclaiming the Chinese Revolution," *The Journal of Asian Studies* 67.4 (November 2008): 1147–64. Perry points out that recent development in history studies tend to "put our faith in institutions such as markets and courts of law, looking to 'democratic transitions' rather than to social revolutions as the path toward political progress. . . . These days we recoil from the senseless violence of the revolutionary past, and place our hopes for the future in liberal democratic reform. But this repudiation is a fairly recent phenomenon."
103 Diana Taylor, *The Archive and the Repertoire: Performing Cultural Memory in the Americas*, pp. 79–86.

4 A traveling text: *Souvenirs entomologiques*

1   Walter Benjamin, "The Task of a Translator" (1923), trans. Harry Zohn, in Marcus Bulock and Michael W. Jennings, eds., *Walter Benjamin: Selected Writings* (Cambridge, MA: The Belknap Press of Harvard University Press, 1996), vol. 1 (1913–26), pp. 256–7.
2   Ye Hui 葉輝, *Shuxie fucheng: Xianggang wenxue pinglunji* 書寫浮城：香港文學評論集 [Writing the Floating City: Collection of Articles on Hong Kong Literature] (Hong Kong: Qingwen Shuwu, 2001), p. 349.
3   Ibid., pp. 360–1.
4   Ōgai Kamome, "Yanjiu chujiao de sangeren" [The Three Who Study Antennas], *The Women's Pictorial*, 21 (September 1934): 5–6.
5   Cf. Bennetta Jules-Rosetta, *Josephine Baker in Art and Life: The Icon and the Image* (Urbana: University of Illinois Press, 2007).
6   Guo Jianying, "Hei, hong, rencanxing yu nüxing" [Black, Red, Cruelty, and Women], in Shen Jianzhong, ed., *Shidai manhua, 1934–1937* [Modern Sketch, *1934–1937*] (Shanghai: Shanghai Shehui Kexueyuan Chubanshe, 2004), vol. 1, p. 10. Originally published in *Modern Sketch*, 1 (20 January 1934).
7   Cf. Ueno Masuzō 上野益三, *Nihon hakubutsugakushi* 日本博物学史 [Natural History of Japan] (Tokyo: Heibonsha, 1973).
8   Ōgai Kamome, "The Three Who Study Antennas," pp. 5–6.
9   Besides Ōsugi Sakae and Shiina Sonoji, the other translators are Washio Takeshi 鷲尾猛 (vols 5 and 6), Kinoshita Hanji 木下半治 (vols 7 and 8), Komaki Oumi 小牧近江 (vol. 9), and Doi Itsuo 土井逸雄 (vol. 10).
10 Liuxu 柳絮, "Zhuzhang zuzhi Dadongya wuzhengfuzhuyizhe dalianmeng" 主張組織大東亞無政府主義者大聯盟 [Advocacy of the Alliance of the Anarchists of Greater East-Asia], *Minzhong* 民鐘 [The People's Knell], 16 (15 December 1926): 2–3. For Ōsugi's life, see his *Jijoden* [Autobiography] (1921–22). For an account of his imprisonment, see his *Gokuchūki* 獄中記 [Prison Memoirs] (1919). For English translations see Byron Marshall, *The Autobiography of Ōsugi Sakae* (Berkeley: University of California Press, 1992).
11 Ōsugi Sakae, "Nihon dasshutsuki" [Escapes from Japan] (1923), in *Ōsugi Sakae shū* 大杉栄集 [Selected Works of Ōsugi Sakae], ed. Osawa Masamichi 大沢正道 (Tokyo: Chikuma Shoten, 1974), pp. 297–327.
12 See Ba Jin (Pei Gan 芾甘), "Weida de xundaozhe: cheng tongzhi Dashan Rung jun zhi ling" [The Great Martyr: To the Spirit of Our Comrade Ōsugi Sakae], *Chunlei* [Spring Thunder], 3 (1 May 1924); "Dashanrung zhuzuo nianpu"

大杉榮著作年譜[Bibliography of Ōsugi Sakae], *Spring Thunder*, 3 (May 1924); "Dashan Rung nianpu" 大杉榮年譜 [Annual Account of Ōsugi Sakae's Life], *Mingzhong* [The People's Knell] 1.9 (1 August 1924). These three articles are collected in *Ba Jin quanji* 巴金全集 [Complete Works of Ba Jin] (Beijing: Renmin Wenxue Chubanshe, 2000), vol. 18, pp. 63–76.

13 Ba Jin, "The Great Martyr: To the Spirit of Our Comrade Ōsugi Sakae," in *Complete Works of Ba Jin*, vol. 18, p. 64. Fisher's last words in English are provided by the author in a footnote.

14 Lydia Liu, *Translingual Practice: Literature, National Culture, and Translated Modernity – China, 1900–1937* (Stanford, CA: Stanford University Press, 1995), p. 3. In the quote she comments on Talal Asad's article "The Concept of Cultural Translation in British Social Anthropology," collected in James Clifford and George E. Marcus, eds., *Writing Culture: The Poetics and Politics of Ethnography* (Berkeley: University of California Press, 1986), pp. 141–64.

15 In "L'étique du souci de soi comme pratique de la liberté" [The Ethics of the Concern for the Self as a Practice of Freedom], an interview in 1984, Foucault confesses that there has been a shift in his idea concerning subjectivity and truth since the time of *Les mots et les choses* [The Order of Things] (1966). In contrast to his previous position of "les pratiques coercitives" (coercive practices), as in psychiatry or the penitentiary system, his lectures at Collège de France began to develop the concept of "les pratiques de soi" (practices of self) and "les pratiques de liberté" (practices of freedom), which allow individuals to modify power relationships. To distinguish the difference between liberation and practices of freedom, he says, "La liberation ouvre un champ pour de nouveaux rapports de pouvoir, qu'il s'agit de contrôller par des pratiques de liberté." (Liberation opens up a ground for new power relationships, which must be regulated by practices of freedom.) The idea is that power relations are mobile, except in extreme cases such as psychiatry or the prison system, where mobility is totally blocked. (Of course, one can argue that, even in psychiatry and the prison system, power relations are not totally rigid.) To Foucault, this concerns how the human subject enters into "les jeux de vérité" (games of truth), and, furthermore, practices of freedom and games of truth are closely related to ethics. According to him, freedom is the ontological condition of ethics, while "l'éthique est la forme réfléchie que prend la liberté" (ethics is the form freedom takes when informed by reflection). See Michel Foucault, *Dits et écrits, 1954–1988* (Paris : Gallimard, 2001), vol. 2, pp. 1527–48. For English translation, see "The Ethics of the Concern for Self as a Practice of Freedom," trans. Robert Hurley et al., in Paul Rabinow, ed., *Ethics: Subjectivity and Truth* (London: Allen Lane, 1997), pp. 146–65. Here I am altering somewhat the English translation in Rabinow's volume.

16 Ōsugi Sakae, *Jijoden* (Tokyo: Sekkasha, 1967).

17 Ōsugi Sakae, "Yakusha no jo" [Translator's Preface] (1922), *Konchūki* [Book of Insects] (Tokyo: Meiseki Shoten, 2005), pp. 5–14.

18 Ibid.

19 The hunting-wasps include species such as le Cerceris buprestide, le Cerceris tubercule, le sphex à ailes jaunes, and le sphex languedocien.

20 Ninagawa Yuzuru 蜷川譲, *Pari ni shisu* パリに死す [Death in Paris] (Tokyo: Fujiwara Shoten, 1996).

21 Ibid.

22 Ibid.

23 Dr. G.-V. Legros, *La Vie de J.-H. Fabre, naturaliste, par un disciple* [Life of J.-H. Fabre, Naturalist, by a Disciple] (Paris : Librairie Ch. Delagrave, 1913).

24 Shiina Sonoji, *Fāburu no shōgai, kagaku no shijin* [Life of Fabre, Poet of Science] (Tokyo: Sōbunkaku, 1925).

25 Legros, *Fabre, Poet of Science*, trans. Bernard Miall (New York: The Century Co., 1913).
26 Legros, *Life of J.-H. Fabre, Naturalist, by a Disciple*, pp. 2–3.
27 *Kunchongji*, trans. Yang Shouqiang 楊守鏘 et al. [Book of Insects] (Beijing: Huacheng Chubanshe, 2001).
28 Lu Xun, *Lu Xun riji* 魯迅日記 [The Diary of Lu Xun] (Beijing, Renmin Wenxue Chubanshe, 1959), Part 1, pp. 507, 510, 642, 653, and Part 2, pp. 765, 774, 792, 815, 817, 837, 839, 845.
29 Cf. Zhou Jianren, "Lu Xun yu ziran kexue," in Liu Zaifu et al., eds., *Lu Xun ho ziran kexue* [Lu Xun and Natural Science] (Macao: Eryashe, 1978), p. 3.
30 Shanghai Lu Xun Museum, ed., *Zhongri youhao de xianqu: Lu Xun yu Neishan Wanzao tuji* 中日友好的先驅：魯迅與内山完造圖集 [Pioneers of the Friendship between China and Japan: Picture Collections of Lu Xun and Uchiyama Kanzō] (Shanghai: Renmin Meishu Chubanshe, 2000), 2nd edn. First published in 1995.
31 Online posting <http://www.santen.co.jp/company/jp/history/chapter1.jsp> (accessed 29 December 2004).
32 Shanghai Lu Xun Museum, ed., *Pioneers of the Friendship Between China and Japan*.
33 Lu Xun (Mingzhao 冥昭), "Chunmo xiantan" [Random Talks in the Late Spring], *Mangyuan* 莽原 [Wasteland], 1 (24 April 1925): 4–5.
34 Ibid.
35 Ibid.
36 For an account of Eroshenko's connection with the Nakamuraya bakery during his stay in Japan, see Aizawa Genshichi 相沢源七, *Sōma Kokkō to Nakamuraya saron* 相馬黒光と中村屋サロン [Sōma Kokkō and Nakamuraya Salon] (Sendai-shi: Hōbundō, 1982), pp. 89–90; For Eroshenko's activities in Japan, see Fujii Shōzō 藤井省三, *Eroshenko no toshi monogatari: 1920 nendai Tōkyō, Shanhai, Pekin* エロシェンコの都市物語——1920年代東京、上海、北京 [Eroshenko's City Story: 1920s Tokyo, Shanghai, and Beijing] (Tokyo: Misuzu Shobō, 1989), pp. 4–49.
37 Shortly after his first arrival in Japan, Eroshenko met Kamichika Ichiko 神近市子 (1888–1980), the journalist and socialist activist who later stabbed her lover Ōsugi Sakae because of jealousy for another woman in 1916 and served two years in prison. It was through Kamichika that Eroshenko was taken under the roof of Nakamuraya 中村屋, the bakery and literary salon run by Sōma Kokkō 相馬黒光 (1875–1955) and her husband Aizo 愛蔵. He lived there for four years. A haven for literary men, artists, and international exiles, Nakamuraya sheltered famous radicals such as the Korean independence fighter Lim Gyuwan, and the Indian independence movement leader Rash Bihari Bose (1897–1945), who married the Sōmas' eldest daughter Toshiko in 1918. The great Indian poet Tagore also visited Nakamuraya in 1922. Cf. Aizawa Genshichi, *Sōma Kokkō and Nakamuraya Salon*, pp. 76–122; Nakajima Takeshi 中島岳志, *Nakamuraya no Bōsu: Indo dokuritsu undō to kindai Nihon no Ajia shugi* 中村屋のボース：インド独立運動と近代日本のアジア主義 [Bose of Nakamuraya: India's Independence Movement and Modern Japan's Asianism] (Tokyo: Hakusuisha, 2005), pp. 105–58.
38 Zhou Zuoren, "Huai Airoxianko Jun" 懷愛羅先珂君 (Missing Mr Eroshenko), *Literary Supplement to the Morning Post* (7 November 1922): 4.
39 The three poetry collections are *Yoake mae no uta* 夜明け前の歌 (Songs Before Dawn), *Saigo no tameiki* 最後の溜息 [The Last Sigh], and *Jinrui no tameni* 人類の為めに [For Mankind]. See Aizawa Genshichi, *Sōma Kokkō and Nakamuraya Salon*, p. 89.
40 Lu Xun, trans. "Chunye de meng" 春夜的夢 [A Spring Night's Dream], *Literary Supplement to the Morning Post* (22 October 1921): 1–2.

41 Lu Xun, "Ya de xiju" [The Comedy of Ducks], *Funü zazhi* 婦女雜誌 [Women's Journal] 8.12 (December 1922): 83–4.
42 Lu Xun, "Random Talks in the Late Spring," pp. 4–5.
43 Ōsugi Sakae, *Konchūki* [Book of Insects] (Tokyo: Sōbunkaku, 1924), 6th edn, pp. 97–113.
44 Jean-Henri Fabre, *Souvenirs entomologiques : études sur l'instinct et les mœurs des insectes* (Paris : Robert Laffont, 1989), vol. I, pp. 165–73. This edition collects the original 10 volumes of Fabre's work into two volumes. Since in this chapter all who discussed *Souvenirs entomologiques* referred to the original 10 volumes, I refer to the original volume numbers for the sake of discussion and clarity.
45 Ibid., pp. 166–7.
46 Ibid., p. 167.
47 Ibid., p. 169. In note 1 Fabre provides the following reference: *Annales des sciences naturelles*, 3rd series, vol. V. This refers to the collection of the journal (Paris: Chez Béchet, 1824–95). This journal, published in Paris from 1824 to 2000, was founded by Victor Audouin (1797–1841), Jean-Baptiste Dumas (1800–884), and Adolphe Brongniart (1801–76).
48 Ibid., p. 170.
49 Ibid.
50 Ibid., p. 173.
51 Peter J. Bowler, *Charles Darwin: The Man and His Influence* (Cambridge, MA: Basil Blackwell, Inc., 1990), pp. 17–18.
52 Jean-Henri Fabre, *Souvenirs entomologiques*, vol. I, p. 199.
53 Ibid., p. 405. In Chapter 10, Volume 2 Fabre provides a note, confessing that later Charles Darwin wrote him and said his grandfather was actually referring to a wasp (*guêpe* in French) in this episode of his book, *Zoonomia*. Fabre regrets that, reading Lacordaire, who translated the English word "wasp" into "sphex," he was duped into believing that an entomologist as renowned as Erasmas Darwin could have mistaken a wasp for a sphex.
54 Ibid., p. 203.
55 H. P. Blavatsky, *Isis Unveiled: A Master-Key to the Mysteries of Ancient and Modern Science and Theology* (New York: J. W. Bouton, 1877), 2nd edn, pp. 305, 433.
56 David Matual, *Tolstoy's Translation of the Gospels: A Critical Study* (Queenston, Ontario: The Edwin Mellen Press, 1992), p. 23.
57 Ibid., p. 12.
58 Ibid., pp. 1–23.
59 Ibid., p. 13.
60 H. P. Blavatsky, "Is Theosophy a Religion?" *Lucifer* (Nov. 1888), pp. 177–87.
61 Fabre, *Souvenirs entomologiques*, vol. I, p. 392.
62 Ibid., p. 371.
63 Charles Darwin, *The Origin of Species by Means of Natural Selection, or the Preservation of Favored Races in the Struggle for Life* (New York: The Modern Library, 1998), p. 316. Originally published in 1859. Darwin's book title begins with "On the Origin of Species" in the first five editions. It is in the sixth edition published in 1872 that "On" is dropped.
64 Ibid., p. 318.
65 Ibid., p. 330.
66 Ibid., p. 360.
67 Wang Daw-hwan 王道還, "yijiuyiwu nian shiyue shiyi ri *Kunchongji* zuozhe Fabu'er shishi" 一九一五年十月十一日《昆蟲記》作者法布爾逝世 (11 October 1915 – Death of Fabre, Author of *Souvenirs entomologiques*), *Kexue fazhan* 科學發展 [Scientific Development], 358 (October 2002): 72–4.
68 Yves Delange, *Jean Henri Fabre, l'homme qui aimait les insectes* [Jean Henri Fabre,

the Man Who Loved Insects] (Paris : Actes Sud, 1999), pp. 24–7. In Fabre's time there were only three kinds of diploma to be obtained: *baccalauréat*, *licence* (at the third year at the university), and *doctorat* (at the eighth year at the university).
69 Ibid., pp. 28–32.
70 Ibid., p. 51. In the text of Delange's book, it is said that Fabre was awarded the Gegner Prize in 1866, but at the end of the book in the list of "Diplômes, titres et distinctions" (pp. 340–1) it is indicated that in 1866 he was awarded the Thore Prize. From Delange's preface to *Souvenirs entomologiques*, it is clear that Fabre won the Thore Prize with 3000 francs in 1866. Fabre's annual salary at Avignon High School was 1600 francs from 1853 on. His salary at the Collège d'Ajaccio was 1800 francs, but it was cut to half in 1850. When he taught at Carpentras as school teacher, his salary was less than 900 francs. With the copyright he received for *Souvenirs entomologiques*, he bought l'Harmas at 7200 francs and returned to John Stuart Mill 3000 francs, which he had borrowed after being driven out of his home in Avignon. Cf. Yves Delange, "Préface," *Souvenirs entomologiques*, pp. 10–24.
71 Ibid., pp. 164–99.
72 Ibid., pp. 47–9.
73 Ibid., pp. 43, 54.
74 Ibid., p. 57.
75 Ibid., pp. 61–3.
76 Ibid., pp. 58–61.
77 Ibid., p. 43.
78 Charles Darwin, *The Origin of Species*, p. 118. In the first three editions of *On the Origin of Species*, Darwin quoted Fabre but did not refer to him as "that inimitable observer Mr. Fabre." Cf. Darwin, *The Origin of Species by Charles Darwin: A Variorum Text*, ed. Morse Peckham (Philadelphia: University of Pennsylvania Press, 1959), p. 174.
79 Francis Darwin and A. C. Seward, eds., *More Letters of Charles Darwin: A Record of His Work in a Series of Hitherto Unpublished Letters* (New York: Johnson Reprint Corporation, 1972), vol. 1, pp. 385–6. Reprint of the edition by D. Appleton and Company in New York in 1903. See also Frederick Burkhardt and Sydney Smith, eds., *A Calendar of the Correspondence of Charles Darwin, 1821–1882, with Supplement* (Cambridge University Press, 1994), pp. 522, 524, 526, 546. First published in 1985.
80 Moustafa Bayoumi and Andrew Rubin, eds., "Traveling Theory," in *The Edward Said Reader* (New York: Vintage Books, 2002), p. 196.
81 P. Kropotkin, *Modern Science and Anarchism* (London: Freedom Press, 1912), pp. 1–17.
82 Ibid., p. 16.
83 P. Kropotkin, *Mutual Aid: A Factor of Evolution* (London: William Heinemann, 1902), p. iiv.
84 Kropotkin, *Modern Science and Anarchism*, p. 31.
85 Ibid., p. 32.
86 Ibid., p. 99.
87 These articles, originally serialized in Shinchō, were later collected as a volume titled *Furansei bungei inshōki* 佛蘭西文藝印象記 [Impressions of French Literature] (Tokyo: Shinchōsha, 1923). They were collected in volume 3 of Yoshie's complete works. See "Koki" 後記 [Postscript], in *Yoshie Takamatsu zenshū* 吉江喬松全集 [Complete Works of Yoshie Takamatsu] (Tokyo: Hakusuisha, 1936), vol. 3, p. 503.
88 Cf. Yoshie Takamatsu, "Nōmin bungaku" 農民文學 [Peasants' Literature], in *Nan'ō no sora* 南歐の空 [The Sky of Southern Europe] (Tokyo: Waseda University Press, 1929), 45 pp. Each work collected in this book starts at p. 1.

226 Notes

89 Ōsugi Sakae, "Sōzōteki shinka – Anri Beruguson ron" [*Evolution créatrice*: On Henri Bergson], in *Ōsugi Sakae zenshū* [Complete Works of Ōsugi Sakae] (Tokyo: Ōsugi Sakae Zenshū Kankōkai, 1925–26), vol. 1, pp. 187–96.
90 Philip S. Foner, ed., *When Karl Marx Died* (New York: International Publishers, 973), p. 39. Cf. also Margaret A. Fay, "Did Marx Offer to Dedicate *Capital* to Darwin?: A Reassessment of the Evidence," *Journal of the History of Ideas*, 39.1 (January to March 1978): 133–46. The confusion of whether Marx offered to dedicate his book to Darwin arose mainly because Isaiah Berlin, in his biography of Karl Marx, mistook Marx's son-in-law's letter, asking Darwin to accept a dedication in his own book, for Marx's letter. For a clear and simple account of the misunderstanding, see Janet Brown, *Darwin's Origin of Species: A Biography* (New York: Atlantic Monthly Press, 2006), p. 101.
91 See *The Letters of Karl Marx*, trans. Saul K. Padover (New Jersey: Prentice-Hall, Inc., 1979), p. 157.
92 Ōsugi Sakae, "Reikon no tame no senshi" [A Spirit Wrestler], in *Complete Works of Ōsugi Sakae*, vol. 1, pp. 738–6.
93 Lu Xun, "Tongxun" 通訊 [Correspondences] (1925), in *Lu Xun quanji* [Complete Works of Lu Xun] (Beijing: Renmin Wenxue Chubanshe, 1989), vol. 3, p. 25.
94 "L'Harmas" is a word in Provençal, a Romance language spoken in southeastern France. Fabre explains in the text of his book: "Les lieux d'opération étaient une plaine inculte, caillouteuse, un—harmas—comme on dit dans le pays." (The places of operation were an uncultivated plain, covered with pebbles, an 'harmas,' as one says in the country." It is the name of the house and garden Fabre purchased in Sérignan du Comtat in 1879. He lived there from the following year to the end of his life.) Cf. Yves Delange, *Jean Henri Fabre, The Man Who Loved Insects*, p. 165.
95 Fabre, *Souvenirs entomologiques*, vol. I, pp. 319–25.
96 Zhou Zuoren, "(2) Fabuer *Kunchongji*" [Fabre's *Book of Insects*, part 2], in *Literary Supplement to the Morning Post* (26 January 1923), p. 3.
97 Ibid.
98 This debate started with Zhang Junmai's talk titled "Renshengguan" 人生觀 [Outlook on Life] at Tsinghua University 清華大學 in Beijing on 14 Februry 1923. It was then criticized by the geologist Ding Wenjiang 丁文江 in a series of articles published in *Nuli zhoubao* 努力周報 [Endeavor Weekly] from 12 April to 3 June 1923. See Ding Wenjiang, "Xuanxue yu kexue" 玄學與科學 [Metaphysics and Science], *Nuli zhoubao*, nos. 48–9 (12 April to 22 April); "Xuanxue yu kexue – da Zhang Junmai" 玄學與科學 – 答張君勱 [Metaphysics and Science: In Response to Zhang Junmai], *Nuli zhoubao*, nos. 54–5 (27 May–3 June 1923); "xuanxue yu kexue de taolun de yuxing" 玄學與科學的討論的餘興 [The Aftermath of the Metaphysics and Science Debate], in *Nuli zhoubao*, 56 (10 June 1923). These articles and other articles of both sides during the controversy are collected in a volume. See Shi Jun 適君 et al., eds., *Kexue yu renshengguan* 科學與人生觀 [Science and the Outlook on Life] (Shandong: Renmin Wenxue Chubanshe, 1997), reprinted, pp. 41–60, 181–210, 256–62. First published in 1923.
99 Lu Xun (Lü Zhun), "Chi bexiang fan" [Living on Bexiang] (1933), in *Complete Works of Lu Xun*, vol. 5, pp. 208–9.
100 Lu Xun (Ruogu), "Opi" [Bad Habits] (1933), in *Complete Works of Lu Xun*, vol. 5, pp. 81.

5 A traveling disease: the "malady of the heart" and the modern boy

1 For loanwords studies, we are all indebted to Masini's 1993 book, which, covering the period from 1840 to 1898, is a major influence on Lydia Liu's

discussion of neologisms and loanwords and the appendix to her book *Translingual Practice*. He points out the contributions of the Protestant missionaries' lexical inventions and the Japanese influence on the formation of modern Chinese lexicon. For a recent study on loan words from Japan, see Juliette Yueh-tsen Chung. Cf. Federico Masini, *The Formation of Modern Chinese Lexicon and Its Evolution toward a National Language: The Period from 1840 to 1898* (Berkeley, CA: Project on Linguistic Analysis, University of California, 1993); Lydia Liu, *Translingual Practice: Literature, National Culture, and Translated Modernity—China, 1900–1937*, pp. 260–1; Juliette Yueh-tsen Chung, "Eugenics and the Coinage of Scientific Terminology in Meiji Japan and China," in Joshua A. Fogel, ed., *Late Qing China and Meiji Japan: Political & Cultural Aspects* (Norwalk, CT: EastBridge, 2004).
2 Larissa Heinrich's work analyzes the discourse of the "Sick Man of Asia" and visual images connected with the theme. Cf. Larissa N. Heinrich, *The Afterlife of Images: Translating the Pathological Body between China and the West* (Durham, NC and London: Duke University Press, 2008).
3 Cf. Masini, *The formation of Modern Chinese Lexicon and Its Evolution toward a National Language: The Period from 1840 to 1898*.
4 Mu Shiying (1933) "Bei dangzuo xiaoqianpin de nanzi" [A Man Taken as a Plaything], in Yueqi, ed., *A Chinese Neo-Sensation Writer of Genius: Complete Collection of Mu Shiying's Stories*, pp. 151–76.
5 Ibid., p. 151.
6 Ibid., p. 153.
7 Ibid., p. 171.
8 Ibid., p. 159.
9 Ibid., p. 169.
10 Ibid., p. 170.
11 Ibid., p. 152.
12 Ibid., p. 152.
13 Ibid., p. 153.
14 Ibid., pp. 153–4.
15 Ibid., p. 160.
16 Ibid., p. 161; pp. 163, 165.
17 Ibid., p. 159.
18 Before the Shanghai School and Beijing School debate broke out in October 1933, Zhou Zuoren had written an article titled "Shanghai qi" 上海氣 [The Shanghai Style] (1927) to ridicule Shanghai culture as "the culture of compradors, hooligans, and prostitutes." Cf. Zhang Yingjin, "The Haipai Controversy," in *The City in Modern Chinese Literature and Film: Configurations of Space, Time, and Gender* (Stanford: Stanford University Press, 1996), pp. 21–7. Cf. also Peng Hsiao-yen, *Haishang shuo qingyu: cong Zhang Ziping dao Liu Na'ou* 海上說情慾：從張資平到劉吶鷗 [Desire in Shanghai] (Taipei: Institute of Chinese Literature and Philosophy, Academia Sinica, 2001), pp. 95–103.
19 Satō Tatsuya 佐藤達哉, *Nihon ni okeru shinrigaku no juyō to tenkai* 日本における心理學の受容と展開 [The Reception and Development of Psychology in Japan] (Kyoto: Kitaōji Shobō, 2002), p. 30. The quotations include "tianming zhi wei xing, shuaixing zh wei dao, xiudao zhi wei jiao" 天命之為性，率性之謂道，修道之謂教 ["Nature" refers to that which is imparted by heaven, "way" refers to the path which is in conformance with the intrinsic nature of man and things, and "moral instruction" refers to the process of cultivating man's proper place in the world.] See *On the Practice of the Mean*, in Andrew Plaks's translation *Ta Hsüeh and Chung Yung* (2003), with modifications; "xiaoren buzhi tianming er bu wei" 小人不知天命而不畏 [The inferior man, who does not have any idea of the will of heaven, does not fear it], from

Lunyu, *Analects, Translations of Confucian Classics* (Shandong Youyi Chubanshe, 1998); "dao xingshan yan bi cheng yao shun" 道性善必稱堯舜 (Mencius talked to him about the theory that men are born good, always citing the sages Yao and Shun as good examples, from *Mencius, Translations of Confucian Classics*), and so on.
20 Ibid., pp. 31–5.
21 Ibid., p. 34.
22 Cf. Zhang Jingyuan, *Psychoanalysis in China: Literary Transformations, 1919–1949* (Ithaca: Cornell East Asian Program, 1992), pp. 37–8.
23 Scott Sunquist, ed., *A Dictionary of Asian Christianity* (Grand Rapids, MI: William B. Eerdmans Publishing, 2001), p. 916.
24 Yan Yongjing, trans. *Xinlingxue* [Study of the Heart and Soul] (Shanghai: Yizhi Shuhui, 1889).
25 Feng Tianyu 馮天瑜 points out this fact, but he never explains why. See his *Xinyu tanyuan—Zhongxiri wenhua hudong yu jindai hanzi shuyu shengcheng* 新語探源—中西日文化互動與近代漢字術語生成 [Origins of Neologisms: The Interplays between Chinese, Western, and Japanese Cultures and the Formation of Modern Chinese Lexicon] (Beijing: Zhonghua Shuju, 2004), pp. 117–277; 510–11.
26 According to Abe Hiroshi 阿部洋, at the peak of Sino-Japanese scholarly exchange from 1905 to 1907, Japanese teachers in China were between 500 and 600 in number, and most of them taught in normal colleges. Cf. Abe Hiroshi, *Chūgoku no kindai kyōiku to Meiji Nihon* 中国の近代教育と明治日本 (China's Modern Education and Meiji Japan; Tokyo: Fukumura Shuppan, 1990), pp. 151–2; Gao Juefu 高覺敷, ed. *Zhongguo xinlixue shi* [History of Psychology in China] (Beijing: Renmin Jiaoyu Chubanshe, 2005), pp. 378–90; Elisabeth Kaske, "Cultural Identity, Education, and Language Politics in China and Japan, 1870–1920," in David Hoyt, Karen Oslund, ed., *The Study of Language and the Politics of Community in Global Context* (Lanham, MD: Lexington Books, 2006), pp. 215–56.
27 Cf. Zhang Jingyuan, *Psychoanalysis in China: Literary Transformations, 1919–1949*. Zhang's book points out that American-trained psychologists were the dominant force in the discipline of psychology in China after they returned around the 1930s (p. 25), but does not discuss the period before. See also Liu Chi-hui 劉紀蕙, "Yayi yu fufan: Jingshen fenxi lunshu yu Tai-wan xiandai zhuyi de guanlian" 壓抑與復返：精神分析論述與台灣現代主義的關連 [Repression and Revival: Psychoanalytical Discourse and Taiwan Modernism], *Journal of Modern Chinese Literature in Chinese*, 4.2 (2001): 31–61. Liu discusses Chinese psychologists in the 1920s and 1930s, for instance Gao Juefu who translated Freud in 1933 and Zhu Guangqian 朱光潛 who wrote *Biantai xinlixue* 變態心理學 [Abnormal Psychology] in 1926, mostly Euro-American trained. Gao graduated from Hong Kong University in 1923.
28 Cf. Abe Hiroshi, *China's Modern Education and Meiji Japan*, pp. 155–6; and Paula Harrell, "Guiding Hand: Hattori Unokichi in Beijing," online posting < http://www.chinajapan.org/articles/11.1/11.1harrell13–20.pdf > (accessed 28 December 2008).
29 Gao Juefu, *History of Psychology in China*, p. 385; Wang Gui 王桂, ed., *Zhongri jiaoyu guanxishi* 中日教育關係史 [History of the Relationship between Sino-Japanese Education] (Jinan: Shandong Jiaoyu Chubanshe, 1993), pp. 280–682. See Gao's book for the history of the development of psychology as a discipline in China. See Wang's book for a historical account of Japan's influence on China's educational system during the late Qing.
30 Cf., Gao Juefu, ed., *History of Psychology in China*, p. 393.
31 Y, "Foluote xin xinlixue zhi iban" 佛洛特新心理學之一班 [General Ideas of Freud's New Psychology], *Dongfang Zazhi* 東方雜誌 [Eastern Miscellany Magazine], 17.22 (25 November 1920): 85–6; Zhu Guangqian, "Fulude de yinyishi shuo

yu xinli fenxi" 福魯德的隱意識說與心理分析 [Freud's Theory of the Subconscious and Psychoanalysis], *Eastern Miscellany*, 18.14 (25 July 1921): 41–51; Wang Guowei 王國維, *Xinlixue gailun* 心理學概論 [*Outlines of Psychoanalysis*] (Shanghai: Commercial Press, 1907). According to the "Appendix" in Zhang Jingyuan's book, Y's and Zhu's articles were among the early introductory works on psychoanalysis in China. The first full-length study on the subject was probably Wang guowei's book, translated from the English translation by Mary E. Lowndes, who had translated from the German version in 1891. It was originally by the Danish scholar Harold Höffding in 1889.

32 See Fei Xiaotong 費孝通, "Chongkan Pan Guangdan yizhu Ailishi *Xing xinli xue shuhou*" 重刊潘光旦譯注靄理士《性心理學》書後 [Postscript to the Reprinted Version of Ellis's *Psychology of Sex*, Translated and Annotated by Pan Guangdan], in Pan Guangdan, trans. (1939–41) *Xing xinlixue* 性心理學 [*Psychology of Sex*] (Beijing: Sanlian Shudian, 1987), pp. 549–8.

33 See Pan's "Xuyan" 敘言 [Preface] to the 1927 edition of *Xiaoqing zhi fenxi* 小青之分析 [Analysis of Xiaoqing], in *Pan Guangdan wenji* 潘光旦文集 [Collected Works of Pan Guangdan] (Beijing: Beijing Daxue Chubanshe, 1993), vol. 1, p. 3.

34 Pan Guangdan, "Feng Xiaoqing kao" [On Feng Xiaoqing], *Funü zazhi* [Women's magazine], 10.11 (November 1924): 1706–17. It was afterwards published as a volume by Xinyueshe 新月社 [The Crescent Society] in 1927. The 1929 version included in Pan's *Collected Works* is a further revision of the 1927 version.

35 In the *Women's Magazine* edition of "Feng Xiaoqing kao," the English term is misspelled as "Narcism." For a more detailed description of the content of Pan Guangdan's article, see Haiyan Lee, *Revolution of the Heart: A Genealogy of Love in China*, 1900–950 (Stanford, CA: Stanford University Press, 2007), pp. 190–9. The author sees Pan Guangdan's psychoanalytic interpretation of the famous poetess as a paradigm shift from the Confucian interpretation of *qing* 情 (feeling) entertained by the traditional literati.

36 Zhu Xiu 朱橚 et al. [Ming], ed. *Pujifang* 普濟方 [General Prescriptions] (Beijing: Renmin Weisheng Chubanshe, 1982), vol. 221, p. 3416.

37 See Pan Guangdan, trans., *Psychology of Sex*, p. 473; Havelock Ellis, *Psychology of Sex: A Manual for students* (London: William Heinemann Medical Books Ltd., 1933), p. 302. *Psychology of Sex: A Manual for students* is an abridged edition of the seven-volume *Psychology of Sex*.

38 Havelock Ellis, *Studies in the Psychology of Sex* (Philadelphia: F. A. Davis Co., 1905–28), seven volumes. Pan Guangdan claims that in 1920 he saw six volumes of this collection at the library of Tsinghua University when he was studying there, and that in 1928 he saw the seventh volume. See "Yixu" 譯序 [Translator's Preface], in Pan Guangdan, trans. *Psychology of Sex*, pp. 1–7. The whole set was republished in two volumes divided into seven parts by Random House in 1936–42.

39 Zhou Zuoren, "Ailisi de hua" 靄理斯的話 [(Ellis's Words], in *Yutian de shu* 雨天的書 [Book on a Rainy Day] (Hobei: Jiaoyu Chubanshe, 2001), pp. 88–90.

40 Zhou Zuoren, "Ailisi suiganlu chao" 靄理斯隨感錄抄 [Passages from Ellis's Impressions and Comments], in *Yongriji* 永日集 [Everlasting Day Collection] (Hobei: Jiaoyu Chubanshe, 2002), pp. 57–64.

41 Zhou Zuoren, *Zhitang huixiang lu* 知堂回想錄 [Memoirs of Zhitang] (Hobei: Jiaoyu Chubanshe, 2002), pp. 770–3.

42 Cf. Peng Hsiao-yen, "*Sex Histories*: Pornography or Sexology? Zhang Jingsheng's Sexual Revolution," in Peng-hsiang Chen and Whitney Crothers Dilley, eds., *Critical Studies: Feminism/Femininity in Chinese Literature*. Amsterdam: Editions Rodopi B.V., 2002, pp. 159–77.

43 Pan Guangdan, "Translator's preface," in *Psychology of Sex*, pp. 1–7.

230 Notes

44 Washio Hiroshi, trans. *Ningen no seiteki sentaku: Sei no shinri* 人間の性的選擇：性の心理 [Sexual Selection in Men: Psychology of Sex] (Tokyo: Tōkasha, 1921). Freud's *A General Introduction to Psychoanalysis* was translated by Yasuda Tokutarō 安田德太郎 in 1926, probably the first translation of Freud's book in Japan. Cf. Yasuda Tokutarō, *Seishin bunseki nyūmon* 精神分析入門 (Tokyo: ARS, 1928). For a later edition, see the Kadokawa edition in 1953.
45 Havelock Ellis, *Sexual Selection in Man*, in *Studies in the Psychology of Sex* (New York: Random House, 1936–42), vol. 1, pp. 1–212.
46 Cf. Washio Hiroshi, trans., *Sexual Selection in Man: Psychology of Sex*, p. 2.
47 Inoue Tetsujirō, trans. *Shinri shinsetsu* [New Psychology] (Tokyo: Aoki Sukekiyo, 1882), vol. 1, pp. 3–19. For the original work, see Alexander Bain, *Mental Science: A Compendium of Psychology, and the History of Philosophy, Designed as a Text-Book for High-Schools and Colleges* (New York: American Book Company, 1868). The part devoted to the five senses is in Part 2, vol. 1 of the original text.
48 In Nishi Amane's translation, the part on the five senses and the terms *gokan* and *shokkaku* is found in Chapter 3, Part 1, vol. 2. See Nishi Amane, trans. *Shinrigaku* [Psychology] (Tokyo: Monbushō, 1875–76), vol. 2, p. 45. For a discussion of Nishi Amane's translation of *Shinrigaku*, see Satō Tatsuya, *The Reception and Development of Psychology in Japan*, p. 37.
49 Nakajima Rikizō, ed., *Shinri satsuyō* [Essence of Psychology] (Tokyo: Hukūsha, 1898), pp. 40–44. This volume is in the collection of the National Central Library in Taipei. It is based on *Outlines of Descriptive Psychology: A Text-Book of Mental Science for Colleges and Normal Schools*, by George Trumbull Ladd in 1898. Nakajima studied with Ladd at Yale University.
50 Nakajima Rikizō, ed. *Essence of Psychology*, p. 16.
51 Ōse Jintarō, *Shinri satsuyō* [Essence of Psychology] (Tokyo: Seibidō Shoten, 1914), p. 23. This volume is in the collection of the National Central Library in Taipei.
52 Inoue Tetsujirō, trans. *Shinri shinsetsu*, p. iii.
53 Ibid.
54 Inoue Tetsujirō, *Shakāmuni ten* [Biography of Buddha] (Tokyo: Bunmeidō, 1902). There are three versions of this work. The other two were published in 1911 and 1926.
55 Li Dongyuan 李東垣 [Jin], "Dongyuan shixiaofang" 東垣試效方 [Prescriptions Tested by Dongyuan], in Ding Guangdi 丁光迪 and Wen Kui 文魁, eds., *Dongyuan yiji* [The Dongyuan Collection of Medicines] (Beijing: Renmin Weisheng Chubanshe, 1993), vol. 2, p. 422.
56 Feng Menglong [Qing], ed., *Jingshi tongyan* [General Stories to Warn the World] (Taipei: Liren Shuju, 1991), vol. 25, p. 288.
57 Chen Daqi, ed., *Xinlixue dagang* [Outlines of Psychology] (Beijing: Beijing Daxue Bianyihui, 1921), 6th edn, pp. 80–107.
58 Gao Juefu, ed., *History of Psychology in China*, p. 388.
59 Pan Guangdan, trans., *Psychology of Sex*, pp. 41–94.
60 See Havelock Ellis, *Studies in the Psychology of Sex*, vol. 1, part 3, p. viii: "The Sense of Smell in Neurasthenic and Allied States."
61 Washio Hiroshi, trans., *Sexual Selection in Men: Psychology of Sex*, p. 6. Hugh Shapiro points out that it was Sugita Genpaku 杉田玄白 who invented the term *shinkei* 神經 to render "nerves" in his 1774 translation of *Kaitai shinsho* 解體新書 (New Book of Anatomy; Kulmus's *Tables anatomiques*). See Hugh Shapiro, "Neurasthenia and the Assimilation of Nerves into China," presented at the "Symposium on the History of Disease," Institute of History and Philology, Academia Sinica, Taiwan, 16–18 June 2000.
62 Miura Kinnosuke, *Shinkeibyō shindanhyō* [Lists of Diagnosis for Diseases of the Nerves] (Tokyo: Miura Kinnosuke, 1894). It seems to be a book published by the

author himself. Hugh Shapiro mentions the following book using the term *shinkei suijyaku*: Tamura Kasaburō, *Shinkei suijyaku konjihō* [How to Cure Neurasthenia Completely] (Tokyo: Kenyūsha, 1911). This is basically a medical manual listing the methods for curing neurasthenia, e.g., water treatment, electrotherapy, hypnotherapy, injection, and so on. The author was a practicing medical doctor.

63 Miura Kinnosuke, *Lists of Diagnosis for Diseases of the Nerves*, pp. 62–3.
64 Ding Fubao and Hua Wenqi, *Shenjing Shuairuo san da yanjiu* [Three Great Studies on Neurasthenia] (Shanghai: Yixue Shuju, 1910). The first mental hospital in China was established by the American Presbyterian minister John Kerr in 1898 (or in 1897, according to Keinman, p. 6; see the following). Cf. Veronica Pearson, *Mental Health Care in China: State Policies, Professional Services and Family Responsibilities* (London: Gaskell, 1995), pp. 8–29. In 1919 A. H. Woods became the first director of the Departments of Neural Science and Mental Science at Beijing Union Medical University. He began to teach these two courses from 1922 on and was the first professor in China to teach such courses. Cf. Arthur Kleinman, *Social Origins of Distress and Disease: Depression, Neurasthenia and Pain in Modern China* (New Haven: Yale University Press, 1986), pp. 6–7. According to him, the term "shenjing shuairuo" first appeared in an abstract in the section on "Current Medical Literature" in *China Medical Journal* in 1923. It quoted F. Dauwe's discussion on neurasthenia published in a Belgian medical journal. The earliest Chinese document on neurasthenia Kleinman can locate was an article titled "Neurasthenia" by Song Mingtang in *Tongji yixue jikan* (Tongji Medical Quarterly). See Kleinman, *Social Origins of Distress and Disease*, pp. 25–8.
65 Lu Shoujian, *Shenjing shuairuo liaoyangfa* [A Treatment for Neurasthenia] (Shanghai: Zhonghua Shuju, 1917); Inoue Masayoshi, *Shinkei suijyaku eiyō ryōhō* [A Nutritional Treatment for Neurasthenia] (Tokyo: Daigakukan, 1915).
66 Lu Shoujian, "Zongshuo" 總說 [General Statement], in *A Treatment for Neurasthenia*, pp. 1–2.
67 Lu Shoujian, "Xu" [Preface], in *A Treatment for Neurasthenia*, pp. 1–2; pp. 15–32.
68 Wang Xiho, *Shenjing shuairuo ziliaofa* [A Self-Treatment for Neurasthenia] (Shanghai: Commercial Press, 1919), p. 3.
69 Cf. Marijke Gijswijt-Hofstra and Roy Porter, ed., *Cultures of Neurasthenia from Beard to the First World War* (Amsterdam–New York: Editions Rodopi B. V., 2001), pp. 1–76. This is a comparative study of the cultures of neurasthenia in various countries, including Britain, America, Germany, the Netherlands, and France, with the developments in China and Japan in view. Beard's essay, "Neurasthenia, or Nervous Exhaustion," was published in *Boston Medical and Surgical Journal*, 3 (1869): 217–21 (Marijke Gijswijt-Hofstra and Porter, p. 71). For Freud's opinion of Beard, see Philip Wiener, "G. M. Beard and Freud on 'American Nervousness,'" *Journal of the History of Ideas*, 17.2 (April 1956): 269–74.
70 Cf. Philip Wiener, "G. M. Beard and Freud on 'American Nervousness,'" p. 270.
71 Marijke Gijswijt-Hofstra and Roy Porter, eds., *Cultures of Neurasthenia from Beard to the First World War*, p. 54.
72 Beard says, "Hemi-Neurasthenia is a term that I have applied to those cases where the neurasthenia affects one side—usually, if not always, the left—much more than the other." See George Beard, *Sexual Neurasthenia: Its Hygiene, Causes, Symptoms and Treatment, with a Chapter on Diet for the Nervous*, ed. A. D. Rockwell with a preface (New York: Arno Press & the New York Times, 1972), p. 55.
73 Ibid., p. 73.
74 Ibid., p. 66.
75 Ibid., p. 269.
76 Philip Wiener, "G. M. Beard and Freud on 'American Nervousness,'" p. 271.
77 See Hugh Shapiro's discussion on the "explicit link between damage to the brain

and seminal exhaustion" in Western neurology. Similar common sense diagnosis can be found in Chinese medical literature.
78 Zhang Ziping, *Chongjiqi huashi, Feixu, Taili* 沖積期化石、飛絮、苔莉 [Fossils in the Age of Alluvial Clays, Flying Willow Katkins, Taili] (Beijing: Renmin Wenxue Chubanshe, 1988), pp. 426, 429. This volume collects three stories: *Chongjiqi huashi* [Fossils in the Age of Alluvial Clays] is reprinted from the first edition published by Taidong Shuju in 1922; *Feixu* [Flying Willow Katkins] from the first edition published by Xiandai Shuju in 1926; and *Taili* from the third edition published by Creation Society in 1926 and the ninth edition published by Xiandai Shuju in 1931.
79 Yu Dafu, *Chenlun* (Sinking), in *Yu Dafu wenji* 郁達夫文集 [Collected Works of Yu Dafu] (Hong Kong: Sanlian Shudian, 1982), vol. 1, p. 21.
80 *Xinkan Dasong Xuanho yishi* [Anecdotes of the Xuanho Period of the Great Song, Newly Reprinted], in Yang Jialuo, ed., *Songyuan pinghua sizhong* [Four Song and Yuan stories] (Taipei: Shijie Shuju, 1962), p. 137; Zhao Erzhuan 趙爾巽 et al. [Qing], *Qingshigao* 清史稿 [Manuscript of Qing History] (Beijing: Zhonghua Shuju, 1986), vol. 472, p. 12822.
81 Chen Menglei 陳夢雷 [Qing], ed., *Gujin tushu jicheng yibu quanlu* [Collections of Ancient and Modern Books: Complete Records of the Medical Section] (Beijing: Renmin Weisheng Chubanshe, 2000), vol. 124, p. 799.
82 Su Xuelin 蘇雪林, "Yu Dafu lun" [On Yu Dafu], in Chen Zishan and Wang Zili 王自立, eds., *Yu Dafu yanjiu ziliao* 郁達夫研究資料 [Research Materials on Yu Dafu] (Hong Kong: Sanlian Shudian, 1986), pp. 66–77. Originally published in *Wenyi yuekan* 文藝月刊 [Literary Monthly], 6.3 (1 September 1934).
83 Jing Tsu's book has a chapter on modern Chinese writers' involvement with psychoanalysis. To her, "Their involvement was less analytical than inventive, for they sought to incorporate a theoretical model into literary creations bearing their personal imprints." See Jing Tsu, *Failure, Nationalism, and Literature: The Making of Modern Chinese Identity, 1895–1937* (Stanford, CA: Stanford University Press, 2005), pp. 167–94.
84 Hugh Shapiro, naming Natsume Sōseki 夏目漱石, Akutagawa Ryūnosuke, and Tanizaki Junichirō 谷崎潤一郎 as examples of typical neurasthenic profiles in Japan, says, "Neurasthenia in contemporary China, moreover, afflicts a much broader cross-section of patients than it did in these other countries. In the West and in Japan the disorder followed clear gender and occupational lines – afflicting young women, brain-working men, and 'patients of the better classes.' China, however, suggests no typical neurasthenic profile." I doubt if China is that different in this respect. See Hugh Shapiro, "Neurasthenia and the Assimilation of Nerves into China." Sun Naixiu 孫乃修 discusses the influence of Freud on modern Chinese writers such as Lu Xun, Guo Moruo, Yu Dafu, Zhang Ziping, and so on. See Sun Naixiu, *Foluoyide yu Zhongguo xiandai zuojia* 佛洛伊德與中國現代作家 [Freud and Modern Chinese Writers] (Taipei: Yeqiang Chubanshe, 1995).
85 Liu Na'ou, *Diary*, Part 1, pp. 110–18.
86 Lu Xun, *Diary of Lu Xun*, p. 14.
87 Wu Haiyong 吳海勇, *Xiaosheng huo yue huakai hualuo liang yiushi: Lu Xun de shengming zhexue yu juejue taidu* 梟聲或曰花開花落兩由之：魯迅的生命哲學與決絕態度 [Calls of the Owl May Be Saying Let the Flowers Bloom or Die: Lu Xun's Philosophy of Life and Obstinacy] (Guangdong: Huacheng Chubanshe, 2006).
88 Shen Congwen, "Yige tiancai de tongxin" [Letters from a Genius], *Honghei* 紅黑 [Red and Black], nos 6 and 7 (10 June and 10 July 1929). Collected in *Shen Congwen quanji* 沈從文全集 [Complete Works of Shen Congwen] (Taiyuan: Beiyue Wenyi Chubanshe, 2002), vol. 4, pp. 325–72.

Notes   233

89 Ibid., p. 349.
90 "Dou'an shi bushen yaopian" [Doan's Pills for Strengthening the Nerves], Advertisement in *Shenbao* [*Shanghai Post*] (13 May 1930), p. 14.
91 Doan's Backache Kidney Pills (1900) Advertisement, in *The Bulletin*, 13 December. Online Posting < http://www.historypages.net/Pdoans.html#Top > (accessed on 28 May 2008).
92 Bu'erduoshou [Blutose], advertisement, *Shanghai Post* (8 November 1930), p. 7.
93 Fujisawa Tomokichi (2004) "Yūka shōken hōkokusho" 有価證券報告書 [Report on Valuable Securities], Online Posting, 1 April < http://www.astellas.com/jp/ir/library/pdf/f_securities2005_jp.pdf > (accessed on 25 May 2008).
94 Burutōze [Blutose] (1930–43) Advertisement, Online Posting <http://www.east-asian-history.net/textbooks/Slideshows/medicine/medicine_show.pdf> (accessed on 25 May 2008).
95 Mu, Shiying, "A Man Taken as a Plaything," p. 158.
96 See Exodus 20:4–5, *The King James Bible*: "Thou shalt not make unto thee any graven image, or any likeness of anything that is in heaven above, or that is in the earth beneath, or that is in the water under the earth: thou shalt not bow down thyself to them, nor serve them. For I, the LORD thy God, am a jealous God, visiting the iniquity of the fathers upon the children unto the third and fourth generation of them that hate me; And showing mercy unto thousands of them that love me, and keep my commandments."
97 Robert Morrison et al., eds. (1813) *Shentian Shengshu* [The Holy Bible], in *China and Protestant Missions: A Collection of Their Earliest Missionary Works in Chinese* (Leiden: IDC, 1983), microfilm.
98 For Christian influence on May Fourth literature, see Xu Zhenglin 許正林, *Zhongguo xiandai wenxue yu Jidujiao* 中國現代文學與基督教 [Modern Chinese Literature and Christianity] (Shanghai: Shanghai University Press, 2003); For Christian influence on modern Japanese literature, see Xiao Xia 肖霞: *Riben jindai langman zhuyi wenxue yu Jidujiao* 日本近代浪漫主義文學與基督教 [Modern Japanese Romantic Literature and Christianity] (Jinan: Shandong University Press; 2007).
99 Alexander Wylie, *Memorials of Protestant Missionaries to the Chinese: Giving a List of Their Publications, and Obituary Notices of the Deceased* (Shanghae: American Presbyterian Mission Press, 1867), reprinted by Ch'eng-wen Publishing Company in Taipei in 1967, p. 5.
100 Ibid., p. 35. Walter Henry Medhurst and William Milne (1785–1822), among others, collaborated with Robert Morrison on the translation of the Bible. The missionaries collaborating with Medhurst included William Muirhead, Joseph Edkins (1823–1905), and William Charles Milne, son of William Milne. See Wylie, *Memorials of Protestant Missionaries to the Chinese*. For a brief account of the history of Christian missionaries in China and the Protestant Christian literature published in China, see *Records of the General Conference of the Protestant Missionaries of China*, Shanghai, May 10–24, 1877 (Shanghai: Presbyterian Mission Press, 1878), reprinted by Ch'eng-wen Publishing Company in Taipei in 1973, pp. 203–27.
101 R. Morrison, *Dictionary of the Chinese Language* (Macao, China: The East India Company's Press, 1819–23), part 3, vol. 6 (1822), p. 262.
102 Translations of the Bible use various dialects in China as well as Mandarin, including the Ningpo, Fuzhou, Shanghai, Hakka, Amoy, and Jinhua (Kin-hwa) dialects.
103 Sōgō Masaaki, *Meiji no kotoba jiten* (Tokyo: Tōkyōdō Shuppan, 1998), 3rd edn. First published in 1986.
104 Ibid., p. 3.

234 *Notes*

105 W. H. Medhurst, Sen., *English and Chinese Dictionary* (Shanghae: The Mission Press, 1847–48), vol. 2, p. 808.
106 Ibid., p. 602. For the story of Nakamura Masanao's advocacy of Christianity in Meiji Japan, see A. Hamish Ion, "Edward Warren Clark and Early Meiji Japan: A Case Study of Cultural Contact," in *Modern Asian Studies*, 11.4 (1977): 557–72.
107 Yanabu Akira, *Ai* [Love] (Tokyo: Sanseidō, 2001), p. 52.
108 Ibid., p. 53.
109 Ibid., p. 54.
110 Ibid., p. 41.
111 Cf. Haiyan Lee, *Revolution of the Heart: A Genealogy of Love in China, 1900–1945* (Stanford, CA: Stanford University Press, 2007).
112 Yanabu Akira, *Ai*, p. 69.
113 Cf. Nagato Hiroshi 長戸宏, *Yamato kotoba wo wasureta nihonjin* 大和言葉をわすれた日本人 [Japanese Who Forgot the Native Language] (Tokyo: Akashi Shōten, 2002), pp. 159–204. The author tries to clarify the history of the Japanese native language, before *kanji* was introduced into Japan. A Korean scholar maintains that the Japanese native language was connected with ancient Korean language. See Pak Pyŏng-sik 朴炳植, *Yamato kotoba no kigen to kodai Chōsengo* やまと言葉の起源と古代朝鮮語 [The Origin of *Yamato kotoba* and Ancient Korean Language] (Tokyo: Seikō Shobō, 1986). For Ogu Sōrai's 荻生徂徠 criticism of *kunyomi* 訓読み as a method of reading Chinese texts, see Koyasu Nobukuni 子安宣邦, *Kanjiron: Fukahi no tasha* 漢字論：不可避の他者 [On the Chinese Character: The Inevitable Other] (Tokyo: Iwanami Shoten, 2003), pp. 71–100.
114 Ban Gu 班固 [Han], "Biographies of Zhang Qian and Li Guangli" 張騫李廣利傳, in *Xinjiaoben hanshu* 新校本漢書 [Book of Han, Newly Annotated] (Taipei Dingwen Shuju, 1986), vol. 61, pp. 2692 and 2689.
115 Huang Tingjian, "Guitianle yin" 歸田樂引 [The Tune of the Joy of Returning to Farm Life], in Tang Guizhang 唐圭璋, ed., *Quan Song ci* 全宋詞 [Complete Collection of *Ci* Poetry in the Song] (Taipei: Minglun Chubanshe, 1970), vol. 1, p. 407.
116 Wei Furen, "Xiqunyao" 繫裙腰 [Tying the Waist of the Skirt], in Tang Guizhang, ed., *Complete Collection of Ci Poetry in the Song*, vol. 1, pp. 269–70.
117 Diana Taylor, *The Archive and the Repertoire: Performing Cultural Memory in the Americas* (Durham, NC and London: Duke University Press, 2003), pp. 79–86.
118 Homi Bhabha, *Location of Culture* (London and New York: Routledge, 1994), p. 235.
119 Cf. Judith Butler, "Preface (1999)" in *Gender Trouble* (London and New York: Routledge, 2006), p. xxv: "In this text as elsewhere I have tried to understand what political agency might be, given that it cannot be isolated from the dynamics of power from which it is wrought. The iterability of performativity is a theory of agency, one that cannot disavow power as the condition of its own possibility."
120 Homi Bhabha, *Location of Culture*, p. 231: "For what is at issue in the discourse of minorities is the creation of agency through incommensurable (not simply multiple) positions."

Conclusion: to connect

1 Nishiwaki Junzaburō, "Jo" (Preface), in *Chōgenjitsushugi shiron* (*Poetics of Surrealism*) 超現実主義詩論 (Tokyo: Kōseikaku shoten, 1929), in *Complete Works of Nishiwaki Junzaburō: Definitive Texts*, vol. 1, p. 7.

2 Miryam Sas, *Fault Lines: Cultural Memory and Japanese Surrealism* (Stanford, CA: Stanford University Press, 1999), pp. 1–6.
3 Steven Snyder, *Fictions of Desire: Narrative Form in the Novels of Nagai Kafū* (Hawai'i: University of Hawai'i Press, 2000), p. 1.
4 Snyder, *Fictions of Desire*, p. 3; Edward Seidensticker, *Kafū the Scribbler: The Life and Writings of Nagai Kafū, 1879–1959* (Stanford, CA: Stanford University Press, 1965), p. 46.
5 Nagai Kafū, "Hanabi" [The Fireworks], in *Kafū zenshū* 荷風全集 [Complete Works of Nagai Kafū] (Tokyo: Iwanami Shoten, 1993), vol. 14, p. 256.
6 Liang Qichao, *Yinbingshi hoji* 飲冰室合集 [The Drinking Ice Water Room Collection] (Beijing: Zhonghua Shuju, 1989), vol. 1, pp. 70–3. First published in 1936.
7 Haun Saussey, "Death and Translation," *Representations*, 94.1 (Spring 2006): 112–30.
8 Zhang Jungu 章君穀, *Xu Zhimo zhuan* 徐志摩傳 [Biography of Xu Zhimo] (Taipei: Lizhi Chubanshe, 1970), pp. 5–6. Liang Shiqiu 梁實秋, *Tan Xu Zhimo* 談徐志摩 [On Xu Zhimo] (Taipei: Yuandong Tushu Gongsi, 1958), p. 5. Zhang's description of Xu Zhimo is based on Liang Shiqiu's book.
9 Xu Zhimo, "Manshufei'er" 曼殊斐兒 [Mansfield], in *Xu Zhimo quanji* 徐志摩全集 [Complete Works of Xu Zhimo] (Hong Kong: Commercial Press, 1983), vol. 3, pp. 1–25. Originally published in *Xiaoshuo yuebao* [Fiction Monthly], 14.5 (May 1923).
10 Zhang Jungu, *Xu Zhimo zhuan*, p. 39.
11 Xu Zhimo, "Fragments," dated January 1922, in *Xu Zhimo quanji bubian: shuxinji* 徐志摩全集補編：書信集 [Supplements to the Complete Works of Xu Zhimo: Letters], ed. Lu Yaodong 陸耀東 (Hong Kong: Commercial Press, 1993), vol. 4, p. 7.
12 E. B. Browning, "Inclusions," and Maurice Thompson, "Atalanta's Race," trans. Xu Zhimo, in *Supplements to the Complete Works of Xu Zhimo: Poetry*, ed. Lu Yaodong, vol. 1, pp. 197–200.
13 Xu Zhimo, "Yitiao jinse de guanghen: Xiashi tubai" [A Shaft of Golden Light: Monologue in the Xiashi Dialect], in *Complete Works of Xu Zhimo*, vol. 1, pp. 89–92.
14 Cf. Wang Zhongchen 王中忱, *Yuejie yu xiangxiang: ershi shiji Zhongguo Riben wenxue bijiao yanjiu lunji* 越界與想像：二十世紀中國日本文學比較研究論集 [Border Crossing and Imagination: Comparative Studies of Twentieth-Century Chinese and Japanese Literatures] (Beijing: Zhongguo Shehui Kexue Chubanshe, 2001), pp. 27–52.
15 Besides Wang Zhongchen's book, see William Gardner, "Anzai Fuyue's Empire of Signs: Japanese Poetry in Manchuria," in Rebecca Copeland, ed., *Acts of Writing: Language and Identities in Japanese Literature* (West Lafayette, IN: AJLS, Purdue University, 2001), pp. 187–200; and Gardner, "Colonialism and the Avant-Garde: Kitagawa Fuyuhiko's Manchurian Railroad," *Stanford Humanities Review*, Special Issue, *Movements of the Avant-garde*, 7.1 (1999): 12–21. For Manchuria studies, the yearly journal *Shokuminchi bunka kenkyū: shiryo to bunseki* [Studies of Colonial Cultures: Materials and Analysis], established in 2002, is most helpful.
16 C. T. Hsia, *A History of Modern Chinese Fiction* (New Haven: Yale University Press, 1971), 2nd edn. Originally published in 1961.
17 Lydia Liu, *Translingual Practice: Literature, National Culture, and Translated Modernity—China, 1900–1937*, pp. 1–42; Emily Aptor, *The Translation Zone: A New Comparative Literature* (Princeton, NJ: Princeton University Press, 2006). While Lydia Liu emphasizes "historical linkages—rather than commonalities" between East and West, Emily Apter resorts to "universal values."
18 Emily Aptor, "Je ne crois pas beaucoup à la littérature comparée: Universal

Poetics and Postcolonial Comparativism," in Haun Saussy, ed., *Comparative Literature in an Age of Globalization* (Baltimore: The Johns Hopkins University Press, 2006), pp. 54–62. Aptor points out that despite his disbelief in literary comparativism, Alain Badiou still engages in "a kind of *comparatisme quand même*" based on the concept of "poetic universalism."

Bibliography

Abe, Hiroshi. (1990) *Chūgoku no kindai kyōiku to Meiji Nihon* [China's Modern Education and Meiji Japan]. Tokyo: Fukumura Shuppan.
Aizawa, Genshichi. (1982) *Sōma Kokkō to Nakamuraya saron* [Sōma Kokkō and Nakamuraya Salon]. Sendai-shi: Hōbundō.
Aptor, Emily. (2006) *The Translation Zone: A New Comparative Literature*. Princeton, NJ: Princeton University Press.
—— (2006) "Je ne crois pas beaucoup à la littérature comparée: Universal Poetics and Postcolonial Comparativism." In Haun Saussy, ed., *Comparative Literature in an Age of Globalization*. Baltimore: The Johns Hopkins University Press, pp. 54–62.
Asad, Talal. (1986) "The Concept of Cultural Translation in British Social Anthropology." In James Clifford and George E. Marcus, eds., *Writing Culture: The Poetics and Politics of Ethnography*. Berkeley: University of California Press, pp. 141–64.
Ba, Jin (Pei Gan). (1924) "Weida de xundaozhe: cheng tongzhi Dashan Rung jun zhi ling" [The Great Martyr: To the Spirit of Our Comrade Ōsugi Sakae]. *Chunlei* [Spring Thunder], 3 (1 May). In *Complete Works of Ba Jin*, 2000, vol. 18, pp. 63–4.
—— (1924) "Dashanrung zhuzuo nianpu" [Bibliography of Osugi Sakae]. *Spring Thunder*, 3 (May). In *Complete Works of Ba Jin* (2000), vol. 18, pp. 65–8.
—— (1924) "Dashan rung nianpu" [Annual account of Osugi Sakae's Life]. *Mingzhong* [The People's Knell], 1.9 (1 August). In *Complete Works of Ba Jin* (2000), vol. 18, pp. 70–6.
—— (2000) *Ba Jin quanji* [Complete Works of Ba Jin]. 26 volumes. Beijing: Renmin Wenxue Chubanshe.
Bain, Alexander. (1868) *Mental Science: A Compendium of Psychology, and the History of Philosophy, Designed as a Text-Book for High-Schools and Colleges*. New York: American Book Company.
Ban, Gu. (Han) "Biographies of Zhang Qian and Li Guangli." In *Xinjiaoben hanshu* [Book of Han, Newly Annotated]. Taipei: Dingwen Shuju, 1986, vol. 61.
Barsam, Richard M. (1973) *Nonfiction Film: A Critical History*. Bloomington and Indianapolis: Indiana University Press, 1992.
Baudelaire, Charles. (1861) *Les Fleurs du Mal*. In *Oeuvres complètes*, 1990, vol. 1, pp. 1–134.
—— (1863) *Le Peintre de la vie moderne* [The Painter of Modern Life]. In *Oeuvres complètes*, 1990, vol. 2, pp. 683–724.

—— (1954) *The Flowers of Evil*. Trans. William Aggeler. Fresno, CA: Academy Library Guild.
—— (1990) *Oeuvres complètes* [Complete Works]. 2 volumes. Ed. Claude Pichois. Paris : Gallimard.
Beard, George. (1869) "Neurasthenia, or Nervous Exhaustion." *Boston Medical and Surgical Journal*, 3: 217–21.
—— (1972) *Sexual Neurasthenia: Its Hygiene, Causes, Symptoms and Treatment, with a Study on Diet for the Nervous*. New York: Arno Press & the New York Times.
Benjamin, Walter. (1923) "The Task of a Translator." Trans. Harry Zohn. In Marcus Bulock and Michael W. Jennings, eds. (1996), *Walter Benjamin: Selected Writings*. Cambridge, MA: The Belknap Press of Harvard University Press, vol. 1, pp. 253–63.
—— (1938) "The Paris of the Second Empire in Baudelaire." In Michael W. Jennings, ed. (2006), *The Writer of Modern Life: Essays on Charles Baudelaire*. Cambridge, MA: Harvard University Press, pp. 46–133.
—— (1980) "Das Paris des Second Empire bei Baudelaire." In Rolf Tiedemann and Hermann Schweppenhäuser, eds., *Gesammelte Schriften* [Collected Works]. Frankfurt am Main : Suhrkamp, vol. 1, pp. 511–604.
—— (1989) *Charles Baudelaire: A Lyric Poet in the Era of High Capitalism*. Trans. Harry Zohn. London: Biddles Ltd., Guildford and King's Lynn.
—— (2003) *The Arcades Project*. Trans. Howard Eiland and Kevin McLaughlin. Cambridge, MA: Harvard University Press, 4th edn.
Bhabha, Homi. (1994) *Location of Culture*. London and New York: Routledge.
Blavatsky, H. P. (1877) *Isis Unveiled: A Master-Key to the Mysteries of Ancient and Modern Science and Theology*, 2nd edn. New York: J. W. Bouton.
—— (1888) "Is Theosophy a Religion?" *Lucifer* (November): 177–87.
Bordwell, David. (1993) *The Cinema of Eisenstein*. Cambridge, MA: Harvard University Press.
Bowler, Peter J. (1990) *Charles Darwin: the Man and His Influence*. Cambridge, MA: Basil Blackwell, Inc.
Brooks, Van Wyck. (1962) "Earnest Fenollosa and Japan." *Proceedings of the American Philosophical Society*, 106.2 (30 April): 106–10.
Brown, Janet. (2006) *Darwin's Origin of Species: A Biography*. New York: Atlantic Monthly Press.
Burke, Peter. (1992) *The Fabrication of Louis XIV*. New Haven and London: Yale University Press.
Burkhardt, Frederick and Sydney Smith, eds. (1985) *A Calendar of the Correspondence of Charles Darwin, 1821–1882, with Supplement*. Cambridge University Press, 1994.
Burutōze [Blutose]. (1930–43) Advertisement, Online Posting <http://www.east-asian-history.net/textbooks/Slideshows/medicine/medicine_show.pdf> (accessed 25 May 2008).
Butler, Judith. (1990) "Imitation and Gender Insubordination." In Aiana Fuss, ed., *Inside/Out: Lesbian Theories, Gay Theories*. New York: Routledge, pp. 13–31.
—— (2006) "Preface (1999)." *Gender Trouble*. London and New York: Routledge.
Cai, Yuanpei. (1932) "Ti *Liangyou* sheyingtu" [On the Photographs of *The Young Companion*]. *Liangyou* (The Young Companion), 69 (September), inside cover.

Charles-Roux, Edmonde (2004). *Le temps Chanel*. Paris : Éditions de la Martinière.
Chen, Daqi. (1921) *Xinlixue dagang* [Outlines of Psychology]. Beijing: Beijing Daxue Bianyihui.
Chen, Menglei, ed. (Qing) *Gujin tushu jicheng yibu quanlu* [Collections of Ancient and Modern Books: Complete Records of the Medical Section]. Beijing: Renmin Weisheng Chubanshe, 2000, vol. 124.
Chen, Zishan, ed. (2001) *Modern Shanghai*. Guangxi: Guangxi Shifan Daxue Chubanshe.
Chiba, Kameo. (1924) "Shinkankakuha no tanjō" [The Birth of the Neo-Sensation School]. *Seiki* [Century]. In Itō Sei et al., eds. (1968), *Nihon gendai bungaku zenshū* [Complete Works of Modern Japanese Literature]. 108 volumes. Tokyo Kōdansha, vol. 67, pp. 357–60.
Chou, Huiling. (1996) "Representing 'New Woman': Actresses & the *Xin Nüxing* Movement in Chinese Spoken Drama & Films, 1918–49." Ph.D. dissertation, New York University.
Chung, Juliette Yueh-tsen. (2004) "Eugenics and the Coinage of Scientific Terminology in Meiji Japan and China." In Joshua A. Fogel, ed., *Late Qing China and Meiji Japan: Political & Cultural Aspects*. Norwalk, CT: EastBridge.
Clifford, James and George E. Marcus, eds. (1986) *Writing Culture: the Poetics and Politics of Ethnography*. Berkeley: University of California Press.
Cohn, Dorrit. (1983) *Transparent Minds: Narrative Modes for Presenting Consciousness in Fiction*. Princeton, NJ: Princeton University Press.
Collas, Philippe. (2002) *Maurice Dekobra: gentleman entre deux mondes* [Maurice Dekobra: Gentleman between Two Worlds]. Paris : Séguier.
Crémieux, Benjamin. (1924) *XXe Siècle*. Paris : Librairie Gallimard, 9th edn.
Crompton, Louis. (2003) *Homosexuality & Civilization*. Cambridge, MA: Harvard University Press.
Darwin, Charles. (1859) *The Origin of Species by Means of Natural Selection, or the Preservation of Favored Races in the Struggle for Life*. New York: The Modern Library, 1998.
—— (1959) *The Origin of Species by Charles Darwin: A Variorum Text*. Ed. Morse Peckham. Philadelphia: University of Pennsylvania Press.
Darwin, Francis and A. C. Seward, eds. (1972) *More Letters of Charles Darwin: A Record of His Work in a Series of Hitherto Unpublished Letters*. New York: Johnson Reprint Corporation, vol. 1.
Deane, Seamus. (1990) "Introduction." *Nationalism, Colonialism, and Literature*. Minneapolis: University of Minnesota Press, pp. 3–19.
DeJean, Joan. (2005) *The Essence of Style: How the French Invented High Fashion, Fine Food, Chic Cafés, Style, Sophistication, and Glamour*. New York: Free Press.
Delange, Yves. (1989) "Préface". In Jean-Henri Fabre, *Souvenirs entomologiques : études sur l'instinct et les mœurs des insects* [Memories of Insects: Study on the Instinct and Manners of Insects]. Ed. Yves Delange. Paris : Robert Laffont, vol. I, pp. 10–24.
—— (1999) *Jean Henri Fabre, l'homme qui aimait les insectes* [Jean Henri Fabre, The Man Who Loved Insects]. Paris : Actes Sud.
Dikötter, Frank. (2008) *The Age of Openness: China Before Mao*. Hong Kong: Hong Kong University Press.

Ding, Fubao and Hua Wenqi. (1910) *Shenjing Shuairuo san da yanjiu* [Three Great Studies on Neurasthenia]. Shanghai: Yixue Shuju.

Ding, Wenjiang. (1923) "Xuanxue yu kexue" [Metaphysics and Science]. *Nuli zhoubao*, nos. 48–49 (12 April to 22 April). In Shi Jun et al., eds. (1923) *Kexue yu renshengguan* [Science and the Outlook on Life]. Shandong: Renmin Wenxue Chubanshe, 1997, pp. 41–60.

—— (1923) "Xuanxue yu kexue—da Zhang Junmai" [Metaphysics and Science: In Response to Zhang Junmai] *Nuli zhoubao*, nos. 54–5 (27 May–3 June). In Shi Jun, et al., eds., *Science and the Outlook on Life* (1997), pp. 181–210.

—— (1923) "Xuanxue yu kexue de taolun de yuxing" [The Aftermath of the Metaphysics and Science Debate]. *Nuli zhoubao*, 56 (10 June 1923). In Shi Jun et al., eds., *Science and the Outlook on Life* (1997), pp. 256–62.

Ding, Yaping, ed. (2002) *Bainian Zhongguo dianying lilun wenxuan, 1897–2001* [Collection of Chinese Film Theories in the Past One Hundred Years, 1897–2001]. 2 volumes. Beijing: Wenhua Yishu Chubanshe.

Doan's Backache Kidney Pills. (1900) Advertisement. In *The Bulletin* (13 December). Online Posting <http://www.historypages.net/Pdoans.html#Top> (accessed 28 May 2008).

Dong, Bingyue. (2006) *"Guomin zuojia" de lichang: Zhong-ri xiandai wenxue guanxi yanjiu* [Writers' Position as National Subjects: The Relationships between Modern Chinese and Japanese Literatures]. Beijing: Sanlian Shudian, pp. 77–122.

Duchêne, Roger. (2004) *Être femme au temps de Louis XIV* [Being Woman at the Time of Louis XIV]. Paris : Perrin.

Eagleton, Terry. (1990) "Nationalism: Irony and Commitment." In Seamus Deane, ed., *Nationalism, Colonialism, and Literature*. Minneapolis: University of Minnesota Press, pp. 23–42.

Eaton, Richard. (1924–27) *The Best French Short Stories of. . . . and the Yearbook of the French Short Story*. Boston: Small, Maynard & Co.

Ellis, Havelock. (1905–28) *Studies in the Psychology of Sex*. 7 volumes. Philadelphia: F. A. Davis Co.; Forwards by Morris L. Ernst and Havelock Ellis. (1936–42). 2 volumes. New York: Random House.

—— (1933) *Psychology of Sex: A Manual for Students*. London: William Heinemann Medical Books Ltd.

—— (1905) *Sexual Selection in Man*. In *Studies in the Psychology of Sex* (1936–42), New York: Random House, vol. 1, pp. 1–212.

—— (1921) *Ningen no seiteki sentaku: Sei no shinri* [Sexual Selection in Men: Psychology of Sex], trans. Washio Hiroshi. Tokyo: Tōkasha.

Fabre, Jean-Henri. (1879–1907) *Souvenirs entomologiques : études sur l'instinct et les mœurs des insects* [Memories of Insects: Study on the Instinct and Manners of Insects]. 10 volumes. Paris : C. Delagrave.

[Fabre, Jean-Henri] (1922–31) *Konchūki* [Book of Insects], trans. Ōsugi Sakae et al. Tokyo: Sōbunkaku.

—— (1989), *Souvenirs entomologiques : études sur l'instinct et les mœurs des insects*, ed. Yves Delange. 2 volumes. Paris : Robert Laffont.

—— (2001) *Kunchongji* [Book of Insects], trans. Liang Shouqiang et al. 10 volumes. Beijing: Huacheng Chubanshe.

Fay, Margaret A. (1978) "Did Marx Offer to Dedicate *Capital* to Darwin?: A

Reassessment of the Evidence." *Journal of the History of Ideas*, 39.1 (January to March): 133–46.
Fei, Xiaotong. (1987) "Chongkan Pan Guangdan yizhu Ailishi *Xing xinli xue* shuhou" [Postscript to the Reprinted Version of Ellis's *Psychology of Sex*, Translated and Annotated by Pan Guangdan]. In Pan Guangdan, trans. *Xing xinlixue* [Psychology of Sex]. Beijing: Sanlian Shudian, pp. 549–58.
Feng, Menglong, ed. (Qing) *Jingshi tongyan* [General Stories to Warn the World]. Taipei: Liren Shuju, 1991, vol. 25.
Feng, Tianyu. (2004) *Xinyu tanyuan—Zhongxiri wenhua hudong yu jindai hanzi shuyu shengcheng* [Origins of Neologisms: The Interplays between Chinese, Western, and Japanese Cultures and the Formation of Modern Chinese Terminology]. Beijing: Zhonghua Shuju.
Fenollosa, Ernest. (1913) *The Epoch of Chinese and Japanese Art*. London: William Heinemann.
Foner, Philip S. ed. (1973) *When Karl Marx Died*. New York: International Publishers.
Foucault, Michel. (1983) "Leçon du 5 Janvier 1983". In Frédéric Gros, ed. (2008), *Le gouvernement de soi et des autres : Cours au Collège de France, 1982–1983* [The Government of Self and Others: Courses at Collège de France, 1982–83]. Paris : Le Seuil, pp. 3–39.
—— (1983) "Qu'est-ce que les lumières ?" In *Dits et écrits, 1976–1988*. Paris : Gallimard, 2001, vol. 2, pp. 1381–97.
—— (1984) "What Is Enlightenment?" trans. Catherine Porter. In Paul Rabinow, ed., *The Foucault Reader*. New York: Pantheon Books, pp. 32–50.
—— (1984) "Qu'est-ce que les Lumières ?" [L'Art du dire vrai]. *Magazine Littéraire*, 207 (May): 34–39. In *Dits et écrits, 1976–1988*, vol. 2, pp. 1498–1507.
—— (1984) "L'étique du souci de soi comme pratique de la liberté." [The Ethics of the Concern for the Self as a Practice of Freedom]. In *Dits et écrits, 1954–1988*. Paris : Gallimard, vol. 2, pp. 1527–48.
—— (1997) "The Echics of the Concern for Self as a Practice of Freedom," trans. Robert Hurley et al. In Paul Rabinow, ed., *Ethics: Subjectivity and Truth*. London: Allen Lane, pp. 146–65.
Frühauf, Heiner. (1997) "Urban Exoticism and its Sino-Japanese Scenery, 1910–23." *Asian and African Studies* 6.2: 126–69.
Fujii, Shōzō. (1989) *Eroshenko no toshi monogatari: 1920 nendai Tōkyō, Shanhai, Pekin* [Eroshenko's City Story: 1920s Tokyo, Shanghai, and Beijing]. Tokyo: Misuzu Shobō,).
Fujii, Yūsuke. (2007) "Tōji no mippō—bunka kensetsu to wa nani ka?" [The Secret of State Rule—What Is Cultural Construction?]. In Ikeda Hiroshi, ed., *Dai Tōa Kyōeiken no bunka kensetsu* [The Cultural Construction of Pan-Asia Co-Prosperity Sphere]. Kyoto: Jinbun shoin, pp. 11–73.
Fujisawa, Tomokichi. (2004) "Yūka shōken hōkokusho" [Report on Valuable Securities]. Online Posting, 1 April. < http://www.astellas.com/jp/ir/library/pdf/f_securities2005_jp.pdf > (accessed on 25 May 2008).
Fukuzawa, Yukichi. (1885) "Datsuaron" [On Severing with Asia]. In *Jiji shinpō* [Current News Daily] (16 March).
Furen huabao [The Women's Pictorial]. (1934) "Zhongguo nüxingmei zanli" [Odes to Chinese Women's Beauty]. 17 (April, Special Issue): 9–29.

Gao, Juefu, ed. (2005) *Zhongguo xinlixue shi* [History of Psychology in China]. Beijing: Renmin Jiaoyu Chubanshe.
Gardner, William. (1999) "Colonialism and the Avant-Garde: Kitagawa Fuyuhiko's Manchurian Railroad." *Stanford Humanities Review*, Special Issue, *Movements of the Avant-garde*, 7.1: 12–21.
—— (2001) "Anzai Fuyue's Empire of Signs: Japanese Poetry in Manchuria." In Rebecca Copeland, ed., *Acts of Writing: Language and Identities in Japanese Literature*. West Lafayette, IN: AJLS, Purdue University, pp. 187–200.
Garelick, Rhonda K. (1998) *Rising Star: Dandyism, Gender, and Performance in the Fin de Siècle*. Princeton, NJ: Princeton University Press.
Gidel, Henry. (2000) *Coco Chanel*. Paris : Flammarion.
Gijswijt-Hofstra, Marijke and Roy Porter, eds. (2001) *Cultures of Neurasthenia from Beard to the First World War*. Amsterdam and New York: Editions Rodopi B. V.
Goldstein, Joshua. (2007) *Drama Kings: Players and Publics in the Re-creation of Peiking Opera, 1870–1937*. Berkeley: University of California Press.
Gunn, Edward. (1991) *Rewriting Chinese: Style Innovation in Twentieth-Century Chinese Prose*. Stanford, CA: Stanford University Press.
Guo, Jianying. (1934) "Bianji yutan" [Editor's Afterwords]. *Furen huabao* [The Women's Pictorial], 17 (April): 32.
—— (1934) *Jianying manhuaji* [Collection of Cartoons by Jianying]. Shanghai: Liangyou Tushu Gongsi; *Modern Shanghai* [Modern Shanghai], ed. Chen Zishan. (2001) Guangxi: Guangxi Shifan Daxue Chubanshe.
Harrell, Paula. (2008) "Guiding Hand: Hattori Unokichi in Beijing." Online Posting < http://www.chinajapan.org/articles/11.1/11.1harrell13–20.pdf > (accessed 28 December 2008).
Haven, Joseph. (1857) *Mental Philosophy: Including the Intellect, Sensibilities and Will*. Boston: Gould and Lincoln.
—— (1875–6) *Shinrigaku* [Psychology], trans. Nishi Amane. Tokyo: Monbushō.
—— (1889) *Xinlingxue* [Study of the Heart and the Soul], trans. Yan Yongjing. Shanghai: Yizhi Shuhui.
Heinrich, Larissa N. (2008) *The Afterlife of Images: Translating the Pathological Body between China and the West*. Durham, NC and London: Duke University Press.
Horiguchi, Daigaku. (1922) "Hokuō no yo" [The Nordic Night]. *Myojō* [Bright Star] (November): 177–88.
—— (1925) "Jo" [Preface]. *Horiguchi Daigaku zenshū*. Tokyo: Ozawa Shoten, 1981, vol. 2, p. 7.
—— (1925) *Gekka no ichigun*. [Gathering in Moonlight]. Tōkyō: Nihon Kindai Bungakkan, 1969.
Hsia, C. T. (1961; 2nd edn, 1971) *A History of Modern Chinese Fiction*. New Haven: Yale University Press.
Hu, Kao. (1934) "Zhongguo nüxing de zhizhuomei" [Chinese Women's Innocent and Ignorant Beauty]. *Furen huabao* [The Women's Pictorial], 17 (April): 10.
Hu, Shi, trans. (1914) "Bolin zhi wei" [The Siege of Berlin]. *Liangyou* [The Young Companion], 64 (December 1931): 10.
Huang, Chaoqin. (1923) "Hanwen gaige lun" [On the Reform of Classical Chinese]. *Taiwan* (January and February), Hanwen zhi bu [Classical Chinese Section], pp. 25–31, 21–7.
Huang, Jiamou. (1933) "'Xiandai dianying' yu Zhongguo dianyingjie—benkan de chuangli yu jinhou de zeren—yubei geiyu duzhe de jidian gongxian" [*Modern*

Screen and Chinese Movies—The Establishment of This Journal and Its Responsibility from Now on—A Few Contributions Intended for the Reader]. *Xiandai dianying* [Modern screen], inaugural issue (1 March): 1.

—— (1933) "Yingxing yingpian yu ruanxing yingpian" [Hard Films and Soft Films]. *Modern Screen*, 6 (1 December): 3.

Huang, Tianzuo (Suichu). (1940) "Wuo suo renshi de liu na'ou xiansheng" [The Mr Liu Na'ou I Knew]. *Osaka mainichi shinbun* [Osaka Daily], Chinese Edition, 5.9 (1 November): 69.

Huang, Tingjian. (Song) "Guitianle yin" [The Tune of the Joy of Returning to Farm Life]. In *Quan Song ci* [Complete Collection of *Ci* Poetry in the Song]. Taipei: Minglun Chubanshe, 1970, vol. 1.

Huang, Wen-hong. (2006) "Xitian Jiduolang lun 'shizai' yu 'jingyan'" [Nishida Kitarō on "Reality" and "Experience"]. *Taiwan dongya wenming yanjiu xuekan* [Taiwan Journal of East Asian Studies], 3.2 (December): 61–90.

Inoue, Ken. (1994) *Yokomitsu Riichi: hyōden to kenkyū* [Yokomitsu Riichi: A Biographic Study and Research]. Tokyo: Ōfū.

Icart, Louis. (1916) "Dessin de Icart" [Sketch by Icart]. *A coups de Baïonnete* [At the Thrust of the Spear], 4.40 (6 April): 252.

Inoue, Masayoshi. (1915) *Shinkei suijyaku eiyō ryōhō* [A Nutritional Treatment for Neurasthenia]. Tokyo: Daigakukan.

Inoue, Satoshi. (2006) *Yokomitsu Riichi to Chūgoku: "Shanhai" no Kōsei to 5.30 jiken* [Yokomitsu Riichi and China: The Structure of *Shanghai* and the May 30th Incident]. Tokyo: Kanrin Shobō.

Inoue, Tetsujirō, trans. (1882) *Shinri shinsetsu* [New Psychology]. Tokyo: Aoki Sukekiyo, vol. 1.

—— trans. (1902) *Shakāmuni ten* [Biography of Buddha]. Tokyo: Bunmeidō.

Ion, A. Hamish. (1977) "Edward Warren Clark and Early Meiji Japan: A Case Study of Cultural Contact." *Modern Asian Studies*, 11.4: 557–72.

Jing, Tsu. (2005) *Failure, Nationalism, and Literature: The Making of Modern Chinese Identity, 1895–1937*. Stanford, CA: Stanford University Press.

Jules-Rosette, Bennetta. (2007) *Josephine Baker in Art and Life: The Icon and the Image*. Urbana and Chicago: University of Illinois Press.

Kaske, Elisabeth. (2006) "Cultural Identity, Education, and Language Politics in China and Japan, 1870–1920." In David Hoyt and Karen Oslund, eds., *The Study of Language and the Politics of Community in Global Context*. Lanham, MD: Lexington Books, pp. 215–56.

Kataoka, Teppei. (1924) "Wakaki dokusha ni utawu" [Appeal to the Young Reader]. *Bungei jidai* [Literary Age] (December). In Itō Sei et al., eds. (1968) *Nihon gendai bungaku zenshū* [Complete Works of Modern Japanese Literature]. 108 volumes. Tokyo: Kōdansha, vol. 67, pp. 360–4.

Kawabata, Yasunari. (1926) *Kanjō sōshoku* [Decoration of the Emotions]. Tokyo: Kinsedō.

—— (1926) "Shōhen shōsetsu no ryūkō" [The Booming of Palm-of-the-Hand Stories]. In *Complete Works of Kawabata Yasunari*, 1981–83, vol. 30, pp. 230–4.

—— (1930) "Watashi no seikatsu (3): kibō" [My Life, part 3: Hopes]. In *Shinbungei nikki* [New Literary Diary]. In *Complete Works of Kawabata Yasunari*, 1981–83, vol. 33, p. 58.

—— (1938) "Atogaki" [Postscript]. In *Kawabata Yasunari senshū* [Selected Works of Kawabata Yasunari]. Tokyo: Kaizōsha, vol. 1, pp. 405–11.

244 Bibliography

—— (1948) "Atogaki" [Postscript]. In *Complete Works of Kawabata Yasunari*, 1981–83, vol. 11, pp. 401–23.

—— (1972) "Yukigunishō" [The Snow Country Sketch]. In *Sandei mainichi* [Sunday Everyday] (13 August): 50–9.

—— (1982) "Shōhen shōsetsu ni tsuite" [On Palm-of-the-Hand Stories]. In *Complete Works of Kawabata Yasunari*, 1981–83, vol. 32, pp. 543–7.

—— (1981–83) *Kawabata Yasunari zenshū* [Complete Works of Kawabata Yasunari]. 37 volumes. Tokyo: Shinchōsha.

—— (1988) "A Sunny Place." In Lane Dunlop and J. Martin Holman, trans. *Palm-of-the-Hand Stories*. San Francisco: North Point Press, pp. 3–4.

—— (2001) *Tenohira no shōsetsu* [Palm-of-the-Hand Stories], ed. Yoshimura Teiji. Tokyo: Shinchōsha.

Keene, Donald. (1984) *Dawn to the West: Japanese Literature of the Modern Era*. New York: Henry Holt and Company.

Kim, Jina. (2006) "The Circulation of Urban Literary Modernity in Colonial Korea and Taiwan." Ph.D. Dissertation, University of Washington.

Kleinman, Arthur. (1986) *Social Origins of Distress and Disease: Depression, Neurasthenia and Pain in Modern China*. New Haven: Yale University Press.

Kōketsu, Atsushi. (2005) "Taiwan Shuppei no ichi to teikoku Nipon no seiritsu" [Invasion of Taiwan and the Establishment of Imperial Japan]. *Shokuminchi bunka kenkyū: shiryo to bunseki* [Studies of Colonial Cultures: Materials and Analysis], 4 (July): 25–33.

Koschmann, Victor. (1995) "Victimization and the Writerly Subject: Writers' War Responsibility in Early Postwar Japan." *Tamkang Review*, 26.1–2: 61–75.

Koyasu, Nobukuni. (2003) *"Ajia" wa dō katararete kita ka: kindai Nihon no orientarizumu* [How "Asia" Was Formulated in Discourse: Modern Japan's Orientalism]. Tokyo: Fujihara Shoten, pp. 83–147.

—— (2003) *Kanjiron: Fukahi no tasha* [On the Chinese Character: The Inevitable Other]. Tokyo: Iwanami Shoten.

Kropotkin, P. (1902) *Mutual Aid: A Factor of Evolution*. London: William Heinemann.

—— (1912) *Modern Science and Anarchism*. London: Freedom Press.

Kwok, Sze-wing. (2007) "Chi sheyingji de ren: shilun Liu Na'ou de jilupian" [The Man with a Movie Camera: On Liu Na'ou's Documentary]. *Shiji wenxue* [Century Literature], 2.7 (July): 28–32.

Lacroix, Paul, Alphonse Duchesne, and Ferdinand Seré. (1852) *Histoire des cordonniers et des artisans dont la profession se rattache à la cordonnerie* [History of Shoemakers and Craftsmen Whose Profession Is Attached to Shoemaking]. Paris : Librairies Historique, Archéologique et Scientifique de Seré.

Ladd, George Trumbull. (1905) *Outlines of Descriptive Psychology: A Text-Book of Mental Science for Colleges and Normal Schools*. New York: Charles Scribner's Sons.

Lee, Haiyan. (2007) *Revolution of the Heart: A Genealogy of Love in China, 1900–1950*. Stanford, CA: Stanford University Press.

Lee, Leo. (1999) *Shanghai Modern*. Cambridge, MA: Harvard University Press.

Legros, G.-V. (1913) *La Vie de J.-H. Fabre, naturaliste, par un disciple* [Life of J.-H. Fabre, Naturalist, by a Disciple]. Paris : Librairie Ch. Delagrave.

—— (1913) *Fabre, Poet of Science*. Trans. Bernard Miall. New York: The Century Co.

Li, Dongyuan. (Jin) "Dongyuan shixiaofang" [Prescriptions Tested by Dongyuan].

In Ding Guangdi and Wen Kui, eds., *Dongyuan yiji* [The Dongyuan Collection of Medicines]. Beijing: Renmin Weisheng Chubanshe, 1993, vol. 2.
Li, Jin. (2005) "Mu Shiying nianpu jianbian" [Concise Annual Accounts of Mu Shiying's Life]. *Zhongguo xiandai wenxue yanjiu congkan* [Studies of Modern Chinese Literature], 6: 237–68.
Liang, Qichao. (1936) *Yinbingshi hoji* [The Drinking Ice Water Room Collection]. Beijing: Zhonghua Shuju, 1989, vol. 1.
Liang, Shiqiu. (1958) *Tan Xu Zhimo* [On Xu Zhimo]. Taipei: Yuandong Tushu Gongsi.
Liangyou [The Young Companion]. (1933) Inside Cover Advertisement. 73 (January).
Lippit, Seiji M. (2002) *Topographies of Japanese Modernism*. New York: Columbia University Press.
—— (2003) "A Melancholic Nationalism: Yokomitsu Riichi and the Aesthetic of Cultural Mourning." In Dick Stegewerns, ed., *Nationalism and Internationalism in Imperial Japan*. London and New York: Routledge Curzon, pp. 228–46.
Liu, Chi-hui. (2001) "Yayi yu fufan: Jingshen fenxi lunshu yu Taiwan xiandai zhuyi de guanlian" [Repression and Revival: Psychoanalytical Discourse and Taiwan Modernism]. *Journal of Modern Chinese Literature in Chinese*, 4.2: 31–61.
Liu, Lydia. (1995) *Translingual Practice: Literature, National Culture, and Translated Modernity—China,1900–1937*. Stanford, CA: Stanford University Press.
—— (2004) *The Clash of Empires: The Invention of China in Modern World Making*. Cambridge, MA: Harvard University Press.
Liu, Na'ou. (1927) *Rijiji* [Diary]. Ed. and trans. Peng Hsaio-yen and Huang Yingzhe. 2 volumes. In *Complete Works of Liu Na'ou*, 2001.
—— trans. (1928) "Qilou de yundong" [The Exercise of Seven Floors]. In *Seqing wenhua* [Erotic Culture]. Shanghai: Diixian Shudian, pp. 37–53.
—— trans. (1928) "Baoluo Muhang lun" [On Paul Morand]. *Wugui lieche* [Trackless train], 4 (25 October): 147–60.
—— (1932) "Yingpian yishulun" [On Cinematic Art]. *Dianying zhoubao* [Cinéma Weekly], Nos. 2, 3, 6–10, and 15 (1 July to 8 October). In *Complete Works of Liu Na'ou*, 2001, pp. 256–80.
—— (1933) "Ecranesque" [About the Screen]. *Xiandai dianying* [Modern screen], 2 (1 April): 1.
—— (1933) "Lun ticai" [On Subject Matter]. *Modern Screen*, 4 (1 July): 2–3.
—— (1933) "Dianying jiezou jianlun" [A Brief Essay on the Rhythm of the Camera]. *Modern Screen*, 6 (1 December): 1–2.
—— (1934) "Kaimaila jigou—weizhi jiaodu jineng lun" [On the Mechanism of the Camera—The Function of Angle and Position]. *Modern Screen*, 7 (1 June): 1–5.
—— (2001) *Liu Na'ou quanji* [Complete Works of Liu Na'ou]. Ed. Kang Laixin and Xu Zhenzhen. 6 volumes. Tainan: Tainanxian Wenhuaju.
Liuxu. (1926) "Zhuzhang zuzhi dadongya wuzhengfuzhuyizhe dalianmeng" [Advocacy of the Alliance of Great East-Asian Anarchists]. *Minzhong* [The People's Knell], 16 (15 December): 2–3.
Lou, Shiyi. (1931) "Zuopin yu zuojia: Shi Zhicun de xinganjue zhuyi—du le 'Zai Bari Daxiyuan' yu 'Modao' zhi hou" [Literary Works and Writers: The Neo-Sensationism of Shi Zhicun—After Reading "In the Paris Movie Theater" and "The Enchanter"]. *Wenyi xinwen* [Literary News], 33 (26 October): 4.
Lowy, Dina. (2007) *The Japanese "New Woman": Images of Gender and Modernity*. New Brunswisk, NJ: Rutgers University Press.

Lu, Shoujian. (1917) *Shenjing shuairuo liaoyangfa* [A Treatment for Neurasthenia]. Shanghai: Zhonghua Shuju.
Lu, Xun (Luan Tingshi), trans. (1921) "Chunye de meng" [A Spring Night's Dream]. *Chenbao fukan* [Literary Supplement to the Morning Post] (22 October): 1–2.
—— (1922) "Ya de xiju" [The Comedy of Ducks]. *Funü zazhi* [Women's Journal], 8.12 (December): 83–4.
—— (Mingzhao). (1925) "Chunmo xiantan" [Random Talks in the Late Spring]. *Mangyuan* [Wasteland], 1 (24 April): 1–32.
—— (1925) "Tongxun" [Correspondences). In *Complete Works of Lu Xun*, 1989, vol. 3, p. 25.
—— (1929) *Yecao* [Wild grass]. Taipei: Wenxue Shiliao Yanjiuhui.
—— (Ruogu). (1933) "Opi" [Bad Habits]. In *Complete Works of Lu Xun*, 1989, vol. 5, pp. 80–1.
—— (1933) "Chi bexiang fan" (Living on Bexiang), in *Complete Works of Lu Xun*, 1989, vol. 5, pp. 208–9.
—— (1934) "Jingpai yu haipai." [Beijing Types and Shanghai Types]. *Shenbao* [Shanghai Post] (3 February): 17.
—— (1959) *Lu Xun riji* [Diary of Lu Xun]. Beijing: Renmin Wenxue Chubanshe.
—— (1989) *Lu Xun quanji* [Complete Works of Lu Xun]. 16 volumes. Beijing: Renmin Wenxue Chubanshe.
Lunyu. (1998) *Analects, Translations of Confucian Classics*. Jinan: Shangdong Youyi Chubanshe.
Malraux, André. (1933) *La condition humaine*. Paris : Gallimard.
—— (1961) *Man's Fate*. Trans. Kaakon M. Chevalier. New York: The Modern Library.
Mao, Zedong. (1919) "Xuesheng zhi gongzuo" [The Work of Students]. *Hunan jiaoyu yuekan* [Hunan Education Monthly], 1.2 (1 December). In *Mao Zedong zaoqi wengao* [Mao Zedong's Early Writings]. Changsha: Hunan Chubanshe, 1995, pp. 449–57.
Marshall, Byron. (1992) *The Autobiography of Ōsugi Sakae*. Berkeley: University of California Press.
Marx, Karl (1979) *The Letters of Karl Marx*. Trans. Saul K. Padover. New Jersey: Prentice-Hall, Inc.
Masini, Federico. (1993) *The Formation of Modern Chinese Lexicon and Its Evolution toward a National Language: The Period from 1840 to 1898*. Berkeley, CA: Project on Linguistic Analysis, University of California.
Matual, David. (1992) *Tolstoy's Translation of the Gospels: A Critical Study*. Queenston, Ontario: The Edwin Mellen Press.
Medhurst, W. H., Sen. (1847–48) *English and Chinese Dictionary*. Shanghae: The Mission Press, vol. 2.
Mencius (1993) *Mencius, Translations of Confucian Classics*. Jinan: Shangdong Youyi Chubanshe.
Miller, Oscar W. (1956) *The Kantian Thing-in-Itself or the Creative Mind*. New York: Philosophical Library.
Miura, Kinnosuke. (1894) *Shinkeibyō shindanhyō* [A List of Diagnoses for Diseases of the Nerves]. Tokyo: Miura Kinnosuke.
Mo, Ran. (1934) "Zhongguo nanren budong lian'ai yishu" [Chinese Men Do Not Know the Art of Love]. *Furen huabao* [The Women's Pictorial], 16 (March): 9–13.

—— (1934) "Wairen muzhong zhi Zhongguo nüxingmei" [How Foreigners Look at Chinese Women's Beauty]. *The Women's Pictorial*, 17 (April): 10–12.
Morand, Paul. (1922) "La nuit des six-jours" [The Six-Day Night]. In *Paul Morand: Nouvelles complètes*, 1992, pp. 137–49.
—— (1923) "The Six-Day Night." Trans. Vyvyan Beresford Holland In *Open All Night*. New York: T. Seltzer, pp. 118–29.
—— (1928) "Liuri zhi yeh" [The Six-Day Night]. Trans. Dai Wangshu (Lang Fang). In *Falanxi duanpian jiezuoji diyice* [Masterpieces of French Short Stories]. Shanghai: Xiandai Shudian, vol. 1, pp. 1–25.
—— (1929) "Liuri jingzou zhi yeh" [The Night of the Six-Day Race]. Trans. Dai Wangshu. In *Tiannü Yuli* [Yuli the Daughter of Heaven]. Shanghai: Shanghai Shuwu, pp. 53–80.
—— (1945) "Liuri jingsai zhi yeh" [The Night of the Six-Day Competition]. Trans. Dai Wangshu. *Xiangdao ribao. zongho* [Hong Kong Island Daily. Miscellany] (28–30 June and 2–12 July): 2.
—— (1976) "Préface". In *L'allure de Chanel*, 1999, pp. 7–12.
—— (1976) *L'allure de Chanel*. Paris: Hermann, 1999.
—— (1992) *Paul Morand : Nouvelles complètes* [Paul Morand: Complete Short Stories]. Paris : Gallimard.
—— (2001). *Paul Morand : au seul souci de voyager* [Paul Morand: For the Sake of Travel Only]. Ed. Michel Bulteau. Paris : Louis Vuitton.
Morrison, Robert. (1819–23) *Dictionary of the Chinese Language*. Macao: The East India Company's Press, 1822, vol. 6.
—— (1813) *Shentian Shengshu* [The Holy Bible]. In *China and Protestant Missions: A Collection of their Earliest Missionary Works in Chinese*. Leiden: IDC, microfilm, 1983.
Mu, Shiying. (1931) "Shouzhi" [Fingers]. *Qingnienjie* [The World of Youths], 1.3. In *A Chinese Neo-Sensation Writer of Genius: Complete Collection of Mu Shiying's Stories*, 1996, pp. 30–3.
—— (1933) "Bei dangzuo xiaoqianpin de nanzi." [A Man Taken as a Plaything]. In *A Chinese Neo-Sensation Writer of Genius: Complete Collection of Mu Shiying's Stories*, 1996, pp. 151–76.
—— (1933) "Craven 'A.'" *Gongmu* [Public Cemetery]. Shanghai: Xiandai Shuju. In *A Chinese Neo-Sensation Writer of Genius: Complete Collection of Mu Shiying's Stories*, 1996, pp. 205–20.
—— (1996) "Craven 'A.'" In Yueqi, ed., *Zhongguo xinganjuepai shengshou: Mu Shiying xiaoshuo quanji* [A Chinese Neo-Sensation Writer of Genius: Complete Collection of Mu Shiying's Stories]. Beijing: Zhongguo Wenlian Chuban Gongsi.
Mushanokōji, Saneatsu. (1987–91) *Mushanokōji Saneatsu zenshū* [Complete Works of Mushanokōji]. 18 volumes. Tokyo: Shōgakukan.
Nagai, Kafū. (1919) "Hanabi" [The Fireworks]. In *Kafū zenshū* [Complete Works of Nagai Kafū]. Tokyo: Iwanami Shoten, 1993, vol. 14, pp. 252–60.
Nagato, Hiroshi. (2002) *Yamato kotoba wo wasureta nihonjin* [Japanese Who Forgot the Native Language]. Tokyo: Akashi Shōten.
Nakajima, Rikizō. (1889) "Kant's Doctrine of the "Thing-in-Itself.'" Ph.D. dissertation, Yale University.
—— (1898) *Shinri satsuyō* [Essence of Psychology]. Tokyo: Hukūsha.
Nakajima Takeshi. (2005) *Nakamuraya no Bōsu: Indo dokuritsu undō to kindai Nihon*

no Ajia shugi [Bose of Nakamuraya: India's Independence Movement and Modern Japan's Asianism; Tokyo: Hakusuisha].
National Subjects' Daily. (1940) *Guomin xinwen.* 29 June to late September, news coverage on the muders of Mu Shiying and Liu Na'ou.
Needham, Maureen. (1997) "Louis XIV and the Académie Royale de Danse, 1661: A Commentary and Translation." *Dance Chronicle*, 20.2: 173–90.
Ng, Yu-kwan. (1998) *Jingdu xuepai zhexue qijiang* [Seven Lectures on the Philosophy of the Kyōto School]. Taipei: Wenjin Chubanshe.
Ninagawa, Yuzuru. (1996) *Pari ni shisu* [Death in Paris]. Tokyo: Fujiwara Shoten.
Nishida, Kitarō. (1911) "Ninshikiron ni okeru junronriha no shuchō ni tsuite" [On the Thesis of the School of Pure Reason in Epistemology]. In *Nishida Kitarō*, 1970, pp. 234–51.
—— (1914–17) *Jikaku ni okeru chokkan to hansei* [Intuition and Self-Reflexivity in Self-Consciousness]. In *Nishida Kitarō*, 1970, pp. 276–82.
—— (1917) "Shushu no sekai" [Multitudes of World]. In *Nishida Kitarō*, 1970, pp. 264–73.
—— (1970) "Ninshikiron ni okeru junronriha no shuchō ni tsuite" [On the Thesis of the School of Pure Reason in Epistemology, 1911]. In Ueyama Shunpei, ed. *Nishida Kitarō*. Tokyo: Chūō Kōronsha.
Nishiwaki, Junzaburō. (1929) Chōgenjitsushugi shiron [Poetics of Surrealism]. In *Complete Works of Nishiwaki Junzaburō: Definitive Texts*, 1993, vol. 5, pp. 7–88.
—— (1933) *Ambarvalia.* Tokyo: Shiinokisha, 1933. In *Complete Works of Nishiwaki Junzaburō: Definitive Texts*, 1993, vol. 1, pp. 7–81.
—— (1947) *Tabibito kaerazu* [No Traveler Returns]. In *Complete Works of Nishiwaki Junzaburō: Definitive Texts*, 1993, vol. 1, pp. 209–308.
—— (1993) *Teihon Nishiwaki Junzaburō zenshū* [Complete Works of Nishiwaki Junzaburō: Definitive Texts]. 13 volumes. Tokyo: Chikuma Shobō.
Ochanomizu University. (2005) "Higashi-Ajia ni okeru shokuminchideki kindai to modan gāru" [Colonial Modernity and the Modern Girl in East Asia]. Tokyo: Ochanomizu University, an international modern girl project, mid-term report.
Odagiri, Hideo. (1972) "Bungaku ni okeru sensō sekinin no tsuikyū" [Pursuing War Responsibility in Literature]. In Usui Yoshimi and Ōkubo Tsuneo, eds., *Sengo bungaku ronsō* [Postwar Literary Debate]. Tokyo: Banchō Shobō, pp. 115–17.
Odagiri, Hiroko. (1980) *Yokomitsu Riichi: hikaku bungakuteki kenkyū* [Yokomitsu Riichi: A Comparative Literary Study]. Tokyo: Nansōsha.
Ōgai, Kamome. (1934) "Zhonghua ernümei zhi gebie shenpan" [A Personal Critique of Chinese Daughters' Beauty]. *Furen huabao* [The Women's Pictorial], 17 (April): 12–15.
—— (1934) "Yanjiu chujiao de sangeren" [The Three Who Study Antennas]. *Furen huabao* [The Women's Pictorial], 21 (September): 5–6.
Okakura, Kakuzō. (1904) *The Ideals of the East with Special Reference to the Art of Japan.* London: John Murray.
Online Posting (1900). Advertisement for Doan's Backache Kidney Pills. In *The Bulletin*, 13 December. <http://www.historypages.net/Pdoans.html#Top> (accessed on 28 May 2008).
—— (1930–1943). Advertisement for Burutōze [Blutose], <http://www.east-asianhistory.net/textbooks/Slideshows/medicine/medicine_show.pdf> (accessed on 25 May 2008).

—— (1936). "Marie Bell in *La gaçonne*" [Marie Bell in *The Boyish Girl*]. <http://en.wikipedia.org/wiki/La_Garçonne_(1936_film)> (accessed 15 April 2010).
—— (2004). "Yūka shōken hōkokusho" [Report on Valuable Securities]. Fujisawa Tomokichi, 1 April. <http://www.astellas.com/jp/ir/library/pdf/f_securities2005_jp.pdf> (accessed on 25 May 2008).
Ōse, Jintarō. (1914) *Shinri sazuyō* [Essence of Psychology]. Tokyo: Seibidō Shoten.
Ōsugi, Sakae. (1913) "Sōzōteki shinka—Anri Beruguson ron" [*Evolution créatrice*: On Henri Bergson]. In *Complete Works of Ōsugi Sakae*, 1925–26, vol. 1, pp. 187–96.
—— (1919) *Gokuchūki* [Prison Memoirs]. Tokyo: Imamura Takashi.
—— (1921) "Reikon no tame no senshi" (A Spirit Wrestler). In *Complete Works of Ōsugi Sakae*, vol. 1, pp. 738–76.
—— (1921–22) *Jijoden* [Autobiography]. Tokyo: Sekkasha, 1967.
—— (1922) "Yakusha no jo" [Translator's Preface]. In *Konchūki* [Book of Insects]. Tokyo: Meiseki Shoten, 2005, pp. 5–14.
—— (1923) "Nihon dasshutsuki" [Escapes from Japan]. In Osawa Masamichi, ed. (1974), *Osugi Sakae shū* [Selected Works of Osugi Sakae]. Tokyo: Chikuma Shoten, pp. 297–327.
—— (1924) *Konchūki* [Book of Insects]. Tokyo: Sōbunkaku, 6th edn.
—— (1925–26) *Ōsugi Sakae zenshū* [Complete Works of Ōsugi Sakae]. 10 volumes. Tokyo: Ōsugi Sakae Zenshū Kankōkai.
Ōya, Sōichi. (1929) "Hyaku pasento moga" [One Hundred Percent Modern Girl]. In *Ōya Sōichi zenshū* [Complete Works of Ōya Sōichi]. 30 volumes. Tokyo: Sōyōsha, 1980, vol. 2, pp. 10–17.
Pak, Pyŏng-sik. (1986) *Yamato kotoba no kigen to kodai Chōsengo* [The Origin of *Yamato Kotoba* and Ancient Korean Language]. Tokyo: Seikō Shobō.
Pan, Guangdan. (1924) "Feng Xiaoqing kao" [On Feng Xiaoqing]. *Funü zazhi* [Women's Magazine] 10.11: 1706–17.
—— (1927) "Xuyan" [Preface], *Xiaoqing zhi fenxi* [Analysis of Xiaoqing]. In *Pan Guangdan Wenji* [Collected Works of Pan Guangdan]. 14 volumes. Beijing: Beijing Daxue Chubanshe, 1993, vol. 1, p. 3.
—— trans. (1939–41) *Xing Xinlixue* [Psychology of Sex]. Beijing: Xinhua Shudian, 1987.
Pearson, Veronica. (1995) *Mental Health Care in China: State Policies, Professional Services and Family Responsibilities*. London: Gaskell.
Peng, Hsiao-yen. (1994) "Xing qimeng yu ziwuo de jiefang: 'Xing boshi' Zhang Jingshing yu wusi de seyu xiaoshuo" [Sexual Enlightenment and Self-Liberation: "Dr. Sex" and May Fourth Erotic Fiction]. *Chaoyue xieshi* [Beyond Realism]. Taipei: Lianjing Chuban Gongsi, pp. 117–37.
—— (1995) "The New Woman: May Fourth Women's Struggle for Self-Liberation." *Bulletin of Chinese Literature and Philosophy, Academia Sinica*, 6 (March): 259–337.
—— (1996) *Piaobo yu xiangtu: Zhang Wuojun shishi sishi zhounian jinian lunwenji* [Diaspora and Homeland: Commemorating the 40th Anniversary of Zhang Wuojun's Demise]. Taipei: Council of Cultural Affairs.
—— (1998) "Langdang tianya: Liu Na'ou yijiuerqi nian riji" [Flâneur of the World: Liu Na'ou's 1927 Diary]. *Bulletin of Chinese Literature and Philosphy, Academia Sinica*, 12 (March): 1–40.
—— (2001) *Haishang shuo qingyu: cong Zhang Ziping dao Liu Na'ou* [Desire in

Shanghai: from Zhang Ziping to Liu Na'ou]. Taipei: Institute of Chinese Literature and Philosophy, Academia Sinica.

—— (2002) "*Sex Histories*: Zhang Jingsheng's Sexual Revolution." In Peng-hsiang Chen and Whitney Crothers Dilley, eds., *Critical Studies: Feminism/Femininity in Chinese Literature*. Amsterdam: Editions Rodopi B.V., pp. 159–77.

—— (2007) "A Traveling Text: Souvenirs entomologiques, Japanese Anarchism, and Shanhai Neo-Sensationism." *NTU Studies in Language and Literature*, 17: 1–42.

Perry, Elizabeth J. (2008) "Reclaiming the Chinese Revolution." *The Journal of Asian Studies*, 67.4 (November): 1147–64.

Petric, Vlada. (1987) *Constructivism in Film: "The Man with the Movie Camera," A Cinematic Analysis*. Cambridge: Cambridge University Press.

Plaks, Andrew, trans. (2003) *Ta Hsüeh and Chung Yung* [The Highest Order of Cultivation and On the Practice of the Mean]. London and New York: Penguin Books.

Plato. (1999) *The Symposium*. Trans. Christopher Gill and Desmond Lee. New York: Penguin.

Pratt, Mary L. (1992) *Imperial Eyes: Travel Writing and Transculturation*. London and New York: Routledge, 2000.

Prest, Julia. (2006) *Theatre under Louis XIV: Cross-Casting and the Performance of Gender in Drama, Ballet and Opera*. New York: Palgrave Macmillan.

Proust, Marcel. (1921) "Preface." In Paul Morand, *Tendres stocks* [Fancy Goods]. In *Paul Morand: Nouvelles complètes* [Paul Morand: Complete Short Stories]. Paris: Gallimard, 1992, pp. 3–12.

Qin, Xianci. (1996) "Zhang Wuojun ji qi tongshidai de Beijing Taiwan liuxuesheng" [Zhang Wuojun and Contemporary Taiwanese Studying in Beijing]. In Peng Hsiao-yen, ed., *Diaspora and Homeland: Commemorating the 40th Anniversary of Zhang Wuojun's Demise*, pp. 57–81.

Rabut, Isabelle and Angel Pino. (1996) *Le fox-trot in Shanghai, et autres nouvelles chinoises* [The Fox-Trot in Shanghai, and Other Chinese Stories]. Paris: Albin Michel.

General Conference of the Protestant Missionaries of China. (1878) *Records of the general conference of the protestant missionaries of China, Held at Shanghai, May 10–24, 1877*. Shanghai: Presbyterian Mission Press. Reprinted, Taipei: Ch'eng-wen Publishing Company, 1973.

Roberts, Mary Louise. (1994) *Civilization without Sexes: Reconstructing Gender in Postwar France, 1917–1927*. Chicago and London: The University of Chicago Press.

Ruse, Michael. (2005) *The Evolution-Creation Struggle*. Cambridge, MA: Harvard University Press.

Said, Edward. (2002) "Traveling Theory." In Moustafa Bayoumi and Andrew Rubin, eds., *The Edward Said Reader*. New York: Vintage Books, pp. 195–217.

Sas, Miryam. (1999) *Fault Lines: Cultural Memory and Japanese Surrealism*. Stanford, CA: Stanford University Press.

Satō, Tatsuya. (2002) *Nihon ni okeru shinrigaku no juyō to tenkai* [The Reception and Development of Psychology in Japan]. Kyoto: Kitaōji Shobō.

Saussey, Haun. (2006) "Death and Translation." *Representations*, 94.1 (Spring): 112–30.

Seidensticker, Edward. (1965) *Kafū the Scribbler: The Life and Writings of Nagai Kafū, 1879–1959*. Stanford, CA: Stanford University Press.

Shangbanyu. (1936) "Wu linghun de routi" [A Body without Soul]. *Shidai manhu* [Modern Sketch], 29 (20 August). In Shen Jianzhong, ed., *Shidai manhu, 1934–1937* [Modern Sketch, *1934–1937*]. Shanghai: Shanghai Shehui Kexueyuan Chubanshe, 2004, vol. 2, p. 400.

Shanghai Lu Xun Museum, ed. (1995; 2nd edn, 2000) *Zhongri youhao de xianqu: Lu Xun yu Neishan Wanzao tuji* [Pioneers of the Friendship between China and Japan: Picture Collections of Lu Xun and Uchiyama Kanzō]. Shanghai: Renmin Meishu Chubanshe.

Shenbao [Shanghai Post]. (1930) "Bu'erduoshou" [Blutose]. Advertisement. (8 November): 7.

—— (1930) "Dou-an shi bushen yaopian" [Doans' Pills for Strengthening the Nerves]. Advertisement. (13 May): 14.

—— (1940) "Fuzhoulu zuowan xie'an/Mu Shiying zao qiangsha" [Bloody Murder Last Night at Fuzhou Road/Mu Shiying Gunned down]. (29 June): 9.

—— (1940) "Fuzhoulu zuori xie'an/Liu Na'ou bei jisi" [Bloody Murder Yesterday at Fuzhou Road /Liu Na'ou Shot to Death]. (4 September): 9.

Shapiro, Hugh. (2000) "Neurasthenia and the Assimilation of Nerves into China." Presented at the "Symposium on the History of Disease," Institute of History and Philology, Academia Sinica, Taiwan, 16–18 June.

Shen, Congwen (Jiachen). (1930) "Yu Dafu, Zhang Ziping ji qi yingxiang" [Yu Dafu, Zhang Ziping, and their Influences]. *Xinyue* [Crescent Moon], 3.1 (March): 1–8.

—— (1934) "On Mu Shiying." In *Shen Congwen wenji* [Works of Shen Congwen]. Hong Kong: Sanlian Shudian, 1982–83, vol. 11, pp. 203–5.

—— (1929) "Yige tiancai de tongxin" [Letters from a Genius]. *Honghei* [Red and Black], nos 6 and 7 (10 June and 10 July). In *Shen Congwen Quanji* [Complete Works of Shen Congwen]. 32 volumes. Taiyuan: Beiyue Wenyi Chubanshe, 2002, vol. 4, pp. 325–72.

Shen, Xiling. (1933) "Yijiusan'er nian Zhongguo dianyingjie de zong jiezhang yu yijiusansan nian de xin qiwang" [A Summing Up of the Chinese Movie Industry in 1932 and New Hopes for the Year 1933]. *Xiandai dianying* [Modern screen], inaugural issue (1 March): 7–9.

Shi, Yan. (1934) "Hangxianshang de yinyue" [Music on the Cruising Route]. *Furen huabao* [The Women's Pictorial], 21 (September): 7–8.

Shi, Zhicun. (1996) *Zhendan er nian* [Two Years at L'Aurore]. Shanghai: Wenyi Chubanshe, pp. 289–90.

Shih, Shu-mei. (2001) *The Lure of the Modern: Writing Modernism in Semicolonial China, 1917–1937*. Berkeley: University of California Press.

Shiina, Sonoji. (1925) *Fāburu no shōgai, kagaku no shijin* [Life of Fabre, Poet of Science]. Tokyo: Sōbunkaku.

Shokuminchi bunka kenkyū: shiryo to bunseki [Studies of Colonial Cultures: Materials and Analysis]. (2002-present) Tokyo: Fuji Shuppan.

Silverberg, Miriam. (2006) *Erotic Grotesque Nonsense: The Mass Culture of Japanese Modern Times*. Berkeley: University of California Press.

Snyder, Steven. (2000) *Fictions of Desire: Narrative Form in the Novels of Nagai Kafū*. Hawai'i: University of Hawai'i Press.

Sōgō, Masaaki. (1986; 3rd edn, 1998) *Meiji no kotoba jiten*. Tokyo: Tōkyōdō Shuppan.

Spitta, Silvia. (1995) *Between Two Waters: Narratives of Transculturation in Latin America*. Houston, TX: Rice University Press.
Stanley, Rhine. (1998) *Bone Voyage: A Journey in Forensic Anthropology*. Albuquerque: University of New Mexico Press.
Stevens, Sarah E. (2003) "Figuring Modernity: The New Woman and the Modern Girl in Republican China." *NWSA Journal*, 15.3 (Fall): 82–103.
Su, Xuelin. (1934) "Yu Dafu lun" [On Yu Dafu]. In Chen Zishan and Wang Zili, eds. (1986), *Yu Dafu yanjiu ziliao* [Research Materials on Yu Dafu]. Hong Kong: Sanlian Shudian, pp. 66–77.
Sun, Naixiu. (1995) *Foluoyide yu Zhongguo xiandai zuojia* [Freud and Modern Chinese Writers]. Taipei: Yeqiang Chubanshe.
Sunquist, Scott, ed. (2001) *A Dictionary of Asian Christianity*. Grand Rapids, MI: William B. Eerdmans Publishing.
Suzuki, Sadami, ed. (1989) *Modan gāru no yūwaku* [The Modern Girl's Charm]. In Suzuki Sadami et al., eds., *Modan toshi bungaku* [Modern City Literature]. Tokyo: Heibonsha, vol. 2.
Taiwan minbao [Taiwan People's Daily]. (1926) "Liujing zuyesheng songbiehui" [Farewell Party for Taiwanese Students Graduating from Schools in Tokyo], 99 (4 April): 8.
Takesuke, Shibusawa. (1970) *Shi no kongen wo motomete—Bōdorēru, Ranbō, Hagiwara Sakutarō sono ta* [Searching for Poetic Origins: Baudelaire, Rimbaud, Hagiwara Sakutarō, and Others]. Tokyo: Shichōsha.
Tamura, Kasaburō. (1911) *Shinkei suijyaku konjihō* [How to Cure Neurasthenia Completely]. Tokyo: Kenyūsha.
Tanaka, Hisara. (1929) "Mogako to moborō" [Miss Modern Girl and Master Modern Boy]. Ed. Gendai Yumoa Zenshū Kankōkai, *Namita no neuchi* [Values of Tears]. In *Tanaka Hisara gashū* [Collected Paintings of Tanaka Hisara]. Tokyo: Kōdansha, 1978, pp. 129–44.
Tang, Na. (1934) "Qingsuan ruanxing dianying lun—ruanxing lunzhe de quwei zhuyi" [Purging the Soft-Film Theory—The Entertainment Theory of Soft-Film Theorists]. *Chenbao* [Morning Post] (19 June): 10.
—— (1934) "Qingsuan ruanxing dianying lun" [Purging the Soft-Film Theory]. *Morning Post* (19–27 June): p. 10 or p. 12.
Taylor, Diana. (2003) *The Archive and the Repertoire: Performing Cultural Memory in the Americas*. Durham, N.C. and London: Duke University Press.
The Holy Bible: King James Version. (2003) Peabody: Hendrickson.
Tocqueville, Alexis de. (1835) *De la démocratie en Amerique*. 2 volumes. Paris : Librarie Philosophique, 1990, annotated and revised.
Tokyō Asahi, yūkan [Tokyo Morning Sun, Evening Paper]. (1940) "Dai Tōa kyōeiken kakuritsu" [Pan-Asia Co-Prosperity Sphere Established]. (2 August).
Tsurumi, Shunsuke. (1967) "Tenkō no kyōdō kenkyū ni tsuite" [The Joint Research on Turnabout]. In Shisō no Kagaku Kenkyūkai, ed., *Tenkō* [Turnabout]. Tokyo: Heibonsha, vol. 1, pp. 1–27.
—— (1991) *Senjiki Nihon no seishinshi, 1931–1945* [Mental History in Wartime Japan, 1931–45]. Tokyo: Iwanami Shoten.
Ueno, Masuzō. (1973) *Nihon hakubutsugakushi* [Natural History of Japan]. Tokyo: Heibonsha.
Ueyama, Shunpei. (1970) "Zettai bu no kenkyū" [Study of the Absolute Nothingness]. In *Nishida Kitarō*. Tokyo: Chūō Kōronsha, pp. 7–85.

Usui, Yoshimi and Ōkubo Tsuneo, eds. (1972) *Sengo bungaku ronsō* [Postwar Literary Debate]. Tokyo: Banchō Shobō, vol. 1.
Vilmorin, Louise de. (1999) *Mémoire de Coco, le promeneur*. Paris : Gallimard.
Wang, Daw-hwan. (2002) "Yijiuyiwu nian shi yue shiyi ri *Kunchongji* zuozhe Fabu'er shishi" [11 October 1915 – Death of Fabre, Author of *Souvenirs entomologiques*]. *Kexue fazhan* [Scientific Development], 358 (October): 72–4.
Wang, Gui, ed. (1993) *Zhongri jiaoyu guanxishi* [History of the Relationship of Sino-Japanese Education]. Jinan: Shandong Jiaoyu Chubanshe.
Wang, Guowei. (1907) *Xinlixue gailun* [Outlines of Psychoanalysis]. Shanghai: Commercial Press.
Wang, Wenbin. (2005) "Dai Wangshu nianbiao" [Annual Accounts of Dai Wangshu's Life]. In *Xin wenxue shiliao* [Historical Documents on New Literature], 106 (January): 95–105.
Wang, Xiho. (1919) *Shenjing shuairuo ziliaofa* [A Self-Treatment for Neurasthenia]. Shanghai: Commercial Press.
Wang, Zhongchen. (2001) *Yuejie yu xiangxiang: ershi shiji Zhongguo Riben wenxue bijiao yanjiu lunji* [Border Crossing and Imagination: Comparative Studies of Twentieth-Century Chinese and Japanese Literatures]. Beijing: Zhongguo Shehui Kexue Chubanshe.
Washburn, Dennis, trans. (2001) [Yokomitsu, Riichi] *Shanghai: A Novel*. Ann Arbor: MI: University of Michigan Press.
Wei, Furen. [Song] "Xiqunyao" [Tying the Waist of the Skirt]. In *Quan Song ci* [Complete Collection of Ci Poetry in the Song]. Taipei: Minglun Chubanshe, 1970, vol. 1, pp. 269–70.
Wiener, Philip. (1956) "G. M. Beard and Freud on 'American Nervousness.'" *Journal of the History of Ideas*, 17.22: 269–74.
Wu, Haiyong. (2006) *Xiaosheng huo yue huakai hualuo liang yiushi: Lu Xun de shengming zhexue yu juejue taidu* [Calls of the Owl May Be Saying Letting the Flowers Bloom or Die: Lu Xun's Philosophy of Life and Obstinacy]. Guangdong: Huacheng Chubanshe.
Wylie, Alexander. (1867) *Memorials of Protestant Missionaries to the Chinese: Giving a List of Their Publications, and Obituary Notices of the Deceased*. Shanghae: American Presbyterian Mission Press. Taipei: Ch'eng-wen Chubanshe, 1967.
Xiao, Xia. (2007) *Riben jindai langman zhuyi wenxue yu Jidujiao* [Modern Japanese Romantic Literature and Christianity]. Jinan: Shandong University Press.
Xinkan Dasong Xuanho yishi [Anecdotes of the Xuanho Period of the Great Song, Newly Reprinted]. (Southern Song) In Yang Jialuo, ed., *Songyuan pinghua sizhong* [Four Song and Yuan Stories]. Taipei: Shijie Shuju, 1962.
Xin shidai [New Age]. (1931) "Wentan xiaoxi" [News of the Literary Circle]. 1.1 (1 August): 7.
Xizhousheng. (Quing) *Xingshi yinyuan* [Marriages that Awaken the World]. Taipei: Lianjing Chubanshe 1986.
Xu, Zhenglin. (2003) *Zhongguo xiandai wenxue yu Jidujiao* [Modern Chinese Literature and Christianity]. Shanghai: Shanghai University Press.
Xu, Zhimo. (1922) "Fragments." In *Supplements to the Complete Works of Xu Zhimo: Letters*. Ed. Lu Yaodong. Hong Kong: Commercial Press, 1993, vol. 4.
——, trans. (c. 1922) [E. B. Browning], "Inclusions." In Lu Yaodong, ed., *Supplements to the Complete Works of Xu Zhimo: Poetry*, 1993, vol. 1, pp. 197–8.

——, trans. (*c.* 1922) [Maurice Thompson], "Atalanta's Race." In Lu Yaodong, ed., *Supplements to the Complete Works of Xu Zhimo: Poetry*, 1993, vol. 1, pp. 199–200.

—— (1925) "Yitiao jinse de guanghen: Xiashi tubai" [A Shaft of Golden Light: Monologue in the Xiashi Dialect]. In *Complete Works of Xu Zhimo*, 1983, vol. 1, pp. 89–92.

—— (1923) "Manshufei'er" [Mansfield]. *Xiaoshuo yuebao* [Fiction Monthly], 14.5 (May): 1–12. In *Complete Works of Xu Zhimo*, vol. 3, pp. 1–25.

—— (1983) *Xu Zhimo quanji* [Complete Works of Xu Zhimo]. Hong Kong: Commercial Press.

—— (1993) *Xu Zhimo quanji bubian: shuxinji* [Supplements to the Complete Works of Xu Zhimo: Letters]. Ed. Lu Yaodong. Hong Kong: Commercial Press, 4 volumes.

—— (1993) "Fragments," dated January 1922. In *Xu Zhimo quanji bubian: shuxinji* (Supplements to the Complete Works of Xu Zhimo: Letters). Ed. Lu Yaodong. Hong Kong: Commercial Press, 1993, vol. 4, p. 7.

Y. (1920) "Foluote xin xinlixue zhi iban" [General Ideas of Freud's New Psychology]. *Dongfang Zazhi* [Eastern Miscellany Magazine], 17.22: 85–86.

Yan, Jiayan. (1989) *Zhongguo xiandai xiaoshuo liupai shi* [Schools of Modern Chinese Fiction]. Beijing: Renmin wenxue chubanshe.

Yanabu, Akira. (2001) *Ai* [Love]. Tokyo: Sanseidō.

Yasuda, Tokutarō, trans. (1928) *Seishin bunseki nyūmon*. Tokyo: ARS.

Ye, Hui. (2001) *Shuxie fucheng: Xianggang wenxue pinglunji* [Writing the Floating City: Collection of Articles on Hong Kong Literature]. Hong Kong: Qingwen Shuwu.

Yokomitsu, Riichi. (1925) "Shinkankakuron" [On Neo-Sensation]. In *Complete Works of Yokomitsu Riichi: Definitive Texts*, 1981–82, vol. 13, pp. 75–82.

—— (1927) "Nanakai no undō" [The Exercise of Seven Floors]. In *Complete Works of Yokomitsu Riichi: Definitive Texts*, 1981–82, vol. 2, pp. 447–59.

—— (1932) *Shanghai*. Tokyo: Kaizō Bunko.

—— (1935) *Shanghai*. Tokyo: Shomotsutenbōsha.

—— (1940) "Mu Ji'ei shi no shi" [The Death of Mr. Mu Shiying]. *Bungakukai* [Literary World], 7 (September): 174–5. In *Complete Works of Yokomitsu Riichi: Definitive Texts*, 1981–82, vol. 14, pp. 250–1.

—— (1939) "Shinakai" [The China Sea]. In *Complete Works of Yokomitsu Riichi: Definitive Texts*, 1981–82, vol. 13, pp. 437–45.

—— (1981–82) *Teihon Yokomitsu Riichi zenshū* [*Complete Works of Yokomitsu Riichi: Definitive Texts*]. Tokyo: Kawade Shobō.

Yoshie, Takamatsu. (1923) *Furansei bungei inshōki* [Impressions of French Literature] Tokyo: Shinchōsha. In *Yoshie Takamatsu zenshū* [Complete Works of Yoshie Takamatsu]. Tokyo: Hakusuisha, 1936, vol. 3.

—— (1929) "Nōmin bungaku" [Peasants' Literature]. In *Nan'ō no sora* [The Sky of Southern Europe]. Tokyo: Waseda University Press.

Yoshimura, Teiji. (2001) "Kaisetsu" [Exposition]. In Kawabata Yasunari, *Tenohira no shōsetsu* [Palm-of-the-Hand Stories]. Tokyo: Shinchōsha, pp. 553–9.

Yu, Dafu. (1921) *Chenlun* [Sinking]. In *Yu Dafu Wenji* [Collected Works of Yu Dafu]. Hong Kong: Sanlian Shudian, 1982, vol. 1, pp. 17–56.

Zhang, Jingyuan. (1992) *Psychoanalysis in China: Literary Transformations, 1919–1949*. Ithaca: Cornell East Asian Program.

Zhang, Jungu. (1970) *Xu Zhimo zhuan* [Biography of Xu Zhimo]. Taipei: Lizhi Chubanshe.

Zhang, Wenyuan. (1936) "Weilai de Shanghai fengguang de kuangce" [Wild Prophesy

of the Future Cityscape of Shanghai]. *Modern Sketch*, 30 (20 September). In Shen Jianzhong, ed. (2004), *Shidai manhua, 1934–1937 1934–1937* [Modern Sketch, *1934–1937*]. Shanghai: Shanghai Shehui Kexueyuan Chubanshe, vol. 2, pp. 404–7.
Zhang, Yingjin. (1996) *The City in Modern Chinese Literature and Film: Configurations of Space, Time & Gender*. Stanford, CA: Stanford University Press.
Zhang, Ziping. (1922) *Chongjiqi huashi* [Fossils in the Age of Alluvial Clays]. Shanghai: Taidong Shuju. In *Chongjiqi huashi, Feixü, Taili*, 1988.
—— (1926) *Feixu* [Flying Willow Katkins]. Shanghai: Xiandai Shuju. In *Fossils in the Age of Alluvial Clays, Flying Willow Katkins, Taili*, 1988.
—— (1926) *Taili*. Shanghai: Creation Society. In *Fossils in the Age of Alluvial Clays, Flying Willow Katkins, Taili*, 1988.
—— (1988) *Chongjiqi huashi, Feixü, Taili* [Fossils in the Age of Alluvial Clays, Flying Willow Katkins, Taili]. Beijing: Renmin Wenxue ChubanShe.
Zhao, Erzhuan, et al. (1928) *Qingshigao* [Manuscript of Qing History]. Beijing: Zhonghua Shuju, 1986, vol. 472.
Zhou, Zuoren. (1919) "Riben de xincun" [Japanese New Village]. *Xin qingnian* [New Youth], 6.3 (March): 265–77.
—— (1922) "Huai Airoxianko Jun" [Missing Mr Eroshenko]. *Chenbao fukan* [Literary Supplement to the Morning Post] (7 November): 4.
—— (1923) "(2) Fabuer *Kunchongji*" [Fabre's *Book of Insects*, Part 2]. *Literary Supplement to the Morning Post* (26 January): 3.
—— (1925) "Ailisi de hua" [Ellis's Words]. In *Yutian de shu* [The Book in the Rain]. Hobei: Jiaoyu Chubanshe, 2001, pp. 88–90.
—— (1925) "Ailisi suiganlu chao" [Passages from Ellis's Impressions and Comments]. In *Yongriji* [Everlasting Day Collection], 2002. Hobei: Jiaoyu Chubanshe, pp. 57–64.
—— (1944) *Zhitang huixiang lu* [Memoirs of Zhitang]. 2 volumes. Hobei: Jiaoyu Chubanshe, 2002.
Zhu, Guangqian. (1921) "Fulude de yinyishi shuo yu xinli fenxi" [Freud's Theory of the Subconscious and Psychoanalysis]. *Dongfang Zazhi* [Eastern miscellany], 18.14: 41–51.
Zhu, Xiu, et al., eds. (1982) *Pujifang* [General Prescriptions]. Beijing: Renmin Weisheng Chubanshe, vol. 221.

Index

In this index figures are indicated in **bold**; notes by n.

acculturation 25, 199n.1
Aesthetic Outlook on Life, An (Mei de renshengguan) 18, 20
agency
  in translation 131–2, 139–40, 164–5, 175
  personal xi-xii 9, 18, 39, 99
Age of Openness: China Before Mao?, The 128
Ai see Love
ai, and love 188–9
Ai zhi fangshi 37
All Contents in a Modern Woman's Brain Cells (Xiandai nüzi naobu xibao de yiqie) 79–82, **81**, **82**
allure de Chanel, L' 83, 91
Ambarvalia 192
anarchism 137–8, 139, 157
Anarchism and Modern Science 138
androgyny, and Louis XIV 3–4
Annales des sciences naturelles 148
Anzai Fuyue 197
Appeal to the Young Reader (wakaki doksha ni uttawu) 92–3
Archive and the Repertoire, The 191
art, fashion as 90
Aru seinen no yume 123–4 *see also* Young Man's Dream, A
Asakusa Crimson Gang, The (Asakusa Kurenai Dan) 96
Asia Development Board 118
Asianism 117, 119, 122
Atarashiki Mura no seikatsu 123
  see also Life in the New Village
Aufheben 109
Autobiography (Jijoden) 139

Babel 196
Bailingji 181, *see also* Hundred-Year-Old-Machine, A
Bain, Alexander 174–5, 230n.47
Ba Jin 138
Baker, Josephine 88, **88**, 134

ballet, and Louis XIV 4
Baudelaire, Charles 5, 8, 27–8, 31–2, 59
Beard, George 176–7
beauty
  modern girl's 73
  Oriental 72–3
Bei dangzuo xiaoqianpin de nanzi 163, 165–9, 178, 186 *see also* Man Taken as a Plaything, A
Beijing School 43–4, 208n.69
Beijing types 43, 209n.73
Bell, Marie **87**
Benjamin, Walter 5–6, 132
Bergson, Henri 107, 159, 160–1
Best French Short Stories, The 54
bexiang 52, 161, 226n.99
Birth of the Neo-Sensation School, The (Shinkankakuha no tanjō) 92
Black Cat, The 101
Black Peony (Hei mudan or Kuro bōtan) 103
Black, Red, Cruelty, and Women (Hei, hong, canrenxing yu nüxing) 134, **135**
Black Venus **88**
Blancard, Emile 148
Blavatsky, H.P. 150–1
Blutose 182–3, **185–6**
Bōdorēru *see* Baudelaire
body
  mechanical female 38, 39
  as transcultural site 126
Body without Soul, A (Wu linghun de routi) 77–9, **78**
bohème, the 6
Boku no hyōhonshitsu 65 *see also My Specimen Room*
Bow, Clara 82
Bowler, Peter J. 149
Bungaku Hōkokukai 123–4
Bungei jidai 63 *see also Literary Times*
Burutōze **186,** *see also* Blutose

Cai Yuanpei 44, 172
Canton 48
censorship 121
Chanel, Coco 83–91, **89**, 212n.40, 212n.48, 213n.52
Chen Daqi 172
Chiba Kameo 92
Chi bexiang fan 161 *see also* Living on Bexiang
Chinese Women's Beauty in a Foreigner's Eye (Wairen muzhong zhi Zhongguo nüxingmei) 72
Chinese Women's Innocent and Ignorant Beauty (Zhongguo nüxing de zhizhuomei) 72–3
Christian motifs, love 187–8
Chuang zao yuekan 54 *see also* Creation Monthly
Chunlei 138
Chunmo xiantan 144, 145
cinematic art, and Liu Na'ou 45–50
Cinematic Art, On (Yingpian yishulun) 45
cinéma vérité 46
city-state, Shanghai as 100, 215n.6
Collection of Cartoons by Jianying (Jianying manhuaji) 79
Collection of Palm-of-the-Hand Stories; (Zhangpian xiaoshuoji) 63
colonialism 26, 110, 126, 127
Condition humaine, La 100 *see also* Man's Fate
Confucian Society 118
conte, On (Konto ron) 63–4
Craven 'A' 35, 36
Creation Monthly (Chuangzao yuekan) 54
Creation writers 43, 178, 179, 208n.56
creative transformation 8–9, 15, 18, 57, 61, 112, 124, 164–5, 191–2
Crémieux, Benjamin 93
Crescent Moon Society 194
Critique of Pure Reason, The 105
cross-dressing, modern girl 59
crowd, symbolism of 101–2
cultural translation 138–9, 164, 191
cultural translators 18

Dai Wangshu 42, 93, 94–5
dandy *see also* dandyism
  as artist 15
  defined 5, 26
  and modern boy
  and modern girl 13, 30
  old-style 193
dandy/flâneur, and transcultural modernity 5–10
dandy/modernists, and Foucault 9
Dandy, Le 27
dandyism *see also* dandy
  and Baudelaire and Foucoult 4–10
  concept of xii–xiii, 13–15
  defining 202n.17

and Liu Na'ou 26–8, 40–1
as life calling 67–70
and sexuality 4
and transcultural modernity 7, 50, 162, 195–6
in Japan 193
Darwin, Charles, and Fabre 146–56, 224n.53
Darwin, Erasmus 149
Dawn of East-Asian Civilization, The (Tōa bunmei no reimei) 118
Dekobra, Maurice 70–2
de Mattos, Alexander Teixeira 140
Descent of Man 158
Diary of a Madman (Kuangren riji) 180
Diet of the Nervous 177
digger wasps 144, 145, 146–9
Dikötter, Frank 128, 129
direct experience 107
direct reality 107–8
Doan's Backache Kidney Pills **184**
Doan's Nerve Tonic Tablets (Dou'anshi bushen yaopian) 181–2, **183**
dress
  and masculinity/femininity 3
  and modern girl 59, **61**, 86–7
Dr. Sex 18, 173
Duruy, Victor 154–5

East-West divide, scholarship 198
Ellis, Havelock 173
Enchantment of a Machine, The (Jixie de meili) 37–8, **39**
Eroshenko, Vasilii 145, 223n.37
Erotic Culture (Seqing wenhua) 74
Escapes from Japan (Nihon dasshutsuki) 137
everlasting travelers 96–7, 214n.86
everlasting woman, the 76, 77
Evolution, On (Tianyanlun) 160
Exercise of Seven Floors, The (Nanakai no undō) 74

Fabre, Jean-Henri 131, 142
  and Charles Darwin 146–56, 224n.53
  and the Church 152
  life of 154–6, 225n.70
Fāburu no shōgai, kagaku no shijin 141
  see also Life of Fabre, Poet of Science
Falanxi duanpian jiezuoji 94 *see also* Masterpieces of French Short Stories
fashion
  as art form 90
  and modern girl 86–7
  and Neo-Sensation writing 40
Fashion, On 86–91
female dandies 83–91
femininity 1
Femme, La 28, 31–2
femmes fatales 29, 34, 84, 134
Feng Xiaoqing Kao 172–3

Feng Xiaoqing, On (Feng Xiaoqing Kao) 172–3
Feng Xuefeng 43
film industry, and Liu Na'ou 45–50
film-truth 46, 48
Fischer, Adolph 138
flânerie 30, 31, 205n.62
flâneurs
  and Benjamin 9
  as a commodity 5
  and transcultural modernity 5–10
  and the turtle 20–1
Fleurs du Mal, Les 29
floating gaze 55
Flowers of Evil, The 29
Foucault, Michel 6–9, 27, 138–9, 222n.15
free love 190
Freud, Sigmund 178
Fukuzawa Yukichi 117
Funü huabao see Women's Pictorial, The

garçonne, La 87–8, **87**
gender indicators, in Japanese 75
gender triad, the Neo-Sensation 10–15, 115
gigolos 36–7, 59
governance, open 128
Great Martyr: To the Spirit of Our Comrade Ōsugi Sakae, The (Weida de xundaozhe: cheng tongzhi Dashan Rung jun zhi ling) 138
Guo Jianying 37, 63, 79, 134
Guys, Constantin 7–8

Hamada Kōsaku 118
Hangxian-shang de yinue 67
hard films/soft films 44–5, 49–50
Hattori Unokichi 171–2
Hei, hong, canrenxing yu nüxing 134, **135**
Hei mudan 103 *see also* Black Peony
homelessness, and Neo-Sensation writing 56, 96–8, 125–6, 128
Homi Bhabha 191
Horiguchi Daigaku 92, 201n.15
Hormone 79
Huang Chaoqin 42
Huang Jiamou 45, 49–50
Hu Kao 72
Human Life 48
Hundred-Year-Old-Machine, A (Bailingji) 181, **182**
Hu Shi 44
Hybridity
  and the Neo-Sensation language 17, 55
  and literary and linguistic invention 198
  and the macaronic 41, 167
  and the new vernacular 57
  and the semicolonial human landscape in Shanghai 55
  transnational and transcultural 73, 192

Icart, Louis 12
Ideals of the East with Special Reference to the Art of Japan, The 118
ignorance, and modern girl 12–13, 60, 66, 72–4, 82–4
imageries
  technology/Western music 69
  war and hunting 166
imperialism 97, 124, 129, 216n.11
Iñárritu, Alejandro González 196
Inoue Tetsujirō 174–5
insect behaviour, and human behaviour 133
Inspiration 193–4
Intermediary 191, 199n.6
intuitive activating agency 108
Isis Unveiled 150–1
Is Theosophy a Religion? 151
Iwamoto Yoshiharu 189
Izu Dancer, The (Izu no odoriko) 96
Izu no odoriko 96

Japanese language, experimentation with 192–3
Japanese New Village, The 123
Jianying manhuaji 79 *see also* Collection of Cartoons by Jianying
Jijoden 139 *see also* Autobiography
Jindai xin 23 *see* Modern Heart
jingxie shuairuo 173 *see also* neurasthenia
Jixie de meili 37–8, **39**

Kagaku no shijin 140 *see also* Poet of Science, The
kanji terms, use of 69, 75, 167
Kannō to shinkankaku 109 *see also* Sensuousness and Neo-Sensation
Kant, Immanuel 105, 202n.27
katakana terms, use of 75
Kataoka Teppei 92–3
Kawabata Yasunari 63–6, 96
Kawabata Yasunari senshū 65
kino-eye 46–8
kinoglaz 46–7
kino-pravda 46
Kitagawa Fuyuhiko 197
Kitamura Tōkoku 189
Kollontai, Alexandra 37
Konchūki 144 *see also* Souvenirs Entomologiques
Konto ron 63–4 *see also* conte, On
Kropotkin, Peter 138, 157–8
Kuangren riji 180 *see also* Diary of a Madman
Kuro bōtan 103 *see also* Black Peony
Kyōto School 107

language, Japanese 192–3
L'Aurore 42
le réel 8–9
Letters from a Genius (Yige tiancai de tongxin) 181

260 Index

Liang Qichao 193–4
Liangyou 43 *see also Young Companion, The*
Life in the New Village (Atarashiki Mura no seikatsu) 123
Life of Fabre, Poet of Science (Fāburu no shōgai, kagaku no shijin) 141
limit-attitude 9
linguistic innovation, Neo-Sensation writing 17, 55, 167–9
Literary Society for Patriotism 123–4
Literary Times (Bungei jidai) 63
literature
  and Liu Na'ou 53–5
  May Fourth/Chinese 198
  national 197–8
Liu, Lydia 138
Liu Na'ou 22–58, 75
  assassination of 24
  dandyism/misogyny of 26–32
  dandyism/Shanghai type 41–50
  as filmmaker 49
  the macaronic/transcultural modernity 56–8
  and Morand 93
  Neo-Sensation mode/modern girl 32–41
  neurasthenia of 179
  in Shanghai/Tokyo 50–6
  transcultural practice 22–6
Living on *Bexiang* (Chi bexiang fan) 161
Li Yingpu 119
Li Zongda *see* Ōgai Kamone
loanwords 163, 165, 226n.1
Location of Culture 191
Lost Lamb (Miyang) 37
Louis XIV 1–5, **2**, 200n.1
Love 189
love
  art of 71–2
  how to say I love you 185–91
  images for 134
  modern 37
  science of 132–6
  translating 164
Loves of Three Generations, The 37
Lu Shoujian 176
Lu Xiaoman 195
Lu Xun 42
  and dandyism 161–2
  and Fabre 159
  and Konchūki 142–6
  neurasthenia of 180

macaronic, the
  and dandyism, China 193–4
  and literature 196
  and Lu Xun 161–2
  by male narrator 67–8
  the modern girl and the modern boy 167–9
  in modern Japanese 192–3

and Neo-Sensation writing 17–18, 32–3, 34, 136
Shanghai Neo-Sensation stories 68–9
and transcultural modernity 56–8
Madame Wei (Wei Furen) 190–1
Ma Junwu 160
Makura no sōshi 109 *see also Pillow Book, The*
malady of the heart *see* neurasthenia
Malraux, André 100
Man's Fate 100, 101, 102
Man Taken as a Plaything, A (Bei dangzuo xiaoqianpin de nanzi) 163, 165–9, 178, 186
Man with a hat, The see Man with the Movie Camera, The
Man with the Movie Camera, The 47, 48, 49
Manyōshū 190
Mao Dun 44
Mao regime 129
Mao Zedong 123, 220n.87
Marriage in Tears and Laughters (Tixiao yinyuan) 46
Masterpieces of French Short Stories (Falanxi duanpian jiezuoji) 94
Mattos, Alexander Teixeira de 140
May 30th Movement 116
May Fourth China 189–90, 196, 207n.48
May Fourth literature 187–8, 198
mechanical female body 38, 39
Medhurst, Walter H. 188, 189
Medical and Surgical Use of Electricity, The 177
medical terms, use of 167
Mei de renshengguan 18, 20
Memories of Insects *see Souvenirs entomologiques*
men, modern girl's attitude to 36–7, 59
metaphysical sucking cups, the 136
Midnight (Ziye) 44
mini-stories 63–4, 66
misogyny 13–14
  and dandyism 73–4, 77–82
  and Liu Na'ou 28–32
Miss Modern Girl and Master Modern Boy (Mogako to moborō) **14, 16, 17**
Miyako 110–13
Miyang 37 *see Lost Lamb*
Model of Modern Women, A (Xiandai nüxing de muoxing) 79, **80**
modern boy, the 14–15, 21, 51–2, 110–12, 115, 132–6
  and Neo-Sensation writing 165–8, 191
modern girl project 203n.47
modern girl, the
  attitudes to 11–13
  commodifying 74–7
  and the dandy 13, 30
  depictions of 15–18
  and fashion 86–7
  gazing back 59–63

how to be a 70–4
and men 36–7, 59
and Neo-Sensation writing 32–41, 44, 165
as Other 59
perspectives on 11
and World War I 204n.49
Modern Heart (Jindai xin) 23
modernism
    Chinese 200n.8
    Japanese in Manchuria 197
    and Liu Na'ou 25
    non-Western 199n.8
modernist, the 31
modernité 8, 31, 98
Modernité, La 27
modernity, attitude of 9
modernization, and colonialism 26
Modern Science and Anarchism 157
Modern Screen (*Xiandai dianying*) 45
Mogako to moborō 14 see also Miss Modern Girl and Master Modern Boy
monojitai 105, 107–8 see also thing-in-itself, the
monologue form 196
monopoly, of scrutinizing women 70
montage 46
Mo Ran 71, 72
Morand, Paul
    and Coco Chanel 83–91, 213n.40, 213n.52
    and Neo-Sensation 92
    style of 93, 94
    travels of 96–7
Morrison, Robert 188
movie industry, and Liu Na'ou 45–50
Mr Huang, allow me to introduce Miss Chen **62**
Mushanokōji Saneatsu 123
Mu Shiying 35, 43, 102–3, 163, 165–9, 178
Music on the Cruising Route (Hangxianshang de yinue) 67
Mutual Aid: a Factor of Evolution 157–8
My Specimen Room (Boku no hyōhonshitsu) 65

Nagai Kafū 193
Nakajima Rikizō 174
Nakamura Masanao 189
Nanakai no undō 74 see also Exercise of Seven Floors, The
narcissism, of dandy 60
national literature 197–8
Natural Theology 149
natural theology 150
neologisms 167–8
Neo-Sensation, On 104–10
Neo-Sensation, term 10–11
Neo-Sensationalism 203n.46
Neo-Sensation School 10, 23
Neo-Sensation writers 43, 74–5

Neo-Sensation writing 40, 41, 57, 169, 191
    linguistic innovation 55, 167–9
    love stories 37
    and modern girl 32–41, 44
    need for translation 179
    palm-of-the-hand stories 63–7, 167
    Paris/Tokyo/Shanghai 92–5
    use of transliterations 67–8, 75
neurasthenia 163–4, 167, 173, 175–84, 231n.64, 232n.84
    other terms for 173
New Japanese Literary Society 122
New People Biweekly, The (*Xinmin congbao*) 194
New People Style, The 194
New Psychology (Shinri shinsetsu) 174
new sensationisms 216n.11
new sensationists 207n.48
New Sensation writers 217n.25
New Shanghai types 43
New Village movement, the 123, 220n.87
New Woman, the 11–12
New Woman, The (Xin nüxing) 44
Nietzsche, Friedrich W. 106
Nihon dasshutsuki 137 see also Escapes from Japan
Ninshikiron ni okeru junronriha no shuchō nit suite 107 see also Thesis of the School of Pure Rationalism in Epistemology, On the
Nishi Amane 169–70, **170**
Nishida Kitarō 107–8
Nishiwaki Junzaburō 96, 192, 197, 214n.86
Nordic Night, The (La nuit nordique) 92
No Traveler Returns 96
nuit des six-jours, La 94 see also Six-Day Night, The
nuit nordique, La 92 see also Nordic Night, The

Odagiri Hideo 122
Odes to Chinese Women's Beauty (Zhongguo nüxingmei zanli) 70
Ōgai Kamome 72–3, 131, 132–6
Okakura Tenshin 118
On Fashion 86–91
On Neo-Sensation 104–10
On Paul Morand 93
Organization of an Aesthetic Society (Mei de shehui zuzhifa) 18, 20
Origin of Species, On the 153, 160
Ortiz, Fernando 25
Ōsugi Sakae 137–41, 158–9
out of Asia, into Europe 117

Painter of Modern Life, The 5, 28, 31–2
palm-of-the-hand stories 63–7
Pan-Asia Co-Prosperity Sphere 102, 118, 124
Pan Guangdan 172–3
Passer-by, To a 59

Pasteur, Louis 154
Past, The 54
peintre de la vie moderne, Le 5, 28, 31–2, 207n.29 see also *Painter of Modern Life, The*
Pillow Book, The (Makura no sōshi) 109
pleasure, visual/tactile 136
Poetics of Surrealism 192
Poet of Science, The (Kagaku no shijin) 140
Poetry and Poetics 197
poetry, Japanese 197
Potelai'er *see* Baudelaire
power relations 164, 222n.15
psychological terms, use of 167
psychology, in Japan/China 169–74, 228n.27
Pudovkine, Vsevolod 45–6
pure durée 107
pure external objectivity 108
Purging the Soft-Film Theory—The Entertainment Theory of Soft-Film Theorists (Qingsuan ruanxing dianying lun—ruanxing lunzhe de quwei zhuyi) 50
Pursuing War Responsibility in Literature (Bungaku ni okeru sensō seki-nin no tsuikyū) 122

Qingsuan ruanxing dianying lun—ruanxing lunzhe de quwei zhuyi 50

ragpickers 6
Random Talks in the Late Spring (Chunmo xiantan) 144, 145
réel, le 8–9
religion
 and love 187–8
 and science 157
 Theosophy as 150–1
reproductive essence 79
Rigaud, Hyacinthe 1, 2, 200n.1
Ruan Lingyu 44

Said, Edward 156–7
Sanshō 123, 124
Sas, Miriam 192–3
science
 as cultural critique 146
 of love 132–6
 and religion 156–7
Seidensticker, Edward 193
Sei Shōnagon 109
Selected Works of Kawabata Yasunari (Kawabata Yasunari senshū) 65
Self-Treatment for Neurasthenia, A (Shenjing shuairuo ziliaofa) 177
senses, how to name them 174–5
Sensuousness and Neo-Sensation (Kannō to shinkankaku) 109
Seqing wenhua 74 *see* Erotic Culture
Sex Histories (Xingshi) 18, **19**, 173
Sexual Neurasthenia 177

Sexual Selection in Man 173–4, 175
Shaft of Golden Light: Monologue in the Xiashi Dialect, A (Yitiao jinse de guanghen: Xiashi tubai) 196
Shanghai 110–11
 as city-state 100, 215n.6
 Neo-Sensation School 10, 208n.69
 types, and dandyism 41–50
Shanghai 219n.78
Hō Shūran 114–18
the masses 128
Miyako 110–13
Neo-Sensation/symbolism 100–3
Olga 113–14
Sanki/Ōsugi 125–8
symbolism 100–3
Yamaguchi 119–24
Shao Xunmei 42
Shen Congwen 43, 44, 181
Shengzhi Yuansu 79
shenjing shuairuo 173, 176, 231n.64
Shenjing shuairuo liaoyangfa 176
Shenjing Shuairuo san da yanjiu 176
Shenjing shuairuo ziliaofa 177
shōhen shōsetsu 63–4
Shibunkai 118
Shiina Sonoji 140–1, 158–9
Shinkankakuha no tanjō 92 *see also* Birth of the Neo-Sensation School, The
Shin Nihon Bungaku (New Japanese Literary Society) 122
shinrigaku 170
Shinri shinsetsu 174 *see also* New Psychology
Shi to Shiron 197
Shi Yan 67
Short Story Monthly (Xia-oshuo yuebao) 54
Shub, Esther 47
Six-Day Night, The (La nuit des six-jours) 94
Snow Country Sketch, The (Yukiguni-shō) 65
Snyder, Steven 192–3
Souvenirs entomologiques 131, 132
 and Ōsugi Sakae 137–41
 and Shiina Sonoji 141
 as traveling text 156–61
Spleen et idéal 29
Spring Thunder 138
Studies in the Psychology of Sex 173
Study of the Heart and Soul (Xinlinxue) 171
Sun King, The *see* Louis XIV
surrealism 193, 216n.17
Su Xuelin 179

Tanaka Hisara 14, 15
Tang Na 50
Taylor, Diana 191
Tenohira no shōsetsu 64 *see also* palm-of-the-hand stories
Theosophical Society 150

Thesis of the School of Pure Rationalism in Epistemology, On the (Ninshikiron ni okeru junronriha no shuchō nit suite) 107
thing-in-itself, the 105–10, 217n.23
Three Great Studies on Neurasthenia 176
Three Laughs (Sanshō) 123, 124
Three Who Study Antennas, The (Yanjiu chujiao de sangeren) 131, 132–6
Thus Spake Zarathustra 106
Tianyanlun 160 *see Evolution, On*
Tixiao yinyuan 46 *see also Marriage in Tears and Laughters*
To a Passer-by 59
Tōa bunmei no reimei 118
'to connect' 196–7, 198
Tolstoy, Leo 151, 159
topos of absolute Nothingness 108
toshi kokka 100
Touch of 1933, The 37, **39**
Toward the Sun 66, 211n.13
Trackless Train (Wugui lieche) 42–3, 94
transcultural practice
  Liu Na'ou 22–6
  Lu Xun 162
  and the macaronic 191
  Yokomitsu Riichi 108
transcultural site, the
  the body as 199n.6
  and the cultural translator 99, 130, 164–5, 191–2
  and the dandy 5, 15
  definition of x–xiii
  fictional characters as 112–14, 126–9, 169
  and linguistic invention 68, 95
  and the macaronic 61
  and Neo-Sensation writers 18
  and personal agency 9
transcultural modernity
  and artistic invention 90
  and creative transformation 178
  and the cultural translator 191
  and the dandy 10
  and dandyism 13
  definition of x–xiii
  and hybridity 198
  and the macaronic 18, 56–8, 60–1, 98
  and the Shanghai Neo-Sensation School 10
  and "to connect" 196
  and translation 163–5
  Xu Zhimo 195
transculturation 25
transformation, creative 164, 191
translation
  agency in 131–2, 139, 175
  cultural 138, 191
  need for 179
  and transcultural modernity 163–5
  untranslatability of languages 198
translation theory 132

translators, cultural xi–xii 9, 15, 17–18, 99, 129, 132, 165, 191
transliteration 67–8, 75, 167
travel
  and dandyism 95–8
  Paul Morand 96–7
  and texts 156–61
Traveling Theory 156–7
Treatment for Neurasthenia. A (Shenjing shuairuo liaoyangfa) 176
Tsurumi Shunsuke 124
turtle, and the flâneurs 20–1
two-way give and take 25

Uchiyama Bookstore 142–3
Uchiyama Kanzō 142–3
Unknown Singer, The 46
untranslatability of languages 198
  see also translation
Unworldly Poet and Women, The 189

Vampire, Le 29
Vernacular Movement 57
Vertov, Dziga 45–6, 48

Wairen muzhong zhi Zhongguo nüxingmei 72
Wakaki dokusha ni uttawu 92–3
  see also Appeal to the Young Reader
Wang Xiho 177
war is so long, The **12**
war responsibility 122–3
Washio Hiroshi 173–4, 175–6
wasps, digger 144, 145, 146–9
Way of Love, The (Ai zhi fangshi) 37
Weida de xundaozhe: cheng tongzhi Dashan Rung jun zhi ling) 138
Wei Furen *see* Madame Wei
Weilai de Shanghai fengguang de kuangce 18, **19**, **20**
What is Enlightenment 7, 202n.27
Wild Grass (Yecao) 180
Wild Prophesy of the Future Cityscape of Shanghai (Weilai de Shanghai fengguang de kuangce) 18, **19**, **20**
Wille zum Leben, der 108
will to life (*der Wille zum Leben*) 108
women *see also* female dandies; modern girl
  Beijing 32, 33, 34
  and dandyism 28, 38
  and Louis XIV 4, 201n.13
Women's Pictorial, The 44, 57–8, **60**, 63
Wugui lieche 42–3, 94
Wu linghun de routi 77–9, **78**

Xia-oshuo yuebao 54
Xiandai dianying 45 *see Modern Screen*
Xiandai nüxing de muoxing 79, **80**
Xiandai nüzi naobu xibao de yiqie 79–82, **81**, **82**

Xingshi 18, **19**, 173
Xinlingxue 171
Xinmin congbao 194
Xin nüxing 44 see *The New Woman*
Xu Manli 44
Xu Zhimo 194

yamato tamashii 117
Yanabu Akira 189, 190
Yan Fu 160
Yang Kui 26
Yanjiu chujiao de sangeren 131, 132–6
Yan Yongjing 171
Yecao 180
Yige tiancai de tongxin 181 *see also* Letters from a Genius
Yingpian yishulun 45 *see also* Cinematic Art, On
Yitiao jinse de guanghen: Xiashi tubai 196
Yokomitsu Riichi 10–11, 53, 74–5, 92–3, 96

Yoshie Takamatsu 159
Yoshimura Teiji 64
Young Companion, The (Liangyou) 43
Young Man's Dream, A (Aru seinen no yume) 123–4
Yu Dafu 37, 54, 179
Yukiguni-shō 65

Zhang Jingsheng 18–20, 173
Zhang Wuojun 23
Zhang Ziping 37, 54
Zhiangpian xiaoshuoji 63 *see also* Collection of Palm-of-the-Hand Stories
Zhongguo nüxing de zhizhuomei 72–3 *see also* Chinese Women's Innocent and Ignorant Beauty
Zhongguo nüxingmei zanli 70 *see also* Odes to Chinese Women's Beauty
Zhou Zuoren 159–60, 173
Ziye 44 *see Midnight*

For Product Safety Concerns and Information please contact our EU
representative GPSR@taylorandfrancis.com
Taylor & Francis Verlag GmbH, Kaufingerstraße 24, 80331 München, Germany

www.ingramcontent.com/pod-product-compliance
Lightning Source LLC
Chambersburg PA
CBHW070556300426
44113CB00010B/1272